CAMBRIDGE MUSICAL TEXTS AND MO

CU00918327

General Editors: Howard Mayer Brown, Peter le Huray,

The new series Cambridge Musical Texts and Mo₁
centres of interest the history of performance and the history of
instruments. It will include annotated translations of important historical
documents, authentic historical texts on music, and monographs on
various aspects of historical performance.

VIOLIN TECHNIQUE AND PERFORMANCE PRACTICE IN THE LATE EIGHTEENTH AND EARLY NINETEENTH CENTURIES

19.50

Paganini sketched during a concert in Germany, c. 1830

VIOLIN TECHNIQUE AND PERFORMANCE PRACTICE IN THE LATE EIGHTEENTH AND EARLY NINETEENTH CENTURIES

ROBIN STOWELL

Professor of Music, University College, Cardiff

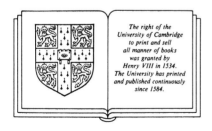

The right of the
University of Cambridge
to print and sell
all manner of books
was granted by
Henry VIII in 1534.
The University has printed
and published continuously
since 1584.

CAMBRIDGE UNIVERSITY PRESS
Cambridge
New York Port Chester
Melbourne Sydney

Published by the Press Syndicate of the University of Cambridge
The Pitt Building, Trumpington Street, Cambridge CB2 1RP
40 West 20th Street, New York, NY 10011, USA
10 Stamford Road, Oakleigh, Melbourne 3166, Australia

First published 1985
First paperback edition 1990

Printed in Great Britain at the University Press, Cambridge

Library of Congress Catalogue card number: 84–14246

British Library Cataloguing in Publication Data

Stowell, Robin
Violin technique and performance practice in the
late eighteenth and early nineteenth centuries. –
(Cambridge musical texts and monographs)
1. Violin – Instruction and study – History
I. Title
787.1.07'14   MT262

ISBN 0 521 23279 1 hardback
ISBN 0 521 39744 8 paperback

Contents

Illustrations

Preface

As a practising violinist I have long been interested in the historical and practical problems of 'authentic' performance but have constantly been disconcerted by the dearth of scholarly material relating to the performance of late-eighteenth- and early-nineteenth-century music for the violin. The years spanning 1760–1840 form a critical period in the history of the instrument which confirmed the ascendancy of the French over the Italian violin school. They witnessed amongst other remarkable developments extensive changes in the instrument and its fittings, the advent of the Tourte bow, the steady expansion of public concert-giving and music publishing, the establishment of numerous conservatoires with their more systematised approaches to musical instruction and the rise of the touring virtuoso; notable amongst such virtuosi was Nicolo Paganini (1782–1840), who represents arguably the summit of *technical* artistry in the history of violin playing (hence his frequent inclusion as a separate entity in my surveys of various technical considerations). The present volume is thus intended to go some way towards filling the gap that exists in modern musical literature by providing a scholarly historical and technical guide both to the manner in which violin instruction was presented in teaching manuals and, from a more practical viewpoint, to the idiomatic performance of violin music composed during that remarkable period of transition.

Although most of the numerous violin treatises and other pedagogical sources of the period fail to provide a true representation of the technical demands of the music of their immediate times, they nevertheless give the most direct access to fundamental technical and interpretative instruction thanks to their non-creative and consolidatory role. As there is no substitute in matters of performance practice for authoritative contemporary sources, my purpose is to provide an overview of the most important aspects of violin technique and some of the often vexing problems of performance practice (for example, interpretative matters for which there are generally few, if any, performance indications) during the period by presenting, wherever possible, substantial extracts from the most important and authoritative treatises (this has proved impractical when dealing, for example, with the diverse theories concerning the *minutiae* of holding the violin and bow, with bow strokes relevant to the myriad pre-Tourte models, or where conflicting opinions result from national or individual preferences). Most extracts are framed with an introduction and commentary and include musical and pictorial examples where applicable, so that the principles discussed may be elucidated, set in historical context, related to other, perhaps contrasting, views and reconciled with the more practical problems of performance on period instruments and bows.

The history of performance practice is an extremely treacherous area, for remarks in treatises are susceptible of different interpretations and the context of application is rarely absolutely clear. The only 'outside' help one has is the attempt, with a suitable instrument and bow, to follow the instructions in the books; this invariably results in a personal, rather than 'scientific' interpretation of the data. My proposed method of presentation demands that the method writers should themselves 'take the stage' with only as much additional support and background commentary from me as available space will allow. As few of the rules disseminated by theorists of the period can be treated as absolute and since there was little unanimity of opinion about many matters of interpretation, readers should be wary of allowing primary sources to lead them blindly or, since musical fashions are so ephemeral, of applying the musical principles of one school or even decade to another. However, given that the presentation of an exhaustive compendium of all the conflicting ideas and side-issues presented in the treatises of this transitional period is inconceivable in one volume, I sincerely hope that my format will cover the main performing trends and serve as a valuable point of departure for deeper investigation by performers, editors and teachers into a substantially authentic technical and stylistic approach to the violin music of the period.

The art of performing was a less formal affair during our period than it is nowadays. If some sections of this book tend to be vague rather than specific, they invariably reflect the very nature of many of the treatises and the late-eighteenth- and early-nineteenth-century approach to violin pedagogy, in which the master–pupil relationship was indispensable. Indeed, several of the non-technical chapters provide not so much comprehensive surveys of such extensive interpretative matters as expression, phrasing or ornamentation as a record of what some violin methods of the period contribute on the subjects, set into a general historical/performance context. Furthermore, detailed discussion of such complex issues as rhythmic alteration, tempo etc. will not be more than briefly touched upon in this summary of fundamental techniques and principles of authentic interpretation, and of their practical application in performance.

Many of the selected extracts in this volume have been translated into English for the first time. All treatises have been consulted in the language of their original publication, except for Campagnoli's *Metodo per violino*, which has been consulted in two authoritative, if stylistically antiquated, nineteenth-century translations. Available modern published translations also have been employed in the cases of C. P. E. Bach's *Versuch* . . . (tr. Mitchell) and J. J. Quantz's *Versuch* . . . (tr. Reilly) but all other translations are my own, unless otherwise attributed.

The task of translating historical source material proved none too easy, especially in the case of some of the redundant and verbose German texts. It is hoped nonetheless that no author's view has been at all misrepresented: to this end, whenever the meaning of the text is ambiguous or a wholly satisfactory equivalent cannot be found in English, the original word or phrase is also given in the printed text. The prime aim has been to provide a clear and accurate translation in fluent and readable English, avoiding, as far as possible, stylistic anachronisms. In this connection I must acknowledge the considerable help of Eileen Schlapp (French and German sources) and John Marsden (Italian sources), both of whom have made many valuable suggestions for the improvement of style and language. Responsibility for any errors that may have crept in, however, must remain my own.

The original sources have been presented as faithfully as space would allow but some editorial licence has necessarily been taken – in such a manner as to preserve the original meaning of the passages in question – in order to maintain conciseness and consistency of approach, notably in the abbreviation of various musical examples, the omission of certain sentences, paragraphs or negligible footnotes which bear no direct relevance to the particular topic under discussion as well as a few musical examples which have been considered superfluous to the needs of this volume, the re-numbering of musical and pictorial illustrations to comply with the schematic outline of the book and, in some cases, the re-positioning of such illustrations in the text for quick and easy reference. All footnotes are editorial unless otherwise indicated.

Each treatise or other source is identified both by its author's surname and an abbreviated form of its title. In some instances authors' names also have been abbreviated for ease of presentation, notably in the case of Rode, Baillot and Kreutzer's *Méthode de violon* (1803), abbreviated to Rode *et al.*, *Méthode* . . . (even though Baillot was its editor and chief contributor), thereby avoiding any confusion between it and Baillot's own *L'art du violon* (1834). Full titles and other relevant details are provided in the handlist of treatises arranged in chronological order by country of publication as an appendix.

I am indebted to my family and many friends and colleagues who have helped and encouraged me during the course of this project. In particular I should like to mention Dr Peter le Huray, who has long fostered my interest in performance practice and has always given generously of his time, advice and experience. I am grateful, too, to the staff of numerous libraries, especially the Pendlebury Library of Music, Cambridge, the University Library, Cambridge, the British Library, the Parry Room Library, Royal College of Music, London and the Bibliothèque Nationale, Paris, for their unfailing assistance. Thanks are also due to Professor David Fuller, for drawing my attention to one extant anonymous treatise, to Professor H. C. Robbins Landon, for the loan of material from his archive and to Professor Alun Hoddinott, for his constant encouragement and support.

Furthermore, I would like to acknowledge an indirect debt to Professor David Boyden, whose masterly study, *The history of violin playing from its origins to 1761* (London, 1965, R/1967) has furnished a reliable and comprehensive background to the early years covered by the present survey. Finally, I must record my gratitude to the staff of the Cambridge University Press, the editors of this series and in particular to Rosemary Dooley, who has cast a careful eye over all stages of the preparation and production of this book.

ROBIN STOWELL

University College, Cardiff

Acknowledgements

Acknowledgement for kind permission to reproduce illustrations and extended quotations is due to the following:

ILLUSTRATIONS

Ashmolean Museum: D. Boyden, *Catalogue of the Hill collection of musical instruments in the Ashmolean Museum, Oxford*, London, Oxford University Press, 1969; © n. d. (Fig. 1)
Music Division, Library of Congress, Washington D. C., U. S. A.: frontispiece
British Library, London: jacket illustration
Kenneth Warren/Novello & Co. Ltd: *The Strad*, vol. 83 (1972) (Fig. 6)

QUOTATIONS

Bärenreiter Verlag: G. Tartini, *Traité des agrémens de la musique*, ed. E. Jacobi, Celle and New York, Moeck, 1961; © n.d.
Dover Publications Inc.: W. H., A. F. & A. E. Hill, *Life and work of Antonio Stradivari*, London, Macmillan, 1902; © 1963
Faber & Faber Ltd.: J. Quantz, *On playing the flute*, tr. E. Reilly, London, 1966
Frits Knuf Publishers: C. van. L. Boomkamp & J. H. van der Meer, *The Carel van Leeuwen Boomkamp collection of musical instruments*, Amsterdam, 1971

Fingering and notation

Violin fingerings are indicated in the usual manner:

0 = open string

1 = the index-finger (not the thumb as in keyboard fingering) and so on.

Pitch registers are indicated by the following letter scheme:

C   c   c¹   c²   c³   c⁴   etc.

Under this scheme the notes to which the violin is normally tuned are represented as g, d¹, a¹, e².

Introduction

At the beginning of the eighteenth century Italy was pre-eminent amongst the musical nations, being represented by such notable composer–violinists as Arcangelo Corelli (1653–1713), Giuseppe Torelli (1658–1709), Antonio Vivaldi (c. 1675–1741), Giovanni Battista Somis (1676–1763), Francesco Geminiani (1680–1762), Francesco Maria Veracini (1690–1750), Pietro Locatelli (1693–1764) and Giuseppe Tartini (1692–1770). Their cultivation of the sonata and the concerto and their styles of composition and performance, incorporating *cantabile* melodies, brilliant figuration, expression and dramatic effects, intended to 'affect the mind and command the passions',[1] strongly influenced the course of music in other countries. Italian musicians filled many of the leading musical posts abroad, especially in Britain, where they were attracted chiefly by the expanding music publishing industry and the flourishing concert life in London and the provinces. Roger North commented (1710): 'It is wonderful to observe what a skratching of Corelli there is everywhere – nothing will relish but Corelli.'[2]

Nevertheless, despite this Italian dominance, traditions of violin playing were beginning to develop in many other countries, including Belgium, Spain, Russia, Switzerland, America, Poland, Hungary, the Netherlands and the Scandinavian countries during the course of the eighteenth century, and Germany could boast a flourishing national school of violin playing with Heinrich von Biber (1644–1704), J. J. Walther (c. 1650–1717) and J. P. Westhoff (1656–1705) as its chief early representatives, culminating in the publication of Leopold Mozart's celebrated *Versuch . . .* (1756). Eighteenth-century France, however, could boast no such heritage. French string music was clearly allied to the dance and only very slowly was the Italian style accepted. Nevertheless, French violinist–composers, many of whom had been trained in Italy, gradually adopted the forms and, to a considerable extent, the techniques of the Italians. The first concertos by a Frenchman were written by Jacques Aubert (1678–1753) (Op. 17, 1735), while François Duval (1673–1728), Sébastien de Brossard (1655–1730), Jean-Féry Rebel (1666–1747) and Elisabeth-Claude Jacquet de la Guerre (1664–1729) were among the first

1. Geminiani, *The art* . . . (1751), preface, p. 1.   2. Wilson, ed., *Roger North on music*, p. xx.

I

French composers to write sonatas, Duval publishing the first collection (1704). With the acceptance of Italian idioms, styles and forms came a dramatic development of violin techniques in France by such violinist–composers as Jean-Marie Leclair *l'aîné* (1687–1764), Louis-Gabriel Guillemain (1705–70), Pierre Guignon (1702–74), Tremais (? – ?) and Jean-Joseph Cassanéa de Mondonville (1711–72). The ascendancy of the French violin school was encouraged by the foundation of the *Concert spirituel* (1725) and other such concert societies and it was confirmed by the publication of the first major French treatise for advanced players, L'Abbé le fils's *Principes* . . . (1761). It was later further consolidated by such notable violinist–pedagogues as Pierre Gaviniès (1728–1800), Isidore Berthaume (1752–1802), Henri Guérillot (1749–1805), Pierre La Houssaye (1735–1818), Marie-Alexander Guénin (1744–1835) and particularly by the remarkable Parisian début at the *Concert spirituel* (March 1782) of the Italian violinist Giovanni Battista Viotti (1755–1824) who, renowned for his noble tone and expressive style, was the first to champion Stradivari's violins in France and was also one of the pioneers in the development of bowing technique after the advent of the Tourte bow. Despite his brief solo career in Paris, his mode of performance became the model for numerous French violinists; notable amongst these were his direct pupils Pierre Rode, Jean-Baptiste Cartier, Auguste Durand, Louis Julien Castels de Labarre, Pierre Vacher, Paul Alday (*le jeune*), Philippe Libon, Friedrich Pixis and André Robberechts, among others, as well as such well-known violinists as Pierre Baillot and Rodolphe Kreutzer. Thus he established the solid technical and stylistic foundations on which the celebrated French school of the nineteenth century was built.

The developments in violin playing during the nineteenth century were aided considerably by the increasing musical and educational interest of the middle classes (throughout Europe but particularly in France), which in turn prompted the emergence of concert-giving as a commercial proposition. Larger concert halls were built to accommodate the ever-increasing audiences and structural alterations to the violin (and many other instruments) became necessary to meet the demand for greater tonal volume. These social and instrumental changes, together with the advent of the Tourte bow, were accompanied by a gradual extension of violin technique, especially in the concerto, where the greater orchestral volume required the soloist to adopt an increasingly brilliant style. Technical developments were also prompted by numerous itinerant virtuosi, many of whom wrote compositions for their own *bravura* performances in the form of concertos, *airs variés*, fantasies, *potpourris*, *souvenirs*, *romances* and the like.

Violinists were also stimulated by the steady expansion of the European music publishing industry, which published much didactic material in the form of studies, exercises and tutors for students of varying standards, thus prompting the gradual fusion of national styles of teaching and playing into a more uniform 'international' approach, and the increasing interest in musical education and pedagogy, especially in France. The new social independence gained by the middle classes as a direct result of the events of the French Revolution (1789) intensified this interest and prompted the gradual acceptance of state control of education, together with the need for free instruction, irrespective of social status. Consequently, a Conservatoire was founded in Paris (established by the *Convention nationale*, 3 August 1795, as the *Conservatoire nationale de musique*) to provide free musical tuition for all who merited it and to train 'artists for the concerts, military bands and theatres of the French republic'.[3] The Conservatoire became the centre of musical instruction in France and the gradual expansion of its own publishing firm, *Le magasin de Musique à l'usage des fêtes nationales*, encouraged the publication of its courses of instrumental study. These took the form of methods, hence the appearance in 1803 of a *Méthode de violon*, written by Rode, Baillot and Kreutzer and edited by Baillot, one of many such works adopted by that institution. The influence of the Paris Conservatoire and its teaching methods was considerable. Most distinguished nineteenth-century French violinists passed through its roll as pupils; some even returned later as teachers, thus ensuring an unprecedented consistency of approach towards instrumental instruction. Its initial success prompted the foundation of similar institutions in other musical capitals, notably Milan (1807), Naples (1808), Prague (1811), Brussels (1813), Florence (1814), Vienna (1817), Warsaw (1821), London (Royal Academy of Music, 1822), The Hague (1826), Liège (1827), Ghent (1833), Geneva (1835), Leipzig (1843) and Munich (1846).

Despite these far-reaching social, instrumental and educational developments, the Italian violin school had begun to decline towards the end of the eighteenth century. The Italian *penchant* for opera and the narrow policies of the conservatoires, directed chiefly towards the cultivation of native singing talent, precipitated this decline, which is reflected in the paucity of pedagogical material (save for the works of Campagnoli and Galeazzi) published in Italy during the period under scrutiny. However, it must be admitted that few violin methods were published in Italy even during the years of the Italian school's greatest influence. This was due no doubt to the traditional master–pupil approach to teaching and the desire to protect pedagogical secrets, as well as to the fact that many leading Italian violinists and theorists occupied important posts abroad and generally published their works in the country of their employment.

The German school continued to prosper in the wake of Leopold Mozart's *Versuch . . . ,* most methods (apart from those of Guhr and Spohr) being of a much simpler technical level, designed more for the instruction of the orchestral violinist (*Ripienist*) than the soloist, and providing a sound but rather limited musical and technical foundation. However, mention must be made

3. *Grove's dictionary . . .* (5th edn), s.v. 'Conservatoire',

of the specialist articles and methods concerning harmonics written predominantly in Germany in the first half of the nineteenth century. Inspired
chiefly by Paganini's virtuoso feats, the articles of Maas and Küster,[4] although
less detailed than the methods of Guhr and Blumenthal, nevertheless played a
significant part in the dissemination of knowledge about harmonics in a country which had been slow to accept such effects into the violinist's repertory.[5]
Meanwhile in Britain, although the concert and publishing climates were
favourable, foreign violinists were still dominant in the early nineteenth
century and no violin methods of any notable merit or significance were
published during that period.

As the main countries to disseminate literature on violin technique and
performance practice c. 1760–1840 were France, Italy, Germany and, thanks
to many of her foreign inhabitants, Britain, this study has been based on the
major pedagogical works that emanated from these countries. These works
were in most cases widely read and were largely responsible for a more systematic approach to violin instruction, exercises, studies, duets and other
compositions being generally provided for the application and perfection of
the techniques discussed. They were for the most part designed as a complement to individual private tuition (the master–pupil relationship was always
considered all-important) and many were intended as guides almost as much
for the teacher as for the student (for example, Spohr's *Violinschule*); thus it is
not surprising that few, if any, were anywhere near comprehensive in content.
Certain technical problems such as shifting were seldom given detailed treatment, whilst interpretative issues determined largely by personal taste and
judgement were rarely discussed in full. The performer was regarded as a
co-partner with the composer in the act of creation; during the eighteenth
century, at least, the performer was, more often than not, the composer and
performance instructions thus proved unnecessary. In any case, educated
musicians were presumed to know the performing conventions of their time
and to possess the judgement required to control their artistic freedom.
Nevertheless, as our period progressed, writers of most nationalities began to
discuss more fully problems of technique (notably of posture, holding the
violin and bow, general left- and right-hand technique, special effects), and of
interpretation (ornamentation, colour and expression, and especially tone
production), skilful management of the bow being the principal factor of
expressive performance. During the period under review some dozen violin
methods of substance were published: it is these that form the backbone of this
study.

4. Maass, 'Ueber die Flaschinettöne, besonders der Saiten', *Allgemeine musikalische Zeitung* (July 1815),
   cols. 477–87; Küster, 'Einiges über die Ausübung der Flageolettöne auf der Violine', *Allgemeine
   musikalische Zeitung* (October 1819), cols. 701–7.
5. See L. Mozart, *Versuch . . .*, ch. 5, §13, p. 107; Spohr, *Violinschule* (1832), p. 108. See also ch. 9,
   pp. 211–22.

The first French tutor of note to be published during the period was *Principes* . . . (1761, 81 pp.) by L'Abbé le fils, alias Joseph-Barnabé Saint-Sevin (1727–1803). This amalgamates the Italian sonata tradition, as represented by the numerous lessons 'in the manner of sonatas', with the French dance tradition, as manifested in the various *Menuets*, *Airs* and *Rondeaux* and in the two suites of *Airs d'opéra*, which also include dances, in the form of advanced duets for two violins. It comprises a rather *ad hoc* mixture of ideas lacking in systematic order with musical content predominating over verbal. Nevertheless, it includes much technical instruction of great consequence, notably that concerning the violin and bow holds, bow management, half position, ornamentation, double stopping and harmonics, supplemented by numerous examples and complete compositions for the instrument.

Michel Corrette's (1709–95) *L'art* . . ., (1782, 91 pp.) is likewise textually sparse, its main substance comprising a collection of compositions for the most part of Italian origins by such composers as Abaco, Alberti, Albinoni, Corelli, Locatelli, Geminiani and Handel as well as the writer himself. Corrette intended the work as a sequel to his *L'école d'Orphée* (Paris, 1738) and it accordingly demands of the student more advanced technical expertise, notably in its bowing requirements, its emphasis on tone quality and expression so characteristic of the French school, its use of high position-work up to the eleventh position, its cadenzas and preludes and its graduated exercises in double stopping.

Jean-Baptiste Cartier (1765–1841) similarly incorporates numerous compositions into his *L'art* . . ., (1798, 287 pp.), which was dedicated to the new *Conservatoire de musique* in Paris, thoroughly commended by that institution's violin professors and consequently adopted initially in its curriculum. The third and most valuable part of this method comprises an anthology of some 140 pieces by members of the French, German and Italian violin schools of the seventeenth and eighteenth centuries. Corelli and Tartini of the Italian school, Stamitz and Mozart of the German school and Leclair, Cartier and Gaviniès of the French school are among the principal composers represented in this section, which embraces a remarkable variety of compositions and styles, ranging from music for unaccompanied violin (comprising works by Stamitz, Nardini, Spadina, Locatelli, J. S. Bach and Moria) to an interesting collection of *chasses* and, as an appendix to the second and later editions of the treatise, an *Adagio* by Tartini complete with eighteen variants as to the possible embellishment of the given melody.

In comparison with this third part the first two are disappointing. The text of the first section, a brief survey of the main principles of violin playing comprising the violin and bow holds, bow division and management, ornaments, expression and other technical and interpretative matters, is especially retrospective. Cartier freely admits that his comments are little more than an amalgamation of extracts from the treatises of Geminiani, Leopold Mozart, Tarade and L'Abbé le fils.[6] It is indeed a curious hotch-potch of ideas from different national schools; as such, however, it nevertheless confirms the advent of a more uniform, international approach to violin playing. The second part, intended primarily to acquaint the student with the geography of the fingerboard, includes nine scales (illustrating the use of position-work) and discusses in turn the fingering of fifths (of all kinds), Italian terms, harmonics, double stopping and ornaments. Three duos by Cartier himself are included for the perfection of slurred bowings (no. 1) and elementary position-work (nos. 2 and 3) together with a survey of various arpeggio bowings.

Michel Woldemar's (1750–1816) *Grande méthode* . . . (c. 1800, 69 pp.), despite its full title, is scarcely suitable for elementary violinists. Although some basic technical problems are discussed, beginners are likely to be defeated both by Woldemar's eccentric style and his advanced technical requirements. The treatise is especially notable for its exhaustive study of scales and its extensive musical content; it concludes with a collection of study material, including exercises, *Le nouvel art de l'archet* (variations on a polonaise, incorporating varied bowings), three *fugues en caprices* and another polonaise with variations. Examples of cadenzas in various keys and suggestions as to varying degrees of ornamentation of a given melody bring the work to a close.

Woldemar also published editions of the treatises by Leopold Mozart and Rode *et al*. His edition of Leopold Mozart's work, entitled *Méthode de violon par L. Mozart rédigée par Woldemar, élève de Lolli* (1801, 81 pp.), reflects many of the technical changes effected since Leopold Mozart's original edition. In fact, Woldemar considered Leopold Mozart's treatise inadequate for nineteenth-century usage, especially the recommended violin hold and many of the principles for fingering and bowing. Concluding with caprices by himself, Hyllverding, Leopold Mozart, Kautz, Christiani, Mestrino, Locatelli and pieces by Corelli and Pagin, his thorough musical and textual revisions result in an edition which bears little resemblance to Mozart's original work in either layout or content.

The *Méthode* . . . (1803, 165 pp.) of Rode *et al*. begins with introductory articles concerning the origins and history of the violin, artistic matters and taste prior to the more practical considerations which form the first part of the work. Basic rules are presented for holding the violin and bow, positioning the arms and hands, finger action (with rather uninteresting exercises, based on scales, in double stopping and in position-work up to seventh position), general posture and bow management, and a description of the various *agrémens du chant* is succeeded in turn by a discussion of bowing principles, nuances and improvised ornamentation. The first part concludes with Baillot's *50 études sur la gamme* while part two deals exclusively with the philosophy

---

6. Cartier, *L'art* . . . (1798), preface, p. ii.

of expression. Despite its deficiencies, this method remained unchallenged as the standard French violin text for approximately thirty years; it was widely read and imitated by many violinists, notably Fauré and Mazas, who include extracts verbatim in their own methods.

Pierre Baillot's (1771–1842) *L'art . . .* (1834, 279 pp.), a conscious attempt to remedy the omissions of the *Méthode . . .* (1803) initially adopted by the Paris Conservatoire, easily surpasses it in content and detail. After an introductory summary of the violin's origins and history and its progress up to Paganini, Baillot divides the main body of his method into two sections. The first part is devoted to the mechanics of violin playing and deals with most technical and stylistic matters in unprecedented detail. Part two concentrates on expression and is essentially a reprint of the relevant section of the *Méthode . . .* with a short introduction by Baillot. Numerous musical examples, studies and compositions are included in this copious volume, which provides a marvellous insight into the technique, style and aesthetics of the period.

François Habeneck (1781–1849) is perhaps best remembered for introducing Beethoven's music to French audiences and continuing to promote it in his various roles as director of the Conservatoire students' orchestra, the *Concert spirituel* (from 1818 onwards) and the *Société des concerts du Conservatoire*. His *Méthode . . .* (c. 1840?, 177 pp.), greatly influenced by the teaching of Baillot, is of special significance as it incorporates facsimiles of extracts from Viotti's unfinished elementary method, presented to Habeneck for publication by Mrs Chinnery, to whom it had been bequeathed. Habeneck's work is divided into three main sections. The first is devoted to fundamental musical rudiments; part two is concerned with violin technique, incorporating information about the violin and bow, an extract from Viotti's treatise, advice about practice, posture, the violin and bow holds, bow management, scales (including another extract from Viotti's method), varied bowings, position-work and shifting. Although the final part chiefly concerns expression and includes practical advice about bow division, dynamics, phrasing, nuances, ornaments and *accent*, Habeneck suddenly reverts to technical considerations quite unconnected with expression, making special studies of double and triple stopping, arpeggios, harmonics, chromatic scales and improvisatory ornamentation, including *préludes* and *cadences*. He concludes with interesting observations on the performing styles of some contemporary violinists, illustrated by extracts from the compositions of Ernst, Vieuxtemps and Paganini.

ITALY

Francesco Geminiani (1687–1762), one of the most prominent Italian violinists at the beginning of the period under study, exerted a remarkable influence on the development of violin technique through his teaching, performance and works, especially his *The art . . .* (1751, 51 pp.). This influence, however, was felt largely in England and Ireland, his adopted homelands, and in countries other than his native Italy; it is therefore evaluated elsewhere.[7]

Francesco Galeazzi's (1758–1819) *Elementi . . .* was published in two volumes (vol. 1, 1791, 252 pp.; vol. 2, 1796, 327 pp.), each divided into two parts. The second volume includes thoughts on the principles of ancient and modern music, coupled with a study of harmony, melody and composition, while the first part of volume one deals thoroughly with general theory and elementary musical grammar and the second part provides a detailed survey of the main technical principles of violin playing and general performance practice. This methodical survey includes informative articles on the construction and main properties of the violin and bow, tuning, intonation, scales, the violin and bow holds, timbre, fingering, position-work and shifting, bow management, harmonics, double stopping, arpeggios, ornamentation, expression and various other considerations. Galeazzi surprisingly considers all ornaments as 'improvisatory' and discusses them in combination with expression, as these factors are considered the two main ingredients of style; this section on ornaments and expression (entitled 'Diminutions and expression') constitutes arguably the most important source of information on improvisation published in Italy in the late eighteenth century. In addition, there are detailed observations on orchestral playing, the duties of the concertmaster, sight-reading, accompaniment, solo playing and an interesting insight into Galeazzi's pedagogical approach, incorporating an hypothetical syllabus for the beginner. This schedule is firmly based initially on the theoretical principles expounded in volume one, part one, and later on the scale, in myriad forms and keys, as a fundamental discipline in the exercise of both left and right hands, especially for purposes of pure intonation, articulation and tone production. Interestingly enough, the second edition of Galeazzi's treatise (Ascoli, 1817, vol. 1 only) incorporates significant improvements in one main area, that of bowing, the author himself admitting in his preface his dissatisfaction with his original survey. Bowing considerations apart, practically all the rest of the material in the revised edition is a verbatim duplication of the original.

Bartolomeo Campagnoli's (1751–1827) *Metodo . . .* (1797?, English translation by Bishop, 131 pp.),[8] strongly influenced by the theories of his teacher, Pietro Nardini (1722–93), appeared in many editions and was widely translated. Subdivided into five parts with an introduction devoted to general technical matters, the first four sections provide detailed systematic instruction regarding the application of the 250 progressive exercises incorporated in part five and an advanced technical standard is reached in the closing exercises.

7. See p. 10.
8. The original date of Campagnoli's method is subject to some disagreement but it was, at the very least, in preparation during the 1790s. See Montanari, *Bartolomeo Campagnoli, violinistica compositore* (1751–1827) (n.p., 1969) and White, *The new Grove . . .*, s.v. 'Campagnoli, Bartolomeo'.

GERMANY

Leopold Mozart's (1719–87) comprehensive *Versuch . . .* (1756, 264 pp.) remained the most important German violin treatise for the advanced player well into the nineteenth century. Four editions appeared before 1800, by which time many of Mozart's technical principles were outdated and suited neither to the demands of the more advanced music of the period nor to the characteristics of the Tourte bow. Each edition includes some revisions which reflect contemporary technical developments. The third edition (1787) contains the most changes, but the differences between this and the second (1769–70) and fourth (1800) editions are negligible. A revised edition of the treatise by Joseph Pirlinger was published under the title *Neue vollständige theoretische und praktische Violinschule für Lehrer und Lernende* (Vienna, 1799–1800) and another such adaptation of the work appeared in Leipzig (1804).

Carl Guhr's (1787–1848) *Ueber Paganinis Kunst . . .* (1829, 61 pp.). an informative account of Paganini's performing style, was the first of two methods of advanced standard published in Germany during the first half of the nineteenth century. It was intended not as a comprehensive violin method but 'merely as an appendix to such as already exist'.[9] Without this study, knowledge of Paganini's technical facility, manner of performance and, indeed, some of his compositions would be slight, since Paganini guarded his works and executive skills with the utmost secrecy. Guhr describes the peculiarities of Paganini's physique, technique and equipment in considerable detail; he isolates the main differences between Paganini's imaginative performing style and that of his contemporaries, emphasising in particular Paganini's tuning of the instrument, bow strokes, combination of left-hand *pizzicato* with bowing, use of harmonics in single and double stopping, *una corda* playing and the extraordinary *tours de force* for which he was renowned.

In complete contrast Ludwig Spohr's (1784–1859) *Violinschule* (1832, 248 pp.) is rather conservative in content, restricted somewhat by the technical and stylistic limitations that he himself imposed. He objected to many of the effects employed by Paganini and other virtuosi, notably 'thrown' bowings, artificial harmonics and suchlike, preferring to cultivate a more 'classical' on-the-string bowing technique and singing tone. His treatise is divided into three sections, the first of which is devoted to the construction, maintenance and constituent parts of the instrument, its arrangement, its strings, the differences in the tonal quality and volume of various violin models, the bow and the use of rosin. The central section comprises progressive and systematic accounts of the basic rudiments of music, the elementary principles of holding the violin and bow, the movement of the right arm, the action of the fingers of the left hand, note values and rests, time-signatures and tempo indications, scales, position-work, extensions, harmonics, varied bowings, double and

9. Guhr, *Ueber Paganinis Kunst . . .* (1829), preface, p. 2.

multiple stopping, arpeggios and ornamentation, especially emphasising the importance of a correct left-hand finger action so that the foundations of pure intonation can be laid. Part three is concerned with style and interpretation and is subdivided into four sections, dealing in turn with interpretation in general, concerto playing, quartet playing and orchestral playing. In addition, Spohr's treatise incorporates extensive exercises for the implementation of his principles and provides considerable advice for parents and teachers concerning practice, regularity of instruction, the ideal starting age and the advantages of parental involvement and encouragement.

GREAT BRITAIN

Violin playing in Britain during the period was dominated by foreign musicians, of whom Geminiani was by far the most important, spreading the technique and style of his master, Corelli, through his compositions, teaching, performance and, above all, his *The art . . .* (1751, 51 pp.). This violin treatise appeared in several editions, including fairly faithful translations into French (first edition, *L'art de jouer le violon*, Paris, 1752?) and German (first edition, *Gründliche Anleitung oder Violinschule*, Vienna, 1782), such minor alterations as they contained reflecting technical changes of the times. In 1769, an abbreviated version of the treatise was published in the United States under the title *An abstract of Geminiani's art of playing on the violin* (Boston, 1769) and there later appeared at least one edited and improved version conforming to the demands of a more advanced technique, notably *L'art du violon ou méthode raisonnée* (Paris, n.d.; Eitner suggests 1803). The title-page states explicitly, 'Originally composed by the celebrated F. Geminiani', and the contents show extensive changes from the original. Plagiarised versions of Geminiani's treatise continued to be published well into the nineteenth century.[10]

10. For a comprehensive list of these pirated adaptations of Geminiani's work, see Geminiani, *The art . . .*, (facsimile ed. Boyden, London, 1952), editor's introduction, pp. x-xi.

I

The development of the bow, the violin and its fittings

The development of a musical instrument is invariably influenced by changing ideals of technique and expression. Instruments either die out or undergo modification if their expressive potential fails to meet the changing demands of musical taste. Nowhere is this interaction between instrument construction and musical style more clearly evident than in the history of the violin and, in particular, the bow during the eighteenth and early nineteenth centuries, a period of experimentation and development marked by flashes of discovery and synthesis.

THE DEVELOPMENT OF THE BOW

The bow was invariably described as 'the soul of the instrument'[1] on account of its vital expressive role in the arts of phrasing, nuance and 'singing'. It underwent considerable variation in size, shape, weight, balance and general construction during the eighteenth century, the preferred design at first varying from country to country in accordance with musical style. Short, straight bows were employed in France, mainly for dance music; long, straight (or slightly convex) bows in Italy, for the sonata and concerto; and rather more solid, convex bows of intermediate length in Germany, probably for greater facility in the execution of the German polyphonic style (the outward-curved 'Bach bow', however, is not a reproduction of a baroque model, but a modern invention designed to facilitate smooth, sustained performances of polyphonic violin music).

The gradual fusion of national styles during the eighteenth century and the demand for increased tonal volume (met also by developments in violin construction), *cantabile* and a wider dynamic range prompted the production of longer and straighter bow sticks, two notable early examples of such models being the bow of c. 1700, accredited to Stradivari, in the Ansley Salz collection (University of California at Berkeley) and one dated 1694 in the Hill collec-

1. See, for example, L'Abbé le fils, *Principes* . . . (1761), p. 1.

II

tion of bows (London). This straightening of the stick required modifications
in the height and curvature of the so-called pike's (or swan's) head, in order to
allow sufficient separation of the hair and the stick; and when, towards the
mid eighteenth century, makers began to anticipate the concave *cambre* of the
'modern' stick, further changes in the design of the head were required for
optimum hair/stick separation at the middle. Fig. 1 clearly illustrates these
developments, ranging from the pike's head of bow A to the modified pike's
head and concave *cambre* of bow B, the transitional bows C (with its raised
pike's head) E and G (with their varying degrees of concave *cambre* and
different dimensions of the pike's head), the hatchet head of bows D and F and
finally the 'modern' head of bows H and I which closely resemble the model
standardised by François Tourte during the 1780s.

   The length of bows employed varied considerably during the first half of the
eighteenth century. Their dimensions were also variable during the latter half
of the century, but, as Sir John Hawkins remarked (1776), there was a growing
trend towards the use of bows with a greater playing length of hair: 'The bow
of the violin has been gradually increasing in length for the last seventy years;
it is now about twenty-eight inches [i.e. 71·12 cm overall length]. In the year
1720, a bow of twenty-four inches [60·96 cm] was, on account of its length,
called a sonata bow; the common bow was shorter; and . . . the French bow
must have been shorter still.'[2] By about 1750 the average playing length of bows
measured approximately 61 cm, although Tourte *père* produced some longer
models, notably bow E (Fig. 1), which is 74·08 cm long overall with a playing
length of hair of 63·92 cm. Table 1 provides a general overview of weights and
measurements of extant bows c. 1700 – c. 1780 and concurs for the most part
with the statistics of the bows illustrated in Fig. 1.

Table 1. *Weights (in g) and measurements (in cm)[3] of bows (c. 1700 – c. 1780)*

	minimum	medium	maximum
Overall length	70.5	72.5	73.9
Diameter of stick at frog	0.85	0.88	0.91
Diameter of stick at head	0.51	0.57	0.70
Hair to stick at frog	1.55	1.77	1.90
Width of hair in frog	0.62	0.82	1.05
Bowing length	60.1	62.5	64.2
Weight	47	51.5	58

   Early-eighteenth-century bows, which were often fluted, were generally
lighter than modern models but were nevertheless strong, if a little inflexible.
Their point of balance was generally nearer the frog than with modern bows
due to the lightness of the head; nearly every model tapered to a fine point at
the pike's head. Snakewood was most commonly employed in bow construc-

2. Hawkins, *A general history* . . ., vol. 2, p. 782.
3. Boomkamp & van der Meer, *The Carel van Leeuwen Boomkamp collection* . . ., pp. 57–8.

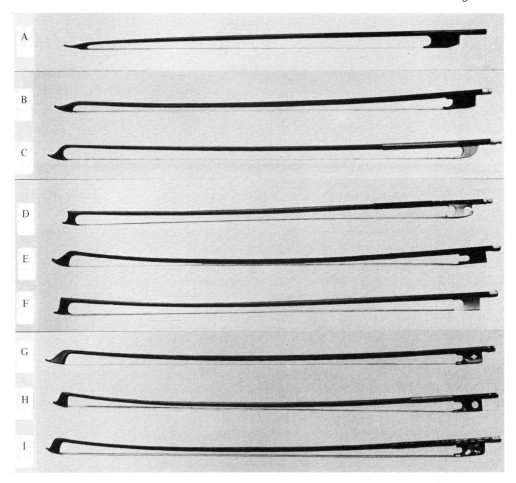

1. Violin bows c. 1700 – c. 1820 preserved in the Hill collection of musical instruments in the Ashmolean Museum, Oxford

		weight (g)	overall length (cm)	playing length (cm)
A	Anon. c. 1700	51	70.4	55.9
B	Anon. c. 1740	58	70.2	59.5
C	Edward Dodd? c. 1750	46	73.0	62.0
D	Anon. c. 1750	52	71.1	63.1
E	Tourte *père* c. 1760	49	73.8	64.4
F	Edward Dodd c. 1775	48	73.4	62.8
G	John Dodd c. 1780	49	73.7	64.1
H	John Dodd c. 1800	53	73.0	63.1
I	Anon. (German) c. 1820	63	74.6	64.5

tion, but pernambuco, brazil wood and plum wood were certainly known and increasingly used as the century progressed.[4] Although bows of pernambuco were rare before c. 1750, the bow attributed to Stradivari (c. 1700), mentioned earlier, is one notable extant example. The modifications in bow design during the century, notably in the shape of the head, the length of the stick and eventually the constitution of the frog (for optimum balance), resulted in an increase in overall bow weight of up to 11 g. (see Table 1). The 'modern' bow averages 56 g.

The type of nut employed for regulating the hair tension varied from a fixed nut to the *cremaillère* device (comprising a movable nut, whose position was adjusted and secured by a metal loop locked into one of several notches on the top of the stick) and, certainly by 1750, the 'modern' screw-nut attachment. The invention of this latter device is erroneously attributed to Tourte *père*; Boyden, however, suggests that it was invented in the late seventeenth century and supplies evidence of a bow in the Hill collection (London), in original condition and date-stamped 1694 on its movable frog, which is adjusted by a screw.[5]

Few bow makers before 1750 stamped their names on their bows and, even by 1800, the naming of bows was more of an exception than the norm. However, although the illustrations provided in eighteenth-century treatises and other contemporary sources fail to match those of extant bows for elegance, they do furnish us with clues as to the main performers who championed the various eighteenth-century developments in bow design. Both Fétis (Fig. 2) and Woldemar (Fig. 3) illustrate four eighteenth-century bow types, named respectively after Corelli, Tartini, Cramer and Viotti,[6] while Baillot (Fig. 4) illustrates six varieties (Corelli, Pugnani, two unnamed transitional types, Viotti and Tourte). That bows were ascribed to well-known violinists as opposed to makers underlines the fact that, with a few exceptions, bow making did not become an organised craft in its own right until the second half of the eighteenth century.

The term 'Corelli bow' appears to have designated the common early-eighteenth-century Italian sonata bow with its straight or slightly convex bow stick and pike's head, while the 'Tartini bow' (Baillot's 'Pugnani bow' looks very similar) appears to have referred to a straight, apparently longer bow of more streamlined design, which, according to Fétis,[7] was constructed from lighter wood and fluted at its lower end in the interests of greater manual control.

The 'Cramer bow' represents one of the many transitional types in bow development between the various Italian models and the Tourte design and

---

4. See Sprengel & Hartwig, *Handwerke und Künste* (Berlin, 1770–3), as quoted in Boomkamp & van der Meer, *The Carel van Leeuwen Boomkamp collection . . .* , p. 59.
5. Boyden, *The history of violin playing . . .*, p. 209 and Plate 29d.
6. In his 'edition' of Leopold Mozart's method (1801), Woldemar illustrates one further type, used by Mestrino, which is similar to though a little longer than the Cramer model.
7. Fétis, *Antoine Stradivari . . .*, tr. Bishop, p. 124.

No 1. — Mersenne, 1620.

No 2. — Kircher, 1640.

No 3. — Castrovillari, 1660.

No 4. — Bassani, 1680.

No 5. — Corelli, 1700.

No 6. — Tartini, 1740.

No 7. — Cramer, 1770.

No 8. — Viotti, 1790.

2. Violin bows c. 1620–1790 as illustrated by Fétis

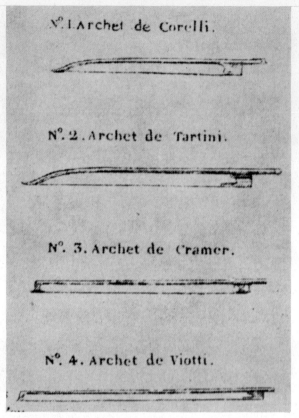

Nº 1. Archet de Corelli.

Nº 2. Archet de Tartini.

Nº 3. Archet de Cramer.

Nº 4. Archet de Viotti.

3. Violin bows of the seventeenth and eighteenth centuries
as illustrated by Woldemar

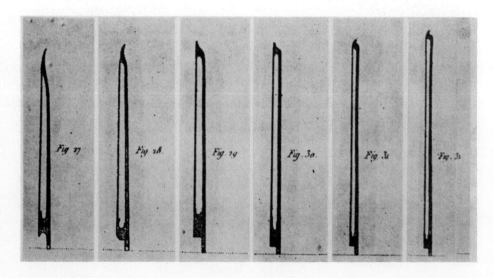

4. Violin bows of the seventeenth, eighteenth and early nineteenth centuries as illustrated by
Baillot

5. Lithograph of Nicolo Paganini by Karl Begas (c. 1820)

was commonly employed between c. 1760 and c. 1785, especially in Mannheim, where Wilhelm Cramer spent the early part of his career. Woldemar confirms that Cramer's bow 'was adopted in his day by most performers and amateurs',[8] and it was certainly well known and commonly employed in London's musical circles after Cramer had settled in the capital in 1772. It was longer than most Italian models but slightly shorter than Tourte's later standardised design, being distinguished also by its characteristically shaped frog, the slight concave *cambre* of its stick and its neat 'battle-axe' head (with a peak in the front matched by a peak in the back of the head proper).[9] Some violinists employed a bow of this type well into the nineteenth century, as Karl Begas's lithograph (c. 1820) of Paganini clearly demonstrates (Fig. 5).

Woldemar claims that the 'Viotti bow' 'differs little from Cramer's in the design of the head [although this is more hatchet-like with a peak in the front only] but the nut is lower and brought nearer the screw attachment; it is longer and has more hair; it looks slightly straighter when in use and is employed almost exclusively today'.[10] However, there is some confusion as to whether Fétis's and Woldemar's so-called 'Viotti bow' with its fully developed hatchet head is actually the Tourte bow in all but name. Certainly Tourte would have been influenced by those performers who frequented his workshops either to suggest ideas and improvements or simply to inspect and play examples of his work. Fétis implies that there was some collaboration between the two personalities: 'at about this time (1780), Viotti came to Paris. Soon convinced of Tourte's superiority over other bow-makers, he asked him to look for a way of preventing the hair from becoming bunched, keeping it evenly spread at the frog.'[11] However, Baillot illustrates the 'Viotti' and Tourte bows as two distinct models, the 'Viotti bow' (c. 72·39 cm) being slightly shorter than the Tourte design (c. 74·42 cm, a measurement which, as Boyden confirms,[12] conforms to that of Baillot's own Tourte bow in the Library of Congress in Washington).

Although both his father (Tourte *père*) and elder brother Xavier (Tourte *l'aîné*) were bow makers, François Tourte (1747–1835) was originally apprenticed to the clock-making trade; after about eight years, however, he gravitated to the family bow-making business as his father's pupil and assistant. The development of the bow had already been forecast by Tourte *père* and his contemporaries (See Fig. 1, bow E, with its fully developed hatchet head) to such an extent that François Tourte can hardly be described as an innovator in this field. His achievement was largely to synthesise his predecessors' work rather than to innovate, as he standardised the dimensions, materials, final design and construction of the bow.

8. Woldemar, *Grande méthode* . . . (c. 1800), p. 3.
9. Boyden, 'The violin bow in the eighteenth century', *Early Music*, vol. 8 (1980), p. 206.
10. Woldemar, *Grande méthode* . . . (c. 1800), p. 3.
11. *Biographie universelle* . . ., ed. Fétis, vol. 7, p. 246.
12. Boyden, 'The violin bow in the eighteenth century', *Early Music*, vol. 8 (1980), p. 210.

Tourte fully understood the needs of contemporary violinists and experimented with various kinds of wood in order to find a variety which provided the lightness, strength and elasticity required for the execution of the increasing variety of bow strokes demanded by changing musical taste. He eventually concluded that pernambuco wood (*Caesalpinia echinata*) best satisfied these requirements and further discovered that, after thoroughly heating the straight stick, he could bend it to the desired concave *cambre*, thus preserving the natural elasticity of the wood. It was vital for the stick to be heated thoroughly, right through the inner fibres, before being bent, otherwise warping or some other malformation might occur. This heating process was apparently unknown to Tourte's predecessors; they carved the stick to the desired curvature or shape, thereby cutting the fibres of the wood across instead of preserving them intact throughout the length of the stick, and thus lost the wood's natural resiliency.

Tourte's bow stick, generally of octagonal design, tapered gradually towards the point; the diameter of the stick measured 8·6 mm throughout the 11 cm length of the lower end. From there to the tip it decreased evenly by 3·3 mm.[13] Vuillaume later proved that, when the bow was unstrung, the stick could be expressed mathematically in terms of a logarithmic curve in which the ordinates increase in arithmetical progression while the abscissae increase in geometrical progression.[14] Such a curve has the general equation of $y = a + b \log x$ and empirically $y = 3 \cdot 11 + 2 \cdot 571 \log x$. William Retford refutes the suggestion that the *cambres* of all Tourte's bows were exactly uniform, close examination with a gauge revealing that no two were exactly the same; however, the taper of each was practically identical, any variation being governed by the balance of the stick.[15]

The pronounced concave *cambre* of the Tourte bow necessitated changes in the design of the head in order to prevent the hair from touching the stick when pressure was applied at the tip. Tourte solved this problem by making the head higher (Fig. 6) (and consequently heavier) than both the pike's head and the early square or hatchet head varieties. This modification naturally affected the balance of the bow and to redress this Tourte added metal inlays (generally in the form of gold, silver or even tortoiseshell ornamentation) to the nut, thus bringing the point of greatest weight close to the hand. The point of balance of the Tourte model thus lies nearer the point (about 19–20 cm from the frog) than that of its predecessors with the smaller, lighter tip.

Tourte also standardised the length and weight of the bow, factors which had varied considerably during the course of the eighteenth century (see Table 1). Tourte determined the ideal length of the bow stick to be between 73·66 cm and 74·93 cm, providing a playing length of hair of approximately 64·77 cm. The optimum weight was approximately 56 g.

13. Farga, *Violins and violinists*, tr. Larsen, p. 92.
14. Fétis, *Antoine Stradivari . . .*, tr. Bishop, p. 124.

15. Retford, *Bows and bowmakers*, p. 48 & p. 28.

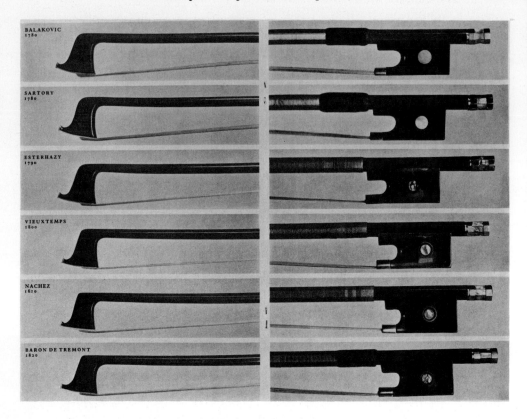

6.   Violin bows (c. 1780–c. 1820) by François Tourte

Tourte also pioneered important changes in the treatment and arrangement of the bow hair. From about the middle of the eighteenth century, the
amount of hair employed in the stringing of bows was gradually increased
(from about 80-100 to 150-200 hairs, although Spohr states 100-110),[16] a
direct result of the contemporary quest for tonal improvement. However, this
increase did not alone solve the tonal problems satisfactorily; a method of
spreading the hair proved essential, as difficulties with the irregular bunching
of the hair were commonly encountered. Tourte's solution was to increase the
width of the ribbon of hair (to measure about 10 mm at the nut and about
8 mm at the point)[17] and to maintain the hair uniformly flat and even by
securing it at the frog with a ferrule, made originally of tin and later of silver.
Louis Tourte (*père*), among others, is thought to have invented the ferrule but
François Tourte was undoubtedly the first bow maker to bring it into general

16. Spohr, *Violinschule* (1832), p. 18.   17. Roda, *Bows for musical instruments of the violin family*, p. 65.

use. A wooden wedge was positioned between the hair and the bevelled portion of the frog so that the hair was pressed against the ferrule by the wedge
and the ferrule itself was prevented from sliding off. A mother-of-pearl slide
was also fitted into a swallow-tail groove in the frog in order to conceal the
hair-fastening and enhance the bow's appearance. Tourte's frogs were generally of ebony, ivory or tortoiseshell, complete with such attachments as a
screw mechanism for adjusting the tension of the hair and in many cases an
ornamental inlay of silver, gold or tortoiseshell.

Tourte devised a unique process for the treatment of the bow hair prior to
stringing his bows. He preferred using French horsehair, as it was apparently
thicker and stronger than that from other countries. Having ensured that the
individual hairs were perfectly cylindrical and of equal length and thickness
throughout, Tourte then scoured them with soap before immersing them in
bran water. After removing the heterogeneous particles which had adhered to
the hairs, he finally plunged them into pure water, lightly coloured with blue.[18]

Although the Tourte bow quickly gained acceptance with those violinists
fortunate enough either to possess one or experiment with one, universal
approval of the new design was slow to materialise. Although Woldemar
claims that the 'Viotti' model was exclusively used (1801),[19] many French
makers continued to make bows modelled on pre-Tourte designs (generally of
brazil wood instead of the more expensive pernambuco) well into the
nineteenth century. Vuillaume's discovery that the taper of the stick generally
corresponded to a logarithmic curve finally provided the impetus for makers
to reproduce the Tourte design, and the publication of Vuillaume's theories
(1856) revealed Tourte's secrets to a wider public of eager craftsmen. It is
therefore not surprising that late-eighteenth-century violin treatises chiefly
discussed bowing techniques relative to pre-Tourte models; it was not until
the *Méthode* . . . (1803) of Rode *et al.* that bow management relevant to the
Tourte bow was examined in any detail, although Campagnoli's instructions
(*Metodo* . . . , 1797?) are fairly advanced.

John Dodd (1752–1839) was probably the first English craftsman to adopt
similar modifications to those introduced by Tourte. Whether Dodd actually
copied Tourte's model or arrived at a similar design quite independently is not
known; legend opts for the latter explanation but, taking into account the considerable influence of touring virtuosi in such matters, it seems doubtful that
English makers would have been ignorant of any noteworthy developments
made by their French counterparts, and vice versa, even though contemporary relations between England and France were hardly conducive to such
a free exchange of ideas. Furthermore, certain differences in the respective
work of the two makers suggest that legend may be correct. Whereas Tourte
cut his sticks straight and shaped them by a process of heating, Dodd is

18. Fétis, *Antoine Stradivari* . . ., tr. Bishop, p. 117.
19. *Méthode de violon par L. Mozart rédigée par Woldemar* . . . (1801), p. 5.

believed (at first, anyway) to have cut out his bow sticks immediately to the
required curvature, thus omitting any such heat treatment. Dodd was also less
consistent than Tourte, experimenting widely with various weights, shapes of
head, lengths and forms of stick and mountings on the nut. Close inspection
of bows G and H (Fig. 1) reveals Dodd's cruder and more primitive approach
to the craft, approximating to the appearance of the Cramer type, which
together with the bows of his father, Edward Dodd (Fig. 1 bow F), most likely
served as his model; his bows are slightly shorter, in both the stick and the playing hair, and lighter than the average Tourte model. In fact, Dodd produced
full-length Tourte-model bows only late in life; bow H (Fig. 1) shows an example (c. 1800) of a fully developed 'modern' bow by Dodd, including slide, ferrule, ornamental effects and the other modifications implemented at that
time.

The Tourte model enabled the performer to control his powers of expression more easily; with its greater length and superior balance it could produce
a stronger tone than its predecessors and was especially well suited to the sustained *cantabile* style dominant in the period of its inception. Its ability to make
smooth bow changes with the minimum differentiation (where required)
between slurred and unslurred bowing brought the later 'seamless phrase'
ideal nearer to reality. A normal straight bow stroke, with the index-finger
pressure and bow speed remaining constant, produced an even tone throughout its length because the shape and flexibility of the stick enabled the index-
finger pressure to be distributed evenly. Variation of this pressure, bow speed,
contact point, type of stroke and other technical considerations provided the
wider expressive range so important to contemporary aesthetic ideals, in
which the element of contrast, involving sudden changes of dynamic or long
crescendos and *diminuendos*, played a significant role.

The hair of most pre-Tourte bows was generally capable of considerably less
tension than that of Tourte models, chiefly because of the shape and consequent inferior strength of the bow sticks employed. Thus, it yields rather more
when brought into contact with the strings and produces, as Leopold Mozart
described it, 'a small, even if barely audible, softness at the beginning of the
stroke'.[20] A similar 'softness' was also perceptible at the end of each stroke,
resulting in a natural articulation provided by the bow itself. The concave bow
stick of the Tourte model, on the other hand, yields very little when pressed on
the string and thus affords a more or less immediate attack. Furthermore, this
quicker take-up of hair, the greater strength (particularly at the point) and the
broader ribbon of hair also contributed to the widening of the bowing vocabulary to include *sforzando* effects (the *sfz* indication was rare in music written
before the last quarter of the eighteenth century) and various accented bowings. The *martelé*, the most fundamental of all modern strokes, formed the

20. L. Mozart, *Versuch* . . ., ch. 5, §3, p. 102.

basis of other important bowings; these included the accented *détaché*, the *fouetté*, *collé* and other accented varieties. Even the *staccato*, the natural stroke of the upper half of most pre-Tourte bows, became a series of small successive *martelé* strokes with the Tourte model.[21] The elasticity of the Tourte bow and the tautness of its hair also led to increased exploitation of various 'thrown' strokes, notably the *spiccato*, *sautillé* and *ricochet* bowings, which rely on the resiliency of the bow stick for their execution.

Thus, the modern violin bow was the product of a number of separate influences, each displaying its own identity until their eventual amalgamation and standardisation by François Tourte. The only later improvements to the Tourte model were the addition of the underslide for the frog, invented by François Lupot junior (1774–1837) to prevent any wear on the nut caused by friction with the stick, the indentation of the channel and track of the frog in the bow, introduced by Jean-Baptiste Vuillaume (1798–1875), and the combination of rear and upper heel plates into one right-angled metal part.[22] Apart from these minor additions and numerous unsuccessful attempts to improve the bow,[23] Tourte's bows were universally imitated as the virtual blueprint for all subsequent bow makers of the nineteenth and twentieth centuries. They have never been surpassed.

THE VIOLIN AND ITS FITTINGS

The mid-eighteenth-century quest for a strong, full tone and sonorous *cantabile* was only partly answered by the various developments in bow design during the century, culminating in the work of François Tourte. Changes also proved necessary in the design and construction of the violin itself in order to enable it to produce sufficient tonal power and brilliance to fill the larger concert halls and compete with the larger concert orchestra of the late eighteenth and early nineteenth centuries.[24] Few of the differences between the 'baroque' violin and its modern counterpart are immediately noticeable, as the fundamental exterior shape of the violin and the length of its body (typically c. 35·6 cm) have remained unchanged to this day.

The extra tonal power and brilliance required was effected chiefly by the greater tensions on the instrument resulting from the introduction of a slightly higher playing pitch, the use of a higher bridge and an increase in the playing length of the strings. The playing length of string of the modern violin is approximately 32·70 cm – 33·02 cm, about 0·64 cm – 1·27 cm longer than the

21. See ch. 8, pp. 182–4.
22. Roda, *Bows for musical instruments of the violin family*, p. 53.
23. See Heron-Allen, *Violin making as it was and is*, pp. 101–2.
24. See Carse, *The orchestra from Beethoven to Berlioz*, London, 1948, p. 18 and Zaslaw's qualifications of Carse in 'The size and composition of European orchestras, 1775–95', *Haydn studies: Proceedings of the International Haydn Conference . . . 1975)*, pp. 186–88, and 'Toward the revival of the classical orchestra', *Proceedings of the Royal Musical Association*, vol. 103 (1977), pp. 179–87.

average 'baroque' model. However, some violinists of the seventeenth and eighteenth centuries obtained a longer playing length of string from the 'baroque' model (approaching and even exceeding the average modern length) by moving the bridge farther back along the belly than is normal today. The placement of the nut may also have been variable.[25]

As a result of a fairly widespread rise in pitch in the last quarter of the eighteenth century,[26] the violin bridge was gradually transformed from the flatter, thicker variety of the early eighteenth century into the thinner, higher (by about 2·1 mm) modern form, with its sweeping curve towards the E string side helping to prevent any undesired 'fouling' of adjacent strings with the bow. Few examples of eighteenth-century bridges are extant but designs varied considerably according to national taste and individual preference; Fig. 8 illustrates the shape of a common baroque bridge, with its high 'eyes' and square feet (above), compared with the low 'eyes' and broad splayed feet of a typical modern model. By the late eighteenth century, the most common bridge type employed closely resembled the modern model illustrated.

The raising of the bridge necessitated a corresponding elevation of the fingerboard in order to enable it to follow more closely the angle of the strings and thus allow clarity of finger stopping. The obvious solution to this problem, insertion of a thicker wedge between fingerboard and neck, proved impracticable because the greater tension of the strings exerted increased pressure on the neck fitting, pressure which the base of the neck, glued to the body and secured by nails driven from inside the block, could barely withstand. Furthermore, the use of a thicker wedge would have proved contrary to the demands of a developing violin technique, which required a thinner, more manageable neck to enable the full range of the instrument to be exploited. Consequently, the wedge idea was rejected and a thinner (by about 3·18 mm) neck employed, tilted back at an angle in order to achieve the required tension (Fig. 7). This 'modern' neck was morticed into the block in order to provide additional strength to counteract the increased tension and was lengthened by 0·64 cm – 1·27 cm (the present standard length is approximately 12·86 cm – 13·02 cm) in keeping with the greater playing length of string. The narrower canted neck facilitated position-work, the adoption of a correct violin hold and performance on the lower strings, which were being increasingly exploited at the time.

The increased string tension exerted greater pressure on both bridge and belly. (The combined tension of the four strings of a violin tuned at modern pitch amounts to at least 50 lb,[27] of which some 20 lb is directed straight down through the bridge and against the belly of the instrument.) To distribute the

25. See Skeaping, 'Some speculations on a crisis in the history of the violin', *Galpin Society Journal*, vol. 8 (1955), pp. 5–6.
26. See ch. 10, pp. 241–5.
27. L'Abbé Sibire (*La chelonomie, ou le parfait Luthier*) estimated the string tension at 64 lb and the vertical pressure on the bridge at 24 lb.

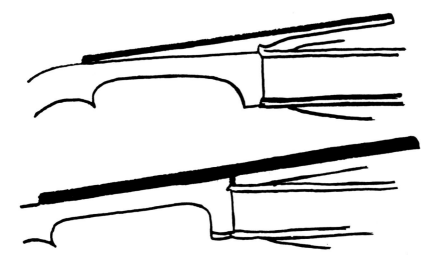

7. Diagram showing the respective angles of the neck and fingerboard of the unconverted 'baroque' violin (above) and the 'modern' instrument

8. Outline diagram of a typical 'baroque' bridge (above) compared with the common modern variety

load and reinforce the instrument against this greater pressure a longer, thicker and stronger bass bar was introduced. The respective measurements of the bass bar were gradually increased until its modern proportions were reached – approximately 26·67 cm long, 0·64 cm broad and 1·11 cm deep in the centre, sloping away to nothing at both ends. The more substantial modern

Table 2. Comparative dimensions (in cm) of baroque and modern bass bars[28]

	length	height in centre	thickness
Average modern bar	26·67	1·11	0·64
N. Amati (1650)	21·91	0·64	0·48
Stradivari (1704)	24·13	0·64	0·48
J. B. Guadagnini (1760)	25·08	0·79	0·48
Gagliano (1780)	26·04	1·11	0·64
F. Gagliano (1783)	30·48	0·95	0·64
F. Gagliano (1789)	27·31	1·75	1·43

bass bar also performed an acoustical function, transmitting the vibrations of the left foot of the bridge to the rest of the instrument. The standardisation of its measurements thus proved an important step towards the late-eighteenth-century sound ideal. The somewhat thicker, more substantial soundpost (c. 1800) also played a significant part.

The longer, narrower neck of the late-eighteenth-century instrument in turn affected the shape of the fingerboard; it, too, was narrowed at the peg-box end, allowing the player greater left-hand facility. The fingerboard was also broadened somewhat towards the bridge and more markedly arched through-out in keeping with the sweeping curve of the 'modern' bridge. Furthermore, it was gradually lengthened by approximately 5·08 cm – 6·35 cm to an average length of 26·67 cm, thus extending the range of the instrument beyond seventh position and affording the violinist greater facility in the exploitation of high position-work. Stradivari's fingerboards had varied in length from 19·05 cm to 21·59 cm;[29] Bornet and Durieu give the fingerboard length as 'neuf pouces' (about 24·13 cm) but Woldemar clearly demonstrates that a fingerboard of modern dimensions was in use by c. 1800, claiming that the violin compass is four octaves and two tones.[30] Many fingerboards and tailpieces were elaborately inlaid and most tailpieces retained the somewhat flatter shape and method of attachment of the old viol tailpiece.

The above modifications in violin design cannot be dated with any positive accuracy but are believed to have been implemented gradually over a substan-tial period of transition between c. 1760 and c. 1830. The new setting of the

28. Examples (with measurements converted to metric units) extracted from Hill, Life and work of Antonio Stradivari, p. 190.
29. Ibid., p. 213.
30. Bornet, Nouvelle méthode . . . (1786), p. 5; Durieu, Méthode . . . (1796), p. 5; Woldemar, Grande méthode . . . (c. 1800) p. 5.

neck appears to have been introduced by French makers,[31] Lancetti remarking (1823) that necks of Italian violins were being lengthened 'according to
the fashion prevailing in Paris'.[32] However, different developments took place
in different cities and at different times. Some Gagliano violins made as early
as the 1780s appear to combine original necks of almost modern dimensions
with fittings of eighteenth-century lightness and the necks of some English
violins were already of modern length c. 1760. The fittings of some other
Gagliano violins matched or even exceeded modern dimensions, notably the
bass bars of the two violins by F. Gagliano listed in Table 2. Whatever the
approximate date of these modifications, most old violins were converted to
comply with the musical ideals and requirements of late-eighteenth-century
musicians. The flat-model Stradivari, primarily designed for the production
of a powerful, brilliant tone, came into its own as a concert instrument, thanks
largely to the highly acclaimed performances of Viotti, who demonstrated the
model's potential to the full; however, the highly-arched models of Stainer and
the Amati family lost their former popularity, due to their comparatively small
tonal potential, suitable only for chamber music and small concert halls.

In spite of all the changes in the various violin fittings, the main body of the
instrument remained unaltered throughout the period of transition;[33] in fact,
this basic design has been unsurpassed to this day despite many attempts at
'improvement'. Spohr confirms that numerous unsuccessful experiments were
conducted c. 1785–9, involving the scraping of the wood inside the sound-
board, in an attempt to increase the tonal potential of the instrument.[34] Spohr
himself recommended hollowing out the fingerboard under the G string to
allow the vibrations of the string to oscillate unimpeded, and Thomas Howell
introduced a shorter tailpiece, glued to the belly of the instrument, in an
unsuccessful attempt at tonal improvement.[35] Numerous other experiments,
many apparently quite ludicrous, were undertaken by other violinists and
theorists, including attempts at constructing violins from such unlikely
materials as earthenware, glass, metal (copper, brass and silver), leather and
even papier-mâché. Several different shapes were also introduced during the
nineteenth century, notably Chanot's guitar-shaped model. Savart's trapezoid
violin, a pear-shaped instrument, a triangular model, a trumpet violin, a fold-
ing violin and many other unusual designs, most of which were intended to
produce greater tonal power, brilliance and sonority.[36] However, none of
these proposed changes in materials or design gained any permanent success
and the popular form of the violin body remained unaltered.

31. See Hill, *Life and work of Antonio Stradivari*, p. 188.
32. Lancetti, *Biographical notices* (Milan, 1823); here quoted in translation from Hart, *The violin: its famous makers and their imitators*, p. 151.
33. This was also a period of great experiment with the piano and many other instruments.
34. Spohr, *Violinschule* (1832), p. 16.
35. *Ibid.*, p. 10 (first introduced by the cellist Bernard Romberg for his C string); Howell, *Original instructions . . .*, p. 21.
36. See Heron-Allen, *Violin making as it was and is*, ch. 5, pp. 104–21.

Although metal strings were readily available[37] and employed in the stringing of many contemporary instruments, late-eighteenth-century violinists
still preferred the gut variety, at least for the upper three strings. The type of
G string employed was either solely of thick gut, sometimes called 'catlines',[38]
or of gut overspun with metal, the latter variety providing greater reliability of
response and invariably greater tonal brilliance, since the higher harmonics
make a greater contribution to the resultant sound. By about 1780, references
to the use of overspun strings for the G and D are more common in contemporary publications;[39] but a gut D (which even today rarely seems to sound
'true') was generally employed until well into the nineteenth century, even
though writers such as Gossec[40] acknowledged numerous disadvantages of
gut strings, notably the need to keep them moist, their tendency to unravel,
their sensitivity to variation in atmospheric temperature, the difficulty in
determining a 'true' string and the common incidence of knots and other
imperfections.

Löhlein states specifically that the G string was wound with silver; Baillot
later cites either brass or silver and Spohr stipulates either plated copper or
solid silver wire, advocating the silver-covered variety 'because they give a
clearer sound and do not corrode or become red and unsightly through long
use'.[41] Twisted silk and silk-covered strings were also available by the end of
the eighteenth century[42] but as these were arguably less resonant, texturally
inferior and more difficult to tune accurately and keep in tune than gut strings
(on account of their unusual elasticity), both the A and E strings were generally of gut and largely remained so until the early twentieth century. The
gradual introduction of the aluminium-covered A and the steel E strings, the
latter accompanied by its metal adjuster for greater facility in fine tuning,
offered players greater reliability of intonation and response as well as a tonal
brilliance better suited to the prevalent sound ideal.

It is impossible to estimate with any positive accuracy the relative thickness
of strings employed during the eighteenth century. Some scholars believe,
probably quite correctly, that eighteenth-century violin strings were generally
thinner than their modern counterparts, in keeping with the smaller string
tension and lower playing pitch of that period;[43] others disagree, some quoting Brossard's statement that the contemporary silver-wound D and G strings
were thinner than their counterparts made simply of gut.[44] One fact, however,

37. See *A musical dictionary*, ed. Grassineau, s.v. 'Wire'; Boyden, *The history of violin playing . . .* , p. 322.
38. See Abbot & Segerman, 'Gut strings', *Early Music*, vol. 4 (1976), pp. 430–7.
39. See *Encyclopédie . . .*, ed. Diderot & D'Alembert, vol. 35, s.v. 'Violon'; Brossard, *Fragments d'une méthode
de violon*, p. 12.
40. *Procès-verbaux de l'Académie des beaux-arts*, vol. 1, pp. 156–61.
41. Löhlein, *Anweisung . . .* (1774), p. 9; Baillot, *L'art . . .* (1834), p. 247; Spohr, *Violinschule* (1832),
pp. 12–13.
42. See Cohen, 'A cache of 18th-century strings', *Galpin Society Journal*, vol. 36 (1983), pp. 37–48; *Allgemeine
musikalische Zeitung*, May 1799, cols. 522–3; *Allgemeine musikalische Zeitung*, August 1801, cols. 781–3.
43. For example, Boyden, *The history of violin playing . . .*, pp. 321–2.
44. Brossard, *Fragments d'une méthode de violon*, p. 12.

is certain; string thicknesses varied considerably according to the pitch in use, the size of the instrument employed, the situation, national or individual tastes regarding string materials and many other variables. Quantz acknowledges the use of both thick and thin strings and Leopold Mozart recommends, for optimum tonal result and reliability of intonation, the use of thick strings for flat pitch and large-model violins and thin strings for sharp pitch and small models.[45] Paganini used very thin strings, as these proved most favourable for his technical exploits, notably his common use of high position-work, natural and artificial harmonics, left-hand *pizzicato* and *scordatura*.[46] However, thin strings produced a rather weak tone and thin E strings were liable to 'whistle' rather than speak clearly, especially in a damp atmosphere; both these disadvantages were common features of Paganini's performances.[47] Spohr claims that the optimum string thicknesses for any instrument can be determined only by experiment, with equal strength and fullness of tone from each string as the ultimate goal.[48] In order to obtain a rich and powerful tone, Spohr employed the thickest strings his violin could bear so long as their response was quick and easy and their tone bright. The optimum string thicknesses once determined, Spohr advises the player to abide by his decision[49] and always measure replacement strings with a string gauge, in order to ensure uniformity in the string thicknesses employed. Spohr is the first to mention the existence of the string gauge, a metal plate (of silver or brass) with a graduated slit, lettered for each string (Fig. 9c). The size of each string was ascertained at the point where it became gently wedged in the gauge.

One device which slightly altered the appearance of the violin at the beginning of the nineteenth century was the addition of the chin rest (*Geigenhalter* – literally, 'violin holder'; see Fig. 9a), invented by Spohr, who states that he and many other violinists had been using it for more than ten years before the publication of his method. He continues:

The modern style of playing, in which the left hand so often changes position, makes it absolutely essential for the violin to be held firmly with the chin. To do this in an unconstrained manner and without bending the head forward presents great difficulties, whether the chin is placed on the right or the left side of the tailpiece or even on the tailpiece itself. One will also run the perpetual risk of drawing the violin away from under the chin when shifting the left hand rapidly downwards from the higher positions, or of disturbing the evenness of the bowing through some movement of the instrument. The chin rest completely rectifies all these evils and allows not only a firm and unconstrained hold of the violin but also has the advantage that one is not compelled to rest one's chin on the belly or the tailpiece, thereby checking the vibration of these parts, to the detriment of the quality and volume of tone of the instru-

45. Quantz, *Versuch* . . ., tr. and ed. Reilly, ch. 17, section 2, §1, p. 215; L. Mozart, *Versuch* . . ., Introduction, section 1, §7, p. 8. See also Reichardt, *Ueber die Pflichten* . . . (1776), p. 86.
46. Fétis, *Antoine Stradivari* . . ., tr. Bishop, p. 74; Guhr, *Ueber Paganinis Kunst* . . . (1829), §1, p. 5.
47. Guhr, *Ueber Paganinis Kunst* . . . (1829), §1, p. 5.
48. Spohr, *Violinschule* (1832), p. 13.
49. Spohr, *Violinschule* (1832), p. 13. See also Baillot, *L'art* . . . (1834), p. 247.

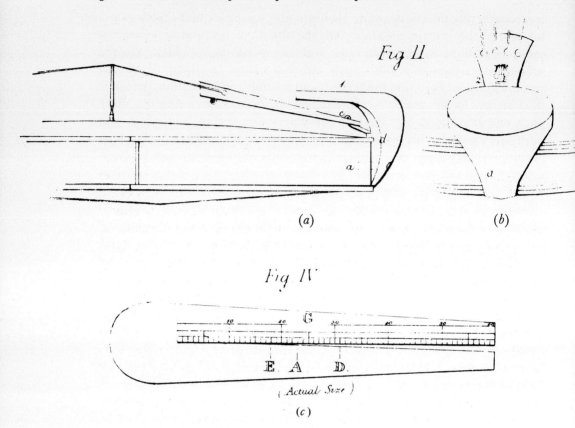

9. The chin rest and its position on the instrument (a, b), and the string gauge (c), as illustrated by Spohr

ment. The bowing, too, gains in freedom and regularity because the violin can be held exactly in the centre, above the tailpiece, and somewhat farther from the face.

(Spohr, *Violinschule* (1832), pp. 8–9)

Spohr's chin rest was made of ebony and was placed directly over the tailpiece, not to the left side as is usual today (Fig. 9b). Although this position of the chin rest must have impeded the violinist to some extent, especially on the lower strings, it nevertheless provided the greater stability required to ensure a more accurate and secure execution of shifts and position-work in the higher registers and greater freedom of the bow arm. However, acceptance of the chin rest was only gradual; some violinists even ignored its use.

Among other essential items of the violinist's equipment was the mute, the use of which was gradually extended from ensemble to solo playing during the course of the eighteenth century. Mutes were generally made from wood or metal and underwent no fundamental change in design until the mid nineteenth century, when the frustrations and inconvenience of manually applying or removing a mute during performances prompted Vuillaume to invent his *Sourdine pédale*. However, the latter, enabling the performer to bring the mute in contact with the bridge by means of gentle pressure with the chin on the tailpiece, gained, like Bellon's invention,[50] only ephemeral success and never came into general use.

The changes in the design and construction of the violin and its fittings and the advent of the modern (Tourte) bow brought greater tonal power, brilliance and sonority to the instrument but at the expense of the overtones structure, thereby sacrificing the clarity and the more relaxed, transparent viol-like characteristics of the baroque violin sound. Whereas the fundamental exterior shape of the violin body remained substantially unaltered throughout the period, that of the bow underwent dramatic transformations. Acceptance of the Tourte bow was inevitably slow to materialise; thus, baroque, transitional and Tourte models co-existed in most orchestras and in solo spheres, as did violins with baroque, transitional and/or modern dimensions and fittings, well into the nineteenth century. Galeazzi claims that each school of violin playing had its own preferred type of bow and the best orchestras were those in which all the violinists were trained in the same school,[51] but it is doubtful if many contemporary orchestras could have attained such an ideal. However, a review of an orchestral concert in 1810 by students of the Paris Conservatoire claims that the student violinists, trained individually by different professors who nevertheless had drawn inspiration from a common source (Viotti), played in a much more polished and unified manner than the violinists formerly of the *Concerts Cléry*, who subscribed to different bowing schools and hence adopted different approaches to bowing techniques.[52] Certainly, the full potential of the Tourte model was not realised until c. 1800 onwards, when its inherent power, its expressive and other qualities could be implemented on an instrument modified to fulfil similar ideals. Nevertheless, one discovers that many of the Paganini caprices, for example, are more easily played with some transitional bows than with the Tourte model and it is probably no coincidence that the bow illustrated in Begas's well-known portrait of Paganini (Fig. 5) is a transitional type believed to be by Sirjean.[53] However, with the advent of the Tourte model, the viability of the violin as a solo instrument increased considerably, allowing violinists to compete on equal terms with the enlarged symphony orchestra of the time[54] and the technique of the instrument was developed accordingly, as some of the succeeding chapters will affirm.

50. See Heron-Allen, *Violin making as it was and is*, p. 194. See also ch. 9, p. 240.
51. Galeazzi, *Elementi* . . . (1791), vol. 1, pt. 2, pp. 76–7 & p. 211. Spohr also shares Galeazzi's opinion – see ch. 11, p. 281.
52. *Les tablettes de Polymnie* (April 1810), pp. 3–4.
53. Liivoja-Lorius, Editorial, *The Strad*, vol. 93 (1982), p. 377.
54. See n. 24 above.

2

The posture of the player

During the first three quarters of the eighteenth century the posture of the player was discussed only in very general terms, normally incorporating reference to the undesirability of unnecessary body movements, facial contortions and any unnaturally constrained or ungraceful playing positions. The latter part of the century witnessed increased interest in posture but provided only two detailed surveys of note, those of Campagnoli and, in particular, Löhlein. Campagnoli refers to the general requirement of an easy and noble posture with graceful hand movements and summarises the main matters for consideration, namely the upright position of the head and body with special reference to the left shoulder (which should be only slightly advanced), the distribution of body weight towards the left side (in order to allow the right arm greater mobility) and the avoidance of all affectation and carelessness.[1] Löhlein, however, goes one step further and provides the most detailed eighteenth-century survey, devoting a whole chapter to posture and expanding the concept to include the basic techniques of holding the instrument. Since the presentation of Löhlein's survey in full would involve undesirable duplication of the material of subsequent chapters, an abbreviated version follows, focusing purely on matters of stance.

15. All mechanical activities achieve their simplicity and pleasing manner by the skilful employment of the relevant limbs, and the simplest activity performed in a clumsy manner is repugnant to the beholder; whereas a natural and unconstrained posture can simplify even the most difficult activity and make it a pleasure to watch. The following questions may therefore be raised here:
(1) What is the subject?
(2) What is its ultimate purpose?
(3) By what means can this be achieved?
As the subject under discussion here is violin playing, the first thing to be observed is how to hold the instrument, by a skilful placing of the body and use of the arms, in a position where the aim of producing a tone such as will flatter the ear may be achieved most comfortably.

16. One should consequently stand upright, but in such a way that the upper part of the body is bent slightly forward . . . [p. 12, §16, sentence 2 to p. 13, §18, sentence 1 omitted]

1. Campagnoli, *Metodo* . . . (1797?), tr. Bishop, Introduction, 'Of the attitude in general', p. 2.

[18.] 'One can never watch too closely to ensure that a beginner, when he positions his instrument, does not raise or twist his shoulder-blade when he supports it. For with a young person whose growth is not yet settled, a high shoulder can easily result from bad posture of this kind. One should therefore adjust one's posture so that the shoulders remain in their natural position.' [quotation marks original]

19. The elbow of the arm holding the violin is turned in towards the body, and it is wrong when many violinists lift it up, which apart from looking clumsy has also the disadvantage that it is uncommonly tiring. Others move it up and down like a bird trying out its wings for the first time; this habit also must be avoided. The elbow must therefore lie quite easily against the side of the body, without, however, pressing into it so firmly or so apprehensively that it looks as though one had stomach-ache. One must at first resign oneself to the fact that with an unfamiliar activity that has still to be learned, even the most unconstrained posture will cause some constraint – this is inevitable with any new way of moving the limbs, as e.g. in fencing, riding and danc- ing. Once one has become properly accustomed to it by diligent and correct practice, all will be well. So now we know how to hold the violin. Still to be considered there- fore are (1) the placing of the feet and (2) the position of the fingers which are to touch the strings.

20. The placing of the feet depends on the direction in which the face is turned when reading the music. If this direction is to the left, then the left foot must be placed in front of the right; if it is to the right or straight forward, then it is better to put the right foot in front of the left, as in this way the body's centre of gravity, accord- ing to the rules of mechanics, always lies between the two feet and makes for a good, firm stance.

It is incredible how much a pleasing manner can improve something, however mediocre its execution; whereas a clumsy manner can ruin anything, however well done. If it happens in addition that poor execution is accompanied by a clumsy manner, then not only the ear but also the eye is insulted, and instead of pleasure, disgust is aroused and one is laughed at into the bargain. 'For this reason one should take the utmost care to avoid all unseemly or oafish attitudes of the body, all distor- tions of the features and all lumbering, superfluous or ridiculous gestures; and one should make only such movements as are simply adequate to achieve one's purpose. One should not always assume that activities that are easy and pleasant to watch being executed are therefore easy in themselves. No! On the contrary, they acquire the appearance of ease and pleasantness from the master hand that executes them, and who will have devoted himself with great diligence to achieving the mastery required. Whereas if the activity is still master over the person who is trying to pursue it, a tension must always result between the two and this breaks out in visible contortions. One can thus conclude with certainty that the less constraint there is perceptible in the execution of anything, the more the executant has it within his power; and the more constraint one sees in it, the less it is within the power of the executant.' [quota- tion marks original]

21. Now anyone who plays with any sensitivity will know how very careful one must be to keep control over one's facial expression and not let other parts of the body participate visibly either. Yet to be able to stand there cold and changeless like a statue or a picture that always has only the one expression is uncongenial to a sensi- tive nature; and it would also betray a great lack of sensitivity, which is as inimical to a good musician as poor hearing. It will therefore be to the credit of a sensitive soul if he can be seen to move gently, in accordance with the emotions of the music; and one may observe with the best musicians that they do this, and often involuntarily. As long as it does not tend to become comical, it is quite acceptable. Let others pride

themselves on their statuesque immutability if they will, and put up as best they can with the not unjustified suspicion that they are wooden musicians!

(Löhlein, *Anweisung* . . . (1774), pp. 12–15)

The question of posture generally received more detailed attention in nineteenth-century violin methods, in particular those of Rode *et al.*, Mazas, Baillot, Habeneck and Froehlich; the position of the head, shoulders and trunk, the distribution of body weight and the placement of the feet are the main considerations generally reviewed. Baillot's account is perhaps the most comprehensive, especially when, as is the case below, his rather terse, but nevertheless explicit, initial summary is amalgamated with his subsequent rather more general observations.

Posture

1. The body and the head upright.
2. The chest open and advanced.
3. The shoulders drawn back.
4. Position yourself at a distance of about a foot, 8 or 9 inches, from the stand, facing it but a little to the left, about 4 to 5 inches from point A to point B, in order to be able to read the two pages of music without disturbing the position of the neck of the violin (see Fig. [10.9]).
5. The bottom of the stand on which the music is placed should be level with the pit of the stomach, or a little below it.
6. The weight of the body carried on the left leg, but without the body leaning to one side.
7. The left foot, placed in front of the stand, that is to say perfectly square with it.
8. The right foot in line with the left and in a natural position, pointing slightly outwards.
9. The distance between the inside of the heels should be between $4\frac{1}{2}$ and 5 inches (see Fig. [10.10]).
10. Avoid as much as possible bringing forward the left hip.
11. Keep the body somewhat arched and supported on the loins (see Fig. [10.1 & 3]).

(Baillot, *L'art* . . . (1834), p. 11)

On posture in general

A noble and relaxed *posture* encourages the development of all the skills, allows gracefulness to accompany the movements of the arm and bow and increases the charm of the performance by making it evident that one has made oneself master of the instrument and that one can surmount all the difficulties without any effort.

One should avoid adopting either any affectation of the posture, which would become ridiculous, or any casualness, which one must never permit oneself when appearing in public.

When one is fairly certain about how one comes to hold the violin and about the evenness of movement in one's fingers and bow, it is then useful to play in front of a mirror, in order to see if one's posture is elegant and graceful and to keep watch for any contractions in the face or limbs, sure signs of stiffness. The best thing to do in order to judge oneself properly being to stand so to speak at a distance from oneself, we are able to do this physically by means of the reflection of our image.

But this method, when applied to the finer details, might lead to error in that it would lack fidelity, owing to the fact that a mirror changes the position of objects from right to left and consequently gives the lines of movement an appearance contrary to the truth. One should therefore play in front of a mirror only in order to watch over one's posture in general.   (Baillot, L'art . . . (1834), pp. 15-16)

Baillot's engraving (Fig. 10.6-8) admirably illustrates the seated playing position but he provides surprisingly little textual comment, merely remarking that the right wrist and elbow must be bent rather more when bowing in this position.[2] Admittedly, the basic essentials of this seated position closely resemble those of Baillot's stance, since the body weight is supported by the left leg and the feet take up a similar position. Notable, however, is the bending of the right leg slightly inwards, in order to avoid contact between the knee and the bow when bowing at the point on the upper strings, and the use of a footstool to support the left leg, and hence the body weight, enabling the trunk to remain erect.

The scope of Baillot's survey is further widened by his disapproval of unnecessary movement such as tapping the foot or moving the violin in order to maintain a sense of rhythm, surprisingly advocated by Martinn and evidently practised by many violinists,[3] and his subsequent consideration of the optimum position for a soloist to adopt in concert.

Ways of standing in order to project oneself

There are two ways of standing for playing in public:

One involves holding the violin with its strings facing the audience so that the sound reaches directly into all parts of the hall.

The other involves standing facing the audience, which is the natural position for all who aim to reach their audience.

The first way has the advantage of allowing none of the smallest details of the sound to be lost, the sound waves being directed towards the majority of the listeners. But it has the disadvantage of obliging the violin soloist to turn his back on the director of the orchestra [presumably the 'concert-master' or leader], thus hindering achievement of the complete ensemble necessary between soloist and his accompaniment.

The second way seems to be preferable to us in that it is more natural and convenient with regard to the audience; it also offers more scope for the accompaniment, and if the orchestra is arranged in the theatre pit, the violin soloist, alone on the stage, is so much in evidence there that none of his delicate playing will be lost and that, standing thus, he will always be able to reach his audience sufficiently, seeing that he has their attention already.   (Baillot, L'art . . . (1834), p. 257)

Most nineteenth-century surveys closely resemble Baillot's theories in general content, if they are perhaps found somewhat lacking in specific detail by com-

2. Baillot, L'art . . . (1834), p. 13.
3. *Ibid.*, p. 253; Martinn, *Méthode élémentaire* . . . (c. 1810), art. 4, p. 6.

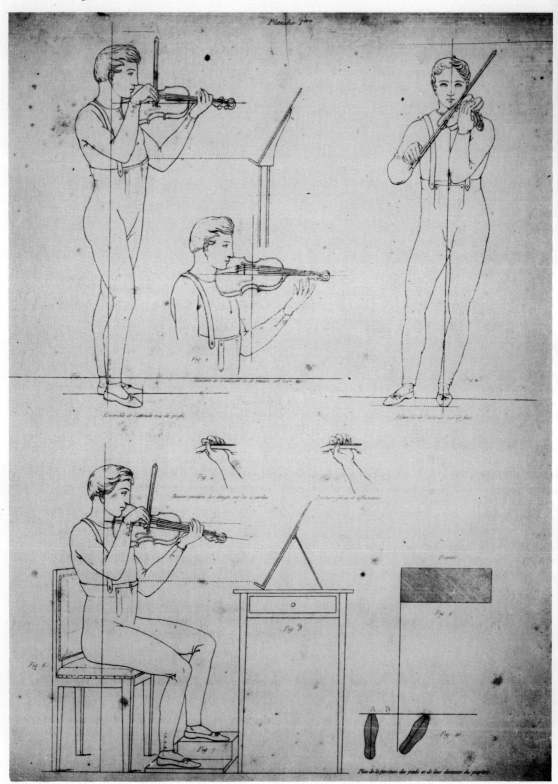

10. Posture and the violin hold as illustrated by Baillot

parison, although opinions concerning the position of the feet are by no means unanimous. Froehlich, for example, reverts to Löhlein's philosophy, relating the position of the feet to that of the head, whilst Pastou claims that the right foot should be advanced in order for the main body weight to be taken on the left side.[4] According to most documentary sources, Paganini also thrust his right foot well forward and rested his body weight on the left hip, bringing the left elbow close in towards the trunk in front of the body, with the upper arm turned inwards. His rather unorthodox posture was determined by his abnormal physique. When standing upright, his left shoulder was apparently an inch higher than his right, a natural conformation quite favourable to the adoption of a relaxed stance.[5] Although many contemporary illustrations depict Paganini in rather ungainly attitudes, Guhr records that his posture was 'unrestrained, although not so dignified as that of *Baillot*, *Rode* and *Spohr*. He also supports the weight of the body on his left side, but he bends forward the left shoulder more than the aforementioned masters.'[6] However, Paganini appears to have contracted such bad habits as beating time with his right foot and twisting his body into the most ungainly attitudes with his head and his right foot forward to form a kind of triangle.[7] Nevertheless, this 'triangular' position probably helped Paganini to stabilise the instrument more easily, especially during the execution of the fingerboard gymnastics for which he became renowned.

Modern theory concerning posture represents a synthesis of late-eighteenth- and early-nineteenth-century ideals. Writers nowadays prescribe rather more flexible guidelines regarding the position of the head, shoulders (although the shoulders should never be raised) and trunk, aiming above all at comfort but recommending that facial contortions should be avoided and that movement of the body should be limited (for aesthetic reasons and practical bowing considerations) but never suppressed. Any one of three positions of the feet is acceptable:[8] (1) with the feet close together and almost at right angles to each other (as in Fig. 21); (2) with one foot slightly advanced, thereby throwing most of the body weight on to the other side and causing the body to bend forward somewhat (as described by Löhlein); (3) with the feet in line but slightly astride (see Fig. 10) and the body weight fairly evenly distributed but with a bias towards the left side. The last-mentioned position is generally preferred because it affords the player superior balance and freedom of movement.

4. Froehlich, *Vollständige theoretisch-praktische Musikschule* (1810), vol. 4, §2, p. 14; Pastou, *Méthode . . .*, art. 8, p. 5.
5. See Bennati, *Notice physiologique sur Paganini*.
6. Guhr, *Ueber Paganinis Kunst . . .*, §5, p. 6.
7. See de Saussine, *Paganini le magicien*, tr. Laurie, p. 111.
8. Flesch, *The art of violin playing*, tr. Martens, vol. 1, p. 14.

3

Holding the violin

Although the violin hold remained unstandardised throughout the eighteenth century, positions varying for the most part between those at the breast, the shoulder or the neck (and all with differing degrees of support), the seeds of modern methods of holding the instrument were eventually sown; the vital stimulus was provided by the gradual establishment of an optimum chin position and manner of supporting the instrument.

POSITION OF THE CHIN

L'Abbé le fils demonstrates the progressive nature of his treatise by recommending, arguably for the first time,[1] the modern violin hold with the chin presumably gripping the instrument (although such a grip is not specified) on the left side of the tailpiece:

The violin should be placed on the collar-bone in such a way that the chin rests on the side of the fourth string; the E string side should be slightly lowered; the right hand should be almost at neck height; the neck [of the instrument] should be held without excessive force between the thumb and the first joint of the index-finger; the part of the neck on this side of the thumb should be on the fleshy protuberance of the first joint; care should be taken to place the thumb opposite the A natural on the G string.
(L'Abbé le fils, Principes . . . (1761), p. 1)

L'Abbé le fils's violin hold was not endorsed by all his successors, some of whom favoured the 'old-fashioned' chin position on the right of the tailpiece[2] but the position of the chin on the left side of the tailpiece was adopted by most late-eighteenth-century writers, notably Löhlein, Galeazzi, Campagnoli,

1. Recent research has thrown up some earlier sources which advocate violin holds resembling modern methods (i.e. a chin-braced grip on the left side of the tailpiece), notably Johann Berlin's *Musicaliske Elementer* (Trondheim, 1744) (pt. 2, ch. 3, §10) and Prinner's (or Brinner) manuscript treatise *Musicalisch Schlissel* (1670), but further contemporary evidence is required to substantiate their content, given their relatively early dates, particularly of the Prinner. See *Early Music*, vol. 7 (1979), pp. 561–2; vol. 8 (1980), pp. 429–30.
2. For example, Kobrich, *Praktisches Geigfundament* . . . (1787), §12, p. 11; Hiller, *Anweisung* . . . (1792), pp. 5–6; Signoretti, *Méthode* . . . (1777), pt. 2, pp. 1–2; Philpot, *An introduction* . . . (1766), p. 5.

Cambini and, perhaps most surprisingly, Roeser in his edition of Leopold Mozart's method (thereby contradicting the principles expounded in the original text).[3] Galeazzi, in particular, is adamant that a chin position on the right side of the tailpiece should not be encouraged because it results in the violin being placed almost on the left shoulder (as opposed to its more central position in relation to the body with L'Abbé le fils's method), necessitating excessive raising and lowering of the right arm when bowing on the outer strings and causing the aural sense to be dulled, owing to the instrument's close proximity to the ear.[4] Cartier likewise advocates the left side of the tailpiece as the most convenient place for the chin, but he also includes an alternative 'old-fashioned' method, involving the placement of the violin against the chest.[5] Bornet provides an interesting variation which may have adversely affected the tuning of the strings, recommending a chin position over the tailpiece 'in such a way that the button is approximately in the middle of the violinist's neck'.[6] Woldemar's edition of Leopold Mozart's work compromises between old and new methods of holding the instrument, advocating a chin position on the left side of the tailpiece but adding that this position is not suitable at first for very young pupils, presumably because the need to bring the left arm well under the violin could cause unnecessary arm-ache; in such cases, chin placement on the right side of the tailpiece is recommended.[7] In his own method Woldemar goes further, echoing Durieu's theory that it does not matter which side of the tailpiece the chin is positioned: 'It is immaterial whether one places the chin on the right or the left part of the violin, as Tartini, Frantzl [sic] and Cramer used to place it on the right and Locatelli, Jarnovick and Viotti placed it on the left. This latter manner is the most general.' (Woldemar, Grande méthode . . . (c. 1800), p. 2; see also Durieu, Méthode . . . (1796), p. 2) Furthermore, Rangoni disagrees with the principle of prescribing general rules for holding any musical instrument, favouring the concept that each performer should adopt a position suitable to his own constitution.[8]

Nevertheless, the chin position prescribed by L'Abbé le fils appears to have become orthodox practice by about the beginning of the nineteenth century and was adopted in particular by professors at the Paris Conservatoire, as indicated in the various methods written for that institution. Baillot, for example, isolates each important step to be observed and adds a further note of advice, expounded also by Jousse and Martinn amongst others, for students of small stature:

3. Löhlein, Anweisung . . . (1774), p. 12; Galeazzi, Elementi . . . (1791), vol. 1, pt. 2, art. 4, p. 89; Campagnoli, Metodo . . . (1797?), tr. Bishop, Introduction, 'On the manner of holding the violin and playing upon it', no. 2, p. 1; Cambini, Nouvelle méthode . . . (1803), Introduction, §1, p. 2. Compare L. Mozart, Méthode raisonnée . . ., tr. and ed. Roeser, §2, p. 1 and L. Mozart, Versuch . . ., ch. 2, §2, p. 53.
4. Galeazzi, Elementi . . . (1791), vol. 1, pt. 2, art. 4, pp. 84–5.
5. Cartier, L'art . . . (1798), pt. 1, art. 1, p. 1.   7. Woldemar, ed., Méthode . . . (1801), p. 6.
6. Bornet, Nouvelle méthode . . . (1786), p. 5.   8. Rangoni, Essai sur le goût . . ., p. 48.

1. The violin should be placed on the collar-bone,
2. inclined towards the right at approximately 45 degrees,
3. pulled in against the neck,
4. held firmly by the chin, on the left side and close *against* the tailpiece; the chin leaning on the violin but not on the tailpiece,
5. the chin should not protrude and should grip the violin – without too great a pressure – with its most salient part and not with the side . . .

(Baillot, L'art . . . (1834), art. 2, p. 11)

Note: If the pupil is a child or if he is of small stature, he will not be able to use the bow
right up to its point without changing its direction by pulling it back; it is thus necessary to see to it that he only uses a bow of length proportionate to that of his arm. It
may even be necessary to position the violin for him as a result and make him keep his
chin on the E string side [of the tailpiece] until he is big enough to play without
difficulty with his chin on the G string side. But if he uses a small-model violin, he
will hold it in the manner generally employed and prescribed in article 2.[9]

(Baillot, L'art . . . (1834), p. 15)

Evidence suggests that Paganini, who did not employ a chin rest, likewise
normally placed his chin on the left side of the tailpiece, since the varnish on
his favourite Guarnerius violin is heavily worn on that side. However, such
evidence is by no means conclusive, as this wear may well have been caused by
previous owners of the instrument. Furthermore, contemporary illustrations
are quite contrary, some clearly showing Paganini's chin positioned on the
tailpiece itself and others depicting a chin position on either side of the
tailpiece.

There were, of course, exceptions to the orthodox nineteenth-century chin
position, Fenkner and Schiedermayer, for example, recommending chin
placement on the right side of the tailpiece and Lottin implying that the chin
should adopt a redundant position either on the left or right side of the tailpiece.[10] Such indecision about the optimum chin position persisted with a
small minority of violinists well into the nineteenth century; a sketch by Adolf
von Menzel, entitled 'Violin Concerto', clearly reveals Joachim's playing position with his chin on the right side of the tailpiece, even as late as 1854.
Furthermore, Spohr's invention of c. 1820, the chin rest, was originally
designed to be placed over the tailpiece in the centre of the violin (see p. 29 and
Fig. 9b). Spohr also advises: 'If the pupil does not wish to use the chin rest, his
chin should then be placed partly on the belly to the left of the tailpiece, partly
on the tailpiece itself.' (Spohr, *Violinschule* (1832), p. 24)

SUPPORT

The chin-braced grip implied by L'Abbé le fils, previously employed only as a
momentary aid to shifting and position-work (in order to prevent the instrument slipping away from the player), along with the chin position to the left of

9. The salient points mentioned in art. 2 are reproduced above and on p. 43.
10. Fenkner, *Anweisung* . . . (1803), 'Einleitung', §5, p. 2; Schiedermayer, *Neue theoretische und praktische
Violinschule* (c. 1815), p. 6; Lottin, *Principes* . . . (1808), art. 14, p. 8.

the tailpiece, gradually came into more general and consistent use; the gains were a firmer and more stable manner of supporting the violin and the freeing of the left hand (although, in most cases, this hand still provided some support for the instrument), which formerly had to 'crawl' warily from position to position (especially when shifting downwards) to exploit the full range of the instrument. The gradual adoption of the chin-braced grip is confirmed by consulting selected editions of Geminiani's violin treatise; the first edition clearly states that 'the violin must be rested just below the collar-bone'.[11] The various French editions of the work quote an exact translation of this text but the third edition (1763?) includes a frontispiece illustration (Fig. 11) of a violinist employing a chin-braced grip at the centre of the violin or perhaps a little to the right of the tailpiece. A later German edition (1782) categorically states that the violin should be held 'between the collar-bone and the jaw-bone',[12] with the chin on the right side of the tailpiece. While it would be erroneous to attribute the changes in these posthumous editions to Geminiani himself, such modifications admirably illustrate the direction in which the violin hold was progressing.

Thus, the violinist's shoulder, chin and left hand generally combined to support the instrument (except, of course, in the old 'breast' position where the instrument was supported by the left arm only) but the degree and manner of support afforded by each member naturally varied according to the *minutiae* of the violin hold and chin position employed. Cambini, for example, recommends chin, shoulder and additional wrist and (at the neck–body joint of the instrument) heel-of-the-hand support, whereas Galeazzi disapproves of such left-hand contact, preferring the use of the thumb as an additional means of support.[13] However, like Campagnoli, most writers are agreed that excess chin pressure should be avoided:

2. The back of the violin is placed on the left collar bone, and the chin pressed lightly on the belly, on the side of the G string close to the tail piece.
3. It is necessary to avoid drawing the chin too near the collar bone, and thereby holding the violin constrainedly; but it should be so directed, that the head of the performer may remain as nearly upright as possible.
(Campagnoli, *Metodo* . . . (1797?), tr. Bishop, Introduction, 'On the manner of holding the violin and playing upon it', nos. 2 & 3, p. 1)

In the early nineteenth century, the left hand was gradually relieved of its supporting role, no doubt in response to increased technical demands, although Rode *et al.* and Mazas recommend supporting the violin with the left hand and chin[14] and Paganini, it appears, stabilised his violin partly with his upper arm, which maintained constant contact with his trunk with additional support from the chin and left hand. The chin rest proved a further invaluable

11. Geminiani, *The art* . . ., Ex. I (B), p. 1.
12. Geminiani, *Gründliche Anleitung* . . ., Ex. I (B), p. 1.
13. Cambini, *Nouvelle méthode* . . . (1803), Introduction, section 3, p. 3.; Galeazzi, *Elementi* . . . (1791), vol. 1, pt. 2, art. 4, pp. 87–8.
14. Rode *et al.*, *Méthode* . . . (1803), art. 1, p. 5; Mazas, *Méthode* . . . (1830), art. 1, pp. 1–2.

11.   Frontispiece to the third edition of Geminiani's *L'art du violon* (Paris, 1763?)

aid towards the comfortable support of the violin; Spohr, however, never dis-
counts the role of the left hand, although he chiefly advocates the use of the
chin and shoulder in supporting the instrument:

The left shoulder is brought forward slightly in order to support the base of the violin
and to incline it to the right (at an angle of between 25 and 30 degrees). The neck of
the violin rests between the thumb and index-finger of the left hand and is lightly held
above the first joint of the thumb, and by the third joint of the index-finger, in order
to prevent it from sinking down to the bottom of the hollow between the thumb and
finger [see Fig. 12].   (Spohr, *Violinschule* (1832), p. 24)

Baillot prescribes an experiment to ensure that the correct method of support
is employed and in this connection ranks as one of the first writers to suggest
the use of a shoulder pad to facilitate the comfortable support of the instrument. Unlike Habeneck,[15] Baillot does allow some left-hand and, in particular, some thumb participation in supporting the instrument in the higher
positions:

(6) With the elbow well forward under the middle of the violin, the left shoulder
should automatically adopt a suitable position to support it [the violin], and one will
thus not need to raise the shoulder – which would constrict the chest.
                                                (Baillot, *L'art* . . . (1834), art. 2, p. 11)

In order to make certain whether the violin is well supported between the shoulder
and the chin and by both, one must test it by letting go of it with the left hand, which
one should keep open in readiness close to the neck as a precaution; if all the condi-
tions are fulfilled (when we say all, we mean that we include the posture of the body
supported from the hips, the angle of the head etc.) the violin will support itself
horizontally [see Fig. 10.2].   (Baillot, *L'art* . . . (1834), p. 12)

Children or young people whose shoulders are not yet broad enough to support the
violin, and women who play this instrument and who have nothing in their attire to
help them hold it easily and inclined to the right, may fill in the existing gap between
the left shoulder and the violin by placing a thick handkerchief or a kind of cushion
there; experience has proved to us that this method offers great advantages without
any inconvenience, and that, with the handkerchief placed under the clothing on the
shoulder, it should not even be noticed . . .   (Baillot, *L'art* . . . (1834), p. 16)

In difficult passages up to the third position, which can be found quite accurately, one
should rest the lower part of the left hand firmly and quite strongly against the body
of the violin where the ribs join the neck; for the higher positions, it is no longer the
hand that is rested against the ribs but the thumb, which one slides along up to the
end of the neck (if one is moving towards the bridge), and it is this [the thumb] which
in turn acts as a point of support for the hand.
    The performer will recognise those passages where one has to hold the violin more
firmly, tucked well into the neck and held securely by the chin, while at the same time
the hand adds to this firmness by its pressure against the top of the ribs; in this way,
he will give greater security to his playing and greater freedom to his fingers, but he
must nevertheless guard against exaggeration if he wants to play with grace and
facility.
    It is also up to him to judge when to úse skill in those more frequent cases where

15. Habeneck, *Méthode* . . . (c. 1840), p. 30.

12.   Posture and the violin hold as illustrated by Spohr

the movement of the hand, as it stretches out and draws back, is so favourable to extensions and position changes that it would be practically useless to press the chin on the violin if this pressure did not give sureness of execution in difficult passages.

(Baillot, *L'art* . . . (1834), p. 149)

THE LEVEL OF THE VIOLIN

The level at which the violin was held naturally varied according to the chin position and means of support employed. The adoption of a chin-braced grip on the left of the tailpiece, later combined with either chin-rest and/or shoulder-pad support, led to the general recommendation that the violin should be held horizontally (allowing, of course, for the necessary inclination of the instrument towards the right) at about shoulder height, a position which afforded the player optimum freedom of left-hand movement, especially in shifts and *sul G* playing, and flexibility in bowing:

The scroll of the violin should describe a horizontal line level with the mouth; any higher or lower and the instrument would no longer have this balance and this steadiness which are necessary for the bowing hand to find the right level in order to cross the strings with more facility, whether one wishes to attack them together or separately.   (Cambini, *Nouvelle méthode* . . . (1803), Introduction, p. 2)

Roeser allows the player a little more flexibility:

The scroll of the violin should be held level with the mouth, or, at the very most, the eyes and it should not be allowed to come lower than the chest. In consideration of this, one should place the music one wants to play quite high in front of oneself.

(Mozart, *Méthode raisonnée* . . ., tr. & ed. Roeser, p. 1)

However, in spite of numerous emphatic statements regarding the optimum height of the violin scroll, many contemporary illustrations, notably the frontispiece of the third French edition (1763?) of Geminiani's treatise (Fig. 11), the frontispiece of Veracini's *Sonate accademiche* Op. 2 (London & Florence, 1744) and most illustrations of Paganini's unorthodox playing position, with his left elbow close to his trunk and the violin partly supported by his upper arm, reveal that the scroll was invariably lowered somewhat. Such lowering of the scroll was in some cases the natural result of a lack of chin support; in other cases it was intentional: Baillot, for example, surprisingly allowed such licence in his seated position for attaining greater facility in straight bowing.[16] The weight of the instrument was thus distributed towards the left hand, allowing the bow in many cases to slide along the string towards the fingerboard of its own accord, thereby altering the bowing angle and hampering good tone production. By keeping the scroll at or slightly above face height, the weight of the instrument was directed towards the player's neck and shoulder and bow placement maintained fairly constant. However, whilst accept-

16. Baillot, *L'art* . . . (1834), art. 4, no. 12, p. 13.

ing these benefits, many writers warn that holding the violin up too high can lead to fatigue in the bowing arm.[17]

THE DIRECTION OF THE VIOLIN

Late-eighteenth-century writers provide little information regarding the direction in which the violin should be positioned (a factor which affected bow management, especially bowing at right angles to the string) and the position of both the left and right arms. This direction of the instrument was dependent in turn on the violin hold employed; a chin position on the right side of the tailpiece would inevitably result in the violin being directed towards the left of the player, whereas the use of the 'breast' position or a chin-braced grip on the left side of the tailpiece would enable the player to hold the instrument straight out in front of him. With the standardisation of the violin hold and the gradual adoption of the chin-braced grip on the left side of the tailpiece, violinists began to hold the violin almost directly in front of them at practically a ninety-degree angle to the left shoulder, as implied by Rode et al.: 'The extremity of the neck of the violin is directly opposite the middle of the shoulder.' (Rode et al., Méthode . . . (1803), art I, p. 5)

THE INCLINATION OF THE VIOLIN

L'Abbé le fils, like his predecessors, required the E string side of the violin to be lowered somewhat in order to avoid excessive raising of the right arm when playing on the G string. This inclination of the instrument, which also facilitated fingering on the G string, was a direction common in most treatises of the period (as it is, indeed, in modern methods) and the only conflicts of opinion concerned the recommended angle of inclination. Baillot prescribes an inclination of forty-five degrees, a considerably greater angle than in modern technique, which more closely approximates Spohr's recommendation of twenty-five to thirty degrees.[18]

THE POSITION OF THE ELBOW

The position of the elbow naturally depends on the violin hold employed. The direction of the violin, the position of the fingers, the size of the hand and fingers, the chin position, the inclination of the instrument and whether or not a chin-braced grip is employed are just a few of the numerous variables which directly affect its placement. It was generally positioned well under the middle

17. For example, Löhlein, Anweisung . . . (1774), p. 12.
18. Baillot, L'art . . . (1834), art. 2, no. 2, p. 11; Spohr, Violinschule (1832), p. 24.

of the instrument, as dictated by the 'Geminiani grip', recommended by many writers in order to allow the fingers to fall perpendicularly on the strings (see Ex. 1). However, the position of the elbow could never have been absolutely rigid; it must have moved to accommodate the position-work and string employed, although such movement is not generally acknowledged in methods of the period. The elbow naturally comes further towards the body as the higher positions are reached, causing the thumb to move down the neck; furthermore, it is most conveniently moved to the right for G string passages and to the left for E string passages.

At the beginning of the period under study, the elbow was generally held quite close to and not away from the body as today, no doubt in order to provide the extra stability required to hold the violin freely and comfortably. It was probably positioned further to the right than nowadays (although this also depended on the length of the player's arm), especially when an inadequate chin/shoulder support was employed and the scroll thus held below chin level. Campagnoli admirably summarises late-eighteenth-century opinion, confirming that the upper arm in many instances acted as a kind of crutch to support the instrument:

9. The elbow must be held turned inwards towards the body as much as possible, so that the point may fall nearly in the middle of the chest; it may even lean against it, if necessary. Care must be taken neither to hold the violin too high nor too low, but in such a manner that the scroll may be nearly opposite the middle of the chest.

10. The upper part of the arm rests lightly against the side of the breast, where it must always remain immoveable [sic].

(Campagnoli, *Metodo* . . . (1797?), tr. Bishop, Introduction, 'On the manner of holding the violin and playing upon it', nos. 9 & 10, p. 1)

With the gradual acceptance of the chin-braced grip on the left side of the tailpiece, the placing of the left elbow and arm was necessarily modified. The upper arm was no longer required to stabilise the violin and so adopted a more relaxed, natural position slightly away from the body in order to hold the instrument horizontal. The left elbow took up a natural (but not inflexible) position vertically beneath the middle of the instrument, a technique endorsed by, among others, Rode *et al.*, Mazas, Baillot, Habeneck and Spohr, the last adding a significant warning regarding the level of the instrument:

The elbow of the left arm should be drawn inwards until it is under the middle of the violin; but it must not rest against the body, because then the violin would slope downwards too much towards the neck [see Fig. 13].

(Spohr, *Violinschule* (1832), p. 24)

There were, of course, exceptions to the above principles. Guhr, while acknowledging the normal contemporary elbow position, describes Paganini's as 'more forced, as he presses the point of his elbow quite close to his body, with the upper part of the arm turning outwards'.[19] Furthermore, some

---

19. Guhr, *Ueber Paganinis Kunst* . . . (1829), §3, p. 6.

13.   The violin and bow holds as illustrated by Spohr

nineteenth-century writers still advocate an elbow position close to or against the body[20] and Baillot himself isolates two exceptions to his prescribed elbow position, 'with the elbow well forward under the middle of the violin';[21] the first involves high position-work on the G string and the second concerns finger extensions on the lower strings:

If one places the fingers one after another on the notes illustrated below and leaves them there, the elbow will be vertically under the middle of the violin; this should be its usual position [see Fig. 20.13].

Ex. 1

(Geminiani)

20. For example, Keith, *A violin preceptor* (1813), p. 12.
21. Baillot, *L'art* . . . (1834), art. 2, no. 6, p. 11.

But when one is obliged to ascend very high on the G string, the elbow will need to help the hand position and thus move forward more or less according to the register of the notes that one needs to reach.   (Baillot, *L'art* . . . (1834), art. 3, no. 4, p. 12)

The third type of *extension* is the one made on all four strings; one should not forget to bring the left elbow forward sufficiently so that the little finger can easily reach the lower strings.   (Baillot, *L'art* . . . (1834), pp. 150–1)

THE POSITION OF THE WRIST

The position of the wrist was only rarely discussed in late-eighteenth-century methods, probably because it was directly determined by both the desired elbow position, close to the body, and the optimum position of the fingers, directly above the strings. Contact between the palm of the hand and the violin neck, which would result in an incorrect and sluggish finger action, was, however, definitely avoided. Campagnoli explains:

7. The wrist must be well turned inwards, that the palm of the hand may not touch the neck, but remain at as great a distance from it as possible.
8. The back of the hand must be turned towards the body of the player, making an opposite movement to the elbow [Fig. 14].
                              (Campagnoli, *Metodo* . . . (1797?), tr. Bishop, Introduction
                       'On the manner of holding the violin and playing upon it', nos. 7 & 8, p. 1)

The normal early-nineteenth-century position of the elbow slightly away from the body necessitated a corresponding modification in the shape of the wrist, so that it generally described practically a straight line with the forearm.[22] There were probably exceptions to this rule, for example in half position or in the higher positions, but these are not documented in contemporary methods; however, they are perhaps accommodated in the common recommendation of a natural hand and wrist position, as described and illustrated by Baillot:

It is a common enough fault to draw the wrist back when making an extension or placing the little finger on a low string; this results in an effect contrary to what is desired, since whilst trying to move the finger forward one is really moving it away [see Fig. 15.25 & 26].   (Baillot, *L'art* . . . (1834), art. 3, no. 3, p. 12)

THE POSITION OF THE THUMB AND INDEX-FINGER ALONG THE NECK

The violin neck was held between the thumb and the index-finger in such a way that it was not allowed to sink into the hollow between them and excessive gripping of the neck was avoided in order not to restrict the movement of the hand for shifts and *vibrato*. Indeed, the extent of such gripping inevitably varied according to whether or not a chin-braced grip was employed; with a

22. See, for example, Habeneck, *Méthode* . . . (c. 1840), p. 30.

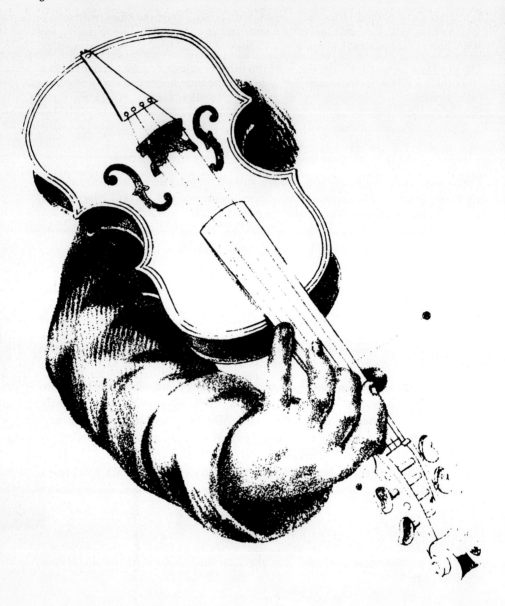

14.   The position of the left wrist and fingers as illustrated by Campagnoli

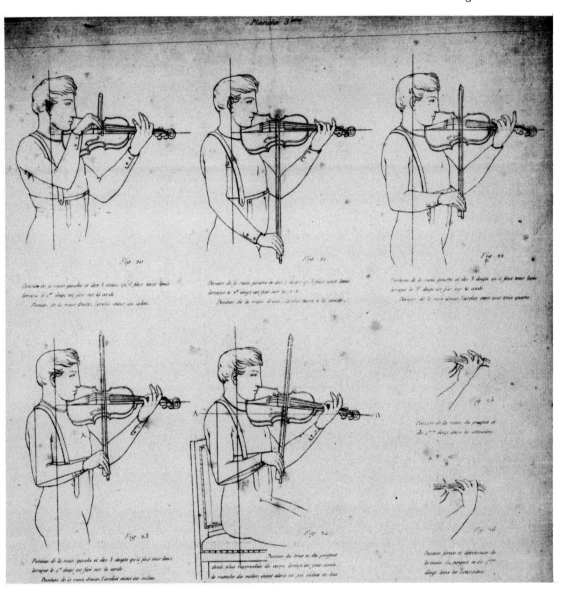

15. Bowing and the position of the left hand as illustrated by Baillot

firm chin-braced grip, the thumb merely provides additional support for the instrument and a counter-pressure against the pressure of the fingers. Baillot concisely voices the opinion of most writers:

1. Support the violin, without gripping it, between the middle of the first joint of the thumb and the middle of the third joint of the index-finger.
2. Do not allow the neck to touch that part of the hand which joins the thumb to the index-finger. Here, one should leave a gap large enough to pass the point of the bow through it. It is well worth attempting this from time to time.

(Baillot, *L'art* . . . (1834), art. 3, pp. 11–12)

The thumb was generally not allowed to project too far over the fingerboard in order to avoid any 'fouling' of the G string. There were three schools of thought regarding the point at which the thumb and index-finger should contact the violin neck (that is, in first position; the contact point naturally varies according to the position employed because from about fourth position upwards the index-finger no longer contacts the neck), some writers recommending a contact point between the bottom joint of the thumb and the base of the index-finger[23] and others advising a point between the middle of the upper joint of the thumb and the middle of the lowest joint of the index-finger.[24] Many writers omit comment about this subject, no doubt preferring to leave the player to cater for his own constitution in the most natural and comfortable way.

Writers express similar divergence of opinion regarding the position of the thumb along the fingerboard. Rode *et al.*, Baillot and Spohr, among others, omit mention of this thumb position (even though Spohr and Baillot provide detailed illustrations), which is necessarily relative to the technical requirements of the fingers of the left hand; many provide flexible instructions, allowing for the constitution of the player's hand and fingers,[25] whilst others are more specific. L'Abbé le fils requires the thumb to be placed 'opposite the A natural on the G string';[26] Cartier attributes to Leopold Mozart a recommendation (although no such recommendation appears in the original edition of 1756), later implied also by Habeneck,[27] that 'the thumb should be placed between the first and second fingers';[28] and Mazas prescribes a thumb position 'straight, but not stiff, opposite the second finger'.[29] This advanced thumb position, admirably illustrated by Campagnoli (Fig. 16), was most commonly employed at the time, allowing the hand greater freedom of action and facility in extensions. Significantly, the following amendment appeared in the 1787 and 1806 editions of Leopold Mozart's method:

23. For example, L. Mozart, *Versuch* . . ., ch. 2, §4, p. 54; Rode *et al.*, *Méthode* . . . (1803), art. 2, p. 5.
24. For example, L'Abbé le fils, *Principes* . . . (1761), p. 1; Baillot, *L'art* . . . (1834), art.3, no. 1, p. 11; Spohr, *Violinschule* (1832), p. 24.
25. For example, Campagnoli, *Metodo* . . . (1797?), tr. Bishop, Introduction, 'On the manner of holding the violin and playing upon it', no. 1 p. 1.
26. L'Abbé le fils, *Principes* . . . (1761), p. 1.
27. Habeneck, *Méthode* . . . (c. 1840), p. 30.
28. Cartier, *L'art* . . . (1798), pt. 1, p. 1.
29. Mazas, *Méthode* . . . (1830), art, 2, p. 2.

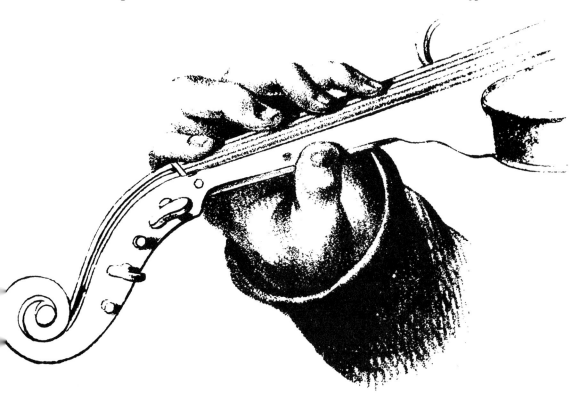

16.   The position of the left thumb and fingers as illustrated by Campagnoli

The thumb must not project too far over the fingerboard; otherwise it gets in the way when playing and robs the G string of tone. It must also be held more forward towards the second and third fingers than back towards the first; because the hand thus achieves greater freedom in stretching. One need only try it and the thumb will generally come to rest opposite the second finger, when it stops f¹ or f sharp¹ on the D string.   (Mozart, *Versuch* . . . , ch. 2, §4, p. 54.
The last two sentences are the additions of 1787 and 1806)

Paganini appears to have adopted a novel thumb position some distance along the neck from the nut. Available evidence is not conclusive on this matter and some sketches completely disprove this theory; nevertheless, such a thumb position seems both possible and likely, since the peculiarities and extraordinary flexibility of Paganini's thumb, fingers, wrist and other joints were apparently such that he could 'bring the thumb of his left hand over the middle of the fingerboard in such a way that he could play, at pleasure, in the first three positions without the "extension"'.[30] Thus, the thumb acted both as a supporting agent for the violin neck and scroll, and as a pivot about which the fingers were perfectly free to extend or contract as required. Many

30. Here quoted from Istel, 'The secret of Paganini's technique', *Musical Quarterly*, vol. 16 (1930), p. 114.

sketches suggest that Paganini actually gripped the instrument between his thumb and index-finger. This may well have been so, but such a grip would not have offered his fingers that complete mobility over the fingerboard which they undoubtedly possessed. It is more likely that the extension and contraction of the fingers in turn involved a sympathetic movement of the thumb, which was generally caused to bend as if to grip the instrument (without actually doing so) when the fingers were contracted and to straighten somewhat when the fingers reached the higher positions. Thus the impression of gripping the instrument would have been given, without such constrictions actually taking place, and Paganini's exceedingly supple fingers were offered that complete freedom of movement essential to his mode of performance.

THE POSITION OF THE FINGERS

Although rather demanding for the budding child violinist, the 'Geminiani grip' is still retained by most writers throughout the period as a guide to the correct placing of the fingers and thumb on the fingerboard in first position. It emphasises the close relationship between the relative positions of the elbow and hand, ensuring that the elbow is held well under the instrument and that the fingers are properly curved and the little finger well extended, factors continually stressed by contemporary writers. Furthermore, in setting the violinist's playing position, it automatically compensates for any physical abnormalities, such as a small hand or short finger span. Significantly, Leopold Mozart includes the 'Geminiani grip' for the first time in his 1769–70 edition, incorporating it into an exercise for perfecting the playing position:

The first finger is placed on the f² of the E string, the second on the c² of the A string, the third on the g¹ of the D string and the fourth or little finger on the d¹ of the G string, but without lifting any again until all four fingers at once are resting correctly on their prescribed places. Then one should try to lift the first, then the third, then the second and then the fourth and let each drop back again immediately, yet without moving the other three away from their places. The finger should be lifted only so high as not to touch the string: and it will be seen that this exercise is the quickest way to acquire the true position of the hand and that in this way one achieves an extraordinary facility in playing double stopping in tune when the time comes.

(Mozart, *Versuch* . . . (1769–70), ch. 2, §4, p. 54)

The 'Geminiani grip' was likewise commonly employed as finger exercise material by numerous other writers, notably by Baillot, who makes many such references to that hand position, two of which are reproduced below:

In order to be sure that the elbow and the left hand are well positioned and that the fingers are placed upright, each on a single string, the following passage, cited in article 3,[31] should be practised.

31. See p. 48.

Ex. 2

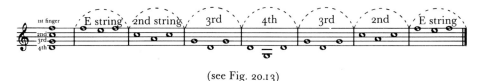

(see Fig. 20.13)

Raise only one finger at a time leaving the three others in position.
(This passage is taken from *Geminiani's* method.)

(Baillot, *L'art* . . . (1834), art. 8, p. 15)

Before moving on to the next lesson, it is necessary to position the left hand as has
been indicated in article 8[32] in order to be sure that each finger touches only one
string at a time, which can be tested by playing the following passage:

Ex. 3

Leave all the fingers in position, then raise only that finger which allows the open
string to sound.

(Baillot, *L'art* . . . (1834), p. 18)

Campagnoli, whilst recommending the 'Geminiani grip', further suggests
fastening two small circular pieces of wood to the neck, one opposite B on the
G string, the other facing the nut on the E string side (Fig. 14), in order to
reassure the student of the correct finger positions,[33] while Signoretti amends
the 'grip' slightly, substituting f sharp[2] for f natural[2] with the first finger, thus
forming a slightly different hand contour.[34] However, Spohr surprisingly
provides little information regarding the position of the fingers and is one of
the few to omit mention of the 'Geminiani grip'; he merely writes:

The part of the hand holding the little finger is brought as close as possible to the
fingerboard, so that this shorter finger may fall straight down onto the strings with its
joints bent, as well as the others.   (Spohr, *Violinschule* (1832), p. 24)

Although myriad ways of holding the violin coexisted during our period,
they were gradually superseded by the typical modern method, with chin-
braced grip on the left side of the tailpiece, the elbow well under the instrument and slightly away from the body, the wrist describing practically a
straight line with the forearm (except of course in half position, the higher
positions or, for example, in cases when multiple stopping necessitates the use
of unorthodox fingerings), and the violin inclined towards the right and held

32. See p. 54.
33. Campagnoli, *Metodo* . . . (1797?), tr. Bishop, Introduction, 'remark', p. 2.
34. Signoretti, *Méthode* . . . (1777), pt. 2, p. 1.

at shoulder height, at practically a ninety-degree angle to the left shoulder. The chin, shoulder and left hand had normally combined to support the instrument, but the left hand, with thumb and fingers so positioned as to achieve optimum 'hammer-like' action (invariably dictated by the 'Geminiani grip'), tonal and expressive potential, technical facility and, above all, comfort, was gradually relieved of its supporting role, due mainly to the increasing demands of an ever-developing technique. Towards the end of our period some violinists began to make use of such further means of support as the chin rest and/or the shoulder pad.

Modern treatises tend to be more flexible regarding the manner of holding the instrument; many writers deliberately refrain from prescribing exact rules (apart from prohibiting chin pressure on the tailpiece), thus leaving the player to adopt a method appropriate to his own natural constitution, particularly with regard to methods of supporting the violin and the relative positions of the hand and elbow. The hand and elbow positions are determined essentially by the placement of the fingers, which is influenced in turn by the wrist, normally held as described above. The fingers should normally fall almost perpendicularly on their tips and on no account should the thumb be allowed to grip the neck of the instrument, a fault which would severely restrict the action of the left hand.[35]

35. See ch. 5.

4

Holding the bow; the fundamental bow stroke

The beginning of our period coincides with a growing interest, especially in France, in the potential of the bow and its expressive powers. L'Abbé le fils calls the bow 'the soul of the instrument it touches, as it is used to give expression to the sounds, sustain them, swell and diminish them',[1] an opinion shared by many other writers; skilful bow management, mastery of a variety of bow strokes and a suitably natural and flexible bow hold were crucial in securing such dynamic control.

To some extent, the methods of holding the violin and bow were (and still are) necessarily related; the violin hold inevitably affects the position of the right hand and arm and the manner in which they are required to act. This close relationship between the violin and bow holds is clearly illustrated by writers' views concerning the position of the right arm and elbow in relation to the body.

THE POSITION OF THE ARM AND ELBOW

The very fact that violinists were advised to incline the violin towards the E string side, in order to prevent the bow arm from being raised excessively high for execution on the G string, suggests that the right elbow was generally positioned fairly close to, but nevertheless detached from, the body in a natural, unconstrained manner and below the level of the bow stick. L'Abbé le fils confirms that 'the elbow should always be detached from the body'[2] and Campagnoli further prescribes two rules:

1. The arm which supports the bow must neither be held too high nor too low, but remain in a natural position.
2. The thumb, the hand, the elbow, and the entire portion of the arm which sustains the bow, must be kept quite on a level; or, in other words, at the same height.

(Campagnoli, *Metodo* . . . (1797?), tr. Bishop, Introduction,
'Position of the right arm', nos. 1 & 2, p. 1)

1. L'Abbé le fils, *Principes* . . . (1761), p. 1.   2. *Ibid.*

57

The common early-nineteenth-century position of the instrument, almost directly in front of the player at practically a ninety-degree angle to his left shoulder, required the right elbow to be lowered somewhat; this in turn resulted in that elbow taking up a position nearer to the body than before, with the bow seemingly hanging from the wrist.[3] Spohr confirms: 'The wrist must . . . be raised, but the elbow lowered and kept as near as possible to the body' (see Fig. 13). (Spohr, *Violinschule* (1832). p. 25) It is interesting to note that the normal modern elbow position represents the opposite extreme to Spohr's recommendation; thus, it can be concluded that the common eighteenth-century elbow position was neither as close to the body as in the nineteenth century, nor as far from the body as in modern practice. Whatever the elbow position employed, the importance of a natural and relaxed position of the right arm, elbow, hand, wrist and fingers is consistently stressed by writers as a prime technical consideration.

Paganini's extraordinary physique and his unorthodox violin hold naturally affected the position of his right arm, resulting in a somewhat cramped-looking bowing style. Guhr explains:

His right arm lies quite close to his body and is hardly ever moved. He allows free play only to his very bent wrist, which moves extremely easily, and guides the flexible movement of the bow with the greatest rapidity. It is only in strong and drawn-out *chords*, for which the lower part of the bow near the heel is used, that he lifts his hand and lower part of his arm somewhat higher, and moves his elbow away from his body.

(Guhr, *Ueber Paganinis Kunst* . . . (1829) §4, p. 6)

Contemporary illustrations are somewhat contrary concerning the bowing position depicted but most confirm the position described by Guhr.

THE POSITION OF THE HAND, THUMB AND FINGERS ON THE BOW

At the beginning of the period, the position of the hand, thumb and fingers on the bow varied considerably according to national style, the demands of the music, personal taste, the size of the violinist's hand and fingers and the balance (and hence the type) of the bow itself, although bow weights and bow construction were gradually standardised towards the end of the eighteenth century. The increasing popularity of the sonata and concerto in France and the expressive ideals of the period led to the replacement of the old French grip – with the thumb placed under the bow hair – a relic of the popular dance styles of previous years but still recommended by Brijon (1763),[4] by a grip similar to that employed by the Italian school. With the gradual fusion of national styles and the standardisation of bow construction in the late eighteenth century came a corresponding, if gradual standardisation of the

3. See Babitz, 'Differences between eighteenth-century and modern violin bowing', *The Score*, vol. 19 (1957), Fig. 1A, p. 36.
4. Brijon, *Réflexions* . . . (1763), art. 7, p. 19.

bow holds employed, especially regarding the respective positions of the hand, thumb and fingers on the bow.

THE POSITION OF THE HAND

In view of the close relationship between the violin and bow holds, it is hardly surprising that L'Abbé le fils, who anticipates the modern violin hold, also recommends a bow grip foreshadowing modern concepts:

The end of the little finger should be placed on the part of the bow fastened to the frog; the index-finger should be placed in such a way that the bow is in contact with the second joint of this finger, which, in order to gain greater power, must be slightly separated from the others. The thumb should be opposite the middle finger and must take the full weight of the bow.   (L'Abbé le fils, *Principes* . . . (1761), p. 1)

L'Abbé le fils's instructions imply that the hand should be placed at the frog and not slightly above it as Geminiani, Corrette and Leopold Mozart had advised. This bow grip gradually gained acceptance towards the end of the century as violinists recognised its superiority in accomplishing the various musical and expressive effects desired.

Italian writers also adopted a progressive attitude in this matter and generally advocated bow grips more akin to modern methods, except that the thumb, and consequently the hand, was normally placed on the stick a short distance away from the frog (Fig. 17). German writers, however, were more conservative, still advocating well into the nineteenth century a hand position *near* rather than *at* the frog. Löhlein's bow grip clearly shows the hand positioned some distance from the frog (Fig. 18), affording arguably a more even balance of the bow but effectively eliminating use of the *true* middle of the bow, the point at which the clearest articulation could be made, and forcing the player towards the tip for detailed passage-work:

The bow is held with the right hand, that is in the following manner: it is held with the thumb and the first two fingers, just where the frog ends and not almost in the middle, in such a way that it lies inside the first joint of the index-finger. The second finger is placed some distance from the first and is somewhat more bent than the first, in such a way that it touches the bow curved round. With these two fingers, especially with the tip of the second, one presses the bow against the thumb, which makes a counter-pressure against the two fingers if one turns in the top segment of the thumb somewhat and pushes the bow upwards from below between the two fingers: being held in this way the bow is bound to take up a firm position so that it cannot waver to and fro. The two remaining fingers rest on the bow quite gently and serve only to give it a more definite direction. This will be easier to understand from the accompanying illustration.   (Löhlein, *Anweisung*. . . (1774), ch. 5, §30, pp. 18–19)

By the beginning of the nineteenth century, most writers were advocating a hand position right at the heel either directly or by implication in a recommendation such as the following:

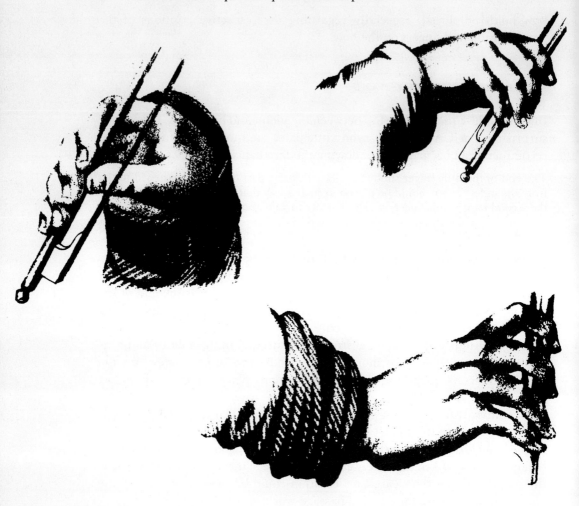

17.   The bow hold as illustrated by Campagnoli

The bow should be supported by all the fingers; care should be taken to place the side and the tip of the thumb against the frog and opposite the middle finger.

(Rode *et al.*, *Méthode*. . . (1803), art. 3, p. 5)

However, there were numerous exceptions, Mazas and Bruni among many writers recommending a thumb/hand position near but not right at the frog. Furthermore, many bows, including a Tourte known to have been used by Viotti, have wrappings covering almost half the stick, thus indicating that many nineteenth-century performers held the bow in the 'old' manner even with the 'new' Tourte bow. Spohr reports that F. W. Pixis held the bow a hand's

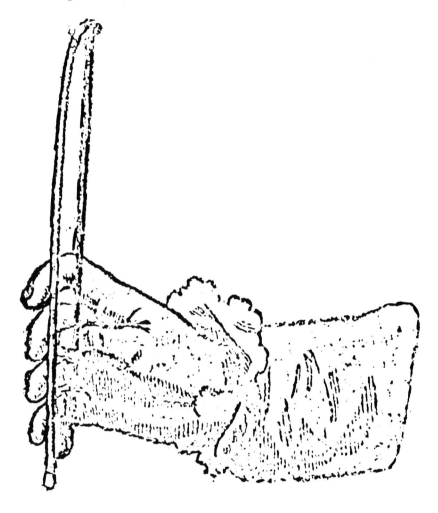

18.   The bow hold as illustrated by Löhlein

breadth from the frog,[5] and Flesch claims that Dancla (as late as 1890) held his bow three inches above the nut.[6] Paganini, too, adopted such a bow grip and this undoubtedly facilitated the execution of the various 'thrown' bowings for which he became renowned, offering greater bow control and more subtle expressive effect within a limited dynamic range. However, it also certainly adversely affected Paganini's tone (as did his use of thin strings and his adoption of light, fast bow strokes, especially suitable for harmonic effects), which, by most contemporary accounts, was lacking in fullness and volume.

5. See Mayer, *The forgotten master . . .*, p. 196.
6. Flesch, *The art of violin playing*, tr. Martens, vol. 1, p. 60.

THE POSITION OF THE THUMB

The thumb's principal tasks were to help support the weight of the bow and provide counter-pressure to that exerted by the index-finger. Contrary to modern practice, it was generally not markedly bent (although some illustrations are somewhat ambiguous on this point) but kept fairly straight, so that the bow could be gripped more securely without causing stiffness in the hand, fingers or wrist. Löhlein is one of the few eighteenth-century writers to recommend bending the thumb (see Fig. 18) but Mazas later advises that the thumb should be bent slightly[7] and Spohr remarks: 'The thumb is placed, bent, with its tip against the bow stick, close to the nut opposite the middle finger' (see Fig. 19). (Spohr, *Violinschule* (1832), p. 25)

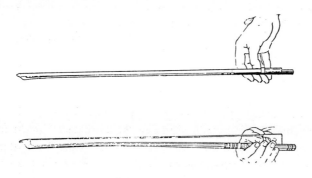

19.   The bow grip as illustrated by Spohr

However, these writers' views are exceptions rather than the rule, although the use of a bent thumb naturally allowed the wrist and fingers greater flexibility and control for the execution of smooth bow changes and other subtle bowing effects so vital to modern technique.

   The position of the thumb depends to some extent on the hand position adopted by the player, the length and point of balance of the bow, the size of his hand, the musical effect desired and many other variables. Consequently, even after the virtual standardisation of bow construction and bow grips in the early nineteenth century, there were differences of opinion as to which thumb position offered greatest freedom in bowing without constriction of the wrist. L'Abbé le fils, for example, is one of many writers to prescribe a thumb position opposite the middle (second) finger,[8] whilst Cartier states: 'The thumb should be [positioned] between the index-finger and the middle finger and should support the whole weight of the bow.' (Cartier, *L'Art*. . . (1798), pt. 1, art. 6, p. 1) Baillot gives perhaps the most detailed survey of the period,

7. Mazas, *Méthode* . . . (1830), art. 3, p. 2.
8. L'Abbé le fils, *Principes* . . . (1761), p. 1; see also Rode *et al.*, *Méthode* . . . (1803), art. 3, p. 5; Mazas, *Méthode* . . . (1830), art. 3, p. 2; Spohr, *Violinschule* (1832), p. 25.

advocating, like Habeneck, a thumb position between the second and third fingers:

2. When the hand is extended to grasp the bow, it will be evident that, if in this inverted hand position one wants to pass the thumb under the fingers, it will take up a sideways position, and that if one then places the bow stick between the four fingers which will be above it and the thumb which will be below, it will come to rest on the fleshy part of the thumb, which is next to the nail, and not quite at its tip, for the thumb should extend approximately 2 *lignes*[9] beyond the stick. It is at this point that it has the most strength to grip the bow when necessary.

3. Avoid bending the thumb.

4. Place it against the frog so that it touches it lightly at its upper extremity without, however, allowing it to enter the opening; those who have neglected this principle have been at fault; in this position the hand better controls the pressure and restraint on the bow; a little practice will soon make the player fully aware of its advantages. When the hand, which always tends to slide, comes to move away from the frog, one should not neglect to put the thumb back in its place.

(Baillot, L'art . . . (1834), art. 4, p. 12)

THE POSITION OF THE FINGERS

Recommendations concerning the position of the fingers on the bow varied considerably during the period; some writers prescribe measurements for the optimum distance between each pair of fingers on the bow stick[10] whilst others recommend a natural finger position, thereby allowing the player licence to adopt a position appropriate to the size of his hand. However, only the basic bow grip is described and little allowance is made for adjustments to the shape of the fingers during certain bow strokes.

The index-finger

Writers continually stress the importance of the index-finger in the control of bow pressure and, hence, tonal quality and volume. Leopold Mozart notably adds in his edition of 1787 that 'the first finger must contribute most towards increasing and diminishing the tone'.[11] The general late-eighteenth-century trend was to separate the index-finger slightly from the other fingers on the bow stick in order for it to control the tonal volume by applying or releasing pressure as required. L'Abbé le fils confirms:

the index-finger should be placed in such a way that the bow is in contact with the second joint of this finger, which, in order to gain greater power, must be separated slightly from the others.   (L'Abbé le fils, *Principes*. . . (1761), p. 1)

Naturally, the further apart the thumb and index-finger were placed, the

9. A *ligne* = 2·25 mm.
10. For example, Bornet, *Nouvelle méthode* . . . (1786), p. 6; Bruni, *Nouvelle méthode* . . . (1806), p. 19.
11. L. Mozart, *Versuch* . . ., (1787 edn) ch. 2, §5, p. 56.

greater would have been the pressure at the point of the bow;[12] however, the stretching out of the index-finger was universally recognised as a technical fault, causing constrictions in the free movement of the wrist and fingers and impeding the player's bow control.

Contrary to most eighteenth-century writers, Rode *et al.*, Baillot, Mazas and Spohr warn against separating the index-finger from the others on the bow stick. Spohr suggests: 'the tips of all four fingers should be so brought together that there is no space between them' (see Fig. 19). (Spohr, *Violinschule* (1832), p. 25) Baillot remarks: 'Avoid separating the index-finger from the other fingers, which, as already discussed, should neither be bent nor stretched but left naturally rounded.' (Baillot, *L'art.* . . (1834), art. 4, p. 12) With the Tourte bow, the separation of the index-finger from the others was no longer necessary in order to realise adequate pressure at the point, due to that model's powers of even pressure-distribution throughout its length.

Some writers maintain that the bow pressure on the string should be regulated by other members, Cambini specifying the importance of the wrist, Campagnoli emphasising that of the thumb, and Rode *et al.*, Mazas and Baillot, among others, advocating the use of thumb, index-finger and wrist-joint pressure.[13] Such variations are reflected to some extent in the recommended contact points of index-finger and bow stick, the three main schools of thought prescribing contact between the first and second joints (Bornet, Cambini and Campagnoli), on or near the middle of the second joint (L'Abbé le fils, Corrette, Lorenziti, Rode *et al.*, Mazas and Baillot), or between the second and third joints of the index-finger (L. Mozart and Signoretti). Spohr, however, suggests one further possibility, a contact point on the first joint of the index-finger, his adoption of a bent thumb probably accounting for this slightly different index-finger position.[14]

The fourth (little) finger

The little finger was generally required to rest on the stick, acting as a balancing agent and affording the player additional bow control. Its role remained unchanged throughout the period even though its position underwent modification in line with the position of the right hand. Baillot provides perhaps the best survey:

2. The little finger supports the weight of the bow when the heel approaches the bridge; as the heel moves away from it [the bridge] in the down bow, the little finger ceases to support the stick, until its pressure becomes useless when playing at the

12. Galeazzi, in his *Elementi* . . . (1791), for example, recommends not only advancing the index-finger along the stick but also pulling the thumb further backwards from below the index-finger or second finger to the third finger for even greater weight.
13. Cambini, *Nouvelle méthode* . . . (1803), §6, p. 4; Campagnoli, *Metodo* . . . (1797?), tr. Bishop, Introduction, 'Position of the right arm', no. 6, p. 1; Rode *et al.*, *Méthode* . . . (1803), art. 6, p. 7; Baillot, *L'art* . . . (1834), art. 7, nos. 3 & 4, p. 15; Mazas, *Méthode* . . . (1830), art. 8, p. 6. See also ch. 6, p. 141.
14. Spohr, *Violinschule* (1832), p. 25.

point; it can then be raised without disadvantage in some arpeggios, but it should be replaced immediately afterwards on the stick and pressed a little against the bow when changing from one string to another . . . because . . . the little finger helps to detach the note in an up bow and to convey the bow immediately afterwards on to the other string.   (Baillot, L'art. . . (1834), art. 8, pp. 14–15)

The other fingers

The respective positions of the second and third fingers on the bow were essentially determined by those of the thumb, little finger and index-finger and the size of the player's hand. The second and third fingers, naturally rounded, rested on the bow without exerting any pressure to guide and control its movements. Campagnoli provides a detailed description of the bow hold:

3. The bow must not be held entirely with the ends of the fingers, but with the fingers a little bent, in a natural position, and in such a manner that the nut may remain beyond the hand . . .
7. The fingers must not be drawn too close together, but be distributed on the stick of the bow, at a little distance from each other. The first joint of the three first fingers must be placed on the stick, the points of the fingers being slightly bent inwards towards the thumb, and the fingers themselves turned along the stick a little, in the direction of the nut. The second joint of these three fingers must be slightly bent within the hand, so that externally they may assume a curved form [see Fig. 17]. . .
(Campagnoli, Metodo . . . (1797?), tr. Bishop, Introduction,
'Position of the right arm' nos. 3 & 7, pp. 1–2)

He later suggests:

5. To make sure of holding the bow correctly, and of distributing the fingers properly on the stick, let three little concave incisions be made on the latter, for the thumb, the first finger, and the little finger, and the other two fingers will consequently fall in their proper places.
(Campagnoli, Metodo . . . (1797?), tr. Bishop, Introduction,
'Management of the bow' no. 5, 'Remark', p. 2)

THE DIRECTION OF THE BOW

Writers are unanimous that the best tonal results are gained by drawing the bow straight across the strings, parallel with the bridge. Löhlein gives a detailed explanation and recommends a device of his own invention as an aid towards the correct implementation of his principles:

Should a beginner, having spared no effort, still not succeed in drawing the bow straight, a means can be used, which, strange though it may seem, nevertheless brings about the desired result. Namely, a strip of pliable wood, e.g. willow or a hazel switch or, even better, whalebone, is fastened in the f-holes at a suitable distance from the bridge, so that it is arched across the bridge at some three horizontal fingers' width above it. Thus, the bow is prevented from moving too near or too far from the bridge or from wandering up and down; and it is bound to keep straight when moved backwards and forwards against this arched stick, so that eventually a perfectly straight bow and good tone will result.   (Löhlein, *Anweisung* . . . (1774) ch. 5, §34, p. 21)

Likewise, Paine recommends his invention, 'the bow guide', to ensure straight bowing,[15] while Spohr stipulates a specific right-hand technique:

it is necessary to move the bow to and fro between the thumb and middle finger. In a down bow therefore, the stick gradually advances towards the middle joint of the index-finger, while the little finger withdraws more and more from the stick; in an up bow, however, the stick should gradually recede into the hollow of the first joint of the index-finger while the little finger moves slowly back with its tip a little over the stick.

(Spohr, *Violinschule* (1832) p. 25)

THE INCLINATION OF THE BOW

Another significant advance in L'Abbé le fils's bow hold was his recommendation to incline the bow towards the fingerboard and thus use chiefly the distant edge of the bow hair:

When placing the bow on the string, the stick should not be perpendicularly above the hair, but must be inclined slightly towards the fingerboard.

(L'Abbé le fils, *Principes* . . . (1761), p. 1)

This advice was endorsed by most of his successors but the degree of inclination recommended, if discussed at all, varied considerably according to personal taste. Campagnoli, like Galeazzi, relates the degree of inclination to the weight of the bow:

The bow must be held with the stick turned a little towards the strings on the side of the finger board, so that the hair may be inclined towards the bridge; and the heavier the bow is, the more must it be turned in the manner here described.

(Campagnoli, *Metodo* . . . (1797?), tr. Bishop, Introduction,
'On the management of the bow', no. 4, p. 2)

Löhlein and Baillot, on the other hand, relate the degree of inclination to the contact point and the musical effect desired. Löhlein claims:

Here I must make a necessary remark, namely that the further one moves the bow away from the bridge the duller and more muted the tone becomes. On the other hand, the closer it is brought to the bridge the sharper and more penetrating the tone. It should also be observed here that whenever the bow is moved away from the bridge [the pressure] should be decreased and the stick tilted towards the bridge; whereas, when it is brought close to the bridge, it should be pressed on the string more firmly and the stick tilted towards the fingerboard. This is to be observed particularly carefully with *vibrato* and also with long held notes; for, by means of this advantage, one can cause the tone to increase and diminish as one deems good.

(Löhlein, *Anweisung* . . . (1774) ch. 12, §100 (n), p. 109)

Baillot points out that it can prove advantageous to tilt the bow only slightly:

The bow stick should be held slightly tilted towards the upper part of the fingerboard;

15. Paine, *Treatise on the violin* . . . (c. 1815), p. 47.

but for the lightly detached strokes in the middle, it should be held closer to or further from the perpendicular, in order to allow more or less elasticity in the action of the stick or the springing of the bow.   (Baillot, *L'art* . . . (1834), art. 4, no. 9, p. 12)

Rode *et al.* provide further reasons, essentially related to the length of the player's arm, for varying the degree of tilt:

The bow stick should be kept inclined towards the fingerboard and the bow should always be parallel with the bridge. However, in order to avoid stretching the arm forward, and thus intersecting the string obliquely at the angle most detrimental to the purity of the sound, there are cases when a slight forward inclination may be given to the point of the bow, in order that, at the same time, a stronger tone may be obtained in those strokes taken at the point.   (Rode *et al.*, *Méthode* . . . (1803) art. 3, p. 6)

Although the inclination of the bow became general practice towards the end of the eighteenth century, especially in France, it was not unanimously accepted, ostensibly because of its detrimental effect on tone quality. Leopold Mozart, Reichardt and Lolli are among those writers who discouraged this practice in the interests of producing a strong, virile and even tone from the full ribbon of hair.[16] The basic scientific reasoning is admirably explained by Donington:

The more tilted the angle of the hair to the string, the narrower the band of hair in contact at normal pressures, the less damping of the very high harmonics, but also the less ample exciting of the lowest harmonics, so that more colour but less solidity is yielded. The less tilted the angle of the hair to the string, the wider the band of hair in contact, the more damping of the very high harmonics (such as are produced by very short lengths of the string), but also the more ample exciting of the lower harmonics (especially the fundamental), so that less colour but more solidity is yielded.[17]

THE FUNDAMENTAL BOW STROKE

The fundamental short bow stroke of the period was executed only by the wrist and forearm but the upper arm and in some cases the shoulder were also employed, albeit indirectly, in the execution of longer strokes, this upper arm movement naturally being upwards and downwards but never lateral. Campagnoli provides perhaps the most detailed late-eighteenth-century account:

9. The wrist must act with the greatest possible address and facility. It must be considered as a spring which directs all the elastic movements of the bow.
10. The arm which conducts the bow may be allowed a slight movement upwards or downwards; but any lateral motion of the upper part of the arm is prohibited; so that the elbow joint should remain free and bend easily, it having to effect the entire operation of playing, without communicating any of its motion to the upper part of the arm.
11. The whole arm, as well as the hand, must make four slight degrees of movement, both in rising and falling, whilst the bow passes from one string to another.

16. L. Mozart, *Versuch* . . ., ch. 2, §6, p. 55; Lolli, *L'ecole* . . . (c. 1760), no. 4, p. 1; Reichardt, *Ueber die Pflichten* . . . (1776), pp. 4–5.
17. Donington, *String playing in baroque music*, p. 28.

12. It is requisite, however, carefully to avoid drawing back the elbow behind the body, as this would entirely derange the direction of the bow.

(Campagnoli, Metodo . . . (1797?), tr. Bishop, Introduction,
'Position of the right arm', nos. 9–12, p. 2)

In comparison, Baillot's step-by-step survey provides a traditional nineteenth-century viewpoint:

1. Start the bow stroke at the beginning of the hair with the wrist rounded; in the down bow, leave the joint of the wrist a little higher than the bow stick, up to and including the end of the bow, so that this joint has the necessary play to enable the hand to move freely and rapidly when required, from right to left for the down bow and from left to right for the up bow (see Figs. [15·21 and 20·11 & 12]).

2. The forearm and wrist must maintain the utmost flexibility.

3. The upper arm and the elbow should never take part directly in the movements of the forearm. To this end, the elbow should be allowed to fall effortlessly into a state of complete passivity.

Passages to practise for this purpose:

Ex. 4

(Viotti: Trio no. 2)   (Viotti: Trio no. 4)

To play from the arm (that is to say, from the upper arm and elbow) is one of the greatest faults one can have. One must constantly try to avoid it. When one plays on the lower strings, the wrist is raised to reach them, the forearm merely follows it, yet this movement is almost non-existent when one has to pass quickly from one string to another as in these passages.

Ex. 5

(Fiorillo: Étude no. 30)

(Baillot, L'art . . . (1834), art. 5, pp. 13–14)

Baillot later continues by discussing the role of the little finger in bowing and then turns his attention to the preservation of the bow's direction parallel to the bridge:

it is necessary (with an up bow and when about two thirds of the bow have been used) to draw the forearm gradually towards the chest and towards the upper arm, and to arch the hand flexibly towards the chin as the heel of the bow is reached; the right elbow will have moved forward a little to effect this. By arching the top of the hand and keeping the joint of the thumb raised from five to six *lignes* [i.e. 11·25–13·5 mm] above the top of the bridge, one will avoid forcing the position of the wrist when the heel of the bow approaches the strings (see Fig. [15·20]).

But when the bow is drawn right to the point, the elbow must continue to remain in a line perpendicular to the shoulder (see Fig. [15·21]).

The same applies when using the middle of the bow (see Fig. [15·23]).

The position of the upper arm is incorrect in Fig. [20·17]).

That indicated in Fig. [20·18] is equally so in that, like the previous one, it causes the forearm to move incorrectly and the bow to lie at the wrong angle across the strings. (Baillot, *L'art* . . . (1834), art. 8, no. 5, p. 15)

By contrast, Spohr's account comprises a *mélange* of traditional methods and a rather more individual approach. He stresses the non-participatory role of the upper arm in the execution of short strokes in the upper third of the bow and emphasises the importance of straight bowing.[18] He claims that the elbow need not be moved when bowing short strokes on the upper two strings but must inevitably be raised for execution on the lower two strings; it should never follow the movement of the forearm but should, together with the upper arm, remain still in order to preserve straight bowing.[19] He includes some surprising observations concerning the movement of the bow between the thumb and middle finger in order to ensure that the bow remains parallel with the bridge and at right angles to the strings.[20] Unlike French writers, Spohr claims that full bow strokes require movement of the upper arm:

Begin by playing an up bow. The upper arm should be kept still during the first third of the bow, but should follow through the continuation of the stroke, with the elbow moving forward but the hand continuing in its original direction towards the strings. Continue the stroke with the bow always parallel to the bridge until the nut reaches the strings, then play a down bow in the reverse manner; the upper arm is lowered to its previous position and then remains immovable during the last third of the bow stroke. (Spohr, *Violinschule* (1832), pp. 28–9)

It is interesting to note that Habeneck recommends the student to use chiefly the middle of the bow at the outset in order both to avoid stiffness of the elbow and wrist and to assist in making the necessary bowing adjustments for the variety of note lengths encountered in passages of sight-reading.[21] Furthermore, some writers go so far as to suggest ways of immobilising the upper arm in order to help the student to adopt a correct position and proper action of the right arm when practising. Löhlein, for example, recommends resting the shoulder against a wall in order to ensure that only the wrist is used, while Campagnoli advises the student to tie a cord round the elbow and secure it to

18. Spohr, *Violinschule* (1832), p. 25.
19. *Ibid.*, p. 27.
20. See p. 66.
21. Habeneck, *Méthode* . . . (c. 1840), p. 38.

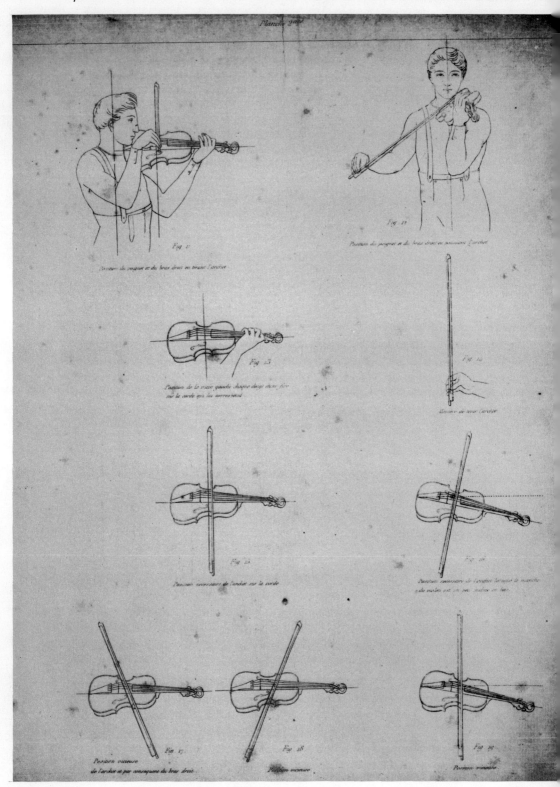

20. The bow hold and bowing as illustrated by Baillot

a button on his clothing (see Fig. 21).[22] At first, students were generally advised to practise bowing on the open strings before undertaking the additional problems of fingering. The A and E strings were generally considered the most convenient strings for this elementary bowing practice, in contrast to the modern preference for the A and D strings, which avoids the extreme bowing angles occasioned by the G and E strings.

THE FLEXIBILITY OF THE WRIST AND FINGERS

The wrist

The need for freedom and suppleness of the wrist is continually emphasised by writers but little additional explanation is generally provided, members of the eighteenth-century French and German schools being particularly unhelpful on this score. No direct mention whatever is made of the degree of wrist turn-in towards the body.

Campagnoli provides perhaps the most explicit eighteenth-century account of the wrist action:

> 1. In commencing a down bow, the joints of the elbow and of the hand should be turned in an entirely opposite direction. The joint of the arm must be well bent inwards, thereby forming a very acute angle; and the hand must be much turned outwards, so that the length of the thumb may be parallel to the direction of the strings.
> 2. When the down bow is finished, the curve of the arm and hand should form nearly a semicircle; hence the hand will be found a little turned inwards.
> 3. In conducting the bow, therefore, the joints of the arm and of the hand must always make two opposite movements: thus, in the down bow, the joint of the arm will be gradually opened and the hand turned inwards; and, in the up bow, the hand will be turned outwards, imperceptibly, and the arm closed.
>
> (Campagnoli, *Metodo* . . . (1797?), tr. Bishop, Introduction, 'On the management of the bow', nos. 1–3, p. 2)

Mazas adopts a somewhat different pedagogical approach, with observations typical of the French school:

> The hand should be kept arched in such a way that it is always slightly above the level of the stick. It is useful to tilt the wrist slightly towards the chin when beginning a note at the heel of the bow, but one should avoid exaggerating this position, which is required, on the contrary, simply in order to give grace to the action of the arm and chiefly to prevent any wavering in the direction of the bow.
> The arm must be allowed all its flexibility and care must be taken neither to raise the elbow nor to bring it too close to the body. Since the violin itself must remain always in the same position, the elbow, the forearm and the wrist will naturally rise to different heights in order to play on each of the four strings.

---

22. Löhlein, *Anweisung* . . . (1774), p. 110; Campagnoli, *Metodo* . . . (1797?), tr. Bishop, Introduction, 'On the management of the bow', no. 5n, p. 2.

’1. Method of immobilising the upper arm when bowing as illustrated by Campagnoli

Essential remarks on holding the bow

Several people, believing that they are bending the wrist, unconsciously bend their fingers over the bow stick instead. This is a very faulty method; it has the disadvantage, in a fast movement, of making the bow whip on to the strings.

It must be borne in mind that the wrist moves in two quite distinct ways that must not be confused. It bends upwards and downwards, and from right to left. When a note is begun at the heel of the bow, the wrist must bend to the right on approaching the chin, and when it is ended with the arm extended, it [the wrist] must bend in the opposite direction while still maintaining the position which keeps it above the stick. The little finger should then scarcely touch it [the bow stick] or even leave it altogether in order to maintain the parallel direction of the bow.

All these movements should be effected without any change in the manner of holding the bow; it is however necessary to avoid any kind of stiffness and, even when using most pressure, to make sure that this is still done with flexibility.

(Mazas, *Méthode* . . . (1830), art. 4, p. 41)

Baillot provides clear diagrams, in accordance with Mazas' principles, to illustrate the optimum wrist positions for bowing at the heel and point respectively (Fig. 20.11 & 12). Pastou, however, whilst acknowledging that the wrist and forearm should act with suppleness, considers that any bending of the wrist joint will be harmful to the tone quality and strength. He maintains that the wrist joint should act only when one is playing at the heel; then, the wrist alone is bent, in order to preserve the direction of the bow parallel to the bridge; but as soon as the middle of the bow is reached, only the forearm should be moved.[23]

Paganini generally kept his upper arm close to his body and employed mainly his wrist (and inevitably his lower arm to some extent) in bowing. With the elbow held low, Paganini's wrist was so remarkably arched that any preservation of suppleness seems practically impossible. He raised his hand and forearm and moved his elbow away from his body only for the execution of strong chordal or other passages involving the lower part of the bow. Nevertheless, despite his apparent awkwardness and stiffness of attitude, contemporary critics constantly remarked on the suppleness of his bowing mechanism and concluded that such an unorthodox technique was the result of intensive study rather than any bodily malformation.[24]

The fingers

It was (and still is) vital for the fingers to be kept flexible and free from stiffness for the satisfactory execution of smooth bow changes, string-crossing and suchlike, especially since most players kept the right thumb fairly straight and not bent as today. L'Abbé le fils was the first writer to acknowledge this:

The bow should be held firmly but without stiffening the fingers; on the contrary, all

23. Pastou, *Méthode* . . . (1830), art. 5, pp. 2–3.
24. See de Saussine, *Paganini le magicien*, tr. Laurie, p. 174.

their joints should be very free; by observing this, the fingers will instinctively make imperceptible movements which will contribute considerably to the beauty of the sounds.   (L'Abbé le fils, *Principes* . . . (1761), p. 1)

Although largely neglected by eighteenth-century German writers, the role of the fingers in bowing is clearly emphasised by the Italian school, Cambini, for example, stressing that the fingers are the springs (*ressorts*) which set the bow in motion.[25] Furthermore, Baillot and Habeneck are adamant that the fingers should not grip the bow too tightly and that the hand should be rounded naturally in order to avoid stiffness in the wrist and arm.[26] However, reference to the various instructions concerning the execution of the fundamental bow stroke reveals that attention is focused more on the role of the wrist than that of the fingers. This is not to say that the 'imperceptible movements' of the fingers, advocated by L'Abbé le fils and his successors, are rejected by early-nineteenth-century writers; on the contrary, they became a natural result of the nineteenth-century manner of holding the bow and executing the whole bow stroke. Nevertheless, the fingers generally played a less significant role in bow management than in modern technique. Spohr is one of the few writers to pinpoint finger movement during the course of the bow stroke in his instructions regarding the movement of the bow parallel to the bridge.[27]

Flexibility, naturalness and suppleness appear to be the keys to bowing instructions of the period, such recommendations being extended in the nineteenth century to the right side of the body by Rode *et al.*, in order to gain the utmost freedom of the right arm, to the lower arm by Baillot, in order for it to follow the wrist freely in all its movements, and to the arm and elbow by Habeneck, in order to obtain the optimum bowing facility.[28]

THE BOW CHANGE

The technique of negotiating the bow change is poorly documented by eighteenth-century writers. Apart from emphasising the need for suppleness and flexibility in the wrist and fingers, writers give no further guidance, merely remarking that the wrist should follow the movement of the arm. The articulated, *non-legato* stroke of the pre-Tourte bow perhaps rendered such directions unnecessary, since smooth separate bowings were only rarely employed before c. 1760, even though Leopold Mozart implies their use:

Through diligent practice of these *divisions* of the bow stroke one becomes skilful in controlling the bow: and by means of this control one achieves *purity of tone*. The

25. Cambini, *Nouvelle méthode* . . . (1803), §4, p. 3.
26. Baillot, *L'art* . . . (1834), art. 4, no. 1, p. 12; Habeneck, *Méthode* . . . (c. 1840), p. 31.
27. See p. 66.
28. Rode *et al.*, *Méthode* . . . (1803), art. 7, p. 7; Baillot, *L'art* . . . (1834), art. 5, nos. 1-2, pp. 13-14; Habeneck, *Méthode* . . . (c. 1840), pp. 31-2.

strings stretched on the violin are set in motion by the violin bow; these vibrating strings divide the air and thus the sound and tone given by the strings when touched originates. Now if a string is bowed several times in succession and is in consequence brought each time from its previous vibration into a new, or similar, or slower, or faster movement; then according to the nature of each successive stroke, each stroke must necessarily be started gently with a certain control and [taken in such a manner that][29] even the strongest stroke brings the already vibrating string quite imperceptibly from its present movement into the next. This is what I meant by the kind of softness I was referring to in §3.[30]

> (Mozart, *Versuch* . . . , ch. 5, §10, p. 105 (p. 106 in the 1787 edn))

Tartini endorses these remarks and follows them up with a somewhat puzzling and sweeping suggestion:

in cantabile passages the transition from one note to the next must be made so perfectly that no interval of silence is perceptible between them . . . To decide whether the style is cantabile or allegro [meaning not only fast in tempo but also cheerful, lively or gay], apply the following test: if the melody moves by step, the passage is cantabile and should be performed legato; if, on the contrary, the melody moves by leap, the passage is allegro and a detached style of playing is required.

> (Tartini, *Traité* . . . (1771), ed. Jacobi, p. 55)

In any case, L'Abbé le fils's appreciation of the use of finger movement in bowing and the emphasis in contemporary methods on the importance of the flexibility of the wrist was gradually reflected in the adoption of smoother bow strokes as a contrast to the normal articulated stroke of the pre-Tourte bow, in which bow changes were emphasised by the bow's characteristic attack and natural *diminuendo*.

The execution of smooth bow changes was greatly facilitated by the Tourte bow, which contributed considerably towards the fulfilment of the *cantabile* aims of contemporary theorists. Consequently, nineteenth-century writers provide more detailed accounts of bow-changing technique, focusing their attention on the wrist since this member automatically affects in turn the relative positions of the fingers, hand, forearm and in some cases the elbow.

Baillot is the most explicit; as we have seen,[31] he recommends beginning a down bow with the wrist rounded naturally, leaving the wrist joint raised slightly above the bow stick throughout the length of the stroke in order to effect the necessary hand movement from left to right for the change to an up bow at the point. The elbow meanwhile should remain unmoved, perpendicular to the shoulder. Baillot prepares for the bow change at the heel when some two-thirds of the up bow have been completed, bringing the forearm gradually in towards the chest and upper arm and, on reaching the heel, turning the hand in towards the chin; the right elbow may move forward naturally in order to effect this (see Fig. 15.20–23). Such a hand movement, together with

---

29. In the 1787 edition, the following words occur at this point: 'without the bow being lifted, played with such a smooth connection that . . .'.
30. See p. 22.
31. See p. 68.

an additional ploy of raising the thumb joint slightly, should eradicate any unnatural wrist actions which may adversely affect the smoothness of the bow change. In making the bow change, Baillot, like Mazas, emphasises the importance of varying the hand weight and finger pressure on the bow stick:

Avoid making audible the change of bow or the slightest jerk either at the heel or at the point; to this end, press the thumb against the stick when the heel approaches the bridge, in order to prevent it [the stick] from being too heavy on the string; and when the change of bow is executed at the point, lighten the hand quickly so that the beginning of the up bow is not audible.

Increase the finger pressure against the stick as the bow comes towards the point; you will then obtain a sound which will have absolutely the same degree of intensity throughout the whole duration of the note.   (Baillot, L'art . . . (1834), p. 131)

Interestingly enough, no writer suggests the ploy, common nowadays, of decreasing the bow speed shortly before the bow change.

The type of bow hold adopted during the period depended on several factors, especially the method of holding the violin and the type of bow in use. However, with a number of transitional bows and certainly with the gradual emergence of the Tourte model, a bow grip right at the heel was most commonly employed. Nevertheless, a variety of bow holds coexisted in the early nineteenth century, in keeping with the prevailing situation regarding the use of violins, bows and fittings in varying degrees of transition. The bow itself was generally not held as firmly as is customary nowadays and the position of the arm and elbow, always relaxed, was never as far from the body as in modern practice, with every effort being made to immobilise the upper arm as much as possible. Late-eighteenth- and early-nineteenth-century writers display more flexibility over the position and curve of the thumb, which most modern players generally place opposite the middle finger in a bent position (the amount of bending depending entirely on the length of the thumb in relation to the hand). The position of the fingers differed considerably according to the various methods of controlling bow pressure, which was never as heavy on the string as with the Tourte model held in the modern manner.

Perhaps the most common bow hold in use nowadays is the so-called Russian method, disseminated largely by Leopold Auer. This involves the index-finger as the main pressure agent, pressing on the bow stick at its second joint with the thumb opposite the middle finger. When playing at the point, the second and third fingers, closely spaced and wrapped around the stick, are in contact with the bow diagonally at an angle of approximately forty-five degrees while the little finger touches the stick (for purposes of balance and effecting a smooth bow change) only when the lower half of the bow is employed (except perhaps in certain 'thrown' bowings). Such a bow grip allows the forearm to turn inwards from the elbow joint, the amount of pronation varying according to the part of the bow being used, and enables the index-finger to maintain its pressure on the bow without the least tension in the hand. Bowing at the heel requires the least pronation, since the weight of the bow, controlled by the little finger, provides most, if not all, of the required pressure. Bowing in the upper third requires up to forty-five-degree pronation of the arm so that it can compensate for the lack of bow weight on the stick by supplying the necessary pressure, controlled through the flexible joints of the index-finger, for satisfactory tone production.

The cultivation of a bow stroke parallel to the bridge, with the bow inclined slightly towards the fingerboard, and flexibility of wrist and fingers are still part and parcel of modern technique, but the increased recognition nowadays of the importance of the arm in bowing, notably in the lower third of the bow, has necessitated the development of a coordinated wrist and finger movement and marked pronation of the hand and forearm, the essential principle being to maintain the forearm, wrist and hand as nearly as possible in the same plane as the bow. It should also be noted that there have been recent advocates (for example, Heifetz, Szigeti) of the introduction of the shoulder into the mechanics of bowing for the purpose of equalising tone, but it must be said that such a technique is an exception rather than the rule.

5

Fundamental left-hand technique

Throughout the period under discussion, the finger joints were often likened to 'small springs' (*petits ressorts*),[1] whose function could be impaired by any stiffening of the wrist or any participation of the wrist or palm in the movement of the fingers. Thus, the hand and fingers generally described a curve with the fingers well over the strings, each knuckle being bent so that the top joints of the fingers were allowed to fall straight down on to the strings from the same height. There was some difference of opinion concerning the optimum height of the 'non-playing' fingers and the degree of finger pressure on the strings, as illustrated in the contrasting accounts by Campagnoli and Baillot to follow.

Two extracts from Campagnoli's treatise emphasise the need for a strong, but not over-firm, hammer-like finger action with minimal uplift of the fingers in order to obtain clear articulation and tone production:

12. The fingers must always be kept over the strings and never be suffered to leave them. By this means, they will always be ready when required and the performance will be accomplished with less fatigue and with the greatest promptitude.

13. The fingers must not be pressed on the strings more firmly than is necessary, in order that the vibrations of that part of the string which extends from the finger to the bridge may not be communicated to the part intercepted between the nut and the finger.

14. In playing, the fingers must be but very slightly raised above the strings, just sufficient not to touch them.

15. It is an established rule, always to keep the fingers on the strings, and not to raise them without necessity; as also to keep those fingers firmly pressed down which will again be required, although other notes may intervene . . .

(Campagnoli, *Metodo* . . . (1797?), tr. Bishop, Introduction, 'On the manner of holding the violin and playing upon it', nos. 12–15, p. 1)

4. The motion of the fingers commences at that joint which connects them with the hand. The perfection of this mechanism consists in the facility it affords of raising or pressing down each finger independently of the others.

1. For example, Signoretti, *Méthode* . . . (1777), pt. 2, p. 2.

78

The fingers placed on the strings form, as it were, a moveable [*sic*] nut. They must act with energy, and their first joint fall perpendicularly on the strings like a hammer.

To acquire the capability of placing the fingers on the four strings in all positions, and without touching the adjacent strings, this exercise [Ex. 6] should be studied, observing not to touch the semibreves with the bow during the performance of the quavers and semiquavers.

Ex. 6

Ex. 7

Different positions of the fingers

5. This [Ex. 7] is another highly useful exercise for acquiring facility in the different positions of the fingers. Each of the four notes should be played alternately with its open string, and without deranging the other fingers, which are intended to remain fixed in the prescribed position.

In general, it is very essential that the fingers, after having taken their places on the strings, be not removed until the moment when they have to be otherwise employed.

(Campagnoli, *Metodo* . . . (1797?), tr. Bishop, pt. i, nos. 4 & 5, p. 3)

Baillot's account implies a higher finger action for the acquisition of evenness, flexibility and clarity of articulation with the finger pressure being adjusted according to the prevailing dynamic (but not, it seems, to the pitch of the note or the string on which it is played)[2] and normally exceeding the bow pressure on the strings:

1. Let the fingers fall from a sufficient height for them to have a little impetus, the first joint upright on the string, but without attempting to make it perpendicular (see Fig. [10·4 & 5]).

2. Apply more or less pressure with the fingers according to whether you are playing quietly or loudly; but, however, apply enough [pressure] for the finger pressure to exceed that of the bow.   (Baillot, *L'art* . . . (1834), art. 6, p. 14).

---

2. See ch. 6, p. 130.

The need for finger strength and a firm finger action is continually stressed by most writers and exercises are invariably provided to cultivate strength, discipline and independence of finger movement as well as suppleness of the hand. However, as in modern methods, the student is normally cautioned against raising the fingers too high[3] and adopting excessive finger pressure[4] (except perhaps when a percussive effect, special accent or specific tonal effect is desired), faults which might cause stiffness and fatigue. The inherent weakness of the fourth finger is commonly emphasised but it is allowed no reprieve, Spohr among others insisting that, like the other fingers, it 'must fall straight down on to the strings with both joints bent, and should never be allowed to lie flat, even on the G string'.[5]

As in keyboard technique, unnecessary finger activity was avoided, the general rule applying that the fingers should not be raised from the strings without good cause.[6] Although this rule inevitably has some disadvantages,[7] it is still relevant to, though not rigidly applied in, modern technique, either as a guide for accuracy of intonation or as an aid towards greater security and facility in shifting. However, strict adherence to it stiffens the hand somewhat and can thus restrict *vibrato* movement; indeed, probably for this very reason Baillot relates finger activity to considerations of tempo:

> 3. Keep the fingers down in fast ascending scales; in descending scales, raise only one at a time and leave the others down.
> 4. But when playing at a slow or moderate speed and *during long notes* at any speed, when only one finger is stopped, *the three other fingers should be kept in the air* (their height corresponding to their natural position), so that they may fall again when required, with the independence they thus acquire, and so that they articulate the notes clearly, above all in slurred passages when they have to contribute everything in this respect (see Fig. [15.20–23]). (Baillot, *L'art* . . . (1834), art. 6, p. 14).

This raising of the redundant fingers in slower tempos and during long notes probably achieved more than just clarity of articulation and independence of the fingers; it also no doubt allowed the hand greater freedom and flexibility for the cultivation of *vibrato*, most commonly employed in slow tempos and on long notes, although writers fail to mention such a connection in their methods.

Habeneck gives the most detailed discussion concerning economy of finger action, recommending placing as many fingers as possible on the fingerboard simultaneously in order to facilitate independence of the fingers and accuracy of intonation. He subdivides his discussion into two parts (ascending and descending scales) and provides numerous fingering rules and exercises, involving scales and various intervals, for use during the initial stages of violin study:

3. For example, Mazas, *Méthode* . . . (1830), art. 5, p. 4.
4. For example, Galeazzi, *Elementi* . . . (1791), vol. 1, pt. 2, art. 4, p. 240.
5. Spohr, *Violinschule* (1832), p. 34.
6. For example, L'Abbé le fils, *Principes* . . . (1761), p. 1.
7. See Flesch, *Violin fingering* . . ., pp. 128–30.

56. Ascending scale

    1. When playing the ascending scale, leave down successively all the fingers that you place on a string.

    2. When you have to change string, transfer your first finger before moving your other three fingers and follow the indications in the example below for their transposition to the next strings.

Ex. 8

As early as the first lessons I advise you to adopt the use of the 4th finger on all the strings; a good hand position immediately results, which is a great compensation for the difficulty that one experiences.

57. Descending scale

    The descending scale presents even more difficulty than the ascending scale.

    1. Because there is no other way of ensuring the position of the hand and the intonation than with the first finger, which may be transferred from one string to another without disturbing the wrist.

    2. Because when it is a matter of moving from the E string to the 2nd string, one is obliged to begin with the 4th finger, which is the weakest and the most unreliable of all.

    Here are the rules which must be followed if the difficulty of this scale is to be overcome:

    1. Always begin the descending scale immediately after playing the ascending scale.

    2. When you have your four fingers placed on the E string and it is necessary to move back down, remove the fingers one by one down to the first finger, which you should leave in place.

    3. Now place the 4th, 3rd and 2nd fingers simultaneously on the second string, the first finger being left on the E string to serve as a guide for their placement.

    4. Withdraw the first finger from the E string only at the moment when you play c^2 on the second string, because at this moment this finger must be moved to the second string to play the b^1.

5. Follow the same procedure for the other strings until the scale is completed, just as I indicate in the following example:[8]

Ex. 10

58. Complete scale with markings in accordance with the rules I have put forward.

Ex. 11

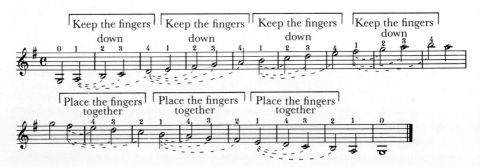

8. These rules, like those for the ascending scale, are the fruits of the observations that we have made of the differences in execution between violinists of great talent, some of whom had more vivacity than others in certain passages, like these for example of this type:

Ex. 9

In studying their respective techniques, we have noted that this difference resulted solely from the fact that some left their fingers on the a, b, c[1] in ascending, whilst others lifted them unnecessarily. It is evident that anyone who lifts his fingers on a, b, c[1] will be obliged to make a second movement in order to replace the same fingers on c[1], b, a, where they were a moment before, and this useless movement must inevitably cause uncertainty and sluggishness. (Habeneck's footnote)

59. Here now are the practical exercises that must be played until the hand position and the intonation of the scale of G are firmly established.

The exercise and the two scales which follow must be played with the full length of the bow.

Ex. 12

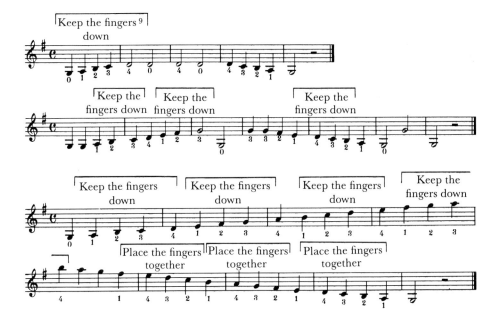

60. In the next three scales, only the part of the bow between A and B should be used, as indicated below:

This is what for the rest of this book I shall call playing with the middle of the bow. [10]

9. Beginners in general have a tendency to pull back the wrist when they wish to place the 4th finger on the lower strings. Their teachers should warn them against this habit by demonstrating that by pulling back the wrist they actually pull back the little finger at the same time, instead of stretching it forward. (Habeneck's footnote)

10. It is essential to accustom the pupil at an early stage to playing with the middle of the bow; then he will not risk developing a tendency to stiffness in the elbow and the wrist and will be better prepared to execute with ease all kinds of music at sight; for there are numerous cases where the combination of long and short notes is a source of embarrassment for those who play at the point. To take one example only, let us consider the following passage:

How could one play the semibreve that comes after the bar of separate semiquavers if one were playing at the point? Whereas if one plays at the middle there is enough bow left to give the long note its full value. One might say that two of the semiquavers could be slurred, thus ending with an up bow; but apart from the fact that this would no longer accord with the composer's intentions, there would always be a problem in anticipating the need for it soon enough when sight-reading. (Habeneck's footnote)

Ex. 14

Ex. 13

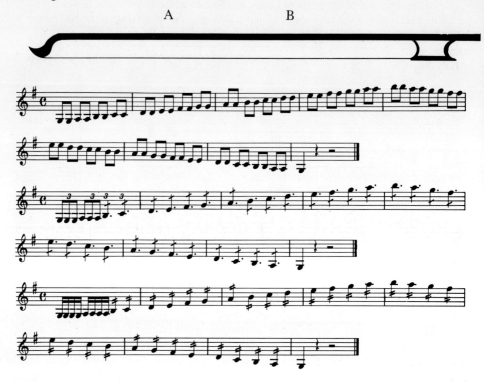

61. After the pupil has practised this first scale long enough to ensure correct placing of the fingers, intonation and handling of the bow, he may then move on to the following exercises on intervals, which are calculated to strengthen him in the practice
of the principles I have put forward concerning the movement of the fingers.

Third section

On intervals

62. When you need to stop the 2nd finger, place the 1st finger behind it at
the same time.
When you need to stop the 3rd finger, place the 2nd and 1st fingers behind it at the
same time.
When you need to stop the 4th finger, place the 3rd, 2nd and 1st fingers behind it at the
same time – all according to the scale of the key in which you are playing.
We recommend that teachers should observe these rules strictly; they are, so to
speak, a technical method of helping the student more rapidly to train his ear and his
fingers in [good] intonation.[11]

11. In making this recommendation, we do not mean to say that in future the fingers must never be kept
off the strings; but these are some elementary rules which should be followed strictly at least until the
fingers are absolutely secure in their placement; and we will add that besides a greater facility in intonation, they will also have acquired by this process an independence which will be invaluable in the
future. (Habeneck's footnote)

Ex. 15

Exercise on the
interval of a
3rd[12]

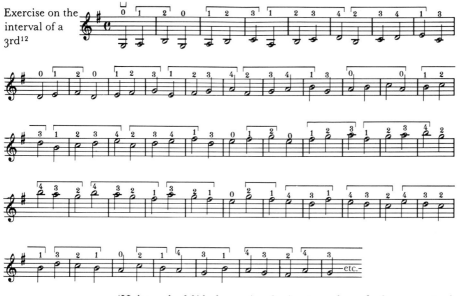

(Habeneck, *Méthode* . . . (c. 1840), pt. 2, ch. 5, §2 & 3, pp. 37-9)

THE POSITIONS

The terminology employed during the eighteenth century to denote positions
varied from country to country and even from violinist to violinist according
to the 'school' by which he was influenced. The various French terms are especially confusing, some writers (for example, L'Abbé le fils, Bailleux and
Tarade) describing modern second position as *première position*, modern third
position as *seconde position* and so on, whilst some (for example, Bornet) call
modern second position *La demie position* and others (for example, Woldemar
and Bedard) name the positions as today.

The corresponding German terminology was *Applicatur, halbe Applicatur*
generally describing either second position or, collectively, the second, fourth
and sixth positions and *ganze Applicatur* normally denoting either third position or, collectively, the third, fifth and seventh positions. However, German
writers did not use this terminology exclusively; Kürzinger, for example,
describes three types of *Applicatur* in the French manner, his first, second and
third positions corresponding to modern second, third and fourth positions
respectively, while Hiller approaches modern terminology, referring to *dritte
Lage* (third position).[13]

12. This sign ⌐¬ should always be understood as indicating that the fingers included under it must be
    kept down as one places them in ascending and that they must be put down together and lifted one
    after the other in descending. (Habeneck's footnote)
13. Kürzinger, *Getreuer Unterricht* . . . (1763), p. 67; Hiller, *Anweisung* . . . (1792), p. 18.

The Italians employed several terms to denote positions, the most common being *portamento, posizionè* and *smanicatura*. Tartini describes modern first position as *luogo naturale* (natural position), second position as *mezza smanicatura*, third position as *seconda smanicatura* and fourth position as *terza smanicatura*. Signoretti, like some German writers, describes three basic positions, *L'entière* (whole), *La demie* (half) and a mixed, compound position called *composée*,[14] whilst the terminology of other writers (for example, Cambini and Lorenziti) betrays French influence.

English players generally adopted the phrase *natural position* to denote modern first position; *half shift* implied modern second position and *whole* or *full shift*, third position. Higher positions were described as *compound positions*, but modern sixth position was sometimes called *double shift*; *last shift* denoted seventh position.

The terminology of the various positions was gradually standardised around the turn of the century, most writers (but not all) adopting that most commonly employed by the ascendant French violin school and, in particular, the Paris Conservatoire. Spohr provides reason enough for this standardisation:

These notes which extend above 𝄞 can only be reached and stopped by the fingers if the hand is shifted from its original position and moves to a greater or lesser extent closer to the bridge. These different positions of the hand are called *Applicaturen*. Formerly, they were divided into half and whole positions. Half position meant the position of the hand in which the g² of the E string 𝄞 is stopped with the first finger; whole position that in which the first finger is placed on the a² of the E string 𝄞 . The next position was again called half, the next one after that again whole position and so on. To distinguish these higher positions of the hand from the lower ones of the same name, they were also called second half or second whole position.

But as this designation of the positions is confusing, I adopt those of the French violin school, which denotes the various positions of the hand as first, second and so on.

The lower position of the hand, in which all the exercises have hitherto been played, is therefore called first position; when the hand is moved just so much nearer the bridge that the first finger falls on the g² or g sharp² of the E string 𝄞 , it is in the second position; on 𝄞 a flat², a² and a sharp² in the 3rd; on b flat² and b natural² 𝄞 in the 4th; on 𝄞 c³ and c sharp³ in the 5th; on 𝄞 d flat³, d³ and d sharp³ in the 6th; on e flat³, e³ and e sharp³ 𝄞 in the 7th, on 𝄞 f³ and f sharp³ in the 8th and so on.   (Spohr, *Violinschule* (1832), pp. 88–9)

Most advanced treatises incorporate discussion (albeit generally sparse) of position-work up to at least seventh position and this conservative limit is invariably extended in various exercises or complete compositions included for further study. Indeed, the scope of some writers' surveys extends to eleventh position and, in some cases, the inclusion of some fingerings beyond

---

14. Signoretti, *Méthode* . . . (1777), pt. 3, p. 1.

this up to thirteenth position.[15] However, the scaling of such heights was quite exceptional before the last decade of the eighteenth century, as musicians were not unanimously appreciative of excessively high position-work. Tarade and de Béthizy, for example, freely admit their dislike of the high registers of the instrument[16] and Galeazzi claims the natural practical range of each string to be two octaves, describing any notes beyond that range on the E string as 'whistles' rather than true notes and substituting harmonics for them.[17] Bornet, describing the normal violin range as the open G string to three octaves above middle C, adds:

> These octaves give approximately the full range of the violin; one cannot extend any lower, but one can still extend higher; when this happens, the composer is at fault, for the sounds are no longer distinguishable and are offensive to the ear.
>
> (Bornet, *Nouvelle Méthode* . . . (1786), p. 2)

The shorter eighteenth-century fingerboard may account for such a comment, making performance in the higher registers a rather precarious operation, in which clarity of fingering was difficult to achieve.

'Of all the positions to which it is necessary to shift on the E string, it is the third . . . which is used the most.'[18] Third position was surpassed only by first position for convenience and simplicity, as the rib of the violin could be used as a possible support (although this is not recommended in modern methods) and intonation guide for the left hand. However, modern second position gradually assumed greater importance from c. 1760 onwards and was consistently employed in compositions of the period, helping to avoid constant shifting between first and third positions, awkward extensions of the hand from first position and unnecessary string-crossing. The difficulties of second position, in which the left hand and fingers have no real guide and means of support to facilitate accuracy of intonation, were gradually overcome, probably owing indirectly to the emergence of the chin-braced grip and the consequent liberation of the left hand.

Half position was also more widely used from c. 1760 onwards. Whilst L'Abbé le fils cannot claim to have discovered it, he was certainly the first to categorise its use:

Scale in the key of G sharp melodic minor

All the fingers employed in this scale are borrowed fingers, that is to say that these fingers are used to stop notes other than those they normally stop.

In order to play this scale [Ex. 16], it is necessary to ensure that the hand is moved back close to the nut.

The sharp major and minor keys very often bring about these borrowed fingerings.

15. For example, Campagnoli, *Metodo* . . . (1797?).
16. Tarade, *Traité* . . . (1774), art. 16, p. 50; Béthizy, *Exposition* . . ., p. 305.
17. Galeazzi, *Elementi* . . . (1791); 2nd edn (1817), vol, 1, pt. 2, art. 6.
18. Corrette, *L'art* . . . (1782), p. 2.

Ex. 16

One is obliged to implement them in certain passages, in order not to shift the hand.

Ex. 17

(L'Abbé le fils, *Principes* . . . (1761), p. 5)

L'Abbé le fils's appreciation of the merits of half position was later shared by many of his compatriots but textual documentation is nevertheless sparse. Curiously enough, Leopold Mozart had earlier omitted mention of this position in his method and appears to have avoided its use (Ex. 18), but his com-

Ex. 18

patriot, Schweigl, calls the position *Zurückweichung der Hand*[19] and testifies to its increasing employment towards the end of the eighteenth century in order to avoid the awkward movements and smudged *glissando* effects caused by the consecutive use of one and the same finger.

SHIFTING

Smooth execution of shifts depends not only on the technical facility of the performer but also his choice of rational fingerings, an individual matter which hinges in turn on the conformation of his hand, the structure, size and strength of his fingers and his musical intentions. Consequently, Tartini claims that it is impossible to give any hard and fast rules regarding shifting:

The student should adopt whatever method he finds most comfortable in each case, and he should therefore practise the hand shifts in every possible way so that he is prepared for every situation that may arise. (Tartini, *Traité* . . . (1771), ed. Jacobi, p. 56)

19. Schweigl, *Verbesserte Grundlehre* . . . (1786), p. 44.

Some years later, Jousse, among other writers, maintains that 'the rules for shifting depend on the expression to be given to a passage and on the quantity of notes, which for the sake of smoothness ought to be played on the same string'.[20] However, available evidence clearly shows that shifts were generally made on repeated notes (Ex. 19), by the phrase in sequential passages (Ex. 20) so that each phrase was played consistently with identical fingering,[21] after an open string (Ex. 21), a rest or pause between *staccato* notes,[22] or after a dotted figure, when the bow was generally lifted off the string (Ex. 22).[23] Thus the actual shift was rarely audible even though a slight break was generally made for articulation purposes, resulting in a system of articulation comparable with keyboard fingering. Extensions were commonly used in order to avoid or facilitate shifts, but natural harmonics were rarely employed for this purpose.

Ex. 19

Ex. 20

Ex. 21

Ex. 22

Eighteenth-century violinists appear to have selected fingerings with much closer attention to the musical phrase than their modern counterparts. This was no doubt due mainly to the inferior stability of the violin hold of the time, even the chin-braced grip, which afforded the player less manoeuvrability in

20. Jousse, *The theory and practice* . . . (1811), pt. 2, p. 70.
21. Tartini, *Traité* . . ., ed. Jacobi, p. 56.
22. *Ibid.*, p. 58.
23. See, for example, L. Mozart, *Versuch* . . ., ch. 8; Reichardt, *Ueber die Pflichten* . . . (1776), p. 34; Campagnoli, *Metodo* . . . (1797?), pt. 3, no. 161; Galeazzi, *Elementi* . . . (1791), vol. I, pt. 2, art. 8, pp. 131-2.

shifting than its modern equivalent. Consequently, as Galeazzi here confirms, eighteenth-century violinists tended to choose, if at all possible, one position to accommodate an entire phrase without shifting the hand:

Rule X

119. To work out the fingering of a passage, it is necessary first to ascertain its limits, that is, to find in fact those notes which are the highest and lowest of the given passage, from which it is easy to work out which position is most convenient for the passage . . . [sentence omitted]

Explanation

It may be that a correct position is sought for this passage (as illustrated in Ex. [23]); we will take note first that the highest note is a³ and the lowest g¹. Therefore, we must search in the table of positions[24] to find that to which this range, g¹–a³, belongs, and we discover that it is the seventh position. So, that is the correct position for this passage. This rule, which needs no further explanation, is applicable to all those passages in which is found the entire range of a position.

Ex. 23

(Galeazzi, *Elementi* . . . (1791), vol. 1, pt. 2, p. 137)

Comfort and economy of shifting therefore seem to have been valued more highly than timbre and tone colour in the selection of fingerings; however, the aim of playing an entire phrase in one position in many cases created unnecessary and even insurmountable difficulties, a shift being required at the beginning of the phrase irrespective of convenience, in order to accommodate the *tessitura* of that phrase (Ex. 24). In Ex. 25, the fingering marked *, involving the

Ex. 24

L'Abbé's fingering

two possible modern fingerings

Ex. 25

24. Galeazzi's 'table of positions', a simple guide to the range of each position, is not essential to our requirements and is thus not included here.

use of consecutive fourth fingers in different positions across the strings, is actually impossible to play properly slurred.

The increased stability of the common early-nineteenth-century violin hold afforded greater scope for the implementation of shifts but, allowing for individual variations, economy of shifting was still relevant to the technique of the period, invariably overshadowing the desire for uniformity of tone colour because of the greater surety of intonation offered. The first two sections of Baillot's survey of fingering confirm this, whilst the final section illustrates how general practices of shifting nevertheless varied from player to player, good taste being the overall determining factor.

The surest fingering

If the composer has determined the *fingering* himself in a difficult passage or phrase, it should be followed as much as possible in order to become identified with the composer's style, the *fingering* being one of the means which serve to characterise the style.

But if the *fingering* is not indicated, it will be necessary to choose the one which offers the most security of intonation.

By trying out a passage several times in different ways one will avoid being satisfied with one's habits and one will see which may be the best means to use for shifting upwards, downwards or remaining in the same position, according to the observations made above.

Furthermore, here are some general principles which will ease the task of achieving this goal.

1. It is better to shift upwards or downwards by semitones or to the positions which offer support for the hand, such as the third and first positions.

Ex. 26

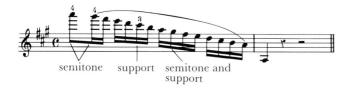

2. [It is better] to change position regularly, using the same finger each time; this repeated movement gives the passage a smoothness of action, which makes it secure.

Ex. 27

3. [It is better] to stay in the same position when the passage allows; as this method is the simplest, it must generally be preferred, except when the known habits of the composer or the character of his music require the contrary: thus, *Viotti* remained almost always in the same position, which compelled him to play on several strings, whereas *Rode* often played on one and the same string, which compelled him to change position.

If it is desired that compositions should be performed in a manner approximating as closely as possible to their true meaning, one must try to work out *fingering* in accordance with the style, well known, of each composer.

The easiest fingering for small hands

But these methods of achieving sureness cannot be the same for everyone and lack of suppleness or the smallness of the hand often militate against employing them. It is then that sureness has to be sought by exceptional, completely individual methods.

Expressive fingering as a characteristic of each composer

By studying the music of different composers, the differences which exist in their manner of *fingering* will be bound to have been noticed; according to the feeling that they wished to give to their phrases, they made use either of the same position, or the same string, or took various positions in the same passage, in order better to convey their character. In order to perform their works in the spirit which has dictated them, it is necessary to use similar methods to those which they have themselves used, otherwise one could not fail to misrepresent their intention and fall into a confusion of styles, the most fatal error in an art which is based on true feeling that cannot be altered without destroying every manner of interest.

Application of the three kinds of fingering

If all the special considerations of *fingering* were to be entered into, one would lose oneself in a mass of details. Thus we shall confine ourselves to giving examples of the three kinds of *fingering* which everyone will apply for himself by making himself familiar with their principles and by making use in addition of the general rules which have just been expressed.

The most reliable fingering and the easiest fingering for small hands

Ex. 28

(Viotti: Concerto no. 1)

Ex. 29

(Viotti: Rondo from Concerto no. 4)

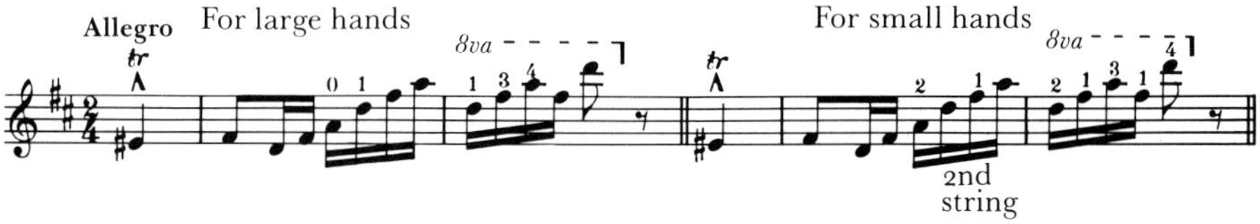
Allegro
For large hands
For small hands
8va
2nd string

Ex. 30

(Viotti: Concerto no. 15)

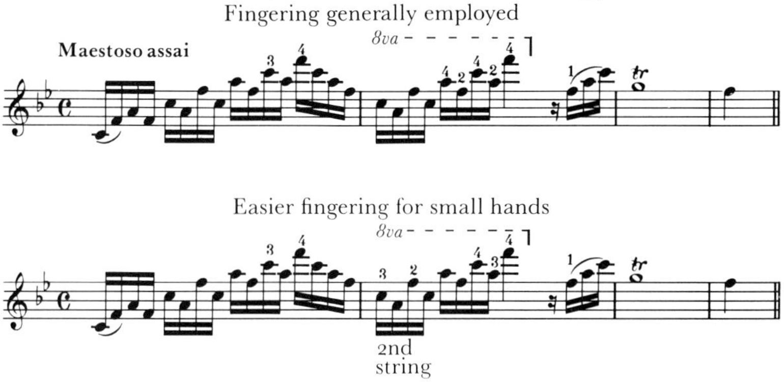
Fingering generally employed
Maestoso assai
8va
Easier fingering for small hands
8va
2nd string

Ex. 31

(Viotti: Concerto no. 10)

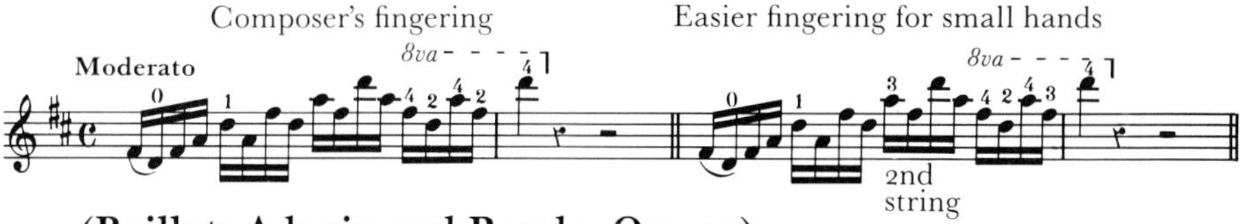
Composer's fingering
Easier fingering for small hands
Moderato
8va
8va
2nd string

(Baillot: Adagio and Rondo, Op. 40)

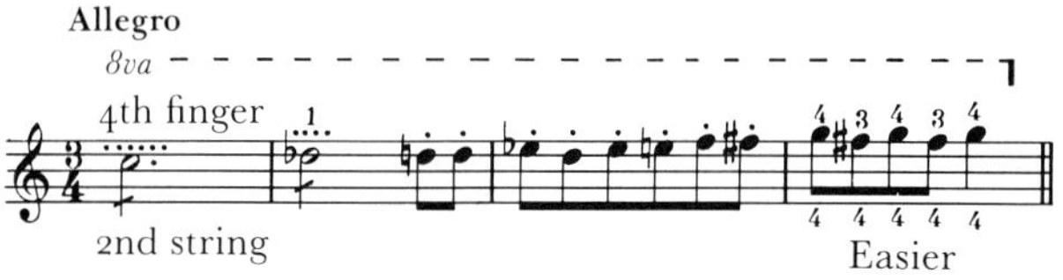
Allegro
8va
4th finger
2nd string
Easier

Ex. 32

(Habeneck, sen.: *Fantaisie Pastorale*)

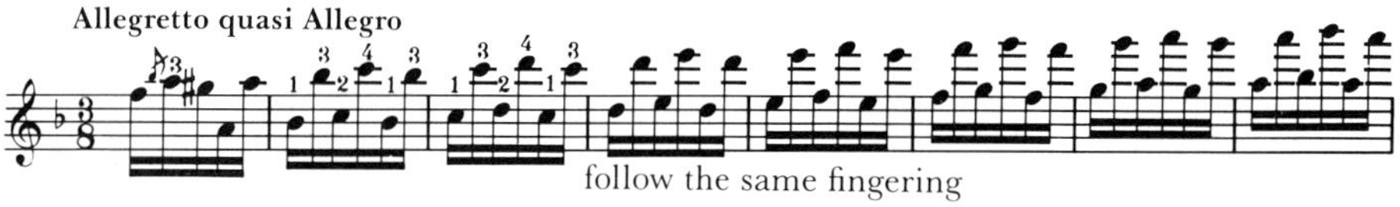
Allegretto quasi Allegro
follow the same fingering

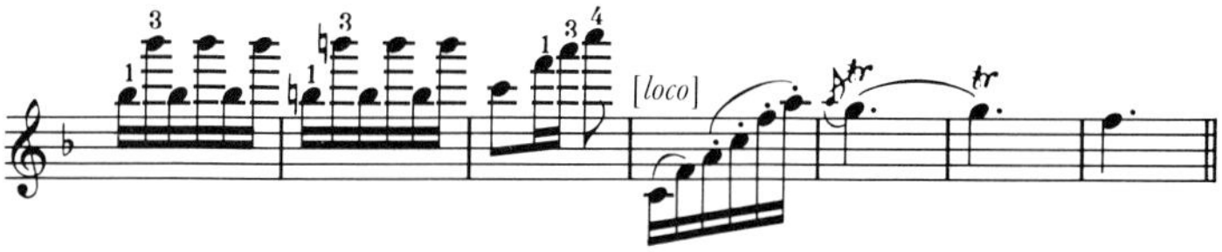
[loco]

The composer's own fingering, easier in that returning to a lower position is avoided.

Expressive fingering as a characteristic of each composer

We have said that *Viotti* remained almost always in the same position, that is to say he avoided shifting his hand, which compelled him to change from one string to another. Simple melodies and phrases receive in this way an expression which preserves the character of each string as well as the different timbre that each string adopts at different positions. This character, hardly perceptible in 1st position, alters in proportion as a higher position is reached; it has something full and mellow, favourable to the composer's style of expression.

Ex. 33

(Viotti: Concerto no. 27)

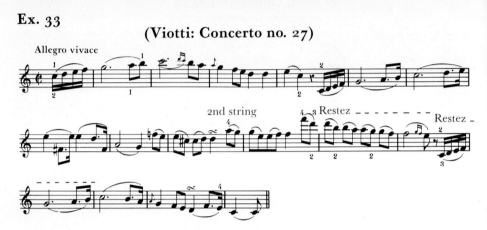

The *fingering* marked *above* is that which we have seen used by the composer. When trying that marked *below*, the disadvantage is immediately felt and one is struck by the character given to the melody by the 1st *fingering*.

The following passage is yet another remarkable example of this: the *fingering marked above* is that employed by the composer. That indicated *below* is marked only in order to make the difference felt.

Ex. 34

(Viotti: Rondo from Trio no. 14)

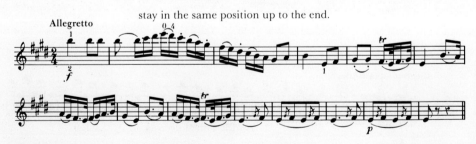

Kreutzer frequently changed position on all the strings, which is appropriate for brilliant melodies and bold passages. [Ex. 35]

Here is an expressive *fingering* by the same composer that one ought indeed to beware of changing. [Ex. 36]

Ex. 35

(Kreutzer: Concerto in G)

Ex. 36

(Kreutzer: Concerto in C)

Rode changed position on the same strings, a style which favours the *portamento* in graceful melodies and gives to these melodies a certain unity of expression as a result of the uniformity of sound coming from the same string.

Ex. 37

(Rode: Sonata no. 1)

(from the same sonata)

It is by observing in each composer the differences which determine their choices of position, string and finger, that one will be able so much the better to add fingering to one's own music according to the kind of expression one wishes to give to it.

Ex. 38

**(2nd edition of the 1st *Méthode de violon* by
Baillot: *50 Études sur la gamme*)**

(Baillot, *L'art* . . . (1834), pp. 146–9)

The mechanics of shifting are only rarely mentioned in treatises of the period and then in hardly any detail. Perrin, for example, emphasises the importance of preparing the hand, where possible, for a shift, moving it in those cases some notes before the position change is actually made, but fails to provide any further, more detailed advice as to how this should be achieved.[25] Those few writers who include such information place most stress on the importance of the thumb in leading the hand smoothly through the lower positions before adopting a comfortable position either beneath the neck or, if necessary, on the rib of the instrument, according to the extent of the shift.[26] Furthermore, they consider it preferable in most cases to establish positions with the first finger, both for reasons of convenience and security of intonation.[27]

Upward shifts generally caused few problems, for if anything they increased the stability of the instrument against the player's neck thanks to the movement of the hand up the fingerboard towards his body. However, downward shifts, particularly when without the help of a chin rest or even a chin-braced grip, required a special technique of the left hand; because of its semi-supporting role, the left hand was generally more in contact with the violin than in modern playing and thus had to crawl back from the high positions 'caterpillar fashion', and invariably between bow strokes, through skilful manipulation of the thumb, index-finger and wrist. Some late-eighteenth-

25. Perrin, *Méthode* . . . (c. 1815), p. 108.
26. For example, Galeazzi, *Elementi* . . . (1791), vol. 1, pt. 2, art. 8, p. 242; Cambini, *Nouvelle méthode* . . .
      (1803), pt. 1, p. 14; Cartier, *L'art* . . . (1798), pt. 2, p. 13; Spohr, *Violinschule* (1832), p. 89.
27. Galeazzi, *Elementi* . . . (1791), vol. 1, pt. 2, art. 8, p. 131.

century violinists gave the instrument occasional support by touching the tailpiece with the chin but continuous chin pressure was still not considered
necessary by many.

   Thus the violinist's fingering and articulation were influenced considerably
by the violin hold employed, invariably resulting in a system of articulation
comparable with keyboard fingering. Like Leopold Mozart,[28] most writers
prefer the smaller upward hand shifts, using adjacent fingers (2 3 – 2 3 or 1 2 –
1 2), to the bolder leaps prescribed by Geminiani and Tessarini (Exx. 39 & 40),

Ex. 39

Ex. 40

a.

b.

even though the gradual adoption of a chin-braced grip encouraged attempts
at more virtuoso technical feats; an illustration would be the larger leaps
(1 2 3 4 – 1 2 3 4 or 1 2 3 – 1 2 3) of Corrette's *tours de force*, in which the possibilities
of one position are generally exhausted before moving to another (Ex. 41).

Ex. 41

Furthermore, the choice between a small or large shift was naturally determined in many cases by the tempo of a piece or the speed of a particular
passage; Cambini, for example, advocates the use of large shifts in quick
movements and small shifts in slow movements.[29] However, most writers

28. L. Mozart, *Versuch* . . ., ch. 8, section 1, §9–12, p. 156.
29. Cambini, *Nouvelle méthode* . . . (1803), pt. 1, p. 13.

appear to have preferred large leaps (4 3 2 1 – 4 3 2 1) in descending passages, whatever the speed, Galeazzi being a notable exception on account of his preference for the 2 1 – 2 1 – 2 1 fingering in descending scales. Nevertheless, the increased use of the semitone shift in the early nineteenth century helped to avoid wide leaps and shifts of the hand and disagreeable string changes, and facilitated the cultivation of the contemporary *legato* style.

Baillot provides some interesting clues as to the mechanics of shifting in his discussions of the *port de voix*[30] and of expressive fingerings.[31] One example of the latter (see Ex. 94) uses anticipatory notes to indicate the recommended method of shifting, Baillot advising the player to slide a stopped finger forwards or backwards in order to substitute skilfully another finger for it; the written-out anticipatory notes were not to be sounded.

Spohr also recommends the use of anticipatory notes (unsounded) to facilitate shifting, especially for rapid position changes involving wide leaps from a low to a high position in slurred bowing (Ex. 42). The finger stopping the

Ex. 42

5th position

lower note is moved rapidly up the string, avoiding any *glissando* effect, until it reaches its rightful place in that position required by the higher note. Spohr also gives an example (Ex. 43) in which the highest note of a phrase is a har-

Ex. 43

monic; he advises the student to make a fast shift, in order to avoid any *glissando*, and to take the finger and bow off the string immediately the harmonic has been sounded, thus allowing the harmonic to ring freely.[32] Spohr's final example involves the use of detached bowing to facilitate shifting; the bow should be stopped momentarily during the shift (Ex. 44), thus making the shift movement inaudible.[33]

Whether or not *portamenti* generally accompanied shifts is a controversial point about which available evidence is conflicting. Certainly, the normal instances when shifts were implemented and the more common use of smaller

30. Baillot, *L'art* . . . (1834), pp. 75–8. See pp. 314–18.
31. Baillot, *L'art* . . . (1834), pp. 152–5. See pp. 112–15.
32. Spohr, *Violinschule* (1832), pp. 120–1.
33. *Ibid.*, p. 128.

Ex. 44

upward shifts would have minimised the inclusion, whether accidental or otherwise, of such effects, but some sources suggest that *portamenti* were employed by some violinists, especially in solo contexts, whether as part of the mechanics of shifting or as ornamental or expressive devices. Burney, in his discussion of Geminiani's chromatic fingering, comments:

> Geminiani . . . was certainly mistaken in laying it down as a rule that 'no two notes on the same string, in shifting, should be played with the same finger', as beautiful expressions and effects are produced by great players in shifting, suddenly from a low to a high, with the same finger on the same string.
> (Burney, *A general history of music* . . . , vol. 2, p. 992)

Furthermore, Reichardt implies that many violinists incorporated a *portamento* into the shift, whether intentionally or not:

> Sliding with a finger through various positions is absolutely forbidden [i.e. in an orchestral context], although it is sometimes permissible for the soloist. Great taste is required in order to make it sound bearable to a sensitive ear; the manner in which most violinists execute it makes it sound like a desperate tom-cat wailing on his stubborn sweetheart's doorstep.   (Reichardt, *Ueber die Pflichten* . . . (1776), ch. 3, p. 35)

Woldemar's famous *couler à Mestrino* (Ex. 45), apparently adopted by Mestrino in most slow movements, is a notable adaptation of the *portamento* for expressive purposes; it is an extension of Rameau's instruction, in the first violin part

Ex. 45

of his *Platée* (1749), depicting the words 'Ce sont des pleurs'. Rameau suggests that the phrase in question should be played by 'sliding the same finger, and making audible the two quarter-tones between E and F'.[34] Corrette implies a *portamento* effect with his fingering recommendations for scales in thirds and sixths in the high positions (Ex. 46), whilst Kreutzer, Lolli and even Leopold Mozart (in a cadenza) indicate the use of *portamento* in shifting, using the same finger for both the lower and upper notes of the shift (Ex. 47). Cambini pro-

34. Rameau, *Platée* (Paris, 1749), p. 99.

Ex. 46

Ex. 47

a.

b.

c.

d.

vides a similar example in his discussion of the expressive performance of phrases by Boccherini and Haydn (Ex. 48) – indeed, there are numerous examples of such *portamenti* in Haydn's quartets – and L'Abbé le fils specifically marks a *portamento* in double stopping (Ex. 49), a most unusual shift when compared with a modern fingering of the same passage. Baillot's and Spohr's shift mechanisms, discussed above, seem more likely than not to have encouraged *portamenti*, in spite of their instructions to the contrary, and Habeneck admits their tasteful use, especially in slow movements and sustained melodies when a passage ascends or descends by step (when the *portamento* should be accompanied by a *crescendo* and *diminuendo* respectively) (Ex. 50a). In passages moving by leap (Ex. 50b), good taste must guide the performer to

Ex. 48

Ex. 49

L'Abbé's fingering

Modern fingering?

Ex. 50

ensure that none of the intermediary tones and semitones is heard, as in Ex. 50c.[35] Paganini regularly employed *glissandi* with great effect, both for reasons of showmanship, especially in his compositions for G string alone (Ex. 51), and for the production of a smooth *cantabile* in double stopping (Ex. 52).

Ex. 51

Ex. 52

Counter-evidence is supplied by, among others, Campagnoli and Spohr, the former despising the introduction of *portamenti* in double stopping:

Double stops in thirds which ascend by degrees must be played by sliding quickly for-wards the first and third fingers upon the same strings, and this in such a manner as not to let either the movement of the hand or of the fingers be perceptible.

(Campagnoli, *Metodo* . . . (1797?), tr. Bishop, pt. 3, no. 188)

35. Habeneck, *Méthode* . . . (c. 1840), p. 103.

Given his stand against such effects, Campagnoli indicates a strange fingering for a passage (Ex. 53) involving what he describes as 'compound positions':

When the melody ascends or descends on the same string by an interval of a third, the 1st or the 2nd finger is used twice or a greater number of times in immediate succession.   (Campagnoli, *Metodo* . . . (1797?), pt. 3, no. 166)

Ex. 53

Spohr, meanwhile, is adamant that, contrary to the practice of many contemporary violinists, no sliding effects should accompany his three approaches to shifting described above; however, one of his own fingerings from his Tenth Concerto (second movement) suggests otherwise (Ex. 54), as do his discussion of the 'soft gliding from one note to another'[36] at the opening of the *Adagio* of Rode's Seventh Concerto and certain *sul G* fingerings in the *Minore* section (Exx. 55 & 56).

Ex. 54

Ex. 55

Ex. 56

Finally, Galeazzi mentions the realistic possibility that in certain quick shifts the desired note may not be reached and he suggests how the performer may redeem himself in such a circumstance, either by making the 'false' note

36. Spohr, *Violinschule* (1832), p. 209.

into an *appoggiatura*, a chromatic scale-wise ornament or some other similar embellishment, in order to veil the error.[37]

EXTENSIONS AND CONTRACTIONS

Extensions and contractions were regularly employed as a means of enlarging the range of the hand in a given position, thus lessening the need for shifts. They were naturally easier to accomplish on the 'original' short-necked instrument and were often indicated in French sources by the letter e, which signified 'that it is necessary to extend or draw back the finger indicated by the number, without shifting the hand or any finger other than the one in use'.[38] Finger extensions were particularly helpful to those violinists who persisted with older methods of holding the instrument, in which the left hand, generally required as a means of supporting the instrument, was allowed little scope to shift freely from position to position. Formal shifts could thus be avoided, an extension permitting a change of position without immediately shifting the hand (Ex. 57).

Ex. 57

Two surveys of the period are included here, which between them cover the general technical principles associated with the execution of extensions, notably the advanced thumb position directly under the violin neck, the elbow position well under the instrument, the need for the wrist to be immobile, the suppleness of the hand and, in some cases, the special treatment given to the fourth finger in the interests of greater accuracy of intonation. Galeazzi prescribes some rigid rules:

Rule I

129. The fourth finger extension is used whenever high notes out of position are approached by leap, but if they are approached by step, the upward extension is permitted only in exceptional cases; moreover, a downward extension being very rare, it is better in such cases to make a shift.

Illustration

Upward extensions are made by stretching out the fourth finger a whole tone or a

37. Galeazzi, *Elementi* . . . (1791), vol. 1, pt. 2, art. 9, p. 145. See p. 107 for complete quotation.
38. L'Abbé le fils, *Principes* . . . (1761), p. 18.

semitone beyond the natural limits of a position; however, if this fourth finger is used before or after its normal placement (in the case of a note a step away) a definite slide on the string, difficult to avoid, will almost always be heard and will result in an undesirable effect; but if the note is approached by leap, the finger will come down directly on the note rather than slide; thus there is no opportunity to make the afore-mentioned ugly slide (see Exx. [58–63]). Exx. [58 and 59] illustrate two instances in

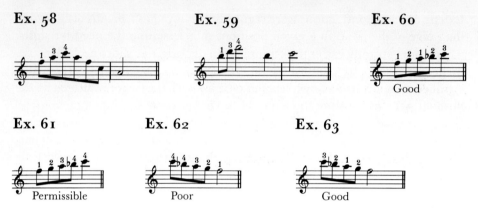

Ex. 58

Ex. 59

Ex. 60

Good

Ex. 61

Ex. 62

Ex. 63

Permissible   Poor   Good

which the extension note, approached by leap, is stopped with the fourth finger. Ex. [60] contains a passage in which the note beyond the position is approached by step. It would be better to finger this passage in two positions than in one alone, as is indicated in Ex. [61]; although, in this last example, it is sometimes permissible to extend the fourth finger, provided that the finger is raised. However, in Ex. [62], since it is almost impossible to raise the finger, which is already extended, the passage is fingered as in Ex. [63] to avoid a slide, which would be faulty.

Rule II

130. Whenever the extension note is the octave above an open string, it is played as an harmonic, although it may be only a step away.

Illustration

If the hand is in third position, it may extend upward to g^1 on the G string, on the D string to d^2, on the A string to a^2 or on the E string to e^3, which are the octaves of their respective open strings, and these notes are fingered as harmonics, although they might be a step away; here is the reason. Extensions are always somewhat difficult to play in tune, as the finger is not in its normal place, but since one property peculiar to a harmonic is that it is never out of tune, we can be sure of pure intonation in the extension to a harmonic. Therefore, such notes may be fingered by extension, although they are a step away, because inasmuch as harmonics do not sound if the finger is not placed in the precise spot, the intermediate pitches will not be heard, even though the finger might be dragged along the string; thus the note will always come out clear and separate from its neighbour. Great attention must be paid to this rule which will be very useful in fast technical or scale passages that extend one step beyond the third position. This is one of the secrets of the art which I here divulge for the advantage of all (but see Ex. [64]).

Ex. 64

Rule III

131. There are occasions when two notes must be played by extension with the third and fourth fingers to preserve uniformity [of tone] or for another reason. This occurs when the two notes are beyond the range of the position on two different strings (see Ex. [65]).

Ex. 65

Explanation and Illustration

In this example, the first position is used to play the second bar. The first finger is held securely to stop f^2 on the E string, the third finger is extended upward on the A string to stop e flat^2 and the fourth finger is extended on the E string to stop c^3. This is based on the rules of uniformity, so it can be seen how necessary it is to know them thoroughly, since they have many applications to other aspects of our art [of violin playing].

Rule IV

132. There are notes that are two or more steps beyond the upper limits of a position; such notes are played quickly in passing and with a small movement of the hand, without, however, quite displacing it from its proper position, or rather, very simply with an extreme extension of the little finger (see Exx. [66, 67 & 68]).

Ex. 66

Ex. 67

Ex. 68

V

Explanation

In Ex. [66], a³ and g³ are played with the extended fourth finger or with a very small leap of the hand. The same is done for f³, g³ and a³ of Ex. [67] and for a³ of Ex. [68]. These are called *notes beyond a position*. The proof is based on Rule II, Article VIII.[39]

Rule V

133. When there is a passage in which the notes are so disjunct and distant that they cannot be fingered in one position only, neither with a shift by step nor with a leap of a third, it is acceptable, then, as there is no alternative, to take up the position known as *di posta*, that is to say, with a violent leap of the hand, always taking care in such circumstances to make the leap as small as possible.

Explanation

This can happen in two ways, that is, from low to high or, vice versa, from high to low (see for both cases Exx. [69 & 70]). In Ex. [69] there is a shift from the first position to

Ex. 69

I   VII

Ex. 70

a³ in the seventh position. In Ex. [70] there is a twofold example. The hand in the ninth position must, without shifting, finger the two notes beyond the position, e⁴ and g⁴, and then as quick as a flash shift down to the second position with the first finger to c² on the A string.

134. As these shifts are extremely hazardous, they must be made only out of dire necessity. Only an expert teacher can contemplate such risks, although frequently

39. This rule states that, where practicable, a position change should not be implemented for only one note.

even he will be subjected to considerable anxieties. However, in such a circumstance he knows very well how to redeem himself if he should shift incorrectly. If, with his quick and skilful ear, he perceives that he has shifted flat or sharp, he should pretend to make an appoggiatura, a chromatic scale-wise ornament or other similar ornamentation; thus he can veil his error so that no one is the wiser, but he must be the first to perceive it and in this lies the art of the great performer. Bad intonation is an affliction of all, but to remedy it before the audience hears it is for the few and these few are the real professionals.

135. With reference to difficult passages, it would now be appropriate to discuss consecutive octaves and tenths and other similar distortions and extensions of the hand, which are traps for the finest performers and the most agile hands. To begin with, consecutive octaves are the most difficult of all, although the distortion of the hand is not as great as in tenths, etc.; nevertheless, the sensitiveness of this consonance is such that every minute defect of intonation is exposed. Passages of consecutive octaves, by step or by leap (see Exx. [71 & 72]) are always fingered with the

Ex. 71

Ex. 72

first and fourth fingers, if there are no open strings, changing positions generally with every octave. Sometimes, however, there are octave passages which can be fingered without hand movement and then it is well to avail oneself of such a fingering. Here is an example (Ex. [73]) which can be executed entirely in the second position.

Ex. 73

136. A very beautiful effect can be produced in an octave passage by the addition of an *appoggiatura* from below to the top note, both notes being slurred together.

137. As for consecutive tenths, they are easier than octaves; since tenths are imperfect consonances, they do not expose accuracy of intonation as much, but for their part they demand a much greater distortion of the hand which renders them awkward beyond measure. There are many who believe that it is necessary to have a hand that will span exceptional lengths to perform octaves, tenths and twelfths. To give the lie to such a fallacy we shall establish the following.

Rule VI

138. Whenever a great distortion of the hand is necessary to form extensions or consecutive octaves, tenths, etc., first remove the thumb from around the neck of the violin and place the tip of the thumb directly under the neck itself. This is done even
when the extension of the hand occurs in the lower positions.

Illustration

When the thumb is placed under the neck, the hand pulls away from the neck and
consequently is in a position to dominate the strings entirely. As a result, it finds itself
in a position to perform any extension without discomfort and to reach wherever
desired, whether one has a very small hand or very short fingers. So, there is not a
performer who, however unhappy at having a hand which cannot extend an octave
and tenth, cannot do so, if he will practise what we have taught in this rule.

139. The major difficulty encountered in the performance of passages in octaves
and tenths is that, as the intonation or, more to the point, the distances [on the finger-
board] between the sounds is always diminishing as one ascends to the higher positions, the hand, shifting upwards, must always be contracting and, vice versa,
expanding whenever it returns from the higher towards the lower positions. Nothing
but great experience and lengthy practice can teach the precise amount of such
progressive expansion or contraction of the hand. Therefore, it can generally be said
that the ability to produce good octaves and tenths does not prove that one is a fine
performer but only that one has practised assiduously such manual dexterity, for this
is all it is.

140. Below are two examples (Exx. [74 & 75]), one a passage of tenths and the
other an extraordinary distortion of the hand from a passage in a concerto of the
celebrated Antonio Lolli of Bergamo, who in this genre is truly unique, possibly also
aided even by physical advantages.

Ex. 74

Ex. 75

(Galeazzi, *Elementi* (1791), vol. 1, pt. 2, art. 9, pp. 142–7)

Baillot adopts a more flexible approach and distinguishes five types of
extension:

The term *extension* is given to the action of extending one or several fingers, without
changing the position of the hand, in order to reach a note more or less distant from

the position in which one is playing. The extension is most usually made with the little finger; however, it has also been used with the 3rd finger. It is used with the little finger for tenths and with the 3rd for octaves.

It is necessary to train small hands to make *extensions* at an early stage in order to give them flexibility and to stretch the 3rd and 4th fingers through frequent use.

The 1st *extension* to practise is that *of a semitone*.

Ex. 76

Extension of
a semitone

The 2nd *extension* is that *of a tone*.

Ex. 77

Extension of
a tone

The 3rd type of *extension* is that which is carried out on all 4 strings; in order that the little finger reaches the lower strings easily, one must not forget to bring forward the left elbow sufficiently. Many people, when making *extensions*, acquire the bad habit of bending back the wrist when they want to use or stretch out the 4th finger, which takes it further away from the note instead of bringing it nearer to it; it is a very bad fault since it causes the wrist to make an unnecessary and hence potentially harmful movement. In order to avoid this, the following exercises should be done, taking care to move only the fingers (see Fig. [15.25 & 26]).

3rd type of extension
Stretch out the little finger without bending back the wrist.

Ex. 78

Extension on
all the strings

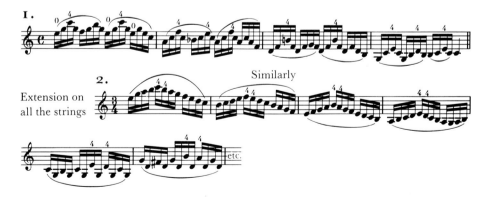

4th type
Succession of extensions in tenths

Ex. 79

Extensions
in tenths

(Note) In order to avoid bending back the wrist when attempting to place the 4th
finger as discussed in the preceding article, it is necessary with tenths to put down the
4th finger first.

Ex. 80

(Baillot: Op. 2, Caprice no. 12)

5th type
Extensions in octaves

In the article about *fingering* we gave as an example the following passage, where the
extension is made with the 3rd finger in a succession of octaves and where, by this
means, shifting down to a lower position is avoided.

Ex. 81

(Habeneck, sen.: *Fantaisie Pastorale*)

Extensions
in octaves

(Baillot, *L'Art.* . . (1834), pp. 150–2)

Baillot later considers another application of the extension principle, the stopped unison; he explains the scientific principles of sympathetic vibrations causing the different timbres produced by stopped unisons and octave fingerings, but although he provides several illustrative examples and studies,[40] little further technical information concerning extensions is included.

Paganini, aided by the extraordinary suppleness of his wrist and fingers, was one of the most remarkable nineteenth-century exponents of extensions. The stretching capacity of his hand was enormous[41] and he was able to adopt an advantageous thumb position and stop a span of three octaves with ease (Ex. 82). Guhr provides various examples of extensions employed by Paganini (Exx. 83–88), some of which (notably Exx. 87 & 88) render the recognition of a definite concept of positions practically impossible.

Ex. 82

Ex. 83

Ex. 84

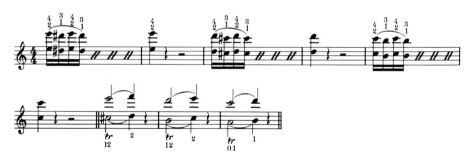

Ex. 85

40. Baillot, L'art . . . (1834), pp. 206–16.
41. See Bennati, Notice physiologique sur Paganini.

Ex. 86

Ex. 87

Ex. 88

EXPRESSIVE FINGERING

Baillot is the only writer of the period to devote a special section to expressive fingering, other writers choosing to discuss many such fingerings in the context of other technical problems rather than as a separate entity. He suggests eight specific principles as guides to the selection of expressive fingerings in accordance with the character of the music:

The fingers and the bow have a simultaneous movement. But independently of this unanimity that they must have, the fingers have a movement peculiar to themselves and from which a great deal can result when true feeling and enlightened taste direct its use. This movement occurs in different ways and must always originate from the nature of the passage whose expressiveness one wishes to convey to best advantage. The bow sustains the sounds like a voice and sings; the fingers articulate like the speech they pronounce and at times appear to speak.
    Here are some methods whose success depends on their correct application.

1st Method

        Drop the fingers on the string from a sufficient height so that they have a little power, much flexibility and so that their movements are extremely even; the result is:
    1. That the fingers fall with impetus and independently hit the exact point for *intonation* more reliably than when they are placed timidly on the string.

2. That *steadiness* is a consequence of this evenness in the movement of the fingers.

3. That since the notes are all extremely well articulated by the fall of the fingers, above all in slurred passages, *clarity* should likewise result from this manner of dropping the fingers on to the strings.

Now, as we have seen in the article about methods of study,[42] these three qualities were the basis of all good performance. All expression which lacked these prime qualities would be poor.

One must therefore consider the *even movement* of the fingers as one of the primary physical means, as indicated in the following example, which should be practised using both fingerings.

Ex. 89

(Note) In the fingering marked above [the notes], attention must be paid above all to the 4th finger, which one should take care to press down rather more than the others because it is weaker.

2nd Method

Shorten the last note of a passage by making the finger fall at the same time as the bow is halted or lifted. This is indicated by a dot or by a small elongated line.

Ex. 90

3rd Method

Make audible, but only barely, a light tapping of the fingers on the string at the same time as the bow produces *flautando* sounds by reason of its lightness and its advanced position about two inches over the fingerboard.

Ex. 91
(Viotti: Trio no. 8)

42. Baillot, *L'art* . . . (1834), pp. 244–63.

4th Method

Drag the same finger from one note to another by imperceptible intervals.

Ex. 92
(Beethoven: Sonata for horn (or violin) Op. 17)

The effect of this passage, which was originally written for the horn, can be conveyed better on the violin by using the fingering indicated above.

5th Method

Slide a stopped finger forwards or backwards in order to substitute another adroitly in its place.

Avoid making audible the small notes in this passage [Ex. 94] marked with a cross, which are sometimes played accidentally when changing position and whose effect is disagreeable.

Ex. 93
(Tartini: L'art de l'archet)

Avoid making audible the small notes.

Ex. 94

6th Method

Drag the same finger almost imperceptibly in passages with ascending or descending semitones.

Ex. 95

Semitone ascending
(Baillot: *Thème varié*, Op. 17)

3rd variation:
Moderato

7th Method

There are some notes which are connected by the same bow stroke; these are slurred notes; the fingers articulate them. There are others which are connected at the same time by the finger and bow; these are '*dragged*' notes; as we have just seen, two notes might often be played in this way. In certain melodic passages, the expression and the relationship of the notes to each other requires that several notes which succeed each other by tones or semitones should be slurred without any articulation using the same finger, dragging it on the string to give this effect and making it slide imperceptibly. There results a great similarity to the voice in expressing these kinds of effects.

Here is an example:

Ex. 96

(Baillot: Étude no. 20)

Adagio cantabile
3rd string

8th Method

Press the finger down and slowly lift it again little by little, without altering the value of the notes.

This method, correctly used, gives the semitones a tender and melancholy expression which generally suits them in slow movements and where one could speak of *minor expression*, recalling what has been said in the article on the *minor mode*.

Ex. 97

(Mozart: Quartet no. 7 [K. 575])

Andante   Press the finger down and slowly lift it again

sotto voce   cresc.

Summary

Expressive fingerings, like all kinds of effects, should be employed with discretion and delicacy. One should therefore avoid using them too often and also sliding the finger either in too forceful a manner or with the slightest affectation. . .

(Baillot, *L'art*. . . (1834), pp. 152–5)

6

Timbre and tone production

TIMBRE

Many violinists of the period thoroughly appreciated the close relationship between fingering and timbre and, with the greater left-hand mobility afforded by the chin-braced grip and eventually (from c. 1820 onwards) the chin rest, began to pay greater attention to the preservation of uniform tone colour within the musical phrase (although security of intonation was naturally a prime consideration, particularly in the earlier years).[1] Spohr, for instance, insists that the positions should be used 'not merely for convenience or facility of playing but also with a view to expression and [quality and evenness of] tone'.[2] Consequently, as verified by the extracts below, the higher positions (especially those up to seventh position) were increasingly exploited for expressive purposes; *una corda* playing gradually reached its zenith, culminating in the *sul G pot-pourris* extravaganzas of Paganini and his fellow virtuosi (for example, Paganini's *Napoleon sonata with variations on the fourth string*, which exploits the full effective range of that string, incorporating harmonics, *glissandi*, *scordatura* and many other effects in unprecedented concentration); sequences were played wherever possible with matching fingerings, bowings and string changes; and concerted efforts were made to avoid, in certain expressive contexts, the stark tonal contrast between open and stopped strings and even to veil the differences in timbre between each string. With regard to the latter, Campagnoli is unique in recommending the cultivation of the unison (Ex. 98) when a change of string proves necessary:

'To diminish the inequality which is perceptible in passing from one string to another, and to correct the natural difference which subsists between the open strings and the strings when stopped by the fingers, and which arises from the different thicknesses of the strings, it becomes necessary to employ the unison which is the origin of concords.'   (Campagnoli, *Metodo* . . . (1797?), tr. Bishop, pt. 1, no. 19)

However, this latter device is of questionable value, for although the unison

---

1. See ch. 5, pp. 89–112.   2. Spohr, *Violinschule* (1832), p. 195.

Ex. 98

would undoubtedly help to veil the differences in timbre between the two strings in question, it would at the same time emphasise that note above all other notes which are stopped normally.

One of the most vexing problems faced by performers concerned the use of open strings. Although open strings were sometimes necessarily employed in the execution of shifts, bariolage, double and multiple stopping, *scordatura* and many other instances, whether for greater facility or effect, they were not generally adopted in instances when stopped notes were technically viable. Roger North (c. 1726), for example, recommends 'sounding all the notes under the touch, and none with the strings open; for those are an harder sound than when stopp'd and not always in tune',[3] and with the gradual introduction of metal covered strings (only by *some* violinists and then generally only for the two lowest strings), the sound of open strings no doubt became 'harder' still. Consequently, the use of unstopped strings was restricted by most violinists and was certainly avoided wherever possible (either by the use of the fourth finger in first position on the lowest three strings, a finger extension or a shift to a higher position) in descending scale passages involving more than one string (especially in slurred bowing),[4] trills (except in double trills where there is no alternative), *appoggiaturas* and other such ornaments and, generally speaking, in most melodic or expressive contexts, in order that the difference in timbre between open and stopped strings should not be starkly exposed. However, it must be admitted that uniformity of tone colour was invariably sacrificed in the interests of accurate intonation and economy of finger movement, but whenever string changes proved necessary, they were made as inaudible as possible.[5]

As chapter seven of his *Elementi* . . ., Galeazzi provides an exhaustive survey (entitled 'Dell'Eguaglianza') concerning tonal uniformity. He prescribes ten rules relating to the cultivation of uniform tone colour and the use of open strings and follows these with lengthy explanations and pertinent musical examples. No doubt modern violinists will be surprised to read of Galeazzi's apparent preference for a trill with the weak fourth finger in first position, rather than a second-finger trill in third position, in his discussion of Rule VIII:

3. Wilson, ed., *Roger North on music*, p. 234. See also L. Mozart, *Versuch* . . ., ch. 5, §13, pp. 106–7; Spohr, *Violinschule* (1832), p. 84.
4. Reichardt, *Ueber die Pflichten* . . . (1776), pp. 30–1.
5. *Ibid.*, p. 38.

89. Here is a matter of utmost importance which, alas, is almost entirely neglected by most teachers, although it is almost certain that the performer will never be able to please his listeners if some natural imperfections inherent in the violin are not first eliminated. One of these imperfections is in fact its unevenness in the volume and quality of the various sounds. We have seen that since all the strings are of the same length and because they must have the same tension so that the violin tone emerges evenly in strength, it becomes extremely necessary to vary their thicknesses in order to achieve the necessary tuning of fifths. In passing then from one string to another, it is inevitable that a sensitive ear hears a certain unevenness of tone which is not very agreeable and which is caused by the difference in the thickness of the strings. Since this is so, because of the nature of the instrument itself, the wise performer must at least modify it [the tone] whenever possible, and the following rules, which we shall call the rules of *equality*, are directed to this end. Under this category come not only all the rules which serve to modify the inequality that is heard in passing from one string to another but also that inequality that occurs naturally between an open and a stopped string.[6] The following is the principal rule and all the others can be considered corollaries of it.

Rule I

90. In expressive passages string changes should be attempted as little as possible; one should not play on four strings that which can be played on three, nor on three that which can be executed on two, nor on two that which can be performed on one.

Illustration

This precept, which is the basis of [tonal] equality, originates naturally from its own definition and from the use to which its rules are directed, since it is evident that the fewer the crossings made from one string to another, the less often unevenness of sound will emerge. However, inasmuch as practical examples are much more useful than the clearest explanations, we shall turn as usual to these for further understanding. We only regret that there are so many and varied combinations of this rule and that its applications are so complicated, that it is impossible to cover them all in a work like this. It will suffice, therefore, to remark that it can be applied to all the positions; in fact, it is the basis of or even the key to the art of position-work, about which I will speak in the following article. He who understands and applies this rule will never err in position-work; at the same time, however, it must be pointed out that in general this and all the other rules of equality apply for the most part only in passages of some expressiveness and in *Adagios* where everything is discernible, for they are not always applicable in fast and loud passages. On the contrary, sometimes the effect of this rule is to produce the very inequality that we must deliberately seek now and then.

Only two examples of equality will be presented here to display its admirable

6. Rousseau is to my knowledge the only writer who has noted the inequality that exists between open and stopped strings (see *Dictionnaire de musique*, article 'vide' where it is expressed thus): 'The sound of open strings is not only lower but more resonant and fuller than when a finger is placed on the strings, which [inequality] is derived from the softness of the finger which impedes and intercepts the play of vibrations. This difference is such that fine violinists shy away from open strings to prevent this inequality of sound, which produces a bad effect when it is not appropriately distributed. This manner of performance requires the use of positions, which increases the difficulty, but when one has formed the habit, one becomes truly the master of the instrument and the most difficult notes are executed like the easiest. (Galeazzi's footnote)

effect. The first, from my Concerto in C (see Ex. [99]), will make it plain that one should not play on two strings what can be done on one. The numbers above indicate the fingering and the roman numerals underneath are the positions, about which we shall write in the following article. The second example (Ex. [100]), a minuet within a rondo from another of my works, the Concerto in D, must be performed only on the G string. . . [sentence omitted]

Ex. 99

Ex. 100

Rule II

91. In the first position, the [notes of the] open strings are played unstopped whenever they ascend by step.

Illustration

When passing from low to higher strings, it is clear that they will blend more easily within the passage whenever it is performed with open strings, which gradually prepare the ear to tolerate the change to a higher string, inasmuch as the open string, in such a case, resembles the sound of the higher string more closely than that of the lower one (see Ex. [101]).

Ex. 101

Rule III

92. On the contrary, if in the first position the [notes of the] open strings descend by step, they must always be stopped with the fourth finger.

Illustration

The reason for this is contrary to the preceding one. It is clear that if, in descending, one passes from an open to a stopped string, there would be a very great inequality, which is unavoidable unless the open string note were stopped with the fourth or some other finger, because this sound would then blend much better with the lower string than if it were open (see Ex. [102]).

Ex. 102

Consequence

93. Descending *appoggiaturas* are therefore always stopped, even though an open string could serve for the *appoggiatura*.

Rule IV

94. Whenever the [notes of the] open strings move by leap, there are two choices: either they are bowed separately or slurred. In the first case the execution is *ad libitum*, either open or stopped if some other reason does not determine the choice; in the second case, there arise again two other possibilities, whether the [notes of the] open strings are slurred to a higher or a lower note. In the first case they will be played open and in the second stopped.

Illustration

If the [notes of the] open strings move by leap and must be played detached, the separation of the bow stroke itself already produces a certain inequality which conceals that between the strings, or, in other words, the small interval which exists between the two bow strokes is bowed so that the inequality of the passage is rendered the least discernible from one string to another; but if it must be slurred, then it is necessary to play it open if it is slurred to a higher note (as §91) and stopped if it is slurred to a lower note (as §92) (Ex. [103]).

Ex. 103

Rule V

95. When an open string [note] which descends or ascends by step is repeated, the first is stopped and the second open in ascending; the reverse is true in descending, the first being open and the second stopped.

Illustration

It is self-evident that, performed in this way, the passage remains much more unified than if played otherwise. The ear, deceived by the perfection of the unison, will not perceive the inequality of the change of strings during the repetition of the open string [notes] (Ex. [104]). The same would apply if one of the repeated notes were an *appoggiatura*.

Ex. 104

Rule VI

96. When two open strings are separated by one or two notes of brief duration, it is better to execute both in the same way, that is to say, either both stopped or both open, the choice being determined by the melody, whether its general tendency is to descend or ascend. This is so, even though previous rules might indicate that it is to be executed otherwise.

Illustration

It would be harsh and unpleasant for the ear to hear the same sound repeated within such a small interval of time in two different ways, hence it is always better in such cases to play the two notes either open or stopped. It appears that this reason gives the lie to the preceding rule but it is not so if one realises that, whenever two sounds immediately follow each other, the perfection of the unison removes the bad effect of the inequality which is even more prominent when some other sound is interposed; this can be experienced by repeating the following and already cited examples several more times (Ex. [105]). The two a¹s in this example can both be played open and both e²s stopped, or vice versa, the two a¹s stopped and the e²s open, although it apparently contravenes the already established rules.

Ex. 105

Rule VII

97. In sequences, all repetitions should be played with the same fingers and the same string changes with which the first figure was executed, or else the execution of the first and following figures should be determined by the repetitions, in such a way that all are similar.

Illustration

For a sequence to be discernible, it is clear that all of its repetitions must give the ear the same sensation, which cannot be obtained unless the execution of these repetitions is exactly the same and of similar equality. If executed otherwise, the sequence becomes ugly and hardly recognisable. In Ex. [106], there is a sequence of two bars

Ex. 106

for each part or limb. Inasmuch as the first of these limbs lies naturally in the first position and all on one string, it would be contrary to the interests of equality to play the second limb in the same position because it would be divided between two different strings, whereas all the first limb remains on the same string; the same can be said for the third limb of the sequence. On the other hand, it is obvious that if the second limb is fingered in the second position and the third limb in the third position, then the whole example will remain on one string and always with the same finger pattern. However, here is a different example (Ex. [107]). Since the first bar is bowed on two strings, it shows us that all the other limbs of the sequence must be bowed likewise on two strings. It would be a mistake to play the second bar in the first position because the passage would then be on one string only and unlike the first limb, but if one takes the positions as they are marked in the example, the whole passage will lie on two strings and will be executed within the rules for sequences. This is an exception to Rule I but this method must be followed for sequences on two or three strings. Another, almost similar, elegant example can be seen in Ex. [108], which is always played on two strings and which may serve as an exercise for the studious.

Ex. 107

Ex. 108

Rule VIII

98. An open string is never trilled, but when a trill is indicated at the pitch of an open string, it should be performed stopped.

Illustration

The unevenness which would arise in trilling on an open string is so obvious that there is no need to demonstrate it. If it is a mistake to play a simple *appoggiatura* with an open string (§93), it would certainly be a bigger mistake to do so in a trill, which is nothing but a repeated *appoggiatura*; therefore, an open string trilled with a stopped note, or a stopped with an open, must be prohibited (Ex. [109]). The first two trills on

Ex. 109

a¹ and e² are played with the third finger in third position and the last trill on d² can be executed in first position with the fourth finger, and thus the rule will be observed.

Rule IX

99. When a sharp precedes the [notes of] open strings, they [the notes] can be played in the first position in two different ways, either with the first finger pulled back or with the fourth finger on the string immediately below. The choice, however, is not *ad libitum* for the performer; it will be noted that if, after the open string with the sharp, [the music] descends by step or leap, it is fingered with the fourth finger; if it ascends by step or leap, it is fingered with the first finger.

Illustration

The reason is the same as that of Rule I; thus, either a change of string is avoided or else, at least, the principal purpose of equality is applied to blend, as it were, as much as possible the sharpened note either with the string above by fingering it with the first finger or with the string below by fingering it with the fourth finger (Ex. [110]). In this

Ex. 110

example, both the d sharp¹ in the first bar and the a sharp¹ in the third bar are fingered with the first finger because they ascend.[7] In the fifth bar the a sharp¹ is fingered with the fourth finger because it descends, as does the d sharp¹ in the antipenultimate bar; however, the d sharp¹ in the penultimate bar is also fingered with the fourth finger in order to avoid the imbalance of hearing two similar sounds in different modes of execution repeated so closely; hence, the same reasons as §96 apply.

7. In the case of the d sharp¹, the use of the fourth finger would also involve a rather pointless double string-crossing. (Galeazzi's footnote)

Rule X

100. Whenever the same passage is repeated several times in a composition, although on different strings or in different keys, one must anticipate it by looking ahead and seeking a position which will ensure that the passage will always be performed with the same tone colour and change of strings in all its repetitions.

Illustration

If a passage is to be clearly recognised for what it is every time it is repeated, it must be played with the same equality, expression and bowing every time, otherwise it would no longer produce the effect of similarity necessarily required by the composition. This passage (see Ex. [111]) is stated three times in a composition, the first in the

Ex. 111

key of C major, the second in F major and the third in G major. The first statement, according to what will be said in the following article, must be played entirely in the second position; therefore, for the other two statements, it will be necessary to choose the position in which each passage will be realised with the very same, in fact exact, change of strings and to see to it that this change of strings occurs, if possible, in the same place. If the second statement is played in the second position, the passage will be in the selfsame circumstances as the first statement; if the third statement is fingered in the third position, it will be played likewise with the same fingers and same changes of strings as were the first two. This rule must never be disregarded unless it is absolutely necessary to do so in a particular case and another strong reason compels a contrary execution.

101. The application of this rule has infinite uses. It brings out the form of a piece of music in which certain passages must necessarily be repeated several times and in various keys, especially in instrumental music in which, generally, the first section closes with the same passages that close the second; in such a case it is always advantageous to play similar passages with the same equality and with the same fingering if possible, although at times it will cause no small difficulty, but the effect must be set above one's own convenience. Yet another example will serve our instruction even better (Ex. [112]). The first statement is fingered in the fourth position; consequently,

Ex. 112

the second statement will also be fingered in the fourth position. It would be a mistake, for equality, to do otherwise, as it would be to execute this passage in the first, second, or third positions, because it would not be analogous to the first statement. This rule merits more attention than is commonly given to it. Since the possibilities are innumerable, it behoves the prudent teacher to remind the diligent student that he must practise very much in order to acquire a perfect equality, which alone will set him apart and raise him above the ranks of ordinary practitioners.

(Galeazzi, *Elementi* . . . (1791), vol. I, pt. 2, art. 7, pp. 122–9)

Although Habeneck's examination of timbre duplicates much of the content of Galeazzi's study, it is particularly interesting for its special emphasis on unity and firmness in bowing and its comparison of satisfactory and unacceptable fingerings for given musical situations:

Achieving even tone and even playing

23. There are two causes of unevenness of tone and execution. The 1st is a result of a lack of unity and firmness in the bowing.

24. When one has to pass from one string to another, the small movement that one is obliged to make with the wrist can bring about a small oscillation to the bow which, by diverting it from its straight line, can cause either an interruption of the sound or a poor tone quality; so that:

    1. One must be particularly careful when changing strings to avoid letting the bow deviate in the slightest from the straight line that it must always follow.

    2. The two notes that follow each other from one string to the next must succeed each other without a break, whether they be slurred or detached.[8]

    3. When the two notes are detached, the 1st must finish soft and quiet and the 2nd should begin likewise soft and quiet, unless the composer has indicated otherwise in order to give a certain intentional accent.

25. The second cause of unevenness of tone and execution is a result of the make-up of the violin itself.

Since for physical reasons the strings of the violin have to be of different thicknesses,[9] a certain unevenness of timbre results which vanishes when one is playing *brilliant allegro* pieces but which can shock delicate ears in *slow* and *gentle* movements.

This disadvantage is inherent in the nature of the instrument, and the skilled artist must apply himself to correcting it.

Observation of the following rule will assist in achieving this end.

Rule

26. In expressive passages, one must continue to change strings as little as possible, and not play on 4 strings what can be played on 3, nor on 3 what can be played on 2, nor on 2 what can be played on one string alone.

27. This rule is the foundation of evenness in playing. But its applications are so numerous that one could write whole books on the subject without managing to

8. It must be observed that the rules given here concerning evenness in playing are to be applied above all in expressive pieces or in *Adagios* where every detail is apparent; while in forceful or brilliant pieces or passages, they can frequently be ignored without disadvantage: and, indeed, there sometimes results from this very unevenness of timbre an effect worth striving after to give variety to one's playing. (Habeneck's footnote)

9. See Rousseau, *Dict[ionnaire] de musique*, article 'Corde'. (Habeneck's footnote)

exhaust the possible combinations. We will content ourselves with the observation that this rule is the most frequent cause of changes in position and that the student who best understands this will also be the one who makes the fewest mistakes in his choice of positions.

Here are some examples which may serve as a guide.[10]

Ex. 113
(Viotti: Concerto no. 7)

This phrase [Ex. 113] encompasses all the 4 strings of the violin; but one can easily convince oneself that if one were to use the E string to play the f^2 and the g^2, the tone would be uneven and the melody would lose its appeal.

Ex. 114
(Haydn: Quartet Op. 20 no. 5)

This phrase would be uneven and lacking in uniformity if one were to play it in the following manner.

Ex. 115

28. In general, one should never use a string for the purpose of playing only a single note.

Ex. 116
(Viotti: Concerto no. 8)

(Viotti: Concerto no. 15)

10. In all these examples, we have put a good fingering alongside a bad one, simply for the sake of comparison, without wishing to suggest that the good fingerings are the only valid ones. (Habeneck's footnote)

29. Generally speaking, whenever a complete phrase can be played on a single string, the use of two strings is to be avoided.

Ex. 117

(Viotti: Concerto no. 7)

30. In passages which form a sequence, it is better to execute the patterns with the same fingers and with the same changes of string.

Ex. 118

(Viotti: Concerto no. 10)

31. In these two examples [one example omitted], the pattern encompasses two strings; each repetition must therefore be played on two strings.

Ex. 119

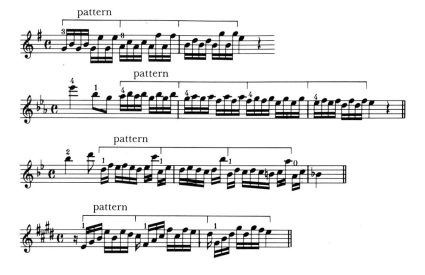

32. In all these examples, the pattern encompasses two strings and each repetition therefore must be played on two strings. Here is an example where the pattern is complete on one string only.

Ex. 120

33. There are certain passages which, without actually being sequential, must be played according to the plan established in the first few notes.

Ex. 121
(Viotti: Concerto no. 11)

This passage must be played entirely on two strings.

34. When a passage happens to be repeated in a piece at the octave, or at a different pitch, one must find a position such that it can be reproduced with the same fingering and the same changes of string.

Ex. 122
(Viotti: Concerto no. 19)

35. This phrase, when put down an octave [Ex. 123], can be played evenly only if one starts in 2nd position on the D string.

Ex. 123

Ex. 124
(Viotti: Concerto no. 6)

36. When this passage is transposed down a fifth in the final solo of this same Concerto, it must be played on the D and A strings with the same fingering and the same positions.

5th position

Ex. 125

(Viotti: Concerto no. 8)

37. This passage, which is transposed down a 5th in the final solo, must be played on the G, D and A strings with the same fingering.

[Habeneck, *Méthode.* . . (c. 1804), pt. 3, ch. 1. §3.,
pp. 103–6) [selected examples only].

TONE PRODUCTION AND SONORITY

Whilst the bow grip and the respective roles of the right hand, wrist and fingers were naturally considered of chief significance in the production of a sonorous tone, the contribution of the left hand towards the attainment of tonal clarity through the firm, hammer-like action of its fingers could not be ignored. Reichardt, for example, evaluates a good full tone as one of the chief requisites of a good orchestral violinist and he devotes a whole chapter of his volume to the basic technical principles of tone production, stressing in particular the importance of cultivating both coordination and independent action of the left and right hands. Whilst his recommendations regarding finger pressure, the use of the full face of the bow hair, the point of contact of the bow on the string and the lifted stroke would not be accepted by most modern writers, his survey is enlightening on many counts, not least in revealing the eighteenth-century German school's rather narrow and retrospective approach to technical matters.

I. *On good, full tone*

A good tone can be produced only if each finger is exactly in the right place, not a fraction sharp or flat, if the pressure of the left hand is as strong as possible, and if the bow is moved in a straight line and is held not too close to the bridge nor too far from it, if it is held firmly but not pressed down too firmly on the strings, if all the hairs touch the strings and not, as is often the case, only the side hairs, and if the bow is not always left resting on the strings, but wherever permissible – and this will be seen later – is lifted off.

Reasons

To put each finger exactly in its right place is essential not only for correct intonation but also, above all, for a good, clear, full tone . . . [sentence omitted]

The pressure of the left hand needs to be as strong as possible because the finger which is stopping the string sets a limit on the vibrations of the string: if this does not happen with total accuracy, then the tone will waver.

The bow must not be moved at an angle, because that will make the tone shrill; it must not be held too close to the bridge, because the strings are too tightly stretched there, and if the bow is used with sufficient strength to convey the vibrations of the whole string – particularly when it is unstopped[11] – it will produce a forceful, grinding tone; but it should not be held too far from the bridge either, because then again this very same strength of bow will not be in correct proportion to the tension of the string.

It is essential for the bow to be held firmly, in order to keep it constantly at a correct angle; but the reason for not pressing the bow too firmly, that is too forcefully, on to the string is that this would make the tone heavy, since the pleasing resonance of the string would be totally lost; except that with short *marcato* notes, where the composer requires them to be played very loudly, a very strong pressure of the bow will not damage the tone, because the bow is at once lifted completely from the string.

The full hairs of the bow must touch the string because a few hairs alone do not have enough strength to vibrate the string sufficiently, particularly when it is to vibrate loudly; but even when quieter passages are being played, the bow must not be tilted in such a way that only the side hairs are touching the string, in order to maintain an even quality and nobility of tone.

The reason mentioned above, namely the resonance of the strings, applies also to lifting the bow off the strings whenever it is permitted rather than leaving it always resting on the strings . . . [rest of paragraph omitted]

11. With the higher notes, where the string is already shortened by half or more, the bow can more readily be allowed to move nearer to the bridge. But then both bow and strings must be in first-class condition. (Reichardt's footnote)

There is nothing more unusual than a violinist or violoncellist with a good full tone. The real reason lies simply in the early instruction; the pupil is not made to spend long enough, or even any time at all, on [playing] his scales. To make it pleasant for him, they give him tunes to play, even difficult pieces, right from the outset. That is as if he were expected to draw people before he can make dots and straight lines. If he eventually gets only to the stage of drawing crooked noses and crooked mouths, then he is certainly never going to learn to draw straight lines. This, and more, is very true of bowing.

(Reichardt, Ueber die Pflichten . . . (1776), ch. 1, pp. 4–8)

Baillot concentrates rather more on considerations of expression, acknowledging that every instrument and each of the four strings has its own natural timbre and demonstrating how this characteristic can be modified, chiefly through skilful bow management, in imitation of other instruments.

The timbre and character of the four strings of the violin

Quite separate from the timbre which belongs to the violin in general, and from that which depends on the construction of each violin in particular, there is a variety in timbre that each of the strings is capable of receiving from the performer and, in this way, as has been said in the introduction, the violin can be given the character of the *oboe*, that of the *flute*, *horn*, *trumpet*, *harmonica* and, where harmony is concerned, the character of the *harp*, *piano* and even the *organ*.

The *E string*, whose timbre is clear and silvery, and some of whose notes can be considered as an extension of the voice, is especially suitable for brilliant passages, opening passages, which become so much more remarkable when they are an octave higher, and seem to a certain extent to be the result of a passionate forward movement which lifts the voice, making it more or less high by the sheer force of the sentiment animating it.

Ex. 126

(Beethoven: Concerto in D, Op. 61)

The E string, by the effect of contrast, gives more sweetness to the expression of the medium notes and brings out the beauty of the low notes better [Ex. 127].

The high notes, used with all the resources of science and genius and rendered with delicacy and purity, have a ravishing effect: there is a remarkable example in the offertory of Mr Cherubini's Requiem Mass, of which we give a few bars here [Ex. 128]:

Ex. 127

(Viotti: Concerto no. 18)

Ex. 128

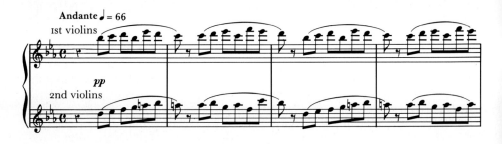

    The timbre of the E string is comparable, in its high notes, with the piccolo, and is suitable for quick pieces that are expressed with lightness [Ex. 129].

    The A string has something sweet and penetrating that gives it the greatest likeness to a woman's voice. It is one of the principal charms of the violin, for all its power is in its sweetness [Ex. 130].

    Sounds analogous to those of the flute are obtainable on the A string, principally after the fourth or fifth note [Ex. 131];

    This string also takes the timbre of the oboe and even that of the bagpipe, the oboe of the mountains.

    In order to imitate this timbre, it is necessary to press the bow a little more than usual, to bring it close to the bridge and to feel that the roughness of the hair delays, so to speak, the vibrations of the string [Ex. 132].

Ex. 129

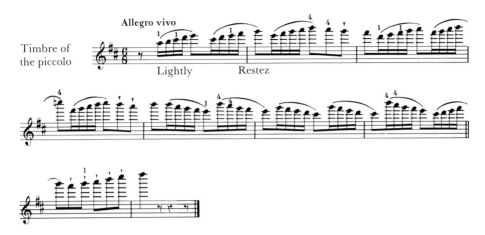

Ex. 130

(Mozart: Quintet no. 7)

Ex. 131

(Mozart: Quartet no. 3)

The D string has the noble and velvety character of the contralto voice; above all, it is suitable to the grandiose style, and though it has not the power or strength of the G string, it has nearly all its majesty [Ex. 133].

This string is the one which best renders flute-like sounds. To obtain these, the bow is drawn across the fingerboard very lightly and rapidly so as to let the string have the

Ex. 132

Timbre of the
oboe and of
the bagpipes

Ex. 133

(Handel: Air)

Original text

Ex. 134

(Baillot: Nocturne no. 2, entitled 'The Dream', Op. 35)

Timbre of
the flute

greatest possible freedom. The tone then has considerably less intensity than it can take on when one wants to produce sounds analogous to those of the oboe; this difference of intensity in the two cases proceeds evidently from the fact that, to produce the tone of the oboe, one sets the string in motion so near the bridge that it is constrained to deviate much more from its position of rest than it does when it is set in motion near the fingerboard and extremely lightly, in order to obtain flute-like sounds [Ex. 134].

The following example requires greater rapidity of bow stroke.

Ex. 135

The G string is the one which proclaims the empire of the violin; there are lower sounds on other instruments but none is found with so much authority. It is the tenor voice in all its beauty. This string holds in its dominion the consonant notes of the higher strings. If it is of a bad quality, it paralyses all that might respond to its voice; if it is pure and sonorous, it gives resilience and life to all the rest. Its energy and its powerful voice make it a whole instrument in itself and the lower this voice is, the more opportunity it gives to expression to attain the sublime [Ex. 136].

The sounds of the G string lend themselves to the imitation of the horn, above all in the slightly higher notes; it is enough to press quite strongly with the fingers and the bow to give some freedom and bite to these sounds when playing fast, and a considerable roundness when playing slowly, and to bring the bow close to the bridge so that the strength of the vibration can render more faithfully the noble and touching sounds of the horn [Ex. 137].

Ex. 136

(J.S. Bach: Sonata no. 4 for violin and harpsichord)

a.

Adagio

4th string up to the end. _ _ _ _

(Viotti: Duo no. 3 'Hommage à l'amitié')

b.

on the 4th string

Ex. 137

(Beethoven: Rondo from Concerto in D. Op. 61)

The sound of the *trumpet* can likewise be produced on the G string by shifting up to the very high notes and by giving more force and movement to the bow.

Ex. 138

(Baillot: Rondo from Concerto no. 2)

Timbre of
the trumpet

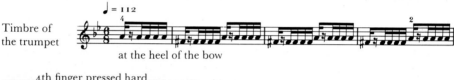

at the heel of the bow

4th finger pressed hard. . . .

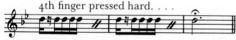

In the articles which deal with *chords* and *harmonic preludes, pizzicato, harmonics,* the *third sound* and *quadruple stopping,*[12] it will be seen how up to a certain point one can continue to imitate on the violin the *piano,* the *harp,* the *harmonica,* and the *organ,* that is to say how one can produce some of the effects of these instruments.

There is little music which does not lend itself to some of these imitations, either indicated by the composer or advertised by him in a general title such as *pastorale, chasse, military piece* etc., or anticipated by the performer who needs no such indication, being familiar with similar pieces. These are riches of which the violin must doubtless take advantage but it must not thereby lose sight of its natural treasures, that is to say, the accents of the human voice for which it is destined to act as a substitute.

Having expounded the resources that are to be found in the various timbres of the four strings of the violin and having shown the advantages that can be derived from them, it is right that we should warn students against abusing this kind of effect: imitation is not the *aim* of art but the *means,* without which there is no art. It is necessary then to use imitations of timbre, with which we are here concerned, only when the subject itself gives rise to them and its character can be better expressed by this means; these imitations become childish from the moment when they are not necessary; they even become dangerous in that they degenerate then into technical passages known under the name of '*string bravura*' (*passages de cordes*) which only too often sacrifice musical thought to false brilliance, which is a fatal way of rendering expressiveness unnatural, of becoming lost in one's own emptiness, and of speaking without saying anything.   (Baillot, *L'art* . . . (1834), pp. 140–4)

12. The reader is referred to some of these articles on pp. 354, 225, 147, 145 & 150.

BOW SPEED, BOW PRESSURE AND THE POINT OF CONTACT

Appreciation of the interdependence of bow speed, bow pressure and the point of contact of the bow on the string is vital for good tone production, for a change in any one of these factors necessitates a corresponding modification in at least one of the others; thus, an increase in bow pressure with the contact point constant requires an increase in bow speed and vice versa; a faster bow speed with constant pressure requires a contact point nearer the fingerboard and vice versa, and so on. Writers of the period omit thorough discussion of the interrelationship between the three factors and their *combined* effect on tone quality and volume, although most examine each aspect separately in varying degrees of detail and many combine two of them together for such analysis.[13] Baillot and Spohr come closest to appreciating this relationship, Baillot quoting Savart:

In order to obtain the greatest possible intensity of sound, all other things being equal, that is to say, the distance from the hair to the bridge and the pressure being the same in all cases, it is necessary to draw the bow more slowly for the low-pitched sounds than for the high-pitched sounds; that is the general principle. But if the pressure of the bow and its distance from the bridge are allowed to vary, very loud shrill tones will then be obtained when the string is attacked very near to the bridge. It would therefore seem that there exists a fixed relationship between the amount of roughness of the hair and the speed communicated to the bow, as well as with the number of vibrations of the string, and this is so true that if the bow is passed lightly and very rapidly over a string, instead of drawing the fundamental sound from it the high octave is normally obtained, and furthermore, when the string is long, often such very high harmonics as the twelfth, and the double and triple octave.

(Baillot, *L'art* . . . (1834), p. 130).

Spohr summarises the relationship between bow speed, bow pressure and the contact point in his brief discussion of tone production:

From the outset, the student should try hard to produce a pure, well-rounded tone. As already observed, the first requisite for this is a straight bow. But it is also necessary to establish how gentle or strong the pressure of the bow on each of the four strings has to be, in proportion to the speed of the bow stroke, in order to make them speak easily and clearly, and to what extent, on the different strings, the hair may be allowed to approach the bridge. As regards the first, the speed of the bow stroke must increase in proportion as the pressure of the bow on the strings becomes greater; and as a thick string is more difficult for the bow to set vibrating than a thin one, the bow should not come so close to the bridge on the lower strings as on the higher ones. The student will find, however, that his own ear, being aware of the need for beautiful tone, will be a better guide to the way the mechanics of bowing can be used to produce such a tone than this or any other theoretical teaching.

(Spohr, *Violinschule*, (1832), p. 26)

Interestingly enough, Perrin is one of the few writers to make the point that playing in the higher positions on the E string requires less bow pressure, a

---

13. For example, Reichardt, *Ueber die Pflichten* . . . (1776), p. 59; Habeneck, *Méthode* . . . (c. 1840), p. 101.

point of contact nearer the bridge (because the length of the string is short-ened in proportion as the stopped finger, acting as a movable nut, advances up the fingerboard)[14] and a corresponding increase in left-hand finger pressure for optimum tone quality, especially in the execution of slow movements; the pressure differences between the two hands are not so marked on the lower strings.[15]

BOW SPEED

The significance of bow speed in relation to tone quality and expression was more fully documented by nineteenth-century writers than by their predecessors, of whom Leopold Mozart and to a certain extent Brijon were among the few to embrace the subject, albeit fleetingly.[16] Baillot's account is most notable for its examination of the relationship between bow speed and tone quality:

Roundness of tone, that is to say the manner of making the string vibrate as evenly as possible, is the principle that is called *breadth* in playing.

This *breadth* consists in grading the duration of the sounds and the length of the bow in proportion to the value of the notes and the grandeur of the style.

It manifests itself at one and the same time both as a restraining force and as a forward movement of the bow. It can only be defined by saying that it is a combination of slowness and speed . . . In the *Adagio*, it is rather more than the normal holding back; in the *Allegro*, it is more than the normal speed of the bow, but with a continuity of vibration that seems to hold back this impulse of the bow and to give back to it in *breadth* what it has to forgo in length.

Sometimes the *length* of the bow stroke is confused with the *breadth of playing*. This length, when it is out of place, is in no way true grandeur but a mere caricature of it, whereas a small amount of bow is very often enough to give breadth to the loftiest thoughts.   (Baillot, *L'art* . . . (1834), p. 130)

Baillot's emphasis here on the importance of dividing the bow according to the length of the notes to be played, in order to maintain an even tone through even bow speed, naturally creates problems in bowing such rhythms as those indicated in Ex. 139, since the player may easily run out of bow or even lose the character of the passage.[17] Baillot's solutions are given in Ex. 140. Habeneck's solutions to such problems are similar, if a little more flexible, since he points out in addition the benefits of changing the bow speed according to the context rather than (like Baillot) keeping it constant. Thus, in Ex. 141a & b, the three slurred notes should be executed with a very much slower bow speed than the separate crotchet; likewise, the dotted crotchets of Ex. 141c & d should be played with a slower bow speed than the quaver which follows, while Ex. 141e essentially involves bow division, the bow being apportioned according to the values of the notes concerned.

14. Gasse, *Méthode* . . . (c. 1839), p. 140.   15. Perrin, *Méthode* . . . (c. 1815), p. 10.
16. L. Mozart, *Versuch* . . ., ch. 5, §7, p. 104; Brijon, *Réflexions* . . . (1763), art. 7, p. 20.
17. Baillot, *L'art* . . . (1834), p. 121.

Ex. 139

a. Presto

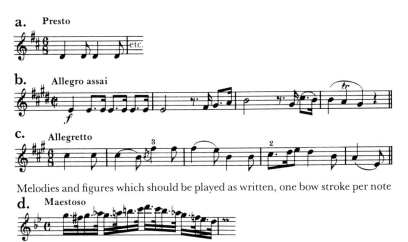

b. Allegro assai

c. Allegretto

Melodies and figures which should be played as written, one bow stroke per note

d. Maestoso

e. Rondo

Ex. 140

a.

b.

c.

Use an up bow for the short note very quickly and very lightly.
Hold the dotted note, spinning it out *piano*

d. Maestoso

very short bow stroke

e. Rondo

Use a down bow for the short note very quickly and very lightly.

Ex. 141

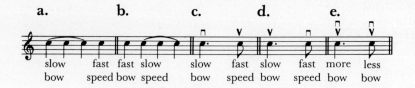

Habeneck provides an interesting survey of the relationship between bow speed, bow pressure, bow apportionment and expression, appreciating in particular that an increase or decrease in bow speed is a most useful means of making short *crescendos* and *diminuendos* in which no change of actual timbre is required.

2. It will have been noticed that the bow does not have the same strength along its whole length.

This length can be divided into three parts:

3. The greatest strength is found at the heel, that is to say from the hand to $\frac{1}{3}$ of the way along.

4. Medium strength exists in the middle, that is in the 2nd $\frac{1}{3}$ of its length.

5. The weakest part is at the point, that is to say in the last $\frac{1}{3}$ of its length.

6. But these three levels of strength are not so inseparable from the portions of the bow to which they correspond that they cannot be modified by means of the greater or lesser speed with which the bow is moved across the strings. For it is a general law of physics that strength increases with the speed of motion, and that it decreases when the motion slows down, and this law is closely applicable to the bow.

7. In practice, say we wish to obtain a soft, gentle sound with the heel of the bow? Then we merely have to move it slowly across the string.

8. Do we want strength at the point? Then we simply move it across the string quickly.

9. Do we want an even level of strength from one end of the bow to the other?

Then a *down bow* should be started slowly and its movement speeded up as one approaches the point, which is the weakest part, *and vice versa*:

An *up bow* should be started rather fast and its movement slowed down as one approaches the heel, which is the strongest part.

10. This then is the theory based on the laws of physics; it is easy to understand but extremely difficult to apply in practice, because it is a question of turning the relationship between strength and speed to advantage in such a way that the result will be the intensity and quality of tone demanded by the expression.

11. In striving to find this relationship there are three hazards that may be met with.

1. If the bow is not moved quickly enough when it is being pressed firmly, the string will squeak.

2. If it is moved too quickly, it will not have enough length to give full value to the note being sustained.

3. If it is held back without being pressed firmly enough, the tone will have neither the intensity nor the carrying power desired.

12. We shall attempt to determine approximately the speed and the gradation of strength to be given to the bow for different kinds of sustained notes, having regard to the value of the notes and the length of bow that must be used to obtain the inflection indicated.

1st Section

On sustained and nuanced notes

13. There are four kinds of sustained note, namely:
  1. The swelled or *crescendo* note, indicated ◁,
which consists in ⎧ beginning *piano*,
            ⎨ becoming gradually louder,
            ⎩ finishing loud.

  2. The diminishing or *decrescendo* note, indicated ▷,
which consists in ⎧ beginning loud,
            ⎨ becoming gradually softer,
            ⎩ finishing *piano*.

  3. The 'spun' note, indicated ◁▷,
which consists in ⎧ beginning *piano*,
            ⎨ becoming louder up to the middle,
            ⎩ becoming softer from the middle to the end.

  4. Note sustained with equ l volume throughout, following Viotti; we will in-dicate it ═ and it consists i⸴ ⎰ sustaining the note with equal volume from
                      ⎱ beginning to end.

14. We have said that the intensity of the note is increased chiefly by the speed of the bow.

Consequently, in the examples which follow to demonstrate this, we have divided the dotted semibreve into 12 quavers which indicate the slowness of the bow when they are close together and show its acceleration as they become further apart. [Ex. 142][18]

15. It will be observed that with all these sustained notes the bow must press more or less firmly on the string corresponding to the greater or lesser speed that we have indicated, and it must be remembered that, to produce a good tone quality, the bow must be gripped between the thumb and the middle finger in proportion to the amount of pressure one wishes to give with the index-finger.

(Habeneck, *Méthode* . . . (c. 1840), pt. 3, ch. 1, §1, pp. 100–2)

BOW PRESSURE

The amount of bow pressure required in the execution of a *piano* as opposed to a *forte* passage actually varies between comparatively narrow limits. It is determined chiefly by the tonal volume desired, the length of the bow stroke, the part of the bow to be used (more pressure is naturally required to compensate for the lightness of the bow stick at the point), the string in use or the

18. We give these relationships as only approximate; for in the various combinations of the number and value of the notes it would be ridiculous to claim that they could be determined with mathematical strictness. (Habeneck's footnote)

Ex. 142

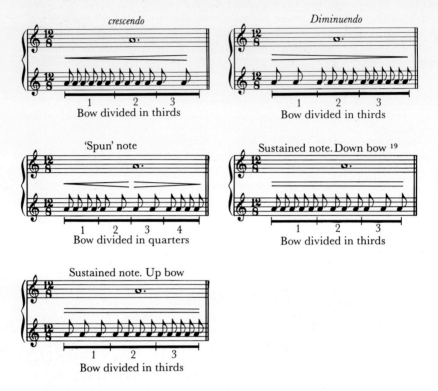

number of strings to be played simultaneously, and the hand position adopted along the fingerboard.

Writers of the period recommend various different methods of bow-pressure regulation. These range from the isolated use of either the index-finger, the wrist or the thumb to the common nineteenth-century compromise, a combination of finger, wrist-joint and especially thumb pressure, as described by Baillot:[20]

3. When it is necessary to give some force to the playing, it should be added solely by the thumb, the index-finger and the wrist; but above all by the thumb. The fore-arm responds to this force while remaining absolutely independent of the upper arm.

4. The four fingers are placed on the stick, pressing the bow in order to set the string in vibration. This pressure, which must sometimes be very strong, would cer-tainly crush the string, if, in order to prevent this, the thumb were not to counter-balance this force by gripping the stick tightly whenever a big sound or a lightening of the bow is desired. Thus, when advised to apply pressure to the bow, it must always be understood that the thumb should then grip the stick strongly from below at the same time as the other fingers press down from above.

(Baillot, *L'art* . . . (1834), art. 7, p. 15)

19. We have used these two parallel lines to indicate a note sustained with equal volume throughout. (Habeneck's footnote)
20. See ch. 4, p. 63.

Nevertheless, many nineteenth-century writers suggest alternatives to the above method. Habeneck, for example, recognises the importance of thumb and index-finger pressure on the bow without mention of wrist pressure, while Spohr recommends the rather outdated use of index-finger pressure only and perpetuates the valid theory of the German school that the thicker strings require slightly more pressure:

As the G string is more difficult than the higher strings to set in vibration, it should be played with a somewhat stronger bow pressure. This also makes it necessary to draw the bow more quickly . . .   (Spohr, *Violinschule* (1832), p. 126)

While index-finger pressure alone is still viable nowadays, most contemporary performers adopt a combination of finger, wrist-joint and thumb pressure, although some, using the middle finger as a pressure agent, place that finger opposite the thumb and create, as Isaac Stern describes it, a 'circle of pressure'. Any slight spread of the fingers on the stick or any pronation of the hand affords additional pressure on the bow.

THE POINT OF CONTACT

The choice of an appropriate contact point of the bow on the string, governed chiefly by the speed of the bow stroke, the tonal volume desired and the length of the string in use, is of great importance in violin playing. While changes of bow speed and pressure are responsible primarily for dynamic shading, variations in the contact point account for the infinite expressive gradations in tone colour of which the violin is capable. The question of variation in the contact point is surprisingly neglected by eighteenth-century writers, the majority describing the normal contact point in a very basic fashion, allowing, like L'Abbé le fils, little variation for differences of string or tonal effect: 'The bow should be drawn straight and always directed over the sound holes of the violin.' (L'Abbé le fils, *Principes* . . . (1761), p. 1) Their nineteenth-century successors, however, adopt on the whole a rather more flexible attitude, generally conceding that the contact point may vary according to the tone quality, volume, effect, dynamic and nuances required and, in some cases, to the thickness of the particular string employed. Baillot, for instance, instructs:

13. Place the hair of the bow between the curve of the f-holes of the violin and the fingerboard, a little nearer to the f-holes than to the fingerboard.
14. Draw the hair nearer to the bridge or further from it according to whether more or less sound is desired in a loud melody. (Baillot, *L'art* . . . (1834), art. 4, p. 13)

Meanwhile, his contemporary, Spohr, perpetuates his compatriots' theory that the optimum contact point depends on the thickness of the strings employed, the bow contacting the string nearer the bridge when playing on the thinner, higher strings than on the thicker, lower strings.[21]

21. Spohr, *Violinschule* (1832), p. 26; see p. 125. See also L. Mozart, *Versuch* . . ., ch. 5, §11, pp. 105–6; Löhlein, *Anweisung* . . . (1774), pp. 19–20.

7

Double and multiple stopping

Double stopping was not unanimously accepted as a valid technical device in the eighteenth century, when many writers disapproved of its use. Avison, for instance, remarked (1753) that 'even in the hands of the greatest masters, double stopping destroys sonority, makes the expression false and slows up execution . . . and brings one good instrument down to the level of two pale reflections'.[1] By the beginning of the nineteenth century, it had received general approbation, Spohr, for example, considering it as one of the principal resources of the violinist and stressing the importance of accurate intonation, facility in shifts (which should be effected without a break), independence of the fingers, mastery of extensions, contractions and bow division, and management of equal bow pressure on both strings, whatever the dynamic.[2]

Double stopping was employed in a wide variety of intervals and forms and was exploited both in a virtuoso manner and merely as a harmonic background either to another melody instrument or even to another melodic line on the same instrument (Exx. 143, 144 & 145). Generally speaking, violin methods of the period are surprisingly lacking in textual instruction regarding the execution of double stopping, although many incorporate exercises to perfect the technique. L'Abbé le fils provides one of the most notable textual surveys, fully appreciating the respective duties of both the right and left hands in a manner hitherto unprecedented:

> To play the double stop to perfection, one must observe three essentials. First, press equally with the two fingers of the left hand and give equal weight to the two strings with the bow. Second, draw the bow perfectly straight, so that the vibration of the two strings is set in motion equally well. Third, raise the bow only in the phrases and figurations which specify the *détaché* [i.e. the *Staccato*].
>
> (L'Abbé le fils, *Principes*. . . (1761) p. 64)

Although L'Abbé le fils's recommendation of equal bow pressure for tonal equality in double stopping is a common concept, it is not endorsed by all of his successors. Campagnoli, for example, directs the player to counteract the

---

1. Avison, *An essay on musical expression*, p. 108.
2. Spohr, *Violinschule* (1832), p. 138.

Ex. 143

Ex. 144

1st violin

2nd violin

Ex. 145

natural tendency to give prominence to the upper note by placing 'the bow upon the two strings, so that its weight may be greater on the lower than on the upper string'.[3]

Baillot's rather more detailed survey, included below, interestingly neglects many of the basic principles and deals with some wider issues of double stopping theory, incorporating exercises and an extended study extracted from Rode *et al.*'s method.

Double and triple stopping

The best preparatory study which can be given for double stopping is one with all the intervals, detached, separated by a short silence which allows checking of the intonation, recognising which of the two notes is out of tune, or if neither of the two is in tune.

Attention should be fixed on the easier note to play and it should be compared with an open string corresponding to the chord being played; by referring to this note, it can serve as a guide for the stopped note.

Try out the c^1 against the open g in this way [Ex. 146].
Try out the e^1 against the c^1 and then against the g [Ex. 147].
The same method should be used in similar passages.

---

3. Campagnoli, *Metodo* . . . (1797?), tr. Bishop, pt. I, no. 20.

Ex. 146

Ex. 147

General observations

Avoid changing the fingers or playing open and stopped notes (those played with the
finger) at the same time.

Ex. 148

(Viotti: Concerto no. 3)

In passages like the following, let the hand lie against the body of the violin and use
the same fingers.

Ex. 149

After having practised the exercises in all intervals, any music of the old masters
which involves double stopping should be studied, choosing the easiest first in order
to succeed gradually in playing pieces of this kind in modern music with the security
of intonation that their complexity makes more difficult.

(Baillot, *L'art. . .* (1834), p. 85)

Finally, mention should be made of two specialised double stopping fingerings; first, the *Überlegung* (otherwise known as *sopradito, croisé, la fausse quinte*)
fingering for diminished-fifth intervals (Ex. 150), which was employed
throughout the period (and still is nowadays) in order to avoid consecutive use
of the same finger, and secondly the technique of fingered octaves, discussed

Ex. 150

for the first time by Baillot[4] and commonly exploited by early-nineteenth-century virtuosi in order to avoid too frequent displacements of the hand and, probably, the continuous *glissandi* which might result from the other fingering ($\frac{1}{4} - \frac{1}{4} - \frac{1}{4}$) between each octave stop, and to gain greater accuracy of intonation.

THE 'THIRD SOUND' (TERZO SUONO)

Discovered by Tartini in 1714 and described fully in his *Trattato di musica* (1754),[5] the physiological phenomenon of the 'third sound' or difference tone, a note of different pitch provided by the inner ear when two loud notes are played simultaneously, was commonly employed as an aid to perfect intonation in double stopping, especially in the higher ranges of the instrument. The phenomenon is such that inaccuracy of double stopping is reflected most noticeably in any fluctuation or 'loss' of the more muffled, lower-pitched 'third sound', since its pitch is determined by the difference of the frequencies of the two notes stopped. In spite of its inestimable value, discussion of the 'third sound' is surprisingly neglected by most writers of the period; only Leopold Mozart, whose by no means flawless survey[6] doubtless was inspired by Tartini (the surveys of both writers include inaccuracies of pitch and/or register in some of their examples of this phenomenon), and, most notably, Baillot provide substantial explanations of the phenomenon, its consequences and examples of its application.

The 'third' sound

Whenever two notes are sounded together loudly, precisely in tune and sustained, the conjunction of resonant waves results in a third note whose pitch geometers and physicists have tried to determine, but so far this question cannot be considered as completely resolved.

We have noted a remarkable effect which we present here as an isolated fact while giving an example of how it can be used to best advantage; it is quite possible that one day it may form part of a general system such as the famous Tartini undertook to establish in accordance with his discovery of the 3rd note heard without any artificial means:

4. Baillot, *L'art* . . . (1834), p. 152. See ch. 5, p. 110.
5. An earlier description appeared in G. A. Sorge's *Vorgemach der musicalischen Composition* (1745–7).
6. L. Mozart, *Versuch* . . ., ch. 8, section 3, §20, pp. 190–2.

When a key 4 or 5 inches long and weighing about 2 ounces is placed on the belly of the violin, on the G string side, close to the bridge and in the line of the f-hole, and two notes are held together evenly and in tune, a third, low note can be heard very distinctly, such as indicated on the 2nd stave in the following examples:

Ex. 151

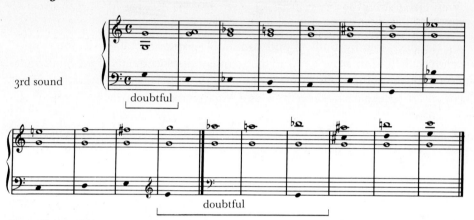

3rd sound

This '3rd sound' can be heard even better as one changes from the first interval to the second and as one returns from the second interval to the first, as the example below demonstrates:[7]

Ex. 152

Moderato

doubtful

7. There is no need to point out that the 'third sound' indicated on the 2nd stave presents here only isolated harmonies and not a harmonic progression. (Baillot's footnote)

While we were enumerating the various characters of timbre which the violin had the property of imitating, we said that it could evoke the harmonious gravity of the organ.

Double stopping is sufficient for this effect to give some idea of the kind of vibrations which distinguish the organ from all other instruments: by pressing the bow firmly on the strings and then bringing it slightly closer to the bridge, the sound takes on something of the *nasard* stop on the organ and the imitation becomes more exact if one can produce undulations in the sound with movements of the left hand. (See article on *undulating sounds*.)[8]

Ex. 153

(Fiorillo: Étude no. 29)

This piece, executed slowly and with full voice, lends itself by its style to the imitation of the organ and can conjure up several of the effects of that most majestic of instruments, which for so many centuries has always been the sublime vehicle of prayer.

Yet again one can find some reminiscence of its most veiled and gentle effects by the method of sustaining chords in *quadruple stopping*, as we have indicated in this example:

Ex. 154

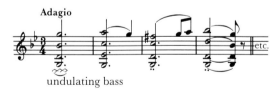

undulating bass

But if one wishes to attempt on the violin to evoke some measure of the power of the organ, success will be all the greater by means of the procedure of which we have been speaking, in that the rumbling occasioned by the movement of the key on the belly of the violin imitates the booming of the organ and in that this imitation can maintain the illusion for several moments, especially if one is playing in a somewhat resonant room.

8. See ch. 9, pp. 208–10.

Here is an example of this type of *effect*.

Ex. 155   **(Chant des Litanies)**

3rd sound

(Baillot, *L'art.* . . (1834), pp. 224–6).

MULTIPLE STOPPING

Due to the somewhat ambiguous and confusing nature of eighteenth- and early-nineteenth-century notation, especially with regard to rhythm, it was not always possible to execute many passages of triple and quadruple stopping literally as written,[9] for polyphony was generally notated in long note values, in order to clarify both the musical progression and the melodic and harmonic functions of the different voice parts. Thus, performers generally spread chords in sustained passages and chord series in triple and quadruple stopping and sustained the principal harmonic and melodic notes where possible for their full written values. However, those using the pre-1780s flatter bridge and pre-Tourte model convex bows (with their slacker tension) would most probably have been able to execute isolated triple stopping without audible arpeggiation, the bow spanning three strings when required without undue difficulty; furthermore, Baillot describes, although not as clearly as he might in the case of quadruple stopping, some interesting methods of sustaining triple and quadruple stopping without arpeggiation.

Triple stopping

In triple stopping, the bow should be placed close to the fingerboard on the D string

9. See Babitz, 'Differences between eighteenth-century and modern violin bowing', *The Score*, vol. 19 (1957), pp. 53–5, for examples (from J. S. Bach's solo sonatas and partitas) in which the exact performance of the written notation is impossible.

at the heel; as the strings are more flexible away from the bridge, it is sufficient to apply pressure to the string which we have just indicated and which is the most raised, for the two other strings to speak at the same time.

Ex. 156

(Baillot: Caprice no. 5)

(Baillot, L'art . . . (1834), p. 85)

Quadruple stopping

The four strings are frequently used in chords but only simultaneously in struck chords; they can be sustained on the violin only with the help of a very simple procedure which does not depart from the normal means of vibrating the strings. We believed that we ourselves had devised it many years ago, having made use of it in the *Adagio* below which was composed by us as an attempt at this procedure. But others having practised it since then, it can be concluded that this procedure was by its nature too much within reach of everyone not to have been discovered simultaneously by a number of people. There are some inventions (if such attempts can so be called) that appear before the player presented by necessity without having to be thought of. For this one perhaps it took only a detachment of the hair or a broken frog to give birth to the idea of remedying the first trouble and doing without the object of the second one by placing the bow stick beneath the violin and holding the ribbon of hair and the stick in the same hand, leaving the fingers positioned more or less as usual.

All the strings can thus be attacked together; one may play on only two or three strings as desired by raising or lowering the right hand. It is a means of giving variety to this kind of effect that is suitable above all to *Adagios* of a gentle, grave or mysterious character and can also be practised at a more or less lively speed.

We have heard some tests performed using this procedure that have not been badly received by the public but which have been confused later on with what is called *charlatanism*. If we understand this word properly, it can be applied only to things that do not correspond to what has been promised, to those things that deceive by an appearance of truth or talent contradicted by the outcome. Now there is clearly nothing in such a procedure that it would be unworthy of true talent to employ; it is of scant importance whether the hair be taut or slack, or whether the stick be placed under the violin instead of being over the strings; the essential thing is to please and to move by whatever means, as long as they contain nothing that is bad in principle or in its effect. The procedure in question enables sounds to be sustained on 4 strings at a time; therein lies the difference from the normal method; it thus offers one more advantage for genius to turn to good account. We are persuaded that in beautiful pieces of music of a calm religious character suited to this manner of playing and rendered with all the requisite nuances and expression, we have here a further technique to add to the effects of the violin and thus increase the charm of its harmony.

Ex. 157

Quadruple stopping for violin solo

(Baillot, *L'art* . . . (1834), pp. 227–8)

Otherwise, chords were spread either upwards or downwards, generally according to the register of the main melody note to be sustained, or played as arpeggios. Since they were generally taken in a down bow (even successions of chords, which involved re-taking the bow), on account of that stroke's greater power, rapid upward 'note-by-note' spreading was the more common practice, as indicated in Galeazzi's thorough if rather long-winded account, included in full later. The respective durations of the two outermost notes of the chord were left largely to the player's discretion, but when spreading the chord upwards, most players appear to have held the lowest note of the chord a little (indeed, in certain circumstances some went as far as holding it for its exact value),[10] presumably to emphasise the harmonic progression, before sounding the other chord members in a rapid cross-string movement; for if estab-

10. See Galeazzi extract quoted on pp. 154–61.

lished well and sounded on the beat, a bass note will stay long enough in the
ear, while the rest of the chord is spread to make harmonic and musical sense.
Interestingly enough, Habeneck defines the harmonic movement more precisely at the outset, sounding the two lowest notes of the chord on the beat, as
in Ex. 158.

Ex. 158

The rapid cross-string movement required for the execution of four-note
chords relied rather more on the use of the wrist than nowadays. Many
modern violinists argue that such independent movement of the hand in the
wrist joint weakens both the volume and quality of the chords. Consequently,
they opt for increased arm involvement, drawing the bow rapidly outwards
and slightly downwards (in a straight line) from the shoulder joint.

Not until Spohr's *Violinschule* is there any evidence of the modern practice of
breaking the chord upwards in twos where the lower two notes (played
together before the beat) are only of short duration while the upper two notes
(played together on the beat) are sustained for their full length. Spohr stresses
the importance of equating bow speed, length and pressure in order to
produce a clear, powerful tone with the full width of hair.

Ex. 159

At the four-part chord of the first bar the bow is placed close to the nut firmly on the
two lowest strings, then pulled down with strong pressure across the two highest ones
and now gently drawn right along to the point on these same two. Although the two
lowest notes are written as crotchets, the bow should not linger on them and their
duration should be a semiquaver's length at the most . . . The chords in crotchets in
the fifth and following bars, however, will all be taken with the down bow, close to the
nut, with strong bow pressure and full width of the hair, sounding [the notes] together
as much as possible in one brisk action and replacing the bow afresh for each [chord].
The bow strokes must not be too short, however, because the chords would then
become sharp and dry.   (Spohr, *Violinschule* (1832), p. 147)

ARPEGGIOS

Some chordal progressions were commonly interpreted as arpeggios, generally indicated by the word *arpeggio* or *arpeggiando* (although such arpeggiation
was not always designated, and its implementation and manner of arpeggiation was invariably left to the performer's discretion and good taste). This fact,
together with the technical skills of pure intonation, deft, flexible and skilful
bow management, equal distribution of the notes in each arpeggio and careful
observance of dynamics and the notes requiring special emphasis demanded
by arpeggios, accounts largely for the importance attached to their study.
Most writers of the period illustrate, either in compositions or in separate sections devoted to the device, a wide range of ways in which chordal passages
can be arpeggiated, embracing various styles and an assortment of bowings
(both slurred and unslurred). Galeazzi, who considers slurring in arpeggios
distasteful, nevertheless provides a notable survey of chord spreading and
arpeggiation, concentrating in particular on bowing, position-work and the
main principles of distributing the notes of the chord satisfactorily.

Of the arpeggio

211. Not content at having brought this instrument to such a degree of perfection
that they could play two parts comfortably at the same time, violinists still strove for
a way of playing three or four; but the unavoidable curvature of the bridge posed an
insuperable problem. The bridge is so made that the bow cannot contact more than
two strings at once and the player desirous of contacting three would have to press the
bow on the strings in such a way that the result would be a strident, harsh and
unbearable sound.

212. So what was to be done in such circumstances? They thought they would
manage to some extent by passing rapidly from one string to the next so that the ear
could scarcely perceive the succession of sounds and think them almost simultaneous, almost as the eye is deceived by children when they rapidly twirl a glowing coal,
which, although it passes through all the points of the circumference of a circle,
appears to the eye to make a continuous, uninterrupted movement. Such a way of
playing is practised on the harp more than on any other instrument, hence the term
arpeggio.

213. Two principal types of arpeggio can be distinguished. The simpler is called
botta or *strappata* by some performers while others call it by the more appropriate
name of *tricordo*. The *tricordo* is an aggregate of three strings or pitches and sometimes
even four (which could then more properly be called *quadricordo* or, after the Greek,
tetracordo). The arpeggio is differentiated from other ways of playing in that each of the
notes of an arpeggio must be situated on a different string; so, if it is desired to arpeg-
giate them, some passages which could be played on two strings must be arranged
and played on at least three strings, otherwise there can be no arpeggio.

214. The manner of bowing the *botta* or *tricordo* is to place the bow firmly on the
bottom string and then, drawing very little bow, lower it suddenly and strike all three
or four strings with a firm, vibrant, short and resolute stroke. Sometimes some *tricordi*
are indicated in white notes, that is, minims and even in semibreves; then the rule is

to hold the bottom note for its correct length and at its very end make the usual quick stroke to sound the others. Moreover, in order to play any arpeggio, all the fingers must be placed at once in their respective positions and not successively as each note is played by the bow.

215. It might be profitable for the reader to find here a series of the most usual principal *tricordi* or *botte* which are played by the violin in *orchestral* music, which is less contrived than that for *solo*. Whoever practises the exercises in this table will be prepared for playing any *tricordo* or *botta* that may occur. And we are all the more eager to present them here in the most usual keys, so that they can also be of greatest benefit to those composers who do not play the violin and therefore sometimes write those useless and awkward combinations of notes which are at times impossible to play. We have arranged these *botte* not only for the tonic of the key but also for the dominant seventh which is used very often.

Ex. 160

216. As the arpeggio is one of the strangest techniques of the art, its [mastery] is indeed a triumph of bowing for whoever understands the most intricate combinations. Its types are so varied that it seems impossible to reduce them to a system and to give them some order; however, we will reduce them to three categories, according to the [bowing] differences that seem most natural, and these are *arpeggi sciolti*, *arpeggi legati*, and *arpeggi misti*.

217. The major difficulty in arpeggios is found in the abbreviations to which they are reduced; they are written so intricately by composers that it is necessary to guess or to possess magic powers to decipher and understand them. For the sake of beginners, we shall attempt as usual with a multitude of examples (since this is the surest way) to make these abbreviations as clear and brief as possible and to give the most precise idea of them.

218. When e^2 or a^1 is seen in an arpeggio, one must always suspect that these notes should be sounded open, which makes it extremely difficult to find the correct position for it. The difficulty is further increased if these same notes are duplicated, because often some are open while others will be stopped. In this case, only wide experience and, above all, some acquaintance with the style of the composer whose compositions one desires to perform will properly help understanding.

219. When a composer wishes an arpeggio to be performed in a given manner and no other, or desires to convey his exact intention to others, he must then write it out in full on the first beat or half bar or sometimes even in a whole bar and then abbreviate the remainder with *segue* written underneath. Then it is perfectly clear that an arpeggio is intended; if it is so notated at the beginning, its bowing, as well as the disposition of the notes, is to be continued throughout the same passage. In order to understand the abbreviations, it is necessary to observe that in every arpeggio there are some changing and some fixed notes; the former notes change for the most part on every crotchet and are indicated with short values such as crotchets or quavers. The stable notes are generally indicated in longer values such as minims or semibreves. These latter values do not indicate, as previously, that they must be sounded for their exact length, which would be impossible after what was said in paragraph 211; it means only that the fingers on these notes must be kept on the strings for their full duration. Here is an example of an *arpeggio sciolto* in which there are changing and fixed notes, which we will explain in detail.[11]

Ex. 161

The first bar is clear enough; there is nothing to mention other than that the a^1 must be stopped with the fourth finger so that the arpeggio, according to its own definition, is taken on three strings. The second bar is merely a replica of the first. In the first half there are two variable and two fixed notes. The two variable notes, a^1 and g^1, change by the quarter bar but since the two notes above, c^2 and e^2 are common for the first half of the bar, they are indicated with minims, although in performance the c^2 is really sounded four times and the e^2 is sounded twice. The same occurs in the other half of the bar where f^1 and d^1 change at each crotchet whilst the third finger must

11. Habeneck, in his *Méthode* . . . (c. 1840), p. 136, uses this very same example for his discussion of arpeggiation.

remain firm throughout the half bar to stop d^2 and a^2. In the third bar there are two variable series, d^3, c^3, b^2, a^2; b^1, a^1, g^1, f^1, while d^2 always remains stable. This finger would never be raised from its placement if the change of position in the middle of the bar did not compel it to stop the first half [of the note value] with the first finger and the other half with the third. The rest of the example is interpreted in the same way.

220. So three things must be observed in an arpeggio: the [finger] position, the disposition or the order of the notes and the strings, and the bowing. With regard to the latter (when the arpeggio is so indicated), if the indication is for separate bows, it should be continued separated; if it is slurred, it is continued with the same bowing that is prescribed at the beginning.

221. In arpeggios, the [hand] position is also deduced from the outer strings, a consideration which was previously neglected because open strings can be most deceptive. For this reason we shall take for consideration the arpeggio in Ex. [162],

Ex. 162

which is one of the most difficult in this genre, and this is how I go about finding its position. In the first two bars I find e^2 duplicated, which tells me or, at least, gives me a strong suspicion (§218) that one is open and the other stopped. In any case, then, I already have one e^2 as an open string. Because of the nature of an arpeggio (§213), the remaining e^2 and g^2 must be fingered one on the A string and the other on the D. Consequently, I must find the position in which this arpeggio is possible. If I finger g^2 on the D string, I will not have e^2 under my hand, hence this is not the correct position. I then finger e^2 on the D string and I find g^2 on the A string under my hand. To make certain that this is the position, it only remains to determine which fingers are to stop the two notes. Although g^2 seems at first glance to be the higher note, it is clear that e^2 on the D string becomes a third higher than g^2 on the A string. Since e^2 is the very note closer to the higher positions, I must finger it with the fourth finger, which is the 'highest' and so I find myself in the fifth position. Having thus found the position for the first beat of the bar, I must be careful not to shift the hand unnecessarily. So, we shall see whether the second beat can be fingered without shifting. One e^2 remains open and the other e^2 is under my fourth finger as the stable note. I sound open a^1 in the middle, hence all remains at ease without shifting. I go on to the second bar. On the first beat I find g^1, a^1, e^2, e^2. The last three are unchanged so they remain as before; only g^1 is variable, which is under the third finger on the G string. By substituting the first finger, I find the last quarter of the bar. We come to the third bar and here is the problem. I cannot finger a^3 in the fifth position where I am, so I must shift, but to where? The highest and lowest notes here are a^3 and d^1, but in the table of positions (§104) there is no position that has such a range, which makes me suspect that the d¹ is open, and so in this case the limits of the position in my passage are no longer d¹ (lowest) and a³ (highest) but rather f sharp¹ (lowest) and a³ (highest). But the sixth position which starts on f sharp¹, terminates, according to Table IV [in Galeazzi's §104] on g³. Thus it is clear that, by extending the fourth finger, I will find the position sought. Now it remains to determine the fingering of the other notes, d¹, f sharp¹, a¹: a¹ is stable so it remains open; d¹ is also open, which was established above; hence f sharp¹ will be stopped with the first finger on the G string, and so the first crotchet beat is fingered. In the second crotchet beat I have the open d¹ and a¹ both unchanged with the highest a³, hence the hand remains inactive holding down only the fourth finger. The following bar is a replica of this bar, and the following four bars are replicas of those previously fingered. So we shall move on to bar 11. From bars 11 to 14 inclusive I find a¹ unchanged and consequently always open; f sharp¹ is stopped with the second finger on the G string and e² with the fourth on the D string, then the following d² is stopped with the third finger and, continuing in this way, the hand shifts gradually downward to the first position, which is very obvious, in bar 15. We shall later return to discuss bar 15; but note for the moment that this arpeggio is executed with separate bows.

222. Having found the position for an arpeggio, one must seek its disposition, that is, the order in which the notes or strings must follow each other, for which the following general rules are established.

Rule I

223. In *arpeggi sciolti* and *legati* disposed across three strings but which must be executed in four bow strokes, the first stroke is for the note on the lowest string, the second is for the note on the string in the middle, the third is for the note on the highest string and the fourth stroke repeats the note on the middle string. If one starts on the highest string this order is reversed.

Illustration

Skipping over strings with the bow hampers uniformity and makes the arpeggios coarse; in addition, it is very awkward. Consequently, one must seek the means to bow neighbouring strings successively. However, the order expounded in the rule is the most natural without skipping over any string and always passing successively from one to another neighbouring string as is apparent when playing; consequently:

Rule II

224. If the *arpeggio sciolto* or *legato* is fingered on four strings and is to be performed in as many bow strokes, it will be necessary to bow the notes two by two, that is, always bowing two at a time so that the last stroke includes the D string.

Illustration

As the *arpeggi sciolti* or *legati* must naturally always start from the outer strings, it is obvious that if one note at a time were bowed, we would find ourselves on the opposite string side at the last stroke, hence the next bow stroke would have to step over two strings to return to the original G or E string, which, as we said in the preceding 'illustration', is coarse and very awkward. However, if the first bow stroke sounds the G and D strings, the second the D and A strings, the third the A and E strings, and the

fourth again the A and D strings, we shall be next to the G string for the following
bow stroke without any skipping or likely inconvenience. The same will be true if we
start on the E and A strings etc. For greater clarity, Ex. [163] shows how an *arpeggio
sciolto*, which is to be bowed in semiquavers, can be distributed across the strings two
by two, starting either from the two lower strings or from the two upper strings, the
choice being left to the performer.[12]

Ex. 163

Yet here is another example [Ex. 164] of an *arpeggio sciolto* which we will give so that
the beginner can better learn to decipher these problems of the instrument. It can be
seen in this example that it is enough to play double stops on the first bow only in
four-string arpeggios to achieve what one wants.

Ex. 164

225. Let us pass on to *arpeggi legati*, which make up the second type, but these are
almost all trivial, commonplace, and in bad taste. Although once much used, they are
now considered insufferable by those of good taste; unless they are executed with
undulating bow, in which case they are difficult but also create a fine effect. Here are
two examples written out in full without abbreviations (Exx. [165 & 166]) for greater
comprehension. The first is slurred eight notes to a bow, down, then up, and the second is slurred only three to a bow, as indicated.

Ex. 165

Ex. 166

12. It will not be difficult to discover that this arpeggio is fingered in the fifth position if one will realise
    that the two 'extremities' are e[1], which must be stopped on the G string because of the very nature of
    the arpeggio, and a[2], which must be stopped on the A string, because e[2], as the stable note, must be
    played as an open E string. It is obvious that such an arrangement between the G and A strings lies
    only in the fourth and fifth positions, but in the fourth position the fourth finger has to be used too
    often; therefore the fifth position will be more convenient. (Galeazzi's footnote)

226. However, there is a bowing which produces a marvellous effect so little known that I have not found anyone who has been able to guess what it is without seeing it written out. Since it is so very unusual and unique of its kind, I willingly publish it here for the greater satisfaction of enthusiasts and serious students, adapting it for an arpeggio [section] inserted in the first fugue of Corelli's Op. V. It can be adapted for all cases by performing it, as is seen (Ex. [167]), with five notes to a bow, regularly down and up; this bowing can also be adapted to four-string arpeggios, seven notes to a stroke, distributing the arpeggio in septuplets (may I be permitted this new term since I cannot find an equivalent elsewhere). Here is a short example to make my meaning clear (Ex. [168]).[13]

Ex. 167

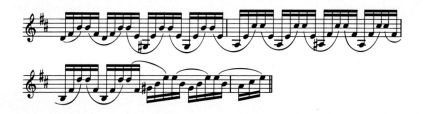

Ex. 168

227. Finally, we come to the most varied and sophisticated kind of arpeggio, called *misto* [mixed] because it is composed of separate and slurred notes. The varieties of this arpeggio are innumerable. As usual we shall be content to show the best, the most common and most tasteful instances, leaving the field free for the industrious performer to find for himself, guided by these, thousands of other unusual combinations so that he may wander freely through such a vast supply to the extent of his talent. So we shall give some examples in groups of three, four and six notes; we shall restrain ourselves, however, from exceeding our proposed limits. We shall first notate them *in full*, then with their corresponding abbreviations, so that such abbreviations can become familiar, since they are generally so notated in the works of those who do not want their exact intentions and manner of bowing revealed. We shall also designate the positions so that the beginner can find them more easily (see Ex. [169]).

228. Here is the place to explain bar 15 of §90 (Ex. [162]). The four notes of the first arpeggio and the first f^2 of the following triplet are bowed down and the two remaining notes are bowed separately as they come. This will produce a very elaborate and highly effective bowing. The two separate notes may also be bowed *picchettare* [slurred staccato] if it is so desired.

---

13. The unusual notation should not seem strange; since all these notes must be given equal value, I cannot find any better expression. (Galeazzi's footnote)

Ex. 169

(Galeazzi, *Elementi . . .* (1791), art. 14, pp. 181–90)

By way of contrast, Baillot's rather more concise survey achieves a fine balance between technical method and musical effect.

Arpeggios

Arpeggios are so called because they sound the notes of a chord one after the other, like a harp.

Arpeggios. Method of execution:

1. *Arpeggios* must be played in general with the middle and even the heel of the bow when their character requires that they should be played *sautillé*.

If one is using a bow that is somewhat heavy at the point, this condition is not necessary since the point will then rebound easily: nevertheless, it should be noted that by using the middle or the heel, the movement made by the wrist when changing from the lower strings to the E string is smaller and this method is consequently preferable.

2. When playing arpeggios one needs the utmost suppleness in the wrist, and one should avoid the slightest involvement of the elbow and upper arm, which must stay without any direct movement when the right hand changes from the lower strings to the E string and from the E string to the lower strings.

3. Most arpeggios should be played with the utmost lightness.

4. In certain arpeggios the low notes should be accentuated most particularly, and in others they should be played out full and roundly.

5. One should pick out an *effect* in them, that is to say something which stands out above everything else. This effect can be produced by emphasising the bass notes and playing the other notes *piano*, by bringing out the melody in the top part, by varying the bow, or indeed by executing all the arpeggios as evenly as possible.

Here are some examples:

Arpeggios

The simplest arpeggios

Ex. 170

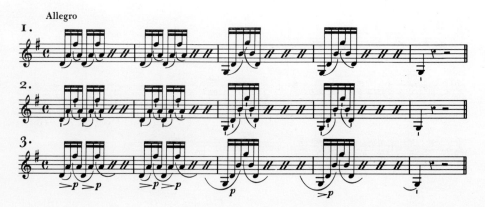

Effects for arpeggios

Emphasise the high detached note and pass at once to the lower note without a break [Ex. 171].

Ex. 171

(Viotti: Concerto no. 13)

Emphasise the 2 high notes quickly and loudly [Ex. 172].

Ex. 172

(Kreutzer: Concerto in F)

Emphasise the low notes fully and make the demisemiquaver fast and accentuated as well as the following note [Ex. 173].

Ex. 173

(Rode: Concerto no. 8)

In the first section [Ex. 174] accentuate the low notes fully and firmly and [play] the other notes *pianissimo*.

In the second section, throw away the first high note quickly and very lightly, make the low notes and all the rest so *piano* that they can barely be heard.

Ex. 174

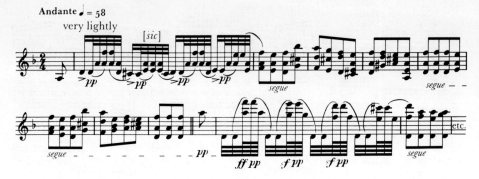

(Baillot: Air and Variations Op. 24)

All the notes very even and extremely clear. [Ex. 175].

Ex. 175

(Habeneck, sen.: Tyrolean Variations)

All the notes even and very light, whether slurred or *staccato* [Ex. 176].

Ex. 176

(de Bériot: Air and Variations Op. 3)

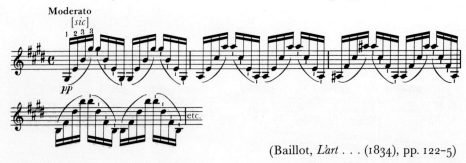

(Baillot, *L'art* . . . (1834), pp. 122–5)

Naturally, the technique involved in the execution of multiple stopping incorporates problems of both left and right hands. Sparing use of the bow was invariably encouraged both for purposes of articulation and for the avoidance of an unwanted arrival at the point for any subsequent passage-work. For reasons of economy in hand and finger movement and greater sonority, open strings were generally employed wherever possible in multiple stopping, which in many cases involved awkward extensions or contractions of the hand. Great finger agility was also required in the execution of a succession of chords and the thumb was sometimes, if only rarely, employed to aid the execution of multiple stops; it generally replaced the first finger on the lowest string when that finger was required on a higher string in certain quadruple stops, as illustrated in Ex. 177, in which 'the G sharp in the first bar . . . should be stopped with the tip of the thumb'.[14] Paganini is believed to have used a similar ploy, which requires great agility and suppleness of the fingers and wrist.[15] Furthermore, Guhr especially emphasises the force with which Paganini held the violin in the execution of passages of sustained triple stopping such as those in Ex. 178. In the execution of the latter example and in quadruple stopping, Paganini was most certainly aided by his use of a flatter bridge, which enabled him to attack chords in such a way that little or no arpeggio effect was audible. Guhr adds weight to this assumption by remarking that, for the execution of strong and drawn-out chords, Paganini used the lower part of the bow and raised the hand and lower part of the arm somewhat higher, bringing his elbow away from his body.[16]

Ex. 177

Ex. 178

14. Petri, *Anleitung* . . . (1767), pt. 3, p. 409. Other well-known eighteenth-century violinists who employed the thumb in this way include Louis Francœur and Jean-Marie Leclair *l'aîné*.
15. See de Saussine, *Paganini le magicien*, tr. Laurie, p. 175; *The Harmonicon*, July 1831.
16. Guhr, *Ueber Paganinis Kunst* . . . (1829), §4, p. 9.

8

Bow strokes and their execution

The various eighteenth-century developments in bow construction and the consequent wide variety of bow types employed complicate considerably any attempt at a comprehensive review of bow strokes and their execution throughout the period. However, it seems perfectly feasible to divide these myriad bow types into two broad categories – pre-Tourte models (embracing the 'Corelli' and 'Tartini' types and all varieties with a pike's head) and Tourte models (including the Tourte, Cramer, Viotti and Dodd types and all varieties with a distinct hatchet head) – and to consider the bowing vocabulary of each category during roughly the years of its greatest influence. In this connection, given that universal approval of the Tourte design was inevitably slow to materialise, the period under consideration can be divided conveniently and justifiably into two 'artificial' sections of roughly forty years each (c. 1760 – c. 1800 and c. 1800 – c. 1840), for it was not until the *Méthode* . . . (1803) of Rode *et al*. – and even then not comprehensively – that bow management relevant to the Tourte bow was examined in any textual detail.

STROKES WITH PRE-TOURTE-MODEL BOWS (C. 1760 – C. 1800)

The number of different bow strokes employed c. 1760 was small and their discussion sparse compared with the wide range afforded by the Tourte bow and the detailed description provided by many early-nineteenth-century authors. Since there is no sufficiently comprehensive late-eighteenth-century survey that warrants independent inclusion here nor any universally accepted terminology or notation, a cross-section of writers' opinions is provided below under general categories of bow strokes relevant to the contemporary violinist's technique and equipment.

SEPARATE STROKES

The normal stroke with the pre-Tourte bow was an articulated *non-legato* stroke, due both to the characteristics of the bow itself and to the manner of holding and drawing the bow. The degree of articulation could be varied by the player and the expression of the stroke could also be modified by the application of nuances appropriate to the length of the note, tempo and the character of the music,[1] as well as by the regulation of bow speed, the point of contact and the pressure used. A considerable variety of effects could thus be obtained from modification of the basic bow stroke. The general vocabulary of separate bow strokes gradually increased in step with the aesthetic conventions of the period and developments in the design and construction of the bow.

Two complementary types of separate stroke, the *brisure* and *batterie*, are worthy of special mention here for the scope they offered in varying passage-work. Employed more commonly at the beginning of our period than later, both strokes required suppleness and agility of the right hand for their optimum execution, the *brisure* (Ex. 179) involving bowing alternately on non-adjacent strings and the *batterie* (Ex. 180) requiring the alternate use of adjacent strings.[2]

Ex. 179

Ex. 180

1. See L. Mozart, *Versuch . . .*, ch. 12, §18, p. 262; Quantz, *Versuch . . .*, tr. and ed. Reilly, ch. 17, section 3, §9, p. 239.
2. See Boyden, *The history of violin playing . . .*, p. 406, for various contemporary definitions of these terms.

STACCATO

The eighteenth-century *staccato* or *stoccato* stroke (virtually synonymous then with the term *spiccato*) ws totally different from modern *staccato* strokes, such as *martelé*, *spiccato*, *sautillé* and other 'thrown' bowings. The pre-Tourte bow was not ideally suited to these latter strokes, for the bow hair and stick lacked the elasticity needed for instantaneous and strong attack. The eighteenth-century *staccato* took the form rather of a certain breath or articulation between notes, somewhat greater than the articulation of the normal bow stroke; this articulation was conveyed in many cases by lifting the bow from the string, especially in slow tempos (in fast movements the bow necessarily remained on the string in the upper half, producing an effect similar to modern *spiccato*), and implied the use of a dry, detached stroke in the lower part of the bow with some feeling of accent but without the sharp attack of the modern *staccato*.

L'Abbé le fils describes this articulated stroke as *détaché* (indicated), a term generally applied to a smooth, separate bow stroke on the string from the early nineteenth century onwards; however, it can also mean 'detached'. Rousseau describes the *détaché* stroke as 'a manner of execution in which, instead of sustaining the notes for their full value, one separates them by silences making up this same value. The quite short and dry *détaché* is indicated on the notes by long dots.'[3] Other terms (*puntato, pointer* etc.) and notation signs (• or ᵛ or ᵛᵛ) were also used to denote the *staccato* stroke and, in some instances, the actual style of the music or context dictated such an interpretation.[4] Nevertheless, contemporary notation for *staccato* effects is confusing, each sign adopting a different and often undefined meaning according to either author or printer.

Few eighteenth-century writers emulate Leopold Mozart and Quantz[5] in their discussions of *staccato* technique but Campagnoli is one notable exception, explaining its execution and uses thus:

This kind of bowing must be made with the point of the bow, and be forcibly articulated. It serves as a contrast to sustained melody and, when judiciously employed, is productive of great effect.

This bowing is also used in triplets. In order to mark it thoroughly, and yet not in a harsh or dry manner, each note must be smartly detached, by attacking the string with vivacity and using sufficient bow to produce a round and full tone. It is also necessary that the notes be perfectly equal as compared with each other; this will be attained by giving greater force to the note played with the up bow, which is naturally more difficult to mark than that played with the down bow.

(Campagnoli, *Metodo* . . . (1797?), tr. Bishop, pt. I, no. 41)

Many writers fail to explain that the manner of performing the *staccato* depends on the tempo of the music; only Quantz, Reichardt and a few other

3. *Dictionnaire de musique*, ed. Rousseau, s.v. 'Détaché'.
4. See L. Mozart, *Versuch* . . ., ch. 1, section 3, §10, p. 39.
5. *Ibid.*, ch. 7, pp. 122–35; Quantz, *Versuch* . . ., tr. and ed. Reilly, ch. 17, section 2, §27, p. 232.

writers acknowledge tempo as a vital factor.[6] Thus, ♩♩♩♩ in moderate tempo was executed ♪♩♪♩♪♩♪♩, with the bow being lifted from the string after each stroke, its motion being controlled by the wrist and fingers. In faster tempos the bow was inevitably kept on the string, the pre-Tourte bow generally producing an effect similar to modern *spiccato*. German writers appear to have adopted a definite terminology to indicate the type of *staccato* stroke required; the terms *gestossen* (or *abgestossen*), *tockiert* or *abgesondert* generally indicate a detached stroke without the bow being lifted, whereas *abgesetzt*, *aufheben* or *erheben* imply the use of a lifted stroke.[7]

ACCENTED BOWINGS

Most pre-Tourte bows were not ideally suited to the production of accented bowings (*martelé*, *sforzandi*, accents and the like), which were used, if at all, only rarely in the modern sense during the eighteenth century. The pre-Tourte bow's inability to distribute hand/index-finger pressure evenly throughout its length or to maintain the width of hair constant, together with its fundamental lightness at the tip rendered it unsuitable for *martelé* bowing, which was generally executed at the point. Tartini confirms the pre-Tourte models' limitations in the distribution of hand/index-finger pressure:

> To draw a beautiful tone from the instrument, place the bow on the strings gently at first and then increase the pressure. If the full pressure is applied immediately, a harsh, scraping sound will result.   (Tartini, *Traité* . . ., ed. Jacobi, p. 56)

Leopold Mozart's indication *fp* (Ex. 181) perhaps most closely approximates the modern *martelé*, but without the latter's biting attack, while Woldemar and Labadens, with bows approximating to the Tourte design, both mention the *martelé* stroke but omit discussion of its execution.

Ex. 181

'THROWN' BOWINGS

Evidence surprisingly suggests that such 'thrown' bowings as *sautillé*, *spiccato* and 'flying *staccato*' were used by virtuosi in *bravura* passages throughout the eighteenth century, the practice being limited to rare occasions in the first half

6. Quantz, *Versuch* . . ., tr. and ed. Reilly, ch. 17, section 2, §7, p. 232; Reichardt, *Ueber die Pflichten* . . . (1776), p. 25.
7. L. Mozart, *Versuch* . . ., ch. 1, section 3, §20, p. 45 & ch. 1, section 3, p. 49, 'Musical technical terms'.

of the century but increasing in step with the developments in bow making, especially with the superior elasticity of the Tourte bow and similar transitional models. Since such 'thrown' bowings were employed only at virtuoso levels during the eighteenth century, they are rarely mentioned in contemporary violin methods; however, Woldemar makes a fleeting reference to *ricochet* bowing within a *col legno* context, recommending the player 'to let the bow stick bounce'[8] (Ex. 182).

Ex. 182

Accompaniment: imitation of the Psalterium by Michael Esser

Lightly hit all notes in the same place with the bow stick.

LEGATO STROKES

Although the normal stroke with the pre-Tourte bow was an articulated *non-legato* stroke, the *cantabile* aims of mid-eighteenth-century theorists gradually encouraged violinists to reproduce *legato* bowings and effects in imitation of the human voice. L'Abbé le fils's use of finger movement to effect a smooth bow change and the contemporary developments in bow design and construction undoubtedly helped to modify the articulated stroke in such a way that it could approximate the modern *legato*, but true *legato* bowing with pre-Tourte models was achieved only by slurring, as Galeazzi confirms:

Rule IV

263. In an *Adagio*, the aim must be above all to play with uniformity of tone not only with the [left] hand but also with the bowing as *legato* as possible. The violin must always sing in an *Adagio* (this is where the greatest attempt must be made to imitate the human voice) and consequently the bow must never be lifted from the strings; on the contrary, it is kept in contact with the strings and (except for the rule in §147)[9] is not allowed to dance about as in an *Allegro*.

Illustration and Observations

There is nothing more difficult than to play a *cantabile* [passage] slowly and well; this is the test of a teacher's skill. There are some who in an *Allegro* will astonish you with

8. Woldemar, *Grande méthode* . . . (c. 1800), p. 48.
9. This rule concerns the cultivation of firm, yet articulated bowing through the release of bow pressure between strokes.

their *bravura*, speed and agility of the left hand and bow but who in an *Adagio* will anger, annoy and bore you and make you hope that at any moment they will finish their wearisome dirge. However, on the other hand, when it is well played, the very style will penetrate our hearts, overcome and take possession of us. But how difficult it is to do this! A volume a thousand times larger than this would barely suffice to present a thesis of all the thoughts that may be expressed concerning a *cantabile* [passage]. This is one of those subjects about which it is better to say nothing than not to say enough, so we will restrict ourselves to making the observation that in a *cantabile* [passage] the song of the human voice must be imitated as closely as possible. If the voice is not to be thought asthmatic or broken, smooth bow changes must be made in order that the melody emerges united and not broken, nor left with those always irritating and unnatural gaps; this unity can be obtained by changing the bow as little as possible and, now and then, by bowing the entire musical idea in only one stroke. In fact, not a little skill is required in changing the bow so that the change may be scarcely discernible.   (Galeazzi, *Elementi* . . . (1791), vol. 1, pt. 2, pp. 201–2)

SLURRED BOWINGS

The Legato slur

The *cantabile* ideals of mid-eighteenth-century theorists led to the increased exploitation of slurred bowings, whether or not so notated, in order to equate the singing qualities of the instrument with those of the human voice, especially in slow movements. Furthermore, the capacity of the slur was enlarged considerably, as Galeazzi confirms:

157. *Legare* or to slur notes means to sound many notes in the same bow stroke without ever raising the bow from the strings and to play them all together and evenly in only one bow . . .

Rule VIII

158. From 2 to 128 notes can be slurred together in only one bow stroke. To slur well one must be careful to conduct the bow uniformly and with great equality as well as to play evenly and correctly all the notes which are slurred. The bow must be released from the string between slurs.

Illustration

The last part of the rule is the only part that requires illustration. Inasmuch as sometimes two, four, six, etc. little slurs of two, three, or four notes are performed all in one bow stroke, it is necessary to lift the bow from the string between slurs, or else each of the shorter slurs would not be heard individually but only as one slur of four, six or eight notes. If, however, the short slurs are played with different strokes, it is obvious that the bow must be released.   (Galeazzi, *Elementi* . . . (1791), vol. 1, pt. 2, p. 156)

   With the general trend towards increased use of *legato* slurred bowing and the enlarged capacity of the slur, the main technical problem was that of dividing the bow according to the tempo, the number of notes to be slurred and their respective dynamic and values.[10] Problems arose, too, with the countless examples of non-uniform slurring notated in autograph manuscripts of the period. Many of Haydn's symphonies are prime cases in point, such lack of uniformity possibly being intentional for reasons of variety and contrast.[11] The development of the Tourte bow further encouraged and greatly facilitated the execution of long phrases involving many notes under a single slur on account of its greater length and ability to distribute pressure evenly throughout.

Bariolage and Ondeggiando

Bariolage, essentially a nineteenth-century term to describe the alternation of notes on adjacent strings, one of which is usually open (Ex. 183), was com-

Ex. 183

monly employed in the eighteenth century, executed either in separate or, more usually, slurred bowing. However, the manner of executing *bariolage*, requiring great flexibility of the wrist and forearm, is not discussed by eighteenth-century writers.

Ondeggiando bowing, similar to *bariolage*, suffered similar textual neglect, despite its common usage, perhaps more so in the first half of the eighteenth century than later (Ex. 184).

Ex. 184

Slurred staccato (le coup d'archet articulé, staccato martellement, notes piquées, Pikiren, Pichettato etc.)

The variety and ambiguity of eighteenth-century notation makes it impossible to reconstruct exactly how slurred *staccato* was performed in specific contexts, but the manner of performance was necessarily governed by the tempo and character of the music. In the eighteenth century, it appears that dots

10. See p. 301.
11. See Barnett, 'Non-uniform slurring in 18th-century music: accident or design?', *Haydn Year Book* vol. 10 (1979), pp. 179–99.

were generally employed under the notes in movements of slow tempo, indicating that the passage should be played on the string rather like a *portato*; strokes under the notes were more common in faster tempos and generally indicated playing in 'lifted' style.[12] However, such a general rule was by no means without exception; L'Abbé le fils, for example, includes numerous *roulades*, slurred in various combinations, using dots under the slurs (Ex. 185), but no such differentiation is discussed or even mentioned by him or his successors.

Ex. 185

When the notes of a *roulade* are slurred, one should begin playing it at half strength and swell the tone as one approaches the last note, which must have the brightest tone; if the *roulade* is not slurred, its tone must be increased, observing the same gradation; but when the notes of a *roulade* or some other brilliant passage are all slurred together in twos, threes etc. and there is a dot on each of these notes, this latter manner of notation indicates the *coup d'archet articulé*; in order to perform this bow stroke well, the wrist should be very free and independent and should articulate each of these notes perfectly evenly, whether with an up or a down bow.

(L'Abbé le fils, Principes . . . (1761), p. 54)

Campagnoli's description of the slurred *staccato* is particularly interesting as three types of *pichettato* stroke are distinguished, the first approximating to L'Abbé le fils's stroke described above; the remaining two resemble the modern 'flying *staccato*', profiting no doubt from the greater resilience of Tourte-like bows, which were becoming increasingly popular in the last decade of the eighteenth century.

The *staccato* style of bowing consists in detaching several notes in the same stroke of the bow. The principle of it is the same as that of the detached bowing (*martelé*); that is, it must be made with the point of the bow, without suffering the latter to quit the string, with this difference, however, that here the least possible length of bow must be used, in order that the notes may be clearly articulated. The first and last note must here also be marked with firmness.

In the *staccato*, all stiffness must be avoided. The bow must have room to play in the hand, and the thumb must be pressed only lightly on the stick. The best way of acquiring this kind of bowing is to practise it slowly and arrest the bow at every note.

2nd manner. The *pichettato* may also be produced by articulating the notes with little movements of the wrist and the fingers, on the stick of the bow, the arm being kept stiff, while the bow is made to skip upon the strings with the greatest lightness, and always in the middle of it.[13]

---

12. Boyden, *The history of violin playing* . . ., p. 416.
13. Galeazzi (*Elementi* . . . (1791), vol. i, pt. 2, p. 157) believes Tartini to be the creator of this stroke, hence its nickname *Note Tartiniate*; it is generally employed in scalic or other such passages of stepwise movement with either an up or a down bow.

3rd manner. The *pichettato* may likewise be made by keeping the bow at an equilibrium, and giving it liberty to skip upon the strings without stopping it. It must be conducted by very slight, elastic movements of the wrist and of the fingers on the stick. This manner may be acquired by practising it, at first, with two notes in a down bow, and two in an up bow; then with 4 and 4, 6 and 6, 8 and 8, on the same string, and with the middle of the bow.

(Campagnoli, *Metodo* . . . (1797?), tr. Bishop, pt. 2, no. 116)

German virtuosi such as Schmelzer, Biber and Walther had developed the slurred *staccato* to a surprising degree prior to the period under scrutiny, Walther's thirty-two notes under a slur (Ex. 186) being a prime example which

Ex. 186

(Walther: *Hortulus Chelicus*)

few violinists matched until the advent of the Tourte bow and the rise of the nineteenth-century virtuoso. Contrary to Leopold Mozart's general principle that the slurred *staccato*, indicated by strokes (Ex. 187), should be played with a 'lifted' bow, most contemporary writers emphasise that the bow should not

Ex. 187

leave the string in the execution of slurred *staccato* bowing. Nevertheless, the lifted stroke remained an important articulation tool, Viotti suggesting that 'at each note the bow should be lifted above the string',[14] whilst L'Abbé le fils explains:

When one finds two notes tied with the ordinary sign, and also separated by a little stroke; example: ♪♪ ♪ ♪ , the slur indicates that the two notes should be taken in the same bow and the little stroke that the bow should be lifted after the first note, which in this case should be played with a full tone; then the short note can be attacked with greater or less force according to the expression one wishes to give it.
Note: It is of no consequence whether these two notes are played in a down bow or an up bow; thus, if they occur readily in a down bow, the student must not attempt to play them in an up bow in order to avoid a down bow on the short note; but he should, on the contrary, take advantage of this opportunity to practise expression on a short note as often with a down bow as with an up bow; although I have said that in principle one should play the short notes in an up bow, there are exceptions to this.

(L'Abbé le fils, *Principes* . . . (1761), p. 10).

14. Here quoted from Habeneck, *Méthode* . . . (c. 1840), p. 26.

Furthermore, the lifted stroke was commonly employed in the execution of a sequence of dotted rhythms such as ♩. ♪ ♩. ♪ , where both notes were generally taken in the same stroke.[15] Lifting the bow after dotted notes and delaying the following short note was a characteristic form of double-dotting described by Quantz and others, especially in respect of French music. Löhlein explains (Ex. 188):

Ex. 188

Here all the dots must be held for half as long again as they are actually written. The following note will then be played correspondingly shorter to allow for the extra length of the dot.

It is possible to play each of these figures in a separate bow, but they will then sound somewhat lame and halting, however smooth the bowing. It is better, therefore, to take these notes two to a bow. The first note with the dot must be played with a long, powerful stroke, since one amplifies the sound in the middle and makes a little *vibrato* with the finger; on the following short note the bow, having come almost to its end with the preceding long note, is raised a very little, so that the sound disappears only until one plays the short note, still with the end of the bow, quite short and clear. Then after this short jerk the full bow is started again on the next long note. These figures need to be practised very diligently if they are to be played coherently; for anything clumsy spoils the effect of a sad melody. They are always a stumbling-block for inexperienced players.

At * the figure is written out as it is to be played in all other similar cases.

(Löhlein, *Anweisung* . . . (1774) ch. 11, pp. 80–1)

The 'Viotti' bowing

The so-called 'Viotti' bowing, related to the slurred *staccato*, was apparently commonly employed during the period by Viotti and his imitators (Ex. 189).

Ex. 189

The grand syncopated bowing as used by Viotti

15. Bailleux (*Méthode raisonnée* . . . (1779), p. 27) is one of the few late-eighteenth-century writers to advocate playing such rhythms with a separate bow for each note.

However, its use is only rarely indicated in Viotti's violin concertos and no directions are provided in contemporary methods regarding its execution, although Woldemar in particular includes numerous examples of its use.

The slurred tremolo

The slurred *tremolo*,[16] referring to the execution of repeated notes on the same string under one slur, is essentially a type of slurred *staccato*, but it can be played either *staccato* or *legato* according to the context or notation. Dots or strokes under a slur generally indicate the use of the *staccato* version, whereas a slur alone implies a *legato* interpretation. Previously, ⌒⌒⌒⌒ was commonly employed to indicate the slurred *tremolo*, but this sign only rarely appears in late-eighteenth-century works. Despite its common eighteenth-century usage, Bailleux is one of the few writers to describe this bowing, calling it *balancement* (Ex. 190):

Ex. 190

The *balancement*, which the Italians call *tremolo*, produces the tremulous effect of the organ; it is several notes of the same value, on the same degree [of the scale], tied together, which one takes in a single bow stroke without leaving the string.

(Bailleux, *Méthode raisonnée* . . . (1779), p. 11)

Portato

The *portato* (Fr. *craquer*) stroke, an articulated, slurred bowing incorporating notes of differing pitches under the slur and generally indicated by dots or lines under the slur, is also closely related to the slurred *staccato*, although its use is confined mainly to slower tempos. Produced by an even series of delicate pressures and relaxations, while the bow is drawn along without interruption, it has great expressive potential if used sparingly.

Galeazzi is one of the few writers to discuss *portato*, even though it was exploited in many compositions, especially in orchestral contexts in an accompanying role:

159. *Note portate*, so-called, are those [notes] which are neither separate nor slurred but almost dragged. They are all played in one stroke without lifting the bow from the string but each note is given a slight articulation with the bow, which is not done in slurring. (*Portato* notes are indicated with simple dots over the notes [under the slur] . . .)   (Galeazzi, *Elementi* . . . (1791), vol. I, pt. 2, p. 156)

16. The term *tremolo* in eighteenth-century methods can refer to trills, *vibrato* and a rapid oscillation of the bow, as well as the meaning under discussion here.

Mixed bowings

Many of the above separate and slurred bowings could be mixed (Ex. 191), especially in passages of double stopping (Ex. 192), providing the performer with remarkable scope for flexibility and variety of bowing. Geminiani and Leopold Mozart in particular took great pains to catalogue many of the bowing variants feasible[17], and works such as Tartini's *L'arte del arco* variations admirably illustrate their employment in appropriate musical contexts.

Ex. 191

Ex. 192

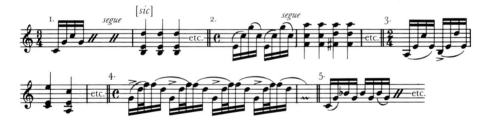

STROKES WITH TOURTE–MODEL BOWS (C. 1800–C. 1840)

It would be impractical to attempt to equate the above subheadings relevant to the pre-Tourte bow with those applicable to bow strokes c. 1800 onwards, given the sharply contrasting properties of the Tourte model, its different technical requirements and its wider bowing vocabulary. Therefore, Baillot's survey, unique in its basic approach of interrelating bow speed and articulation and without doubt comprising the most extensive early-nineteenth-century classification of *détaché* bow strokes, is included here as a point of departure from which to consider the principal bowings and theories of other contem-

17. Geminiani, *The art* . . ., pp. 22–3; L. Mozart, *Versuch* . . ., ch. 7, pp. 122–35.

porary writers. Baillot classified bow strokes under two basic categories, according to speed: slow or fast (a classification that few modern players would endorse).

Two types of bow stroke

Slow and fast bow strokes, the basis for all others

There are two ways to set the string vibrating.
    1. By drawing the bow *slowly*, holding it back to a greater or lesser extent and applying more or less pressure.
    It is thus that one can sing on the violin, in imitation of the voice, which does not act in fits and starts and does not separate the sounds, but sustains them and carries them over from one to another.

Ex. 193

Slow bow stroke

a.

Holding back the bow (Haydn: Quartet no. 26)

b.

Holding back the bow in an *Adagio* determines its character, using the term in its general sense, a character consisting in profound and concentrated emotion, which affords such pleasure that one wishes to preserve it in one's heart for a long time. It is this emotion that the slowness of the bow must express to the full, by relinquishing ·each note only at the last moment and, as it were, with regret.
    This *holding back* of the bow does not, however, in any way exclude those passages expressive of great passion which can be rendered properly only by considerable movement of the bow. Example:

Ex. 194

(Mozart: Quintet no. 8)

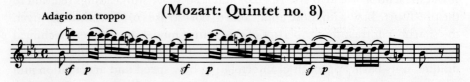

    2. The second way to set the string vibrating is to move the bow *quickly across*; it is in this way that passage-work is played. Most of the bow strokes during these passages should be light; those that require a certain pressure, like the *martelé* or *staccato*, should be executed in such a way that all the notes have *roundness*.

Ex. 195

Rapid bow stroke

(Viotti: Concerto no. 23)

Remain in position – – – – – – –

Ex. 196

(Baillot: Concerto no. 9, Op. 50)

All bow strokes follow of necessity from these two ways of making the string vibrate; their basic principle is *slowness* or *speed*; one must take pains to characterise them carefully so that one may sustain and slur the notes in the *melody* and detach them clearly in the contrasting *passage-work*.

It will be seen in the article on the *détaché* that there are, exceptionally, certain bow strokes which must be *dragged* and which can for this reason be considered as *mixed* strokes, since although they are used in a quick passage they are executed with a little of the holding back that is generally expected in a melodic line.

The composite bow stroke

There is another type of bow stroke which can be called composite, since it consists in employing [elements of] slow and fast bow strokes simultaneously. It requires both speed and holding back at the same time and it is intended to produce the effect of two separate parts, of which the one sings the melody with a dragged bow and the other accompanies with detached notes:

Ex. 197   (Fiorillo: Étude no. 32)

Détaché bow strokes

Clarity is one of the three fundamental elements of technique in every good performance. This clarity depends to a great extent on the manner in which the *détaché* is
executed; therefore, it is essential:

　　1. To know the principle of the *détaché* in general, and the various kinds of *détaché*
which give so much charm and variety to one's playing.

　　2. To know which part or division of the bow one must use in order to characterise
them well.

　　3. To apply oneself to some technical details in order to obtain the means of
achieving them easily.

　　Varied bow strokes, that is those composed of different elements in the same passage, will be the subject of a special article.

　　With regard to *détaché* bow strokes, they do, indeed, offer variety among themselves, but this variety is only relative and they should be considered as *fundamental*
strokes because they have a character of their own which can be used in forming combined bow strokes.

　　It has been seen that two types of bow stroke, the *slow* and the *fast*, were the basis for
all the others.

　　The *fast* bow stroke is essentially the basis for the *détaché* stroke.

　　In accordance with their effect on the string, *détachés* are:

　　Muted (*Mats*), *Elastic* (*Élastiques*), *Dragged* (*Traînés*).

　　The *muted* bow strokes are:
　　1. the *grand détaché* – 2. the *martelé* – 3. the *staccato*

General method of execution

Leave the bow resting lightly on the string.

　　Articulate the notes, by means of a more or less extended movement, with the wrist
and the forearm.

　　Take advantage of the flexibility and 'play' in the stick for each.

　　When the bow hair is left on the string, preventing its vibrations from being
entirely free, this lack of freedom gives to the note thus played an accent that we can
only call a *muted accent*.

　　The *elastic* bow strokes are:
　　1. the *détaché léger* – 2. the *perlé* – 3. the *sautillé* – 4. the *staccato à ricochet* or the *thrown*
and *rebounding staccato*

General method of execution

　　With more play, more *elasticity* of the bow than the preceding [strokes], whose
elasticity was seen to be a little restrained.

　　Sometimes [the bow] is *bounced* enough to leave the string a little, but only in certain passages.

　　The *dragged* bow strokes are:
　　1. the *détaché plus ou moins appuyé* – 2. the *détaché flûté*

These must be considered as *mixed* bow strokes since they are made by dragging the bow across fairly briskly and they thus have something in common with both the *slow* and the *fast* bow stroke.

1 'Muted' détachés

Grand détaché

Division of the *Grand détaché*

1. Attack the string with a down bow,
2. with a little pressure,
3. away from the bridge,
4. very briskly.
5. Make only one stroke audible.
6. Stop the bow short.
7. Leave it on the string without pressure.
8. Do the same with the up bow.

Note: Use more or less bow according to the speed of the passage.

Ex. 198

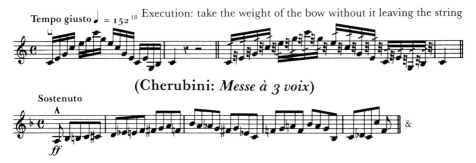

(Cherubini: *Messe à 3 voix*)

Allowing for variations and inconsistencies in the tempo markings recommended (particularly by Baillot), Habeneck endorses Baillot's comments, calling the stroke *grand détaché porté* and relating bow length to tempo.[19] He recommends a method of practising this bowing which involves lifting the bow slightly off the string at the end of each stroke, in order to become accustomed to the lightness of bowing required and to allow the string free vibration.[20] He also mentions a stroke called *suivi* but fails to describe it with sufficient clarity; it seems, however, that this stroke was similar to the *grand détaché* but played faster and with less rigidity and separation.[21]

18. This *grand détaché mat* can be articulated up to a speed of ♩ = 152 on the Maelzel metronome, and even up to ♩ = 160 if the passage is a short one. At higher speeds than this, one can take advantage of the elasticity of the stick to perform the *détaché léger* described in no. 4 of the bow strokes. (Baillot's footnote)
19. Habeneck, *Méthode* . . . (c. 1840), p. 51.   20. *Ibid.*, p. 52.   21. *Ibid.*, p. 51.

Of the other advanced early-nineteenth-century treatises, Rode *et al.* surprisingly omit mention of the *grand détaché* by name and both Mazas and Spohr refer to the stroke only very fleetingly.

2 *Martelé*

Division of
the *martelé*

1. The thumb pressed against the stick.
2. Separate each note sharply and evenly
3. with the wrist, letting the forearm follow a little
4. if the speed is less lively,
5. and if, consequently, the bow stroke is not so short;
6. a little rest between each note.
7. Leave the bow on the string without pressure after the note is played.
8. Lengthen the *martelé* a little on the E string in order to compensate for the thinness of the higher sounds.

Ex. 199
(Baillot: Prelude)

Moderato ♩ = 72
4th string

Habeneck (*martelé* indicated by ᴵ or ·) endorses Baillot's comments but adds that the bow should be stopped prematurely, using less flexibility of the wrist than in *grand détaché* but without the slightest stiffness in the wrist or forearm.[22] Rode *et al.*, Mazas and Spohr opt for a slightly more expressive bias, stressing the need for sufficient bow length to produce a sonorous and full tone and thus avoid harshness and dryness.[23] No mention is made in early-nineteenth-century methods of the modern recommendation of a low wrist position with the forearm slightly pronated for this bowing.

3 *Staccato*[24]

The *staccato* or *détaché articulé* is executed by playing a down bow sharply and strongly on the first note, and attacking all the others evenly in a single up bow like short, quick little *martelés*.

The length of the *staccato* [stroke] is proportionate to the number of notes from which it is composed; examples:

22. *Ibid.*, p. 61.
23. Rode *et al.*, *Méthode* . . . (1803), pt. 1, p. 131; Mazas, *Méthode* . . . (1830), p. 122; Spohr, *Violinschule* (1832), p. 136.
24. The early-nineteenth-century *staccato* is the equivalent of the slurred *staccato* of most eighteenth-century methods.

Ex. 200

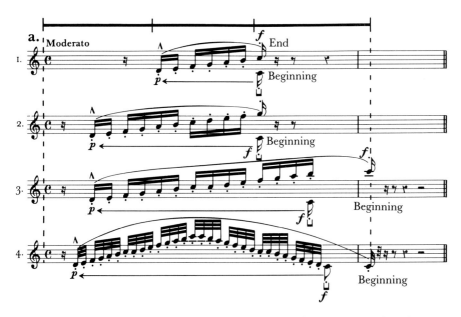

If the character of the piece requires it, however, the *staccato* can be played more broadly, that is to say increasing the duration of each note and the length of the bow; example:

Some people have the faculty of playing a very quick *staccato* quite naturally, that is without the benefit of practice, with a stiff action imparted to the wrist and the arm with a kind of shuddering by means of which all the notes can be articulated with great facility. It is rarely that this can be done keeping in time or achieved other than by chance unless one seeks to control it in the manner indicated below.

The *staccato* that can be acquired by practice is a combination of incisiveness and softness. It is a light, repeated attack on the string effected by a movement of the wrist, followed by a slight relaxing of the bow, which has less support from the thumb during the little stop made on the string at each note. The *staccato* is more easily achieved by exaggerating the attack and the stop on the string until one has the ability to articulate it faster, clearly and lightly.

Method of studying it

1. Grip the bow a little by pressing the thumb against the stick, in order to accent the first note of every beat sharply and loudly and leave some play in the bow for the other notes.

2. Play the down bow on this first note loudly and very quickly.

3. Stop the bow very abruptly on the string each time.

4. Attack all the other notes evenly in a single up bow stroke, but *piano* compared to the first note of the beat.

5. Stop the bow slightly on the string on each of these *piano* notes.

6. Play the last note loudly and very quickly in the up bow, stopping it short like the first.

7. Practise also lifting the bow after the final note, as this also may be required occasionally.

8. Give more or less length to the *staccato* according to the number of notes, following the examples to be found at the beginning of this article.

Practise this passage very slowly at first.

Ex. 201

This alternation of incisiveness and lightness in the use of the bow will soon lead to the ability to play the *staccato* evenly and to keep it in time with the beat of 112 and 152 on the Maelzel metronome in these or similar passages.

Ex. 202

The various kinds of staccato or détaché articulé

Ex. 203

On the same note

a. Moderato

On the same string

(Lafont: Variations – Nocturne sur les Chevaliers de la fidèlité)

b.

In an ascending scale

c.

In a descending scale

d.

In ascending broken chords

e.

In descending broken chords

f.

With few notes (Rode: *Thème varié*)

g.

With a number of notes on the same string

h.

Ex. 203 (cont.)

With a number of notes, changing strings
(Baillot: Étude no. 3)

i.

In arpeggio
(Baillot: Étude no. 1)

j. Maestoso

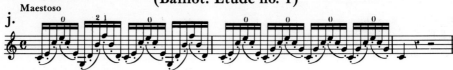

Gently
(Viotti: Concerto no. 11)

k. Allegro maestoso ♩ = 100

At moderate speed
(Fiorillo: Étude no. 3)

l. Allegro

Fast
(Rode: Caprice no. 3)

m. Moderato

Very fast
(D'outrepont: *Thème varié* no. 2)

n. Moderato

Cantando
(Beethoven: Serenade)

o. Adagio

Mellow and expressive
(Baillot: Quartet no. 2)

Broadly and becoming louder
(Viotti: Concerto no. 19)

In a down bow

Varied
(Rode: Caprice no. 7)

A way of varying this *staccato* passage
(Viotti: Rondo from Concerto no. 24)

Alternate up and down bows

The *staccato* or *détaché articulé* can be played with a down bow in most of the passages given above as examples. It is useful to practise this bow stroke in all these ways in order to achieve the appropriate flexibility, speed and lightness in passage-work. This can be achieved by practising it on the pattern of scales, and as in the following example [Ex. 204].

Ex. 204

(The 2nd Kreutzer study can be practised in the same way.)

Ex. 205

Allowing for slight variations in the pressure agent employed, Habeneck, Rode *et al.*, Mazas and Spohr provide similar but less detailed accounts and recommend the use of as little bow as possible for each note, Spohr in particular emphasising that the lower half of the bow should never be required for either up- or down-bow *staccato*.[25] Writers do not mention the modern method of facilitating down-bow *staccato*, in which the bow stick is inclined towards the bridge and the wrist and elbow are dropped sharply below the level of the frog, the fingers being well curved.

Habeneck also refers to another variety of slurred *staccato*, called *notes portées* (i.e. *portato*) which are indicated by the same notation (‿‿‿), but played at a slower tempo and with more bow to each note.[26]

Staccato à ricochet or détaché jetté

The *staccato à ricochet* is played with either an up or down bow, but more generally with a down bow, throwing the bow at the [lower] end of its middle [third] and from about two inches above the instrument on to the string; it then bounces and strikes several notes of its own accord due to the effect of this bouncing; the bow should be lifted quickly from the string at each note played with an up bow.

We have seen it executed in this way by R. Kreutzer in the following passage [Ex. 206].

In this last example the composer has made happy use of *ordinary staccato* and of *staccato à ricochet*.

By means of the bouncing of the bow used in the *staccato à ricochet*, a larger number of notes may be articulated in a single up or down bow; one simply needs to drop the

25. Habeneck, *Méthode . . .* (c. 1840), note b, p. 84; Rode *et al.*, *Méthode . . .* (1803), pt. 1, p. 131; Mazas, *Méthode . . .* (1830) (*coup d'archet piqué*), p. 123; Spohr, *Violinschule* (1832), pp. 132–3.
26. Habeneck, *Méthode . . .* (c. 1840), note b, p. 84.

Ex. 206

(Kreutzer: Concerto no. 10)

a. Allegro moderato

(de Bériot: *Air Varié* no. 5, Variation 3)

b.

bow from a slightly greater height on to the string.[27] Examples can be found in the work of Mr Guhr of Frankfurt.[28]

Hitherto no sign has been used to indicate the *ricochet* other than that used for the *ordinary staccato*.

One might use the following:

4 Elastic détachés[29]
Détaché léger[30]

		Division		

Separate each note, holding the bow very lightly on the string, taking advantage of the elasticity of the stick to give it an imperceptible and slightly lengthened bounce, as was said concerning the division of the bow where this passage was given as an example:

Ex. 207

Allegro ♩ = 108

Execution

27. Mr Paganini is the first whom we have heard make use of this. (Baillot's footnote)
28. i.e. Guhr, *Ueber Paganinis Kunst* . . . (1829).
29. The part of the bow best suited to these strokes essentially varies according to the weight and balance of the bow, the tempo, dynamic and the thickness of the strings employed, but these variables are not acknowledged by writers of the period.
30. This stroke is not discussed by other contemporary writers.

5 *Détaché perlé*[31]

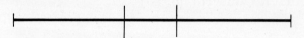

Separate each note in the same way [as for the *détaché léger*], taking advantage of the elasticity of the stick, but allow very little length of bow, bearing in mind the tempo, as was said concerning the division of the bow where this passage was quoted as an example.

Every note even and rounded.

Ex. 208

6 *Détaché sautillé*

Make the bow bounce lightly in the same place and slightly leave the string.

Paesiello requested that this violin accompaniment for a 'Judicabit' of his should be played very *détaché* for sharper contrast with the voice part, which is sustaining semibreves.

Ex. 209

Rode *et al.*, Mazas and Spohr omit reference to this bowing but Habeneck is more explicit, claiming that the stroke is best executed at a point just below the middle of the bow;[32] it is employed in fast movements in passages too fast for the *grand détaché* with lightness and flexibility in the wrist, so that the stick articulates each note, bouncing on the string through its own elasticity.[33] Modern theorists tend not to look on this bowing as an exclusive function of the wrist and advocate the introduction of the forearm into the stroke, the

---

31. This stroke is not discussed by other contemporary writers; see p. 297.
32. Habeneck, *Méthode . . .* (c. 1840), note u, p. 52.
33. *Ibid.*, p. 79.

actual amount of arm movement required depending entirely on the tempo and tonal volume desired. Furthermore, many claim that production of this stroke is greatly aided by turning the forearm inwards, so that the top of the wrist is at an angle of about forty-five degrees to the bow stick.

7 Staccato à ricochet

In presenting a picture of all the kinds of *staccato* we have included the *staccato à ricochet* although it is essentially to be counted among the *elastic* bow strokes, since the notes become articulated through the bouncing of the bow thrown on to the string, as was done using the back of the bow in the passage in the overture to the Caliph of Baghdad [by Boieldieu] that we quoted when speaking of rhythm. How to play the *staccato à ricochet* is indicated following the examples of the *various kinds of staccato* (see *staccato à ricochet* or *détaché jetté*, p. [188].)

Rode *et al.* and Spohr omit reference to this stroke and Mazas refers to it only fleetingly, commenting little about its execution. Habeneck, however, calls it *staccato élastique* and unlike Baillot credits Paganini with its revival, since similar bounding strokes were employed, albeit sparingly, by some eighteenth-century composers. Both Guhr and Habeneck indicate that this stroke is most difficult when combined with string changes. Modern methods generally recommend using the full ribbon of hair for the *ricochet* stroke (with the stick upright and not inclined towards the fingerboard) but no mention is made of this ploy by early-nineteenth-century writers.

8 Détaché traîné ou appuyé

The *détaché traîné* is played at the middle or at the point of the bow, which is allowed greater or less pressure on the string in such a way that there is no separation between each note.

It is used in the *tremolando* and in the semiquavers in a symphony where its effect is enhanced by the number of instruments.

Examples:

Ex. 210

(Haydn: Symphony no. 82)

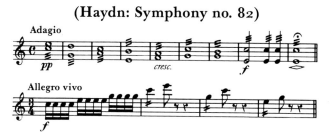

This bow stroke can also be employed in certain passages which require a dragged accent which the composer indicates with the words: *stracinato* or *stracinando l'arco*, *traîné* or *en traînant l'archet*.

For this it is necessary to bring the bow a little nearer the bridge, to play very *piano* and to separate each of the notes by a little silence after drawing them with as little bow as possible.

Ex. 211
(Boccherini: Quintet no. 58)

The *détaché appuyé* is sometimes played at the point of the bow in passages whose character requires a slightly duller sound than in the *martelé*, which makes it necessary to keep the bow constantly on the string.

This *détaché* results from the way in which the composer of the study noted below was in the habit of playing passage-work; it should be used only rarely in compositions other than his.

Ex. 212
(Rode: Caprice no. 10)

The *détaché appuyé* can also be played with the middle of the bow; but it then changes its character and is usually employed in *batteries*, continuous arpeggios in which all the notes are detached.

For *batteries* use the least possible amount of bow.

Articulate all the notes very fast and very cleanly.

Ex. 213
(Baillot: Étude no. 12)

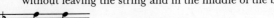

9 Détaché flûté (very lightly dragged)

The *Détaché flûté* is indicated by the words *flautato* or *stracinato, flûté* or *traîné*.

This bow stroke does not produce its complete effect, that is, imitating the flute, except in the middle register, on the A and D strings, as the example below will show.

Place the point of the bow lightly on the fingerboard, approximately one inch from its end.

Lengthen each *piano* note a little, evenly and with a kind of nonchalance.

Ex. 214

(Boccherini: Quintet no. 69)

Minuetto

stracinato

But if one does wish to soften the notes on the E and G strings and make them as flute-like as their register permits, since the corners of the violin get in the way of the bow being placed on the fingerboard when one is playing on these two strings, especially the E string, one will be obliged to come as close as possible to the end of the fingerboard and again to use the same method of dragging the bow.

(Baillot, *L'art.* . . (1834), pp. 97–110)

ADDITIONS TO BAILLOT'S SURVEY

Although Baillot provides an extensive classification of *détaché* strokes, a few additional bowings were discussed by his contemporaries and indeed by Baillot himself, in other places in his method. Some additional bowings considered by other writers, moreover, do not fit easily into Baillot's scheme outlined above.

ACCENTED BOWINGS (OTHER THAN MARTELÉ)

Saccade

Baillot does not include the *saccade* in his working plan, preferring to define it elsewhere in his method:

The *saccade* is a rough and sudden jerk of the bow given to notes, generally in twos, threes etc., and sometimes irregularly, that is to say without symmetry. Harshness must above all be avoided in the *saccade* since it is a primary effect of its nature. The *saccade* is good only in so far as it does not affect the purity of the sound.

When the *saccade* is introduced into an orchestral passage, the effect of the massed instruments gives it in its roughness a fullness of sound which cannot be produced by one instrument alone.

In a violin solo, its function is to break the monotony, to lighten the passage and give it energy. One must take care to correct its normal harshness all the more especially then because the sudden contrast requires a brisk, decisive movement of the bow which would easily make the playing dry and hard if one did not attempt to *blend* the *saccade* into the other notes of the passage.

Saccadé bowings:

Ex. 215

(Viotti: Concerto no. 24)

All the *sf*s on the 1st and 3rd notes
must be played mellowly, with a
slightly longer bow.

Ex. 216

(Rode: Concerto no. 4)

Accentuated *saccadé* indicated by the composer:

(Kreutzer: Étude no. 3)

(Baillot: Concerto no. 5)

Slurred *saccadé* bowing:

Ex. 217

(Baillot: *Air varié* Op. 20)

(Baillot, *L'art* . . . (1834), pp. 125–6)

The execution of accents

Baillot describes the execution of accents simply and concisely: '*Attack* the note
and then draw it out a little for the rest of its value, very softly.' (Baillot,

L'art . . . (1834), p. 270) Like most writers, he commonly employs accented bowings at the beginning of some trills[34] or arpeggios[35] and in certain syncopated passages[36] (Ex. 218) as well as for dramatic and expressive effect.

Ex. 218

(Beethoven: Quartet no. 6)

2nd manner,
attacking
the note
with a *sf* or >

Fouetté

Spohr is one of the few contemporary writers to consider this strongly accented 'whipped' stroke, which is especially suitable in fast tempos (Ex. 219):

Ex. 219

at each note marked > the string is, as it were, whipped by the bow. That is to say, [the bow] is raised above the string and thrown down violently on to it in an up stroke, quite close to the point, so that the bow stick does not develop a shuddering motion. After the attack, it [the bow] is gently moved forward about three inches and then drawn back an equal distance for the second note. . . The difficulty of this bowing consists chiefly in always raising the bow to the same height above the string for each stroke and in making the strokes of perfectly equal length. When well executed, it has an astonishing effect.   (Spohr, *Violinschule* (1832), p. 137)

THE LIFTED BOW STROKE

The lifted bow stroke plays a less prominent role in early-nineteenth-century technique, in which *cantabile* playing and the new resilient qualities of the Tourte bow were increasingly exploited. This is admirably demonstrated by contemporary descriptions of the [♩♪] bowing, which rarely involve a lifted

---

34. Baillot, *L'art* . . . (1834), p. 78.   35. *Ibid.*, p. 124.   36. *Ibid.*, p. 135.

bow stroke; instead, the bow remains on the string and its movement is checked momentarily (for usually no more than a demisemiquaver's duration) between the two notes, the second note being achieved through gentle wrist movement. Habeneck devotes a special section to bowings for such dotted rhythms.

97. When one finds two notes, the first of which is longer than the second, as for example:

Ex. 220

If one arrives naturally at a down bow on the 1st, the 2nd will be an up bow and if one arrives naturally at an up bow on the 1st, the 2nd will be a down bow. Both ways should be practised.

98. There is a third way which is widely used, particularly where there is a long series of these notes of unequal value and where the playing must be louder.

It consists in playing the dotted note and the note following it in the same bow, for example:

Ex. 221

One should use a lot of bow on the first note and play the second with a slight jerk of the wrist.   (Habeneck, *Méthode* . . . (c. 1840), p. 68)

However, lifted strokes were not totally excluded from the violinist's vocabulary; Spohr, among others, includes numerous examples of their use. In Ex. 222, the bow is raised from the string at the quaver rests and the stroke

Ex. 222

continued in the air, so that, at the end of the bar, the whole length of the bow is employed. In Ex. 223, Spohr recommends playing the off-beat triplets in an up bow:

Ex. 223

The bow is raised from the string during the rest, drawn back in the air and is again placed on the string at the point for each triplet.   (Spohr, *Violinschule* (1832), p. 45)

SLOW SMOOTH (LEGATO) STROKES

The Tourte bow was better suited than its baroque counterpart to the execution of slow smooth strokes, because of its greater ability to sustain phrases evenly from end to end.

Curiously enough, Baillot's survey of bowings does not extend to detailed explanation or even classification of these strokes. Referring to them only in general terms, he discusses their sustained *legato* nature and their ideal dynamics in given contexts and emphasises their dependence on smooth bow changes for optimum effect.[37]

SLURRED BOWINGS

The legato slur

Comparison of the original editions of, for example, Haydn's Op. 20 quartets (1769–72) with subsequent early-nineteenth-century editions (for example, Peters) will confirm that slurring was more commonly employed after the advent of the Tourte bow, which was better suited to the production of *cantabile* effects than its predecessors. The capacity of the slur was further enlarged in keeping with contemporary taste (see the extraordinary long slurs in Ex. 224) and although many of these longer slurs are more likely phrase markings, indicating the need for sustained *legato* bowing using more than one stroke, the *cantabile* implication of these long slurs is a vital key to the expressive ideals of the period.

While generally acknowledging the importance of bow-division,[38] early-nineteenth-century writers appear to have been more concerned with the finger pressure and agility of the left hand in their considerations of slurred bowing, in order to achieve clarity, vitality and brilliance. Baillot, for example, recommends: 'In slurred passages, make the fingers fall from a sufficient height for them to have impetus.' (Baillot, *L'art. . .* (1834), p. 19)

Bariolage and ondeggiando

Bariolage, illustrated but rarely discussed in early-nineteenth-century methods, was employed only sparingly, according to the nature and charac-

37. See p. 74.   38. See p. 301.

Ex. 224

ter of the passage. Baillot singles it out for special mention, providing little technical instruction but defining it thus:

The name *bariolage* is given to the kind of passage which presents the appearance of disorder and oddness, in that the notes are not played in succession on the same string where one would expect this (see Ex. [225a]) or when the notes e², a¹, d¹ are played not on the same string as in Exx. [225b & c] but alternately with one stopped finger and the open string (see Exx. [225d & e]), or else finally when the open string is played in a position where a stopped note would normally be required (see Ex. [225f]).

Ex. 225

Ex. 225 (cont.)

Passages
fingered
as they would
normally
be played

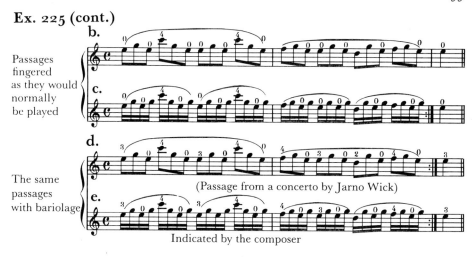

The same
passages
with bariolage

(Passage from a concerto by Jarno Wick)

Indicated by the composer

(Haydn: Quartet no. 66, Trio)

The study of bariolage

Bariolage is not always indicated; it must be used only with extreme caution and only
in certain passages which lend themselves to this changing of strings and this alternating mixture of stopped and open notes. One must above all take account of the
nature of the passage even more than the disposition of the notes. In general, it is
suited only to pieces in a lighter style, and would be out of place in those of a more
severe style where such effects are in no way admissible.

Ex. 226

(Baillot, *L'art.* . . (1834), pp. 126–7)

One of the few early-nineteenth-century writers to mention *ondeggiando* bowing is Habeneck, who nonetheless fails to distinguish it from *bariolage*. However, he deals rather more than Baillot with the technical requirements for its successful execution, emphasising the importance of the freedom of the arm and the flexibility of the wrist for the smooth passage of the bow from one string to another.[39]

The 'Viotti' bowing

Most writers include this bowing in their methods, but Spohr singles it out for special comment;[40] it is similar to but generally more 'symmetrically' employed than Baillot's *saccade* stroke, and is essentially a type of slurred *staccato*. The first note of each pair (Ex. 227) is played softly with little bow

Ex. 227

while the second requires a longer stroke and a considerable degree of pressure for the accent. The addition of this accent deserves special attention as it is rarely included in eighteenth-century versions of this stroke.

The 'Kreutzer' bowing

This bowing, mentioned only by Spohr,[41] is named after the violinist who is said to have first employed it (Ex. 228). Alternate pairs of notes are played *staccato* and *legato*, the second note of the *staccato* pair being played *sforzando*.

Ex. 228

39. Habeneck, *Méthode* . . . (c. 1840), p. 135.
40. Spohr, *Violinschule* (1832), p. 136.   41. *Ibid.*, p. 137.

MIXED BOWINGS

Like their predecessors, many nineteenth-century writers were keen to illustrate the many different ways in which the above bow strokes could be
exploited in combination, in order that audience interest should be sustained
through variety of bowing. Baillot's survey[42] is especially notable for its equation of such mixed bowings with the character of the music (Ex. 229).

Ex. 229

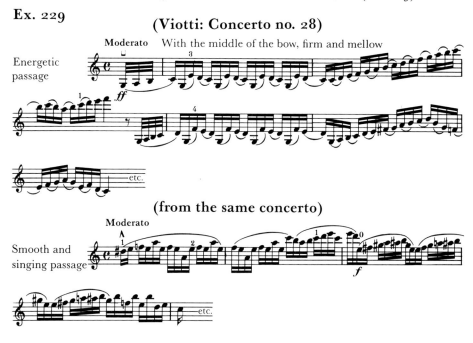

(Viotti: Concerto no. 28)

Moderato   With the middle of the bow, firm and mellow

Energetic
passage

(from the same concerto)

Moderato

Smooth and
singing passage

BOWING INDICATIONS

Signs indicating the type of bowing and articulation required were increasingly and more thoroughly employed during the period in an attempt to avoid
ambiguity of interpretation; however, the respective meanings of these signs
were not consistent. The dot (•) most commonly indicated articulation with
the bow on the string and the wedge (▾) articulation with the bow off the string
(for example, Quantz), but Habeneck, for example, generally employs these
signs conversely (although the use of the dot to indicate the *martelé* and *grand
détaché porté* strokes is an exception). Furthermore, Rode *et al.* do not employ
the wedge at all and thus add to the ambiguity of the dot, while Mazas, Spohr
and other writers likewise increase the confusion, using signs indiscriminately
and inconsistently, without supplying sufficient information as to their
respective meanings. Such failings naturally inflicted extra responsibility on
the performer to interpret the music faithfully according to its true character.

42. Baillot, *L'art* . . . (1834), pp. 111–20.

9

Special effects

The term 'effect', a special means of conveying the character and expression of a composition in performance, had two distinct meanings during the period under discussion. Baillot employs the following two definitions as the basis of his study of 'Effect and means of effect':[1]

Effect, the pleasurable and forceful impression created in the ear and mind of the listener by any good music. One can distinguish under the name *means of effect* all those in which the feeling created seems superior to the methods used to arouse it.[2]

Effects can be associated with any modification of the sound; thus one can distinguish *effects of intonation, rhythmical effects, effects of intensity, effects of timbre, effects of character, simple effects*, resulting from a single one of these causes, *compound effects*, that is to say those resulting from two or a number of causes simultaneously.[3]

In accordance with the views expressed, Baillot divides his discussion of the term into two categories: 'particular effects', comprising such short-term effects as contrasts of low and high range, varied bow strokes or rhythms, nuances (*crescendos, diminuendos,* 'spun' (evenly sustained) sounds, softened or veiled sounds of various timbres), prolonged cadences, surprises, anticipations, retardations and perturbations, and 'general or prolonged effects', comprising unisons and octaves, harmonics, *con sordino, pizzicato,* combination tones, quadruple stopping, the various ways of tuning the violin and rhythm. Baillot stresses the value of such effects in adding striking variety to a composition, notably in a contrasting episode of a cadenza, but warns against their unnatural and excessive employment. He dismisses the first category in few words, claiming that 'particular effects' are the very essence and expression of a composition and cannot be separated for study purposes from their musical contexts. However, he provides such a detailed theoretical and technical survey of 'general effects' that, with certain modifications, it will serve conveniently as a foundation for this chapter. (Double stopping, with its inherent

---

1. Baillot, *L'art . . .* (1834), pp. 205–43.
2. *Dictionnaire de musique*, ed. Rousseau, s.v. 'Effet'; Baillot here uses an abridged form of Rousseau's original, causing a certain ambiguity in the process.
3. *Dictionnaire de musique*, ed. Castil-Blaze, s.v. 'Effet'; again an abridged form is used by Baillot, resulting in a similar ambiguity.

considerations of combination tones and unisons and octaves, multiple stopping and rhythm have warranted separate discussion elsewhere[4] and have
been replaced by two additional relevant categories, special bowing effects
and *vibrato*.)

VIBRATO

Vibrato (otherwise called *tremolo, ondulazione, tremolio, Bebung, Schwebung, tremblement, tremblement serré, balancement, ondulation, flatté,* close shake and other less
common terms), sometimes indicated by the symbol ∿∿ but generally freely
added by the performer, was normally employed somewhat sparingly as an
expressive ornament during the period, despite Geminiani's exceptional
recommendation of what is essentially a continuous *vibrato* in the approved
modern fashion[5] (although Leopold Mozart's reference to violinists who
'tremble consistently on each note as if they had the palsy'[6] nevertheless
proves that Geminiani had some disciples). On the whole, its execution and
application are sparsely documented – Habeneck, for example, among
numerous other notable authors, surprisingly omits mention of the device in
his *Méthode. . .*, published towards the mid nineteenth century – but the surveys of Leopold Mozart, Spohr and Baillot are particularly remarkable for
their informative instruction and musical illustration and, with their varied
individual biases, provide a fine cross-section of *vibrato* theory and practice
throughout the period.

Leopold Mozart's survey, based on Tartini's theories, represents the most
explicit eighteenth-century *exposé* of *vibrato*, dealing with the device in two
different parts of his method. The meat of the subject is discussed early in his
chapter concerning improvised ornaments but a further passing reference is
made to *vibrato* and its relation to bowing and tonal disciplines during his discussion of the various divisions of the bow. Both extracts are cited separately
below, in order to represent Leopold Mozart's theories fully.

1. The *tremulo* is an ornament which arises from Nature herself and which can be
introduced gracefully on a long note not only by good *instrumentalists* but also by skilful singers. Nature herself is our teacher in this. For if we strike a slack string or a bell
firmly, we hear after the stroke a certain wave-like 'beating' (*ondeggiamento*) of the
struck note. And this wavering resonance is called *tremulo*, or also the *tremulant*.

2. With the violin family of instruments one may attempt to imitate this natural
trembling by pressing one's finger strongly down on a string and making a small
movement with the whole hand; which, however, must not move sideways but for-

4. See ch. 7, pp. 144–65 & ch. 11, pp. 272–5.
5. Geminiani, *The art . . .*, p. 8.
6. L. Mozart, *Versuch . . .*, ch. 11, §3. See also Löhlein, *Anweisung . . .* (1774), p. 51; Bremner, *Some thoughts
on the performance of concert music*, pp. i–ii; and alterations (attributed to Bremner) to Geminiani's original text of *The art . . .* in the reissues published by Bremner (after 1777) and Preston (after 1789), as
outlined in Hickman, 'The censored publications of *The art of playing on the violin*, or Geminiani
unshaken', *Early Music*, vol. 11 (1983), pp. 73–6.

wards towards the bridge and back towards the scroll: some mention has already been made of this in the *fifth chapter*. For just as the trembling sound which remains when string or bell is struck does not continue to sound pure as one note but fluctuates sometimes too high and sometimes too low, so one must take pains to imitate exactly this wavering between sounds by the movement of the hand forwards and backwards.

3. Now because the *tremulo* does not sound pure as one note but fluctuates, it would be a mistake indeed to play every note with the *tremulo*. There are already players who use *vibrato* consistently on every note as if they have the palsy. The *tremulo* must be employed only in such places where Nature herself would produce it; namely as if the stopped note were the striking of an open string. For at the end of a piece, or even at the end of a passage concluding with a long note, the final note would inevitably continue to hum afterwards for a fair time if struck, for example, on a pianoforte. Therefore, the closing note or also any other long sustained note may be ornamented with the *tremulo*.

4. However, there is a *slow*, an *accelerating* and a *fast tremulo*. One may distinguish them thus:

Ex. 230

The slow	*uuuu*
The accelerating	*uuxxxx*
The fast	*xxxxx*

The larger signs may perhaps represent quavers, and then the smaller can be seen as semiquavers; and, as many signs as there are, so often should the hand be moved.

5. However, the movement must be made with a strong emphasis of the finger and this emphasis introduced always on the first note of every crotchet beat; but in fast movement on the first note of every quaver beat. As an example I will write here some notes which may very well be played with the *tremulo*; indeed, which really require this movement. They must be played in the whole [i.e. third] position.

Ex. 231

One should execute the *tremulo* thus:

Ex. 232

One makes the movement thus.

In the two examples, the stress of the movement in no. 1 [Ex. 231] falls always on the note marked by the figure 2, because it is the first note of the whole or half crotchet. In Example no. 2 [Ex. 232], on the other hand, the stress falls for exactly the same reason on the note marked by the figure 1.

6. The *tremulo* can also be made on two strings and thus with two fingers simultaneously.

Ex. 233

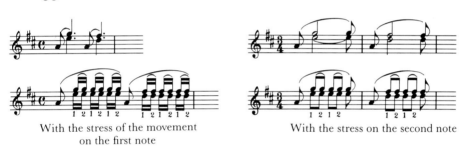

With the stress of the movement   With the stress on the second note
on the first note

7. Before beginning a *cadenza*, which is improvised at the end of a *solo*, it is customary always to sustain a long note, either on the key-note or on the fifth [i.e. dominant]. On such a long sustained note an accelerating *tremulo* may always be employed. For example, the end of an *Adagio* may be played as follows:

Ex. 234

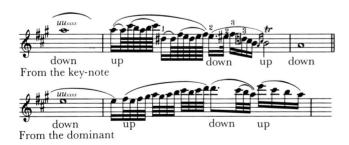

Ex. 234 (cont.)

down   up   down

But the stroke must be started softly and gather in strength towards the middle, so that the greatest stress falls at the beginning of the faster movement; and finally the stroke must end softly once more.   (Mozart, *Versuch*. . ., ch. 11, §1–7, pp. 238–42).

    4. The *first division* can be as follows: the down bow or up bow is started with a pleasant softness; the tone is increased by means of gentle, imperceptible pressure; the greatest volume is produced in the middle of the bow and is moderated by reducing the bow pressure gradually, until finally the tone dies away completely at the end of the bow.
    It must be practised slowly and with as much holding back of the bow as possible, in order thereby to bring oneself to a position where one can sustain a long note in an *Adagio* purely and gracefully, to the great satisfaction of one's audience. Just as it is particularly moving when a singer sustains beautifully a long note of varying degrees of loud and soft without taking breath. But in this matter one should also particularly observe that the finger of the left hand which stops the string should slightly relax [its pressure] in soft playing and the bow should be brought a little further away from the bridge or fulcrum; whereas, for loud volume, the fingers of the left hand should press the string down strongly and the bow must be drawn nearer to the bridge.
    5. In this first division in particular, as also in the following, the finger of the left hand should make a small slow movement; which must not be sideways but forwards and backwards. That is to say that the finger should move forward towards the bridge and backwards again towards the scroll of the violin, in soft tone quite slowly but in loud rather faster.   (Mozart, *Versuch* . . ., ch. 5, § 4–5, pp. 102–3)

    Spohr's short survey closely resembles Leopold Mozart's account at the outset but it later reflects the more expressive ideals of its time, citing a more varied list of uses of *vibrato*, notably for the intensification of notes marked *sforzando*, and four *vibrato* speeds and their respective indications. The textual discussion is succeeded by studies in duet form and interpretative analyses of Rode's seventh concerto and Spohr's own ninth concerto, in which the sparing use of the device at speeds appropriate to the contexts is expertly illustrated (Ex.235).

The *vibrato* (*tremolo*) and the changing of a finger on a note also belong to the group of ornaments.
    When a singer sings with passionate emotion or raises his voice to its greatest volume, a trembling of the voice is noticeable, resembling the vibrations of a powerfully struck bell. The violinist is able to imitate closely this trembling, together with many other peculiarities of the human voice. It consists of a wavering or fluctuation of a stopped note, which sounds alternately a little below and above the true intonation and is produced by a trembling movement of the left hand in the direction from the

Ex. 235

nut to the bridge. However, this movement should not be too vigorous and the deviation from the true pitch of the note should be scarcely perceptible to the ear.

In older compositions one finds the *vibrato* indicated sometimes by a row of dots
. . . . . or by the written word *tremolo*; in more recent works its use has been left
entirely to the player. He should take care, however, not to introduce it too often and
in unsuitable places. The above-mentioned moments when *vibrato* becomes noticeable in the singer apply also to its use by the violinist. He should therefore use it only
in passionate passages and for the strong accentuation of all notes marked *fz* or>.
Long sustained notes may also be made more alive and intense through the use of
vibrato. If such a note *crescendos* from *p* to *f*, it makes a pleasing effect if the *vibrato* begins
slowly and the rapidity of the vibrations increases in relation to the increase in
volume. A *vibrato* which begins fast and becomes gradually slower is also very
effective on a note which starts loud but gradually dies away.

Thus *vibrato* may be divided into four types, (1) fast, for sharply accentuated notes,
(2) slow, for sustained notes in impassioned melodies, (3) beginning slowly and
becoming faster for a *crescendo*, (4) beginning fast and becoming slower for a *decrescendo*
on long sustained notes. These latter two types are difficult and require much practice, in order that the increase and decrease in the vibrations may be completely uniform and do not give rise shall we say to a sudden transition from slow to fast or vice
versa . . . [2 paragraphs omitted].

The fast *vibrato* is indicated ⁓⁓⁓, the slow ⁓⁓⁓, the accelerating ⁓⁓⁓ and
the decelerating ⁓⁓⁓.   (Spohr, *Violinschule* (1832), pp. 175–6)

Baillot's account is especially notable for its expansion of the *vibrato* concept
to include three types of 'undulated sounds', a wavering motion of the bow
caused by variation of pressure on the stick (discussed earlier by Brossard,
amongst others, as a technical device employed in imitation of the tremulant
of the organ and dating back at least to the sixteenth century),[7] the normal
left-hand *vibrato* and a combination of both effects. It is reproduced in full

7. *Dictionnaire de Musique* . . ., ed. Brossard, s.v. 'Tremolo',

below, accompanied by appropriate musical illustrations including an especially instructive example of left-hand *vibrato* technique, which clearly accom-
modates Baillot's theory that notes should be begun and finished off without
vibrato for purposes of accurate intonation. It is also interesting to note that
Baillot appears to be more flexible about *vibrato* speeds, presumably leaving
such decisions to the performer's good taste.

Undulating sounds

There are various ways of *undulating* the sound; these can be achieved by:
1. Pressing the bow on the string by degrees, then similarly lessening this pressure
    and repeating this movement faster or more slowly, more or less often.
2. Giving the left hand a slight rocking or trembling movement which is transmitted
    to the finger placed on the string.
3. Using these *two methods* simultaneously.

1. Undulation produced by the bow

Draw the bow across the string, at first slowly and softly, then louder, and gradually
decrease its pressure; the vibrations will increase and decrease in intensity in proportion to this pressure or to the speed of the bow; the result of this greater or smaller
amplitude in the oscillation of the string will be an *undulation* of the sound, if you
make this undulation quicker by making the stick bend a little and by giving it a kind
of palpitation, indicated by this sign or ⁀⁀ .

   The *undulation* produced by the bow alone conveys calm and purity because, on the
one hand, it generally appears in slow or *moderato* movements and on an open string;
and on the other hand, when it is played with one finger placed on the string and
remaining still, the intonation of the note remains unchanged, whereas in another
type of *undulation* this intonation is momentarily altered, as will be seen in the following article.

Ex. 236
(Boccherini: Quintet no. 75)

2. Undulation produced by the left hand

Place one finger on the string, keep the other three fingers raised, and rock the left
hand as a unit with a more or less moderate movement, so that this rocking or
shaking of the hand is conveyed to the finger on the string. By means of this slight
trembling, the finger, always remaining on the same note, moves forwards and back-

wards a little, and the string, alternately shortened and returned to its original state by this movement, adds an *undulation* to the sound, the approximate effect of which is shown in the following illustration [Ex. 237].

Ex. 237

This *undulation*, produced by the finger with varying degrees of slowness, may express animation, tenderness and sometimes suffering; but the rocking of the finger momentarily affects the intonation of the note. In order that the ear may not be distressed by this and may be consoled immediately, the exact pure note should be heard at the beginning and end. *Undulation*, when discreetly introduced, gives to the sound of the instrument a great similarity to the voice when it is strongly touched with emotion. This means of expression is very powerful, but if employed often it would soon lose its moving quality and would possess only the dangerous disadvantage of making the melody unnatural and depriving the style of that precious naïvety that is the greatest attraction of art, in that it has the capacity always to recall it to its primitive state of simplicity.

Viotti used *undulation* in the manner indicated in the following examples.

Ex. 238

(Viotti: Concerto no. 19)

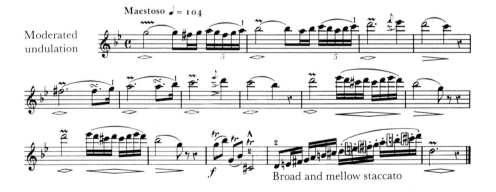

It can be seen from the above example that the *undulation* can be produced at one and the same time by the movement of the finger and by that of the bow, but this latter acts only as a simple *undulation*, that is to say such that it takes place within the 'spun' sound, the *crescendo*, *forte* and *diminuendo*; whereas that which is brought about by the movement of the finger is rapid and may comprise here approximately four rocking movements, one for each semiquaver, but without being precisely measurable.

Ex. 239

(Viotti: Quartet no. 15)

slightly less
moderated
Undulation

With a little slackness

3. Undulation produced simultaneously by the movement of the bow and by the movement of the finger

In this *undulation* the finger and bow act together and more briskly than in the two previous types.

Ex. 240

(Leclair: *Chasse* from Sonata no. 9, Book 3, Op. 5)

Undulation
actuated by the
finger and
the bow.

The *undulation* would be unbearable beyond a certain speed; likewise, it must be rejected in a succession of notes; it gives a good effect only on a long note or when the same note is repeated.

Avoid giving the *undulation* a flabby quality, which would make the playing seem old-fashioned, or a stiffness which would spoil its charm and fluency; above all, avoid making a habit of vibrating the hand, which must be used only when the expression renders it necessary and, furthermore, in compliance with all that has been indicated in order to prevent its misuse.   (Baillot, *L'art.* . . (1834), pp. 137-9)

Violinists of the period thus appear to have been highly sensitive regarding the use of *vibrato*, particularly the use of a *vibrato* speed appropriate to the dynamics of the bow[8] and the tempo and character of the music.[9] The use of

8. Campagnoli, *Metodo* . . . (1797?), tr. Bishop, pt. 2, no. 127.
9. Löhlein, *Anweisung* . . . (1774), p. 51.

the device varied considerably according to region and performer, especially in the late eighteenth century, but available evidence suggests that it was employed sparingly and discreetly to enhance special moments in the music, particularly, it seems, long sustained or final notes in a phrase. Such use of the device for final notes in a phrase, notes which in most contexts are 'phrased off', has puzzled many scholars. However, *vibrato* was never allowed to become a formula to be applied or withdrawn blindly; its inclusion in such circumstances seems to have been for colouristic purposes, tailor-made to help rather than hinder phrasing, and would have been relatively unobtrusive, if handled tastefully.

Some violinists of the period stand poles apart from the recommendations of Geminiani and his disciples,[10] refusing to accept *vibrato* into their technical vocabulary on the grounds that it was lacking in taste and encouraged impure intonation. Quantz, on the other hand, freely admits the use of *vibrato* as a way of avoiding poor intonation![11]

Owing to its limited use overall, especially since it was primarily part of the technical equipment of advanced players and soloists, *vibrato*, with its attendant range of speeds, most probably had a more striking effect then than the continuous variety (with speed variation) practised nowadays. Furthermore, the *vibrato* movement of the time, executed with the fingers and wrist but not with the lower arm, was necessarily somewhat narrower, tighter and less intense than its modern counterpart for two main reasons. First, with the absence of a chin rest (not invented until c. 1820), both the thumb and the index-finger were generally required to come into contact with the thicker violin neck of the period as a further means of supporting the instrument (the modern preference is for such contact between the thumb and violin neck only), thus affording the hand and arm much less freedom of movement; secondly, the use of excessive *vibrato* when playing a violin in original condition, with gut strings tuned at low pitch and with a bow of less hair tension than nowadays, invariably leads to the production of an undesirable 'wobble' in the sound.

The 'authentic' performer's goal, therefore, is to acquire by practice and experiment a wide range of palatable *vibrato* speeds and intensities and to apportion them to the character and myriad expressive requirements of the music.

HARMONICS

Although natural harmonics were exploited long before the beginning of our period, by such composers as Jean-Joseph Cassanéa de Mondonville, Charles

10. Galeazzi, *Elementi* . . . (1791), vol. 1, pt. 2, p. 191 (Galeazzi suggests a type of 'bow undulation' with a tense arm as a more bearable and effective substitute); Bremner, *Some thoughts* . . ., pp. i-ii; Jousse, *The theory and practice* . . . (1811), pt. 1, p. 48.
11. Quantz, *Versuch* . . ., tr. and ed. Reilly, ch. 17, section 2, §32, p. 235.

de Lusse, L'Abbé le fils and Domenico Ferrari,[12] their unanimous acceptance into the violinist's technical vocabulary was slow to materialise, due to their inferior tone quality. Furthermore, the earliest sonata to employ artificial harmonics, the first of Carlo Ciabrano's *Six solos for a violin, with a thorough-bass for the harpsichord*, was not published until 1763; it was followed some ten years later by the first of La Houssaye's *Sei sonate a violino solo e basso*, Op. 1 (Paris, c. 1773). The omission of harmonic effects from many important violin tutors, notably those of Geminiani, Rode *et al.* and, essentially, Leopold Mozart, further underlines their mixed reception, Leopold Mozart expressing particular disapproval of any juxtaposition of harmonics and normally-stopped notes within the same piece or movement.[13] L'Abbé le fils's brief survey of harmonics marks a step forward in the exploitation of the device and, in keeping with Leopold Mozart's views, incorporates a *menuet* written entirely in harmonics, both natural and artificial (Ex. 241). However, as with most other

Ex. 241

eighteenth- and early-nineteenth-century tutors, the accompanying written instruction is sparse, omitting reference to such important considerations as left-hand finger pressure, bow speed, bow pressure and the optimum contact point of the bow on the string. The amount of finger pressure required naturally depends on the type of harmonic desired; otherwise, for the best results, a fairly fast stroke should be cultivated with firm, steady pressure and a contact point near the bridge.

It was left to less reputable musicians like the vagrant Bohemian violinist Jakob Scheller (1759–1803) and virtuosi such as Paganini to arouse public interest in harmonic effects and the various techniques involved in their

12. Mondonville, *Les sons harmoniques, sonates à violon seul avec la basse continue* . . . (c. 1738); de Lusse, *Six sonates pour la flûte traversière avec une tablature des sons harmoniques* . . . (1751); L'Abbé le fils, 'Duo italien de Bertolde' from the *Deuxième recueil d'airs français et italiens, avec des variations pour deux violons* . . . (c. 1754); Ferrari, *VI Sonate a violino solo e basso* . . . *opera I⁰* (c. 1756–60).

13. L. Mozart, *Versuch* . . ., ch. 5, §13, p. 106–7.

mastery.[14] Paganini extended the use of harmonics to the limit of their technical potential and his introduction of artificial harmonics in double stopping,
employing all four fingers simultaneously, was an innovation. Chromatic
slides, single trills (Ex. 242), trills in double stopping (Ex. 243) and double

Ex. 242

Ex. 243

trills, all in harmonics, together with some interesting pseudo-harmonic
effects,[15] were included in his general repertoire; in his compositions for the
G string only, he extended the range of that string to cover at least three
octaves. Such stimulation resulted in the publication of numerous articles and
methods on the subject, especially, and rather surprisingly, in Germany, a
country which had been slow to accept the device.[16] The most significant of
these publications was Carl Guhr's *Ueber Paganinis Kunst, die Violine zu spielen*,
which, although somewhat confusing at times, incorporates an ambitious and
exhaustive survey of harmonic effects – Mazas quite justifiably claims that
some of Guhr's examples are more easily written than played.[17] It served as a
model for many later studies, incorporating not only the artificial harmonic of
the fifth but also that of the octave, as well as double harmonics (natural and
artificial), trills, diatonic and chromatic scales and other effects, entirely in
harmonics. Extended extracts are thus presented below alongside Guhr's
compatriot Spohr's rather brief survey of the same period, in order to represent
and contrast radical and conservative viewpoints about the use and execution
of harmonics.

14. See Mazas, *Méthode* . . . (1830), preface.
15. See Kirkendale, 'Segreto comunicato da Paganini', *Journal of the American Musicological Society*, vol. 18
(1965), pp. 394–407; Guhr, *Ueber Paganinis Kunst* . . . (1829), §13, p. 54.
16. See Kirkendale, 'Segreto comunicato da Paganini', *Journal of the American Musicological Society*, vol. 18
(1965), p. 405.
17. See Mazas's detailed survey, *Méthode* . . . (1830), pp. 115–21.

10. Harmonic playing in single notes

In my introduction I have drawn attention briefly to the advantages of this style of playing and it can be stated with certainty that Paganini has attained his outstanding precision and clarity on the violin above all by playing harmonics, since he possesses an incredible facility in [harmonics] both in single and double stopping and in slow phrases and rapid passages, without missing a single note. Apart from those advantages, there are certain passages, which can be played with comparative ease using [harmonics] but which are otherwise *impossible*, for example, no. 1 [Ex. 244]; others thereby become easier and safer [when harmonics are used]: no. 2 [Ex. 245].

Ex. 244

Ex. 245

on the 4th string

   In view of all that I have said, it remains truly incomprehensible that harmonic playing should have fallen into such *total* neglect in recent times, although it cannot be denied that many will have been deterred largely, one may assume, by the difficulty [of harmonics] and through anxiety about the great effort required for the production of these notes. The matter is simply not as difficult as many may imagine. In fact, in a simple scale the *only* difference between ordinary playing and harmonic notes is that for the former the fingers press *firmly* and for the latter *lightly* [on the strings]. However, the difficulties increase in double stopping for which it is very often necessary to use *four* fingers for *two* notes. An essential difference in playing harmonic notes is that they must always be taken a little higher than normal notes, since to produce harmonics the string is only touched lightly with the tip of the pad of the finger, while in normal playing the tension of the string is increased through the firm pressure of the whole breadth of the finger. But even this also has its advantage, in that the left hand learns thereby to distinguish accurately the greatest subtleties of touch, which are necessary especially in ordinary playing for the high notes at the end of the fingerboard near the bridge.

(A) Natural harmonic notes

Natural harmonics, for which only a lightly placed finger is necessary, are, for each string: the octave (at half the string's length); the second fifth (at $\frac{1}{3}$) from the fundamental note; the second octave (at $\frac{1}{4}$); the 3rd third (at $\frac{1}{5}$); the 3rd fifth (at $\frac{1}{6}$); the 3rd seventh (at $\frac{1}{7}$), but this note is a little lower than shown on our artificial scale; the 3rd octave (at $\frac{1}{8}$); the 4th second (at $\frac{1}{9}$); the 4th third (at $\frac{1}{10}$); the 4th fourth (at $\frac{1}{11}$);

the 4th fifth (at $\frac{1}{12}$); the 4th sixth (at $\frac{1}{13}$); the 4th seventh (at $\frac{1}{14}$); the 4th octave (at $\frac{1}{16}$) and so on. So if we take, for instance, the open G string as our fundamental note, then the following natural harmonics appear upon it *twice*: first from the *middle* of the string to the *nut* and again from the *middle* of the same [string] to the *bridge*. The former, however, gives the notes distinctly only up to the 3rd fifth; the f³ and g³ [*sic*] sometimes sound, but they lie so close to each other that it is not always possible to rely on their immediate production; with the latter even the 4th, 6th, 7th and octave speak clearly.

Ex. 246

If the finger is lightly placed on the string at an equal distance from the nut and the bridge, the *lowest* harmonic notes will be produced, e.g. here the note g¹. This note we will indicate by A¹ (first harmonic) (see i [Ex. 247]); the 2nd harmonic note d² is formed at one third of the string and it is quite immaterial whether the third be reckoned from the nut or from the bridge, A² (k). The same rule applies to the quarter-string g² or third harmonic, (A³) (l); the 4th b² (A⁴) is formed at one fifth of the string (m) and (A⁵) d³ at one sixth (n).

Ex. 247

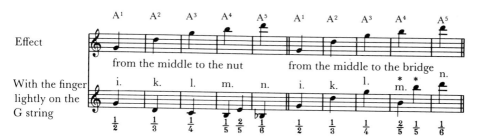

The notes marked * are of course only practicable when the fundamental note is an open string, here G.

The *roman* numerals in no. 5 [Ex. 248] and all following examples indicate the interval to be made by the lightly placed finger with the given fundamental note. The octave VIII, fifth V and the fourth IV are always perfect; the major third is indicated III and the minor III♭.

Ex. 248

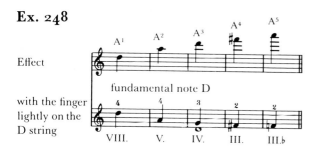

[Similar examples are also provided for the A and E strings but are not included here.]

To put it in a different way, it will thus be seen that the mid-point of the string gives the octave; the [perfect] fifth, reckoned from the fundamental note, gives the second fifth; the [perfect] fourth the second octave; the *major* third the 3rd third; the *minor* third the 3rd fifth.

The difference between the *major* and *minor* third must be observed very carefully to avoid becoming confused by the indications in future musical examples.

(B) Artificial harmonic notes with one firm and one light finger.

When the note a flat is played on the G string, the latter may be considered shortened and its former complete length is somewhat decreased. The finger takes the place of the nut.

The same procedure then takes place as with the previous open G string except that here the first finger must remain firmly pressed down on the a flat.

The halfway point of this shortened string, therefore, touched lightly with the little finger, will give the octave a flat[1] (i) [Ex. 249]. The great stretch required, however,

Ex. 249

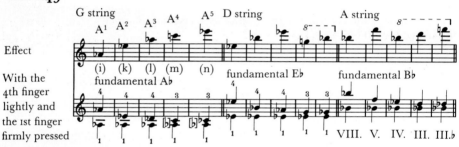

makes this extremely difficult. It is most likely to succeed if one can contrive to stop the fundamental note a flat with only the side of the first finger, for in this way one can reach the mid-point of the string. The third *of the thus shortened string* gives as before the second fifth e flat[2] (k), the quarter the second octave, a flat[2] (l); the fifth the third third c[3] (m), the sixth the third fifth e flat[3] (n) [Ex. 249].

(Guhr, Ueber Paganinis Kunst. . . (1829), pp. 13–15)

Several similar examples are provided for various fundamental notes on all four strings, but particularly the G and D strings, Guhr acknowledging the less frequent use of artificial harmonics from third position upwards on the A and E strings. Subsection C follows, entitled 'Diatonic scales in which natural harmonic notes occupy the principal degrees of the scale, which can be taken only in the third position and are then perfectly easy to play' (Ex. 250).

Most of these scales involve wide stretches for the first four or five notes and illustrate the use of A[1], A[2] and A[3], that is, where the light finger touches the octave (A[1]), the perfect fifth (A[2]) and the perfect fourth (A[3]) above the fun-

Ex. 250

Ex. 251

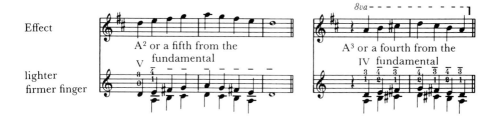

damental note (Ex. 251). Guhr further adds that A⁴ and A⁵ can and must occasionally play their part in the scale, especially for double notes, but warns that A⁵ cannot be introduced satisfactorily in rapid scale passages, due to its unreliable 'speaking' properties; it is only practicable in passages such as Ex. 252.

Ex. 252

Many of Guhr's examples show the various effects that can be produced from the same fundamental note, using A², A³, A⁴ or A⁵ as alternatives, and he especially recommends practising such exercises as Ex. 252, on account of the alternating ³–⁴₁–₂ fingering, and mastering the scales formed by A⁴ (Ex. 253).

Ex. 253

A further subsection regarding chromatic scales incorporates examples in which A^2 (the fifth remaining as fundamental note) is changed to the higher octave by the light touch of the second finger (Ex. 254a); similarly in Ex. 254b by the touch of the second or third finger and in Ex. 254c the A^1 (the octave remaining as the fundamental note) by the touch of the first finger. Guhr concludes section 10 by again stressing the need for the greatest precision of touch.

Ex. 254

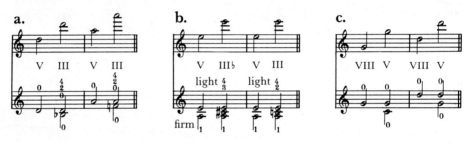

11. On harmonic double stopping

Just as when playing single notes it is clear that one must avoid touching the strings with any finger not absolutely required, so with double notes even greater attention must be given to this point. The principal rule in studying them is first to play each note separately, beginning with the upper note, following with the lower note, then playing both combined together or at least in quick succession. This practice will be found a great aid and simplification in accustoming the hand to the precise touch and fingering.

(A) On combining natural harmonics

The easiest combination is that shown in nos. 1 [Ex. 255a] and 2 [Ex. 255b]. It will be found with nos. 3 [Ex. 255c] and 4 [Ex. 255d] that a more delicate management of the bow and above all a scrupulous correctness of touch are required in order to make the notes speak quickly. To practise in the following way will be found of considerable benefit [Ex. 256].   (Guhr, *Ueber Paganinis Kunst. . .* (1829), p. 24)

Ex. 255

Ex. 256

Guhr concludes this subsection with examples of double-stopped natural harmonics of varying difficulty and then proceeds to double stopping in artificial harmonics, commencing with the easiest interval, the perfect fifth, and dealing in turn with major and minor thirds, perfect fourths, major and minor sixths, major, minor and diminished sevenths, octaves and unisons. He further provides examples of scales in harmonics in thirds and sixths and exercises (including some by Johann Küster) for the perfection of single- and double-stopped harmonics.

Guhr ends his survey with observations regarding the optimum manner of writing harmonics and examples of their effective combination with normal playing:

(D) On the manner of writing harmonics

It cannot be denied that in writing harmonic notes it is best that the eye should see what the ear hears. Therefore, I write a melody in harmonics at the pitch at which the ear perceives it and add the word *Armonica*, or A^1, A^2 and so on, or merely A above it. This manner of writing also gives the player the advantage of choice between normal and harmonic notes, should he not be versed in the latter. But if, for example, g^2 is written ![ARM] or ![notation] then the choice ceases, and besides the ear hears g^2 whilst the eye sees c^1.

When the normal manner of playing succeeds harmonic notes, I put S or Sto., that is *solito* or *maniera solita di suonare* (as normal, or normal manner of playing) e.g.:

Ex. 257

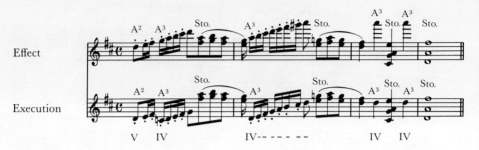

(E) On combining harmonics with normal playing.

Passages like the following [Ex. 258], in which Paganini combines normal playing and harmonic notes, are both pleasing and unusual.

Ex. 258

Ex. 258 (cont.)

d.

Execution

(Guhr, *Ueber Paganinis Kunst* . . . (1829), pp. 38–9)

Spohr, on the other hand, is reserved about the use of all harmonic effects because of their lack of tonal affinity with stopped notes. He particularly disapproves of the performance of entire melodies in artificial harmonics, claiming that such effects adversely affect tonal breadth and sonority and thus degrade the instrument.

Harmonics are produced by touching the string very lightly with the finger, instead of pressing it down firmly on the fingerboard as is the case with other [natural] notes. On account of their brighter sound, they are employed chiefly in order to make one single note stand out more clearly than the others, for example the final note of ascending scales or broken chords.

However, as many of the harmonics that can be produced on the violin are so different in sound from the natural notes of the instrument that they strike the ear immediately as strange and ill-matched to the others, the noble school allows the use only of those to which this does not apply. These are 1) the octave, 2) the fifth of the octave, and 3) two octaves above each string, that is on the G string 𝄞 , on the D string 𝄞 , on the A string 𝄞 , and on the E string 𝄞 . The middle of the string gives the octave; two-thirds of its length gives the fifth of the octave and three-quarters two octaves above, measuring from either the nut or the bridge. However, harmonics must always be taken on the side nearer the bridge because they respond more easily and reliably and have more tonal affinity with stopped notes there than on the opposite side. Thus, all usable harmonics are stopped in the same place as their equivalent sounding 'natural' notes.[18]

(Spohr, *Violinschule* (1832), p. 108)

18. The harmonics cited above have always been used by all good violinists in combination with the natural notes, as they are not very different in sound from the latter. All others, however, and especially the so-called artificial harmonics, must be rejected as unsuitable, because they differ considerably from the natural tone of the instrument. Whenever entire melodies are played in such childish, alien tones, it amounts to degradation of the noble instrument. Admittedly, the celebrated Paganini has caused a great sensation of late through the revival of the antiquated and almost forgotten art of playing harmonics and through his outstanding skill, but however tempting such an example may be, I must still strongly advise all young violinists not to waste time in such study to the neglect of more useful things. In support of this view, I can cite the greatest violinists of all time, e.g. Pugnani, Tartini, Corelli, Viotti, Eck, Rode, Kreutzer, Baillot, Lafont and others, not even one of whom has played harmonics after Paganini's fashion. I might go so far as to say that even if harmonic playing were to be a valuable addition to art and an enrichment of violin playing, sanctioned by good taste, it would still be bought too dearly at the expense of a full, sonorous tone, with which it is incompatible, because the artificial harmonics speak only with thin strings, from which it is impossible to produce a full tone. (Spohr's footnote)

This section should not be concluded without a mention of Galeazzi's unorthodox alternative method of producing harmonics, endorsed by Guhr and Spohr in the extracts cited, which involves bowing near the nut and fingering near the bridge, thus reversing the normal manner of playing the instrument.[19] He even provides two examples to illustrate the theoretical feasibility of his suggestion, although its obvious practical awkwardness would naturally have limited its serious application.

PIZZICATO

Pizzicato with the right hand was commonly employed in violin music of the period but instruction as to its execution was surprisingly neglected in most contemporary tutors. The comparatively few writers who mention the device – the German school is perhaps the best represented – divide themselves basically into three schools of thought, the first advocating the normal violin hold with the right-hand index-finger performing the *pizzicato*[20] and the second recommending the 'guitar position' with the violin held across the body and under the right arm and the *pizzicato* performed by the right-hand thumb.[21] The members of the third faction, mostly writers of the more comprehensive surveys and notably Löhlein, Campagnoli, Spohr and Baillot, incorporate descriptions of both techniques and thus generally adopt a more flexible approach to the execution of *pizzicato*. Löhlein, for example, recommends the normal violin hold with right-hand index-finger *pizzicato* for most *pizzicato* passages but, like Spohr, prefers the guitar position, with the strings plucked by the thumb, for chords.[22] This thumb *pizzicato*, which could be employed with either of the basic right-hand *pizzicato* techniques,[23] depending of course on the musical context, was especially useful for the clear and sonorous arpeggiation of chords or for passages in which a softer tone was required, the fleshy pad of the thumb being far better equipped than the index-finger for this purpose.

Passing mention must be made here of Berlioz's contribution towards extending the range of *pizzicato* techniques.[24] In an effort to achieve more varied and rapid *pizzicato* effects, he suggests a manner of execution closely resembling guitar technique, which involves laying down the bow, using the thumb and the three largest fingers as plucking agents and making the little finger rest on the violin body as support for the right hand. Such a position allows greater facility in the execution of passages such as Ex. 259, with the successive use of the first and second fingers on the same string.

19. Galeazzi, *Elementi* . . . (1791), vol. 1, pt. 2, art. 12, p. 176.
20. For example, Reichardt, *Ueber die Pflichten* . . . (1776), p. 83; Petri, *Anleitung* . . . (1767), pt. 3, p. 413.
21. For example, Hiller, *Anweisung* . . . (1792), p. 10.
22. Löhlein, *Anweisung* . . . (1774), pp. 96–7; Spohr, *Violinschule* (1832), p. 168.
23. See Baillot, *L'art* . . . (1834), pp. 223–4 (presented in translation on pp. 225–6).
24. Berlioz, *A treatise on modern instrumentation*, tr. Clarke, p. 21.

Ex. 259

N.B. Figures = R.H. fingers
+ = R.H. thumb.

The use of the more difficult left-hand *pizzicato* was rare but by no means unknown in the eighteenth century. Tremais, for instance, requires an advanced left-hand *pizzicato* technique in the second sonata of his Op. 4 (in *scordatura*), in which individual *pizzicato* notes are alternated with single bowed notes and sometimes with bowed slurs (Ex. 260). Eighteenth-century

Ex. 260

documentation of left-hand *pizzicato* is very sparse – only Campagnoli and Woldemar[25] mention it in their treatises and then only fleetingly – and many prominent nineteenth-century writers, notably Rode *et al.*, Habeneck, Mazas and Spohr, also fail even to acknowledge the device. However, Johann and Anton Stamitz, Mestrino, Pichl, and other such violinist–composers began to popularise its use at the end of the eighteenth century, preparing the way for its thorough exploitation by succeeding generations of virtuosi.

Left-hand *pizzicato* was one of the most striking ingredients of Paganini's performing style, in which it was sometimes combined even with right-hand *pizzicato*, notably in the fifteenth variation of his *Carnaval de Venise* (Ex. 261).

Ex. 261

25. Campagnoli, *Metodo* . . . (1797?), tr. Bishop, pt. 3, no. 195B; Woldemar, *Grande méthode* . . . (c. 1800), p. 48.

Furthermore, Paganini was perhaps the greatest exponent of left-hand *piz-zicato* and bowed notes in combination (Ex. 262). He exploited this effect with unprecedented intensity in such works as the 'God save the King' variations and the *Duet for one violin*. The former even contains a *pizzicato* melody accompanied by bowed notes (Ex. 263); the melody is later transferred to the G

Ex. 262

Ex. 263

Variation 4: Vivace

string, with *pizzicato* demisemiquavers providing the accompaniment. The climax comprises sustained open notes on the G and D strings with double *pizzicati* in sixths above.

Such astonishing facility in the execution of left-hand *pizzicato* may be attributed in part to Paganini's unorthodox posture and violin hold; his left elbow, positioned against his chest, no doubt acted like a crutch, from which the left hand and wrist could execute *pizzicato* with greater power.

Baillot's account of *pizzicato* techniques is perhaps the most comprehensive and detailed of the period, although Reichardt's right-hand *pizzicato* instruction closely rivals and even surpasses it in some respects. However, as Reichardt understandably omits consideration of left-hand *pizzicato*, for this was never part of the eighteenth-century *Ripienist*'s everyday technical equipment, Baillot's account will form the basis of our survey, together with an extract from Guhr's study, which focuses on Paganini's eccentric and virtuoso application of Baillot's basic principles.

Pizzicato

Pizzicato is accomplished by plucking the string with one finger of the right or the left hand.

Right-hand pizzicato

Pizzicato is usually accomplished with the right hand; it is fuller in tone than left-hand *pizzicato* and, furthermore, it is more sonorous when played by the thick pad of the finger, which rectifies its natural dryness.

This *pizzicato* is generally played with the fleshy part of the thumb, holding the violin like a guitar, that is to say, crosswise under the right forearm. When there are few notes to play, or when the tempo scarcely allows the time to place the violin in this position, the string is plucked with the index-finger or the thumb of the right hand, chiefly for chords, holding the frog of the bow [in the palm] with the last two fingers bent round it. Soft sounds are obtained by placing the thumb near the middle of the fingerboard.

Ex. 264

(Haydn: Quartet no. 40)

Broken chords, as on the harp, plucked with the thumb when ascending and with the index-finger when descending.

Ex. 265

Three notes plucked with the thumb, and the 4th note plucked with the index-finger.

Ex. 266

Chords played alternately with the bow and with the index-finger of the right hand.

Ex. 267

Left-hand pizzicato

The strings may also be plucked with the fingers of the left hand, but with neither the same facility nor so many advantages; since the string does not vibrate as freely near the nut as it does where it lies less close to the fingerboard, the sound produced is dry. This shortcoming cannot be rectified as it can with the right hand, which can set the string vibrating near the middle of the fingerboard in order to produce mellow sounds. Furthermore, the fingers of the left hand, because of their position, cannot call upon the same strength as the thumb and index-finger of the right hand, and even if they are more agile, owing to the assistance that they can afford each other mutually as they pluck the string one after another, they have less control [over their agility].

Stamitz sometimes employed this type of *pizzicato* in his solos in something of the following manner.

All the notes with a dot over them must be plucked with the finger which has played the preceding note; the others are played with the bow.

Ex. 268

When, in an orchestra, the finger is not placed soon enough on the string in order to pluck it with precision, a slight delay results which spoils the ensemble and which should be guarded against with great attention and special care when using this type of effect.

With *pizzicatos* being employed frequently by modern composers, it is very useful to practise executing them well with the right hand; they are susceptible of many nuances which one may not be able to add if one does not possess the technique.

All the necessary exercises for the practice of left-hand *pizzicato* will be found in Mr Guhr's book.   (Baillot, *L'art*. . . (1834), pp. 223-4)

The relevant extract from Guhr's treatise, complete with the exercises recommended by Baillot, is included here as a supplement to Baillot's survey.

9. *Paganini's combination of bowing and left-hand pizzicato*

Although this type of *pizzicato* was frequently employed in the earlier Italian school in Mestrino's day,[26] it has become quite obsolete in the more recent French and German schools. Only Paganini uses it and, as his results prove, with great success. The chief requirement for its accomplishment is that the second, third and fourth fingers of the left hand should pluck the notes *clearly* and *neatly*. Particular difficulties arise with the G and D strings, because they are more difficult to set vibrating, and most of all with notes for which the plucking finger lies next to the one already stopping [the note]. The following exercises will show how this difficulty can be overcome. (The middle of the bow should contact the string with a short, almost springing stroke.)

The noughts here signify *pizzicato* with the 2nd, 3rd and 4th finger, not open strings.

The final A in no. 1 [Ex. 269] should be plucked with the 4th finger.

Ex. 269

on the 2nd string

Ex. 270

It is extremely difficult to play the following passage distinctly on the G string without touching the open D and A:

Ex. 271

Variation sopra 'Nel cor piu non mi sento'

---

26. Fayolle (*Paganini et Bériot*, pp. 49–50), with some reason, considers Guhr's statement regarding Mestrino and the Italian school to be incorrect.

Ex. 271 (cont.)

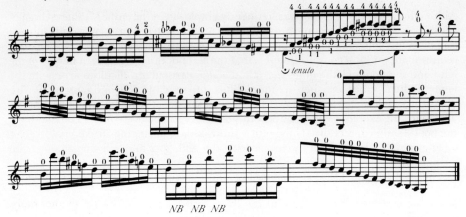

NB NB NB

NB indicates that the open string is played with the bow and the fingered notes
stopped with the first finger and *plucked* with the fourth.

(Guhr, *Ueber Paganinis Kunst. . .* (1829), §9, pp. 12–13)

SPECIAL BOWING EFFECTS

Discussion of effects such as *sul ponticello*, *sulla tastiera*, *flautando*, *col legno* and
tremolo, employed only sparingly in compositions of the period, is generally
omitted by most writers; the sparse documentation that exists is summarised
below.

   Although some writers point out the tonal consequences of drawing the
bow on or near the bridge or over the fingerboard, their intention is merely to
highlight effects which are contrary to the contemporary ideal of a strong,
powerful tone rather than those which are suitable for expressive exploitation.
Boccherini is known to have employed the *sul ponticello* effect[27] and Haydn also
exploits it in the second movement of his Symphony no. 97 in C. Woldemar
provides an example of its use (Ex. 272), attempting to imitate the Jew's harp

Ex. 272

Accompaniment: imitate the Jew's harp by playing
lightly close to the bridge.

normal sounds   Jew's harp

use an up bow
for the 1st

27. Boyden, 'The violin and its technique in the eighteenth century', *Musical Quarterly*, vol. 36 (1950),
   p. 28.

by 'playing lightly close to the bridge'.[28] Writers of the period omit discussion of the value both of inclining the bow stick towards the player for optimum execution of this effect, so that the upper harmonics of the fundamental are given more prominence than the written note, and of employing a light, even bow pressure, the actual amount depending on the instrument in use.

Passing mention of the opposite effect, *sulla tastiera*, is made by Woldemar and Galeazzi[29] but Baillot, who describes the *flautando* or *détaché flûté* separately elsewhere in his method,[30] again provides the best overall description of those effects resulting from a fundamental change in the contact point between bow hair and string.

13. Place the bow hair between the rounded parts of the violin f-holes and the fingerboard, a little nearer to the f-holes than to the fingerboard (see Fig. [20·15])

14. Move the hair nearer to or further from the bridge, according to whether more or less sound is desired for the melody, while playing firmly.

15. It is desirable to bring the bow away from the bridge to achieve mellowness and roundness of tone in the passage-work as well as sweetness in the melodies.

16. By virtue of the bow hair being very near to or very far from the bridge, two opposite effects are obtained; the first is indicated by the words: *sul ponticello, tout contre le chevalet*; by putting scarcely any pressure on the bow at all, the tone has a whistling and nasal [quality]; it is suitable for certain contrasts.

Ex. 273

(Boccherini: Quintet no. 7)

The other is marked *sul la tastiera* [*sic*], *sur la touche*; by using longer, lighter bows, soft, flute-like sounds are obtained.

Ex. 274

(Baillot: *Air varié* Op. 14)

(Baillot, *L'art* . . . (1834), art. 4, p. 13)

28. Woldemar, *Grande méthode* . . . (c. 1800), p. 46.
29. *Ibid.*, p. 47; Galeazzi, *Elementi* . . . (1791), vol. 1, pt. 2, p. 168.   30. See p. 192.

Col legno is mentioned only by Woldemar, Baillot, Berlioz and Howell but little technical instruction is included. Woldemar is perhaps the most explicit, directing the student merely 'to hit all the notes lightly in the same place with the bow stick';[31] Berlioz and Howell[32] confirm that *col legno* was rarely employed at that time, but Howell considers it 'of sufficient importance' and Berlioz indicates that 'it has perceptible effect in a large orchestra'. Boieldieu certainly proved the latter point in his overture *Le Calife de Bagdad* (1800).

The *tremolo* (otherwise called *bombo* or *Schwärmer*), a rapid reiteration of the same note or notes produced by a quick movement of the bow up and down, is another special effect sparingly employed and rarely discussed during this period. It was most commonly used in an orchestral context to heighten the dramatic effect, as in Ex. 275 from the oracle scene of Gluck's *Alceste*. Berlioz, not surprisingly, provides the most comprehensive survey, claiming that the *tremolo*, with its fast, supple and relaxed wrist movement, can express trouble,

Ex. 275

---

31. Woldemar, *Grande méthode* . . . (c. 1800), p. 48.
32. Berlioz, *A treatise on modern instrumentation*, tr. Clarke, p. 12; Howell, *Original instructions* . . . (1825), p. 51.

agitation, terror or a stormy, violent or angelic character, according to its various degrees of pitch and dynamic.[33] Amongst the violin repertory, three of Mazas's *Études d'artistes* are worthy of special mention here, since each is specifically designed for the perfection of one particular type of *tremolo*. No. 67 concentrates on the ordinary *tremolo* effect (Ex. 276a), whilst its immediate

Ex. 276

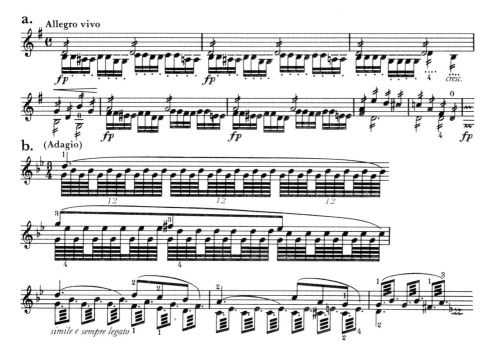

successor deals with left-hand *tremolo* within a *legato* bowing context (Ex. 276b), an effect commonly employed by Paganini (for example, in the Caprice no. 6). The sixty-ninth study is perhaps the most interesting, as it is intended for the practice of the 'tremolo with springing bow', which involves a combination of *ricochet* and *tremolo* techniques (Ex. 277).

Ex. 277

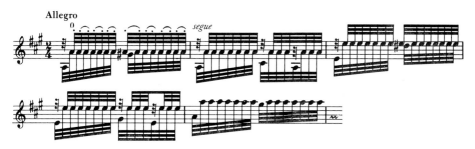

33. Berlioz, *A treatise on modern instrumentation*, tr. Clarke, p. 7.

SCORDATURA

Scordatura, an Italian term designating variations in the tuning of the violin (otherwise called *violon discordé* or *à cordes ravallées* in France and *Verstimmung* or *mit der gebundenen Violine* in Germany), was employed in violin playing as early as the seventeenth century and maintained its popularity until about the end of the eighteenth century. It was inherited from lute and viol technique, the first-known violin composition to include *scordatura* being the second sonata of Biagio Marini's Op. 7 (1629). Composers were attracted to the new colours, timbres and the increased sonority or brilliance offered by the retuning and consequent tension changes of the relevant strings; furthermore, *scordatura* could provide new harmonic possibilities, extend the range of the instrument (for example, by lowering the G string), imitate other instruments or facilitate the execution of whole compositions or certain technical passages, especially those involving wide intervals, intricate string-crossing or double stopping, which might otherwise be impossible. The particular tuning employed was generally indicated at the beginning of each composition or movement, accompanied, in most cases, by a form of tablature indicating a key-signature for each string.[34] With this tablature, the violin was treated as a transposing instrument, the music being notated according to the disposition of the fingers and not according to sound. This method of notation inevitably required the violinist to observe three basic rules in performance: to use first position wherever possible, to use open strings wherever possible unless otherwise indicated and to apply accidentals only to the register indicated. Further technical problems to be overcome involved those of intonation (and, in many cases, retuning in the middle of a composition), and the need to adapt such bowing considerations as the contact point, bow speed and pressure to suit string textures, tensions and thicknesses. When a string is tuned lower than its normal pitch, a richer tone results from the use of a thicker string which in turn requires heavier bow pressure, slower bow speed and a contact point further away from the bridge. The reverse is true when a string is tuned higher than its normal pitch. However, these problems appear to have been neglected by most writers in their methods.

Up to the beginning of the eighteenth century, *scordatura* was most commonly employed by German violinists, notably Nicolas Strungk, J. E. Kindermann, Gottfried Hunger and, most important, Heinrich Biber. However, there are few examples of *scordatura* in eighteenth-century works by German composers; although Quantz mentions *scordatura* briefly in his *Versuch* . . ., Schweigl's *Grundlehre der Violin* (1794-5) was one of the first German violin methods to refer to and illustrate the device.

At the time of its decline in Germany, the use of *scordatura* became more

---

34. See Russell, 'The violin scordatura', *Musical Quarterly*, vol. 24 (1938), pp. 84-96.

popular in Italy, England and France. Tartini, Castrucci, Lolli, Barbella, Campagnoli and Nardini were all prominent Italian exponents of the device. Barbella's and Campagnoli's tunings, derived from the four middle strings of the viola d'amore, were used to imitate that instrument. Campagnoli instructs the player to use thick A and E strings and play *con sordino*, describing the effect as 'an unusual mode of tuning and playing the violin, pleasing and useful from the variety it introduces into the art'.[35] Nardini's tuning, employed in his *Sonate énigmatique*, incorporates the normal tuning for the two upper strings and the viol tuning for the two lower strings, thus enabling the player to provide his own bass line. The music is printed on two staves, which are to be played simultaneously, the bass clef indicating the notes as fingered on a violin tuned normally in fifths (Ex. 278).

Ex. 278

Scordatura was also known in England from as early as the seventeenth century but there is little evidence of its regular use during the eighteenth century. However, Scottish composers employed the device in many of their reels and folk dances, notably *Kilrack's reel* or *Anthony Murrey's reel*, the most common tuning being a–e^1–a^1–e^2.

Michel Corrette's *L'école d'Orphée* (1738) was the first French method to discuss *scordatura*, adopting four different tunings in examples entitled *Pièces à cordes ravallées* (Ex. 279);[36] Corrette employed the fourth tuning again in his

Ex. 279

Premier livre de sonates à violon seul. Other French composers to employ *scordatura* included Jean Le Maire (for example, Sonata I, *Rondeau*), Tremais (for example, Op. 4 nos. 2, 4 and 6) and Berthaume (for example, Op. 2 and Op. 4 no. 2).

35. Campagnoli, *Metodo* . . . (1797?), tr. Bishop, pt. 3, no. 195C.
36. Corrette, *L'école d'Orphée*, pp. 39–41.

Baillot provides the most comprehensive survey of *scordatura* usage throughout the period and beyond, listing nine tunings and discussing the advantages and disadvantages of each:

Tuning of the violin

	Advantages	Disadvantages
1. Universally adopted tuning 	Simplicity . . . Richness. Is composed of only one and the same perfect consonance. Its range gives the notes of tunings nos. 2, 3, 4, 6, 7 and 8, whereas these tunings do not include all the notes incorporated into this range.	This way of tuning the violin has no other disadvantage than that associated with simplicity. It might not always be equally pleasing to imperfect organs, but one never wanders from it without feeling the need to return.

Scordatura or different ways of tuning the violin

	Advantages	Disadvantages
2. Used by Tartini 	Greater vibration of the octaves with the open E and A, just as with the aliquots.	Monotonous . . . Vibrations which, by their great resonance, are suitable only for certain characters of music requiring more sonority than others, and which are harmful, besides, considering that the nuances must depend on the performer, and that no note should speak more than another where the performer does not wish it. One note less at the bottom of the register.
3. Used by Barbella 	Harmonious and sweet, imitating the viola d'amore.	Monotonous . . . Two high notes fewer, one low note less.
4. Used by Nardini 	As the preceding.	Monotonous. Three low notes fewer. Less sweet than the preceding for this reason.

5. Used by Lolli

A low and sweet effect

Limited . . . with the fourth string three tones lower and thus very slack, it does not take the bow.

6. Used by Mr Paganini

One more high note. Very awkward passages rendered easy and incisive by this means. Increased sonority.

Less nobility, due to the raising of the four strings by a semitone and the semitone less in the bass. With the solo violin tuned in this manner and the orchestra preserving the ordinary tuning, the character of the tonality is altered by this combination.

7. Used by Mr Paganini

A different tuning for the G string only; more sonority (with the B natural) and more sense of illusion in the use of the G string alone, in that the high notes appear more difficult than they are in reality, the string being raised a third. Renders easy some passages which would be impractical without this method.

Minor or major third less in the lower register.

8. Used by Messrs Mazas and de Bériot

A similar advantage to the preceding tuning, but not so great for the exclusive use of the G string. Giving more sonority to the other strings.

One less low note.

9. Used by the author of this method

Gives a surprising effect of sweetness. Low note favourable to the arpeggio. Semitone more in the bass.

The G string thus lowered does not stay in tune if the effect is prolonged.

10. Idem

Surprise more prolonged; a sweet and deep effect; favourable to the arpeggio and to the ending of the piece. A fourth more in the bass.

The G string, slackened more than in the preceding passage, stays in tune even less if its use is more prolonged. In order to avoid this disadvantage, one can put on a thicker G string, but it would no longer be in proportion to the other strings and would destroy that smoothness and balance between the strings whose effect is a performance with the greatest sweetness of transition when passing from low to high or high to low notes.

In spite of the disadvantages, more or less great, that we have just described, experience proves that these different *ways of tuning the violin* can sometimes be successfully employed.   (Baillot, *L'art* . . . (1834), pp. 229–33)

The section concludes with compositions or extracts from works by the composers listed above.[37] The two studies by Baillot himself, each requiring a remarkable retuning of the G string during its course, are written out at actual pitch, an unusual practice in *scordatura* writing, as compositions are normally written out as fingered by the performer.

Scordatura gradually lost popularity during the nineteenth century, although it never became obsolete. Paganini was undoubtedly its greatest and most prolific exponent, employing the device to simplify his music and add brilliance to his tone and performing style. For example, Paganini's Violin Concerto no. 1 in E flat major employs the sixth tuning in Baillot's table; this tuning gives the soloist extra tonal colour, intensity and brilliance over the orchestra and facilitates certain virtuoso passage-work, the violinist fingering in D major with the resultant sound in E flat major (Exx. 280 & 281). Abnormal tunings also enabled him to reproduce, on open strings, harmonics which would normally have to be stopped, and Guhr provides numerous other examples demonstrating the advantages of *scordatura* (Exx. 282–4).

Many writers claim that Paganini sometimes retuned his strings during a composition, always with unfailing accuracy,[38] and he adopted a special tuning for his works for the G string only, generally raising that string a minor third to b flat (Ex. 285), or even a major third to b natural. Other works require the G string to be raised a tone to a, notably the three *Airs variés*; simi-

37. Baillot, *L'art* . . . (1834), pp. 234–40.
38. See Istel, 'The secret of Paganini's technique', *Musical Quarterly*, vol. 16 (1930), p. 113.

Ex. 280

Ex. 281

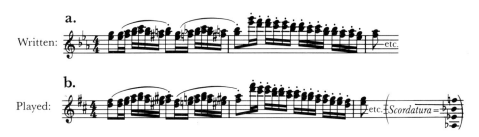

Ex. 282

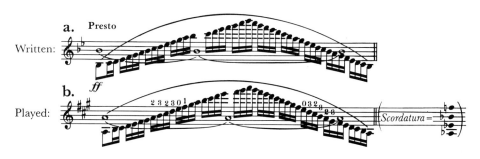

Ex. 283

Ex. 284

Ex. 285

larly, the violin part of his variations on the air 'Di tanti palpiti' (in B flat major) is written in A major for a violin tuned up a semitone. Furthermore, it is quite conceivable that, in his 'Moses' Sonata, Paganini may have tuned the G string up a perfect fourth to c^1.[39] Paganini apparently used even thinner strings for such remarkable applications of *scordatura* and took the precaution of stretching each string to the required pitch before a performance.[40]

Apart from Paganini, examples of violin *scordatura* in the nineteenth century are rare. Mazas, however, employed the device in his *La cloche fantaisie* Op. 76, and Spohr also employed it in some of his duets for violin and harp, raising each string a semitone to correspond with the harp part, written a semitone higher. The raising of the G string was also employed by some violinists, nota-

39. See Rizo-Rangabe, correspondence, *The Strad*, vol. 68 (1958), p. 380.
40. Guhr, *Ueber Paganinis Kunst . . .* (1829), §1, p. 3.

bly de Bériot, Mazas and Prume, whilst Berlioz claims that Winter tuned the G string down a tone in order to produce 'softer and deeper effects'.[41]

CON SORDINO

Mutes were generally made from wood or metal; Leopold Mozart mentions wood, lead, steel or brass, while Rousseau suggests either copper or silver.[42] Quantz favours the steel varieties, provided their weight is proportioned to the size of the instruments.[43] Reichardt, on the other hand, prefers a mute 'of solid, thick and dry wood'[44] on the grounds that metal mutes either veil the sound too much or produce a whistling, rasping tone.

Con sordino was more commonly employed in orchestral and ensemble playing than in solo performance, but, even so, its use was rare, reserved only for special effect. German writers provide the most detailed information about the use of mutes in the late eighteenth century, a subject which was surprisingly neglected in contemporary French and Italian methods. Löhlein, for example, echoes Quantz's advice, recommending that the mute should be used in order to convey the effect of tenderness and flattery as well as more 'violent' emotions such as madness and despair.[45] However, Baillot is one of the few early-nineteenth-century writers to discuss muted effects in any detail; his account outstrips all others of the period and is thus included below.

The mute seems to give the sound a sort of 'minor mode'. Its veiled timbre has something mysterious, sweet and doleful about it. It refreshes and rests the senses which are very wearied by brilliant effects, it prepares the way for other impressions which are then so much the stronger for being induced by a contrast; it inclines one to meditation, it encourages those profound emotions which are so attractive to tender and melancholy souls, because such music can give a feeling beyond pleasure and even have a power for good.

It is therefore essential to use the mute whenever the composer has so indicated his intention; it would be misguided to believe that playing very *piano* would take its place; we think we have made it sufficiently clear that nothing could take the place of this effect of timbre.

(See the *Andante* of the [Haydn's] Symphony in E minor,[46] the introduction to Haydn's Oratorio, *The Creation*, the *Adagio* of Mozart's G minor Quintet, the Trio on the death of Haydn and finally the admirable *Crucifixus* from the Mass in four parts by Mr Cherubini.)

Note: The mute, when placed on the bridge, has several disadvantages.

(1st) It cannot be placed in position without suspending and impeding one's playing.

41. Berlioz, *A treatise on modern instrumentation*, tr. Clarke, p. 4.
42. L. Mozart, *Versuch . . .*, ch. 1, section 3, p. 52; *Dictionnaire de Musique*, ed. Rousseau, p. 461, s.v. 'Sourdine'.
43. Quantz, *Versuch . . .* tr. and ed. Reilly, ch. 17, section 2, §29, pp. 233-4.
44. Reichardt, *Ueber die Pflichten . . .* (1776), p. 86.
45. Löhlein, *Anweisung . . .* (1774), p. 110; Quantz, *Versuch . . .*, tr. and ed. Reilly, ch. 17, section 2, §29, pp. 233-4.
46. Baillot is probably referring to Haydn's Symphony no. 44 in E minor (the 'Trauersinfonie').

(2nd) It disturbs the tuning of the violin.

(3rd) It is as troublesome to take off as to put on.

It would therefore be desirable for violin makers to look for a method which would allow the performer to mute the sound of the violin and to restore it at will to its natural state, *without stopping playing*, preserving all along the special timbre given by the ordinary mute.[47]   (Baillot, *L'art.* . . (1834), p. 223)

47. (This problem has just been solved in the most ingenious and satisfactory manner by one of our worthy violin professors, Mr. Bellon.) (Baillot's footnote)

10

Pitch, tuning and intonation

A confusing variety of pitches coexisted internationally, nationally and even in the same locality in the eighteenth century, the actual pitch adopted normally differing according to the type of music played and, naturally enough, the performing venue. In particular, the relative pitches used in secular and sacred venues were commonly at variance within most localities (church/ organ pitches normally being the highest) and the varied terminology employed in their description (*Cornet-Ton*, *Zinck-Ton*, *Chor-Ton*, quire pitch, *ton de chapelle*, *corista*, *Kammer-Ton*, *ton de chambre*, *Grosskammerton*, *Kleinkammerton*, *tief Kammer-Ton*, *Opern-Ton*, *ton d'opéra* etc.) was open to different interpretation according to date, country, city and venue.

In his thorough survey of these relative standards,[1] devoted to a period spanning more than three centuries, Mendel states that in Germany the pitch of organs was normally called *Chor-Ton*, so named because many old organs had been built at a high pitch to suit the choir (in modal music). Even though this term would seem to imply a substantially standardised pitch, nothing could be further from the truth in the eighteenth century. Furthermore, there were at least two approximate levels of *Kammer-Ton*, a higher variety about a whole tone lower than *Chor-Ton* and a variety a semitone lower still[2] (sometimes differentiated by the word *tief*). Documentation regarding the relative standard of *Cornet-Ton* is more confusing to interpret, some sources implying that it was identical with *Chor-Ton* and others suggesting that it was approximately a semitone higher.

Not until J. H. Scheibler's *Der physikalische und musikalische Tonmesser* (Essen, 1834) did frequency measurements become sufficiently accurate for reliable deductions to be made, but Mendel includes considerable evidence concerning absolute pitches before 1834, concentrating in particular on extant wind instruments and harpsichords, voice ranges and tuning forks in addition to theoretical publications; furthermore, he incorporates an interesting tabular

---

1. Mendel, 'Pitch in Western Music since 1500: a re-examination', *Acta Musicologica*, vol. 50 (1978), pp. 1–93.
2. Adlung, *Anleitung zur musicalischen Gelahrtheit* (Erfurt, 1758; facsimile ed. Moser, Kassel, 1953), p. 387.

outline summary, based on Ellis's work,[3] of the diverse pitches used in different places for various functions during the nineteenth century.

The lack of pitch uniformity during the period often required performers to resort to transposition in ensemble music in order to adapt to other instruments of fixed pitch or finite range (like the human voice); *Kammer-Ton* woodwinds, therefore, would have been required to transpose when employed in ensemble with *Chor-Ton* organs or trumpets, in order to reconcile their relative pitch standards. Such a situation naturally affected singers and wind players (who generally had to be equipped with different instruments at different pitches) rather more than string players, owing to the easier adjustability of string intonation, but Petri's comment about the occasional necessity for strings to be tuned down a tone from *Chor-Ton* to *Kammer-Ton* reveals that string players did not always escape problems of pitch lightly; furthermore, in addition to retuning, they were occasionally required to change from thick to thin strings, or vice versa, in order better to accommodate fixed-pitch instruments.

Quantz was one of the first eighteenth-century theorists to express disapproval of such pitch discrepancies and to recommend the adoption of a uniform pitch standard, although it must be pointed out that Praetorius (1571–1621) had suggested the use of a 'suitable pitch' of $a^1 = 424.2$ Hz as early as 1619; this relates approximately to the pitches of Handel's tuning fork ($a^1 = 422.5$ Hz in 1751) and the so-called London Philharmonic fork ($a^1 = 423.3$ Hz in 1820). Quantz remarks:

The pitch regularly used for tuning in an orchestra has always varied considerably according to the time and place. The disagreeable choir pitch prevailed in Germany for several centuries, as the old organs prove. Other instruments, such as violins, double basses, trombones, recorders, shawms, bombards, trumpets, clarinets, etc., were also made to conform to it. But after the French had transformed the German cross-pipe into the transverse flute, the shawm into the oboe, and the bombard into the bassoon, using their lower and more agreeable pitch, the high choir pitch began in Germany to be supplanted by the chamber pitch, as is demonstrated by some of the most famous new organs. At the present time the Venetian pitch is highest; it is almost the same as our old choir pitch. The Roman pitch of about twenty years ago was low, and was equal to that of Paris. At present, however, the Parisian pitch is beginning almost to equal that of Venice.

7. The diversity of pitches used for tuning is most detrimental to music in general. In vocal music it produces the inconvenience that singers performing in a place where low tuning is used are hardly able to make use of arias that were written for them in a place where a high pitch was employed, or vice versa. For this reason it is much to be hoped that a single pitch for tuning may be introduced at all places. It is undeniable that the high pitch is much more penetrating than the low one; on the other hand, it is much less pleasing, moving, and majestic. I do not wish to argue for the very low French chamber pitch, although it is the most advantageous for the traverse flute, the oboe, the bassoon, and some other instruments; but neither can I approve of

---

3. Ellis, 'A history of musical pitch', *Journal of the Society of Arts*, vol. 28 (1880), pp. 293–336; reprinted in Mendel, ed., *Studies in the history of musical pitch*, pp. 11–54.

the very high Venetian pitch, since in it the wind instruments sound much too disagreeable. Therefore I consider the best pitch to be the so-called German *A* chamber pitch, which is a minor third lower than the old choir pitch. It is neither too low nor too high, but the mean between the French and the Venetian; and in it both the stringed and the wind instruments can produce their proper effect. Although the shape of the instrument would remain, the very high pitch would finally make a cross-pipe again of the traverse flute, a shawm of the oboe, a violino piccolo of the violin, and a bombard of the bassoon. The wind instruments, which are such a special ornament of an orchestra, would suffer the greatest harm in consequence. Indeed they owe their existence to the low pitch. The oboes and bassoons in particular, which were made for the low pitch, would become completely false if forced up by shortening the reeds and mouth pieces. The octaves would be expanded, that is, the lower note of an octave would become lower, while the upper note would become higher; just as in the opposite case, when the reed is pulled out too far and the mouthpiece is lengthened, the octaves contract, and the lower note becomes higher, the upper note lower. The flute has the same peculiarity when its plug is pushed in too deeply or drawn out too far. For in the first case the octaves expand in the manner mentioned above, while in the second they contract. To be sure, smaller and narrower instruments could be made that would improve the high notes; but the majority of the instrument-makers work according to accustomed models that are adjusted to the low pitch, and very few would be in a position to reduce the measurements in a sufficiently correct ratio that would make the instrument high yet also retain its trueness. And even if some were finally to succeed, the question would still remain: would the above-mentioned instruments, if adjusted to the high pitch, produce the same effect as with the old measurements peculiar to them? Partiality for an instrument is indeed in itself good, but only as long as it does not bring detriment to the other instruments. In some parts of Italy they prefer the heightening of the pitch referred to above. For there the wind instruments are less used than in other countries, and in consequence the inhabitants do not have such good taste with regard to these instruments as they have for other things in music. In Rome at one time the wind instruments were banned from the church. Whether the unpleasant high pitch or the manner of playing the instruments was the reason for this I must leave undecided. For although the Roman pitch was low, and advantageous for the oboe, the oboists then played on instruments that were a whole tone higher, so that they were obliged to transpose. And these high instruments produced an effect like that of German shawms against the others that were tuned low.

(Quantz, *Versuch* . . . , tr. and ed. Reilly, ch. 17, section 7, § 6 & 7, pp. 267–9)

Although Quantz's textual exposition of these problems achieved scant immediate reaction, there was a growing tendency for the lower pitches to be preferred (dilapidated organs tuned at high pitches were being replaced with new ones at lower pitches – for example, at St Thomas's Leipzig) and, towards the end of the eighteenth century, for makers of woodwind and brass instruments in each locality to adopt a reasonable uniformity in the respective pitches of their instruments, even though pitches still varied from area to area. Ellis cites Carlo Gervasoni's view of the situation in Italy at the turn of the century:

The tone, commonly called pitch (*corista*), is not the same in all cities, but in some it is higher or lower than in others. The pitch of Rome is, in fact, much lower than that of

Milan, Pavia, Parma, Piacenza and all the other cities of Lombardy, and the pitch of Paris is not only sharper than that of Rome but much sharper than that of Lombardy. A mean pitch (*un corista di mezzo*) which is more generally accepted, is, nevertheless, that of Lombardy, and with this agree, more or less, the pitches of various provinces.

(Gervasoni, *La scuola della musica* (Piacenza, 1800), p. 126, as quoted in Ellis, 'A history of musical pitch', *Journal of the Society of Arts*, vol. 28 (1880), p. 309)

Mendel suggests that the a^1 of Quantz's (and Agricola's) *Chor-Ton* would seem to approximate to our b^1, the a^1 of their *Kammer-Ton* (higher variety) to our a^1, the a^1 of their *Kammer-Ton* (lower variety or *A-Kammerton*) to our a flat^1 and the a^1 of their 'former French pitch' to our g^1. Although there is no question of an extant mean pitch in Europe during the eighteenth and early nineteenth centuries, it is certainly not unreasonable to presume, on the further evidence of many contemporary woodwind instruments, theoretical sources and numerous English and German organs, that pitches approximately a semitone below $a^1 = 440$Hz were most common at that time. However, as Mendel cautiously reminds us, the number of pitches we can claim to know is too small and their distribution as to date, place, and function too uneven for such a statement to be irrefutable.[4]

The gradual emergence of concert-giving as a commercial proposition designed for all rather than for an élite minority, the resulting increase in touring activity of virtuoso performers, the developments in instrument construction and the more systematised approach to musical instruction at the various newly-established Conservatoires at the beginning of the nineteenth century intensified the need for a uniform pitch standard. Baillot, in particular, urged scientists and musicians jointly to determine one:

'The diapason is the fixed point which has been agreed upon as a standard so that the system of intonation shall not undergo any modification either as a whole or in part, and so that the *C* shall never be played at the pitch of a *B* or a *D*. This fixed point can be found by means of a small single-note instrument made of steel, called a tuning-fork, which is so made that it gives out constantly and without the slightest modification the note a^1. This invariable regulator is used for tuning all instruments. The note a^1 was chosen in view of the fact that all stringed instruments have an open string which gives this note.'[5]

This is the diapason as it was intended to be but not as it is in fact, for this invariable regulator may indeed remain the same for any one concert hall or theatre (though even then it may vary with temperature) but each group of musicians also has its own, which gives rise to serious disadvantages, and attempts have been made to remedy these at various times.

In 1812, it was acknowledged that the classes at the Conservatoire needed to adopt a diapason at a level between the lowest and highest then in use; as a result, wind instruments at this pitch were constructed for this school.[6]

4. Mendel, 'Pitch in Western music since 1500: a re-examination', *Acta Musicologica*, vol. 50 (1978), p. 76.
5. *Dictionnaire de musique moderne*, ed. Castil-Blaze. (Baillot's footnote)
6. Ellis gives the pitch standard at the Conservatoire (1812) as somewhere between 439·45 Hz and 439·55 Hz, considerably higher, therefore, than the pitches in use at the *Opéra* in 1810 (423 Hz) and 1811 (427 Hz).

In 1821, a diapason was adopted for the theatre of the *Académie royale de musique* and there was even a statute decreeing that it should be used by royal theatres throughout France. This measure was in force only for grand opera and for only a short time; motives of personal convenience won the day and caused a return to the earlier wind instruments which had been used in the concert halls.

Nevertheless the diversity of pitch has the effect every day of hindering good performance, wearying the voice and giving rise to the feeling that the time must surely be ripe for the adoption of a regulator for pitch just as has been done for time.

Everyone is well aware that there would be great obstacles in the way of achieving this; but it would be a task worthy of our age with its urge for perfection, that it should strive to determine the *absolute pitch* (*le son fixé*) which has so preoccupied the last century, and to establish a pitch which physicists, in agreement with practical musicians, would seek to bring as closely as possible into accord with the range of the voice, and which would at the same time be based on immutable mathematical foundations, in such a way that it could be used to determine pitch just as one can determine the temperature from a thermometer, the beat from a metronome, or the hours in the day from mean time.[7]

A standard pitch fixed in this way with all the assurances that must inspire confidence could be brought into use imperceptibly without the need for any general measures to enforce it; it would be sufficient for authority to favour its use, since innovations are never better received than when people are simply convinced of their usefulness.

(Baillot, *L'art* . . . (1834), p. 191)

However, although a variety of pitches were in use, the prevailing trend was for pitch standards to rise during the early nineteenth century (see Ellis's table with special reference to the Paris *Opéra*), owing largely to the desire for greater tonal brilliance, especially in the brass instruments of the military band, $a^1 = 448$ Hz being adopted at the *Opéra* and $a^1 = 446 \cdot 2$ Hz at the Conservatoire in Paris in 1858. At the recommendation of Sir George Smart, the London Philharmonic Society had temporarily checked such a rise in England (1820–6) with a compromise $a^1 = 433$ Hz and Scheibler, at a congress of physicists held at Stuttgart in 1834, proposed the standard $a^1 = 440$ Hz, which was accepted in principle but not widely implemented. In 1859, a commission appointed by the French government further halted this upward trend and determined $a^1 = 435$ Hz as the optimum pitch standard, this pitch being embodied by Lissajous in a standard fork, *diapason normal*, subsequently calculated to be $a^1 = 435 \cdot 4$ Hz. Nevertheless, the general rise in pitch standards continued unabated, thanks again to pressure from the military bands; not until the development of an international broadcasting network was the desire for world-wide agreement on a uniform pitch standard confirmed, unanimity on $a^1 = 440$ Hz eventually being reached at an international conference held in London in 1939.

A confusing variety of tuning systems also coexisted at the beginning of the

7. *Absolute pitch* has quite recently been once more the subject of research by our most famous physicists. They have finally defined it. We can hope therefore to see the fulfilment of our wishes if only they will apply their discoveries in collaboration with practical artists to the establishment of a standard pitch. *Note*: see the interesting article on this subject by Mr Fétis, published, after the completion of the present work, in the *Revue musicale* no. 47, 21 November 1833. (Baillot's footnote)

period under study,[8] but violin methods provide little explanation, concentrating merely on the violin's melodic role in the tuning of tones and semitones rather than larger intervals, especially fifths and thirds, which are so essential to the more chordal role of keyboard instruments and their tuning systems. Contrary to modern practice, most eighteenth-century violinists adopted a modified type of meantone temperament, in which a sharpened note was considered a 'comma' (i.e. about 22 cents) lower in pitch than the flattened form of the note a tone higher (Ex. 286). As Leopold Mozart remarks:

Ex. 286

On the keyboard, G sharp and A flat, D flat and C sharp, F sharp and G flat, and so on, are one and the same note. This is caused by the temperament. But according to the right ratio, all the notes lowered by a flat are a comma higher than those raised by a sharp. For example: D flat is higher than C sharp, A flat higher than G sharp, G flat than F sharp, and so on. Here the good ear must be judge, and indeed it would be good to introduce pupils to the monochord.

(Mozart, *Versuch* . . . , ch. 3, §6, p. 166)

He provides two scales (Ex. 287), leading through the flats and sharps respectively, intended as an intonation exercise in distinguishing between the large diatonic 'semitones' and the small chromatic 'semitones'.

Ex. 287

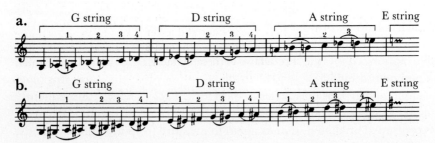

Around the turn of the century, the whole practice was reversed by many theorists and preference was eventually given to tuning sharpened notes higher than the flattened form of the note a tone higher, making diatonic 'semitones' smaller than chromatic ones and inflecting notes such as the leading note and the seventh of the dominant-seventh chord according to their

8. See Boyden, 'Prelleur, Geminiani and just intonation', *Journal of the American Musicological Society*, vol. 4 (1951), pp. 202–19; Chesnut, 'Mozart's teaching of intonation', *Journal of the American Musicological Society*, vol. 30 (1977), pp. 254–71; Barbour, 'Violin intonation in the 18th century', *Journal of the American Musicological Society*, vol. 5 (1952), pp. 224–34.

implied harmonic resolutions. Zaslaw[9] claims that the earliest reference to this modern manner of tuning enharmonic pairs is found in irate remarks made by J. J. Rousseau in the 1770s,[10] but Campagnoli's *Metodo* . . . (1797?) is the first violin method to include an illustration and description of this Pythagorean-type tuning system (Fig. 22).

> Table representing the exact distance which is found between the synonymous notes tuned mechanically on the organ, pianoforte, and harp, set off on the fingerboard of the violin. In adopting the temperament, the fingers must be placed upon the strings between the little lines.
>
> (Campagnoli, *Metodo* . . . (1797?), tr. Bishop, pt. 4, no. 225).

Zaslaw points out[11] that the following remark by Bremner suggests how musicians' ears may have become first accustomed to our present system.

> A teacher instructs his young pupil to make the half note, or semitone, by putting the finger close to the one that it succeeds; and this is the best direction that can be given to a beginner: but when the student is once able to tune his instrument, the insufficiency of that rule should be made known to him. That it is very defective, is plain for this reason: if to make the half note in the first position of the hand, the finger requires to be put close to the finger already down; it must be impossible for the same fingers to play the same notes in tune an octave higher on the same string, the stop there, being but half the length it is below. And yet this same first rule, by which all the sharps are made too sharp, and the flats too flat, even if the fingers are thick, is evidently the only one attended to by many of the *Dilettanti*.
>
> Tune can only be ascertained by comparing one sound with another; for an unconnected sound cannot be out of tune. A gentleman, therefore, by being in the constant practice of tuning his violin, tenor or base, of which the strings are fifths to each other, has got master of a fifth. He likewise can refine an eighth, and this he has acquired by comparing the sound given by the third finger on any of the strings, with that of the open string below it, to which it is an octave. But that performer who thinks he plays in tune, and yet whose ear cannot refine all the concords with the same degree of certainty it can a fifth or eighth, does but deceive himself and disappoint others.
>
> There are seven concords, namely, the greater and lesser 3ds, the 4th, 5th, greater and lesser 6ths, and the 8th, or octave. The 4th, 5th, and 8th are called the greater, and the others the lesser concords. Of two of these, namely, the 5th and 8th, we shall, for the reasons already given, suppose the student to be master. The others are in like manner adjusted by comparing them with one or other of the open strings, they being the tests by which tune can be best ascertained; and therefore I have made use of them as standards in the following examples. In playing these examples, a slow and even bow is recommended, as thereby the fingers will have time to move backward and forward in search of truth, without any failure in sound.
>
> Flat stops of the first and second fingers.

Ex. 288

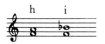

9. Zaslaw, 'The compleat orchestral musician', *Early Music*, vol. 7 (1979), pp. 46–57.
10. Musset-Pathay, ed., *Œuvres complètes* (Paris, 1824), vol. 2, pp. 289–90.
11. Zaslaw, 'The compleat orchestral musician', *Early Music*, vol. 7 (1979), pp. 46–57.

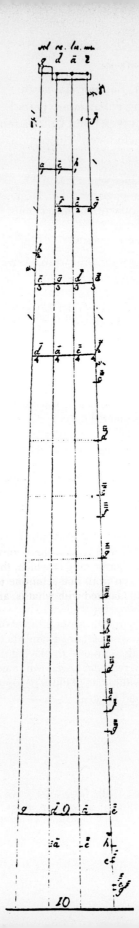

22. Campagnoli's tuning system

The note f¹ is to be so stopped that the open string a¹ may become a perfect 3d to it, (h). This is the major, or sharp 3d, the refining of which will cost some time and attention to the unexperienced. This 3d being thoroughly adjusted, let the finger f¹ remain in its place, to which let b flat¹ be made a perfect 4th, (i). This is a more powerful concord than the 3d, and therefore sooner ascertained. If these two chords are in exact tune, they fix the flat stops of two fingers on all the strings, for the opposite 5ths have the same stops.

Of the three remaining concords two are found by means of the b flat¹.

Ex. 289

The b flat¹ being again adjusted and retained in its place, let g¹ be put in tune by its octave below it, (k); to which g¹, the b flat¹ is a minor, or lesser 3d, (l). Again, the same b flat¹ is a minor 6th to d¹, (m).

The major, or greater 6th, only now remains to be treated of, and may be found thus:

Ex. 290

The note g¹ tuned by its octave, (n). To that g¹, tune b¹ a major 3d, (o); which b¹, is a major 6th to d¹, (p).

If the ear can adjust the above five concords, it will have no difficulty in doing the same in any other part of the instrument; for a 3d is a 3d wherever it is, and so of the others.

As 3ds and 6ths are the most difficult for the ear to perfect, the following example should be much practised; in the performing of which, the finger should be made to slide gently backward and forward from one semitone to the other, till the ear be thoroughly satisfied, and well acquainted with what is, and is not in tune.

Ex. 291

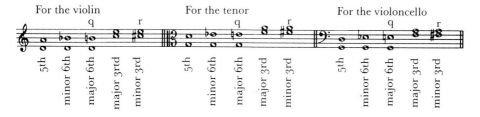

In like manner the student may creep up to the top of his fingerboard, and in every shift of the hand, tune the concords by one or other of the open strings.

The upper note at (q) and the under note at (r) are the sharp stops of the first and second fingers.

That the eye may be satisfied as well as the ear, let the chords below at (s) be put in exact tune, and if the fingers b¹ and c² are retained in their places, it may be seen, that though c² is but a semitone above b¹, yet those fingers are not close to each other. By the chords at (t) the same proof may be made of c sharp² and d².

Ex. 292

I shall only further observe on this very important, though perhaps somewhat tedious head, that if the student makes a point of giving due attention to tune on all occasions, his ear will soon become master of it, whether he plays alone, or bears a part with others; for if alone, he has his own open strings for a test; and when with others, one or other of their parts, to which his may be a concord, will be his guide. It is true his partners may be equally at a loss with himself, and, therefore, not to be depended upon; but even this may tend to his improvement, and of course to theirs, provided they often compare notes and check each other; a liberty which all gentlemen who wish to improve, should give and take without restraint.

(Bremner, *Some thoughts on the performance of concert music* (1777), pp. iv–vi)

TUNING THE VIOLIN

The manner of tuning the violin was rarely discussed in detail in treatises of the period and, more often than not, only the notes to which the strings should be tuned were cited. However, the most common method adopted involved employing a tuning fork or pitch-pipe to determine the pitch of one string (usually the A, although Galeazzi opts for the D and Hack recommends employing four tuning forks, one for each string)[12] and tuning the other strings either by ear from the given note or alternatively by rather more impractical methods such as measurement,[13] mathematical calculation or even, to some extent, pure guesswork, as confirmed by those directions involving tuning the string up 'to as high a pitch as you think it can moderately bear'[14] – as if that point were easy to judge! The two extremes of tuning instruction during the period are provided by Hiller and Baillot. Hiller, imitated later by Fenkner, prescribes the most ludicrously naïve and unreliable method imaginable, advising the student to sing the opening bars of three hymn tunes (*Wir glauben all' an einen Gott, Lobt Gott ihr Christen* and *Nun sich der Tag*), in order to establish the correct pitch for each string. The appropriate pitch for the open D and A strings is sung on the syllables *Wir* and *glau* of the first hymn and that of the E and G strings established on the syllables *Gott* in

12. Galeazzi, *Elementi* . . . (1791), vol. 1, pt. 2, art. 3, pp. 82–3; Hack, *New and original instructions* . . . (c. 1835), p. 12.
13. Jousse, *The modern violin preceptor* (c. 1805), §6n, p. 6.
14. Goodban, *A new and complete guide* . . . (1810), p. 17.

the second hymn and *sich* in the third hymn respectively.[15] Habeneck, on the
other hand, extols the benefits of instruction in *solfège* with regard to tuning,[16]
while Baillot provides a more orthodox and practical approach, emphasising
the importance of acquainting the student with tuning in perfect fifths as soon
as possible:

Tuning the violin is the first thing on which the pupil's attention should be concentrated.
As soon as he is capable of putting the bow on the strings, it will be for the purpose of
playing on the 4 open strings tuned in fifths: *E, A, D, G.* The first exercise of his audi-
tory faculties must therefore be directed to these notes which will be the subject of his
1st lesson, and which will become the foundation of his work through being in tune
with each other.

Nevertheless, a beginner cannot tune the violin himself – this task requires a certain strength and the development of certain skills – but he can be taught to judge the
correct tuning of the fifths by making him say which note to him seems too high or too
low.

His first lesson therefore will be simply an appeal to his awareness, to his sense of
hearing which will soon be the judge of every movement of his fingers.

The teacher will decide the moment when the pupil must make the *tuning of the
violin* a particular study in itself, and he will make him pursue this study for several
days to the exclusion of any other, until he knows how to tune extremely readily, so as
to be hardly audible, and yet with a regularity that is agreeable to the ear, as will be
seen below.

Whatever instrument one plays, *tuning* is the starting point for good intonation,
without which everything sounds wrong; this essential point is unfortunately too
often forgotten when musicians play together; it is the duty of the leader, who is naturally in charge of a concert, to establish good discipline in this matter, and it is the
duty of the true artist to conform to this with the most scrupulous care.

Method of tuning

The violin should be *tuned* in true fifths with the greatest care, very quietly so that it
can hardly be heard, and in as short a time as possible; this is done by proceeding in
the following manner:

Ex. 293

If it is necessary to start again in order to be sure that the fifths are in tune, then
one must try to do it rhythmically and speedily and make the fifths agreeable by playing them extremely delicately and with great purity of sound, however lightly one
brushes the strings.

It should be sufficient to play each of the 3 fifths twice over once one is accustomed
to this procedure and if the pegs of the violin turn with no trouble.

When the strings are thus left to themselves and the fifths are separated by a

15. Hiller, *Anweisung* . . . (1774), p. 2.   16. Habeneck, *Méthode* . . . (c. 1840), p. 24.

silence, one can judge the intonation better, whereas when one plays loudly, the strings stretch and do not produce the true note, and when the bow is left on the strings, their continual and multiplied vibrations make it more difficult to appreciate the correct intonation, in which the slightest little fault is noticeable on the other hand *even at a distance* when one hardly touches the strings.

Fifths repeated briskly and frequently, whether absent-mindedly or from habit, would become in their own different way just as intolerable as they are when played slowly and with full tone; they would prevent full advantage being taken of the method we have described by people of common sense who have no wish to turn into pain the pleasure they are seeking in harmony.

But when it is necessary to play with the full length of the bow on the strings to make the rosin stick, and to prepare oneself to play in a large hall, why should one not try to impart some charm to this succession of fifths whose perfect consonance, taken in isolation, never fails to delight the ear?

It would suffice if 3 small notes were added to these fifths to determine their tonality, in the following manner:

Ex. 294

One cannot acquire too early the habit of *tuning* in the manner described above, to avoid becoming the scourge of one's audience and so that one does not destroy the effect of the music with these repeated fifths which succeed in wearying the ear precisely when it needs to be left in peace. It needs this peace before the music, because the senses require calm if they are to receive agreeable impressions; peace is necessary afterwards, so that the soul may dwell on these impressions and enjoy the benefit they afford. One should bear in mind that the more noise one makes in tuning, the more time one needs to judge the intonation, and the less one finds oneself precisely in tune. Finally, it must be observed that the extreme delicacy of the ear, its great sensitiveness, far from being a fault, is here a precious quality that one must seek to preserve; and since unfortunately one cannot close one's ears as one closes one's eyes, it is all the more important to avoid anything that might offend them and would eventually unsettle them.

The leader of the orchestra must take his a[1] from a *tuning fork* of accepted pitch, and have the others *tune* to the pitch of this note: first the oboe, to which then all the other wind instruments must tune. Then he will turn to the strings who must *tune* to him one after another and then withdraw to one side to finish *tuning* without being heard. The area where tuning takes place should always be well away from the audience. The player who gives the note holds on the a[1] like an organ pipe; the player who is tuning makes the note ring gently; by means of this ringing sound he will be better able to hear the differences which assist in achieving a unison.

But if one is *tuning* to the *piano*, or to someone who is playing the ringing sound instead of the sustained note, then one must sustain the note oneself to give a contrast and to enable one to reach the correct note more easily.

(Baillot, *L'art*. . . (1834), pp. 250–1)

Most writers recommend tuning the strings in the order A, E, D, G; this is contrary to normal modern practice (A, D, G, E), which allows the E string, the most sensitive to tension variations of the other strings, to be tuned last of all.

INTONATION

Intonation problems commonly arose when string players were playing in small ensembles (Quantz confirms that such fine distinctions of pitch were perceptible in small ensembles[17]) with instruments of fixed pitch, especially keyboard and, to a certain extent, wind instruments, because the string players had to adjust to the intonation systems of the fixed-pitch instruments. Although, like Galeazzi, many string players were opposed to the adoption of any system other than just intonation, numerous writers from c. 1830 onwards aimed essentially at the exclusive production of an equally tempered intonation, especially for beginners, thus easing the problems of performing with instruments of fixed pitch so tempered. Spohr remarks in his preface for parents and teachers:

Extreme patience and perseverance must be devoted to the 4th section, which lays the foundations of pure intonation for the student. The teacher can indeed save himself great trouble in the future if he insists with uncompromising strictness right from the outset on the absolutely pure intonation of the pupil's stopped notes.[18]

(Spohr, *Violinschule* (1832), preface for parents and teachers, p. 3)

However, since no violinist can play strictly according to mathematical formulae, the judgement of his ear and innate key-sense were his chief recourses in modifying his intonation, whether consciously or subconsciously, in order to produce the most consonant results. A flexible compromise invariably resulted between meantone temperament (common to most eighteenth-century keyboard instruments), equal temperament and *substantially* just intonation (substantially, because just intonation as a complete system of fixed intervals is an artistic impossibility).[19] Campagnoli confirms the need for such flexibility thus:

Correctness of intonation prohibits temperament on the violin, except in certain cases: 1st, to lessen the movement of the fingers; 2dly, to satisfy the delicacy of the ear, when accompanying other instruments; 3dly, to facilitate performance; for instance, when A flat and G sharp successively occur on the third string, it is not necessary to withdraw the fourth finger in order to employ the third, but the fourth must be kept

17. See Quantz, *Versuch* . . ., tr. and ed. Reilly, ch. 17, section 6, §20, pp. 160–1.
18. By pure intonation is naturally meant that of equal temperament, since in modern music no other exists. The budding violinist needs to know only this one intonation. For this reason neither unequal temperament nor small and large semitones are mentioned in this method because both would serve only to confuse the doctrine of the absolutely equal size of all 12 semitones. (Spohr's footnote)
19. See Boyden, 'Prelleur, Geminiani and just intonation', *Journal of the American Musicological Society*, vol. 4 (1951), pp. 202–19.

pressed upon the string, and its positon be modified as the nature of the harmony
may require.   (Campagnoli, *Metodo* . . . (1797?), tr. Bishop, pt. 4, no. 225)

The addition of *vibrato* is nowadays considered one of the most effective ways of
constantly adjusting string intonation to that of an accompanying medium
but there is no evidence of such a practice being employed during the period
under study.

A similar flexibility of intonation was also naturally required in those
ensembles not involving keyboard instruments and even within the string
quartet. Chesnut cites an A flat or G sharp minor triad in the finale of
Mozart's Symphony in E flat major, K.543 (bar 113) written enharmonically in
mixed notation G sharp – B – D sharp – A flat, together with a comparable
example of a B or C flat major chord, written C flat – E flat – F sharp – B, in
the *Adagio* of Haydn's String Quartet Op. 76 no. 6 (bar 36). The use of a mixed
notation in such cases pinpoints the enharmonic change and alerts the performers into modifying their temperament according to the prevailing harmonic context.[20]

Open strings naturally further complicated matters in such a fluid intonation system, since only one open string of a violin tuned in perfect fifths will
correspond with most common keyboard temperaments. Galeazzi claims that
the violin can be tuned perfectly in fifths only in the key of D major, since only
then are the fifths actually perfect; in other keys, certain open-string tunings
have to be 'tempered' somewhat and this is best achieved by avoiding open
strings and stopping the notes in question (for example, the open a^1 string
note in C major or the open e^2 string note in G major).[21] Petri, among others,
also recommends the avoidance of open strings, especially the A and E
strings, preferring the use of stopped notes for easier intonation adjustment,
whereas Leopold Mozart and Quantz make more positive suggestions.
Mozart implies that the violinist should match the tuning of his open strings
with that of a keyboard,[22] whilst Quantz provides two possible solutions, one
involving the violinist and the other involving the keyboard player:

To tune the violin quite accurately, I think you will not do badly to follow the rule that
must be observed in tuning the keyboard, namely, that the fifths must be tuned a little
on the flat side rather than quite truly or a little sharp, as is usually the case, so that
the open strings will all agree with the keyboard. For if all the fifths are tuned sharp
and truly, it naturally follows that only one of the four strings will be in tune with the
keyboard. If the a^1 is tuned truly with the keyboard, the e^2 a little flat in relation to the
a^1, the d^1 a little sharp to the a^1, and the g likewise to the d^1, the two instruments will
agree with each other. This suggestion is not presented as an absolute rule, however,
but only as a matter for further reflection.
                    (Quantz, *Versuch*. . ., tr. and ed. Reilly, ch. 17, section 7, §4, p. 267)

---

20. Chesnut, 'Mozart's teaching of intonation', *Journal of the American Musicological Society*, vol. 30 (1977),
    pp. 270–1.
21. Galeazzi, *Elementi* . . . (1791), vol. I, pt. 2, art. 6, pp. 118–19.
22. L. Mozart, *Versuch* . . . ch. 12, §6, p. 255.

Referring to the keyboard player, Quantz remarks:

Any keyboard performer who understands the ratios of the notes will also know that subsemitones such as D sharp and E flat differ by a comma, and therefore cause, because of its lack of divided keys, some inequality in intonation upon this instrument as compared with other instruments on which these notes are produced in their true ratios, especially if the keyboard plays them in unison with one of the instruments just mentioned. Since, then, these notes cannot always be avoided, especially in those keys in which many flats or many sharps appear, the accompanist would do well to seek as much as possible either to hide them in a middle or lower part, or, if one of them forms a minor third,[23] to leave it out entirely. For these minor thirds in particular sound very bad and imperfect if they are struck in unison with the principal part in the upper octave.[24] The minor thirds I refer to are principally the C, D, and E of the two-line octave, if a flat stands before them, or, to put it more briefly, C flat, D flat and E flat. But I also refer to g^1 and a^1, and d^2 and e^2, if they are preceded by a sharp; for if they form major thirds, the interval is too large, and they are thus too high. It is true that you cannot perceive this difference as distinctly if you play alone on the harpsichord, or if you accompany a large ensemble, but if these notes are found in unison with another instrument, the difference is all too clearly heard, since the other instruments give them in their true ratios, while upon the keyboard they are tempered; for this reason it is better to omit them entirely than to offend the ear. But let anyone whom the omission does not please at least take the minor and major thirds indicated above in the low register, where the ear will better endure them, as I have indicated for the other subsemitones. Apart from this, the unison does not produce as good an effect with an instrument as with a voice. In addition the poor intonation is not as apparent to the ear in the low register as in the high. To be convinced of this, tune an octave either flat or sharp on one keyboard of the harpsichord, then on the other keyboard tune one string of the high note quite accurately with the low one. Then try the mistuned unison and see if it does not displease the ear more than the mistuned octave.[25]

(Quantz, *Versuch*. . ., tr. and ed. Reilly, ch. 17, section 6, §20, pp. 260–1)

Similarly, in ensembles involving one instrument of fixed pitch, Habeneck opts for concealing the different temperament of the fixed-pitch instrument rather than bring the tuning of the other instruments in line with it:

The intonation of the two scales joined by a bracket { is the same for instruments with predetermined or fixed notes such as the piano or the organ; but it is perceptibly different on the violin or the bass, which, since they are obliged to form their own notes, can modify infinitely the relationships between them.

It is no part of the intention of this work to expatiate on the nature and extent of this difference, particularly since there is no need to take it into account except when the entire harmonic ensemble is produced by instruments with variable notes and one single instrument with fixed notes joins in, whereupon the main object must be to remove the difference forthwith if the intonation is not to be made intolerable; suffice it to say that this is done to prevent students being taken by surprise, which would

23. Quantz seems to mean a minor third in relation to the bass.
24. In other words, the minor third of the keyboard above the bass does not agree with the minor third of the principal part.
25. The organist Sorge, however, disagreed with this solution, maintaining that string players should always be made to adjust their intonation to the keyboard tuning; see Quantz, *Versuch* . . ., tr. and ed. Reilly, Introduction, p. xxxiii.

plunge them into a state of distress and perplexity by making them doubt the accuracy of their own ears.   (Habeneck, *Méthode*. . . (c.1840), pt. 2, §4, p. 78)

Galeazzi should perhaps be allowed the final word, since he at least suggests a useful compromise for making intonation acceptable to the ear. He claims that the greatest accuracy of intonation should be reserved for the characteristic notes of a key – the root, third and seventh – and that the seventh note, when acting as a leading note, should normally be raised slightly in order to please the ear.[26]

INTONATION AIDS

Diatonic scales

Baillot classes intonation amongst the three basic constituents of accuracy in performance,[27] a view endorsed in a variety of phraseology by most writers of the period, some even recommending the use of a fretted or marked fingerboard to facilitate the attainment of such accuracy. The appreciation of scales in the training and discipline of the left hand was not fully acknowledged until the second half of the eighteenth century when, following Geminiani's and Leopold Mozart's surveys, writers normally included scales in some form in their methods in order to encourage the cultivation of accurate intonation, finger independence, elasticity and agility, strong finger action for tonal clarity and many bowing disciplines, notably those of tone quality, bow division and dynamics.

Woldemar devotes almost one half of his method to scales in some form, whether as straightforward scales or as exercises designed to teach basic musical rudiments or perfect certain techniques; he urges teachers 'to apply themselves particularly to scales in order to make pupils well aware of the relationship and the distances between the notes and to avoid the greatest of all faults, unfortunately too common, which is failing to play in tune, above all in the sharp keys'.[28] He subdivides the scale into three main types – diatonic, chromatic and enharmonic – and considers it 'an inexhaustible mine capable of more than a thousand variations',[29] incorporating into his survey syncopated rhythms, triplets, intervals, double stopping in thirds, sixths, and octaves, arpeggios, the *coup d'archet articulé*, *brisure* and other advanced bowings, and gives examples of scales with notes two octaves apart, *Gammes dites du diable* (Ex. 295), and exercises, based on scales, with programmatic aims (Ex. 296).

Galeazzi, who recommends the study of only theoretical principles and scales (in myriad forms) in the first year of violin pedagogy, expounds a rather complex, mathematically-based way of cultivating accuracy of intonation in

26. Galeazzi, *Elementi* . . . (1791), vol. I, pt. 2, art. 6, pp. 121-2.
27. Baillot, *L'art* . . . (1834), p. 252.
28. Woldemar, *Grande méthode* . . . (c. 1800), p. 2.   29. *Ibid.*, p. 24.

Ex. 295

Ex. 296

Scale expressing anger

Allegro

con fuoco   cresc.   poco ƒ

A storm

To play this scale, all the lightning flashes should be taken in an up bow and the first note of the thunder in a down bow.

calando

scale playing in different keys, using pre-marked cards as guides for left-hand finger placement.[30] Baillot's survey is rather more conservative. After preliminary pages of twenty-four one-octave scales in 'all the keys' and four major and two minor scales with key signatures of three, five and seven flats, together with their enharmonically equivalent scales with key signatures of five to seven sharps, 'identical on keyboard instruments but played with different fingering and character on the violin',[31] Baillot later concentrates on two-octave diatonic scales (major and relative minors) in all keys of up to and including six flats and five sharps, simple arpeggios (two and three octaves), scales by thirds in two and three octaves and scales by and in octaves (many of these scale types incorporating various slurred and detached bowings), prefaced by the following introductory comment:

The *scale* is the yardstick of our musical system; it provides in its own right a noble and symmetrical melodic line, capable of much expression and variety; it lends itself to all the movements of harmony, it can accompany any melody, and when one reflects on its limits, one can hardly believe that five tones and two semitones can provide so many combinations and offer so many resources. It can never be studied too carefully, therefore, in all its aspects and all its fortunes; it is the palette on which the colours must be well prepared, so that all the different *tones* and their most delicate shades may be at one's disposal.

When talking of *scales*, the first idea that springs to mind is that of a kind of torture, or at the very least a lengthy tedium which not everyone has the power to tolerate or overcome.

30. Galeazzi, *Elementi* . . . (1791), vol. I, pt. 2, art. 6, pp. 101–22.
31. Baillot, *L'art* . . . (1834), pp. 21–4.

We have acknowledged that the common habit of playing scales slowly was the reason why pupils rejected them or refused to practise them; it has been said elsewhere why scales played too slowly were not as beneficial as those played with sufficient movement to establish their tonality. But it has not proved possible to reject slow scales altogether, since those which are destined to establish good intonation *with regard to harmony* and form part of studies and are in *1st position* must be played with a certain slowness.

So much trouble and patience is required in the arts to obtain good results that no effort should be spared which aims at smoothing out difficulties, cutting short study time and bringing nearer the moment when one can gather the fruits of one's labours.

Nevertheless, these efforts are not as tedious as people imagine; the time spent in playing scales, in memorising, and in the ways we have described, does not require such heroic patience as one might be led to believe.

The longest exercise devoted to these scales, played in succession in all 24 keys according to the formula and speed indicated, lasts only 7½ minutes and the shortest lasts only *one* minute, as can be seen at the top of these exercises.

Allowing that one should take them at first at only half the speed indicated, until the intonation is reliable, the result is that a few minutes' work done with concentration each day will give a sureness and correctness to the playing of elementary studies that would take several years to achieve by any other method known to us.

Finally we recommend constant practice of these formulated studies as being to the art of the violin what *vocalisation* is to the art of singing.

(Baillot, *L'art* . . . (1834), p. 45)

Scales provide the framework for Gasse's *Méthode*. . ., whilst Spohr, unlike most of his compatriots, devotes a special section of his treatise to scales, at the same time discussing key systems, intervals and other basic rudiments. Little written text is included but a number of studies are provided. Especially notable is Spohr's systematic approach to the fingering of three-octave diatonic scales, in which the root position of a four-note chord of the key of the scale in question essentially determines the finger position in which that scale should be commenced: thus, for the scales of B flat major and minor the first position would serve as the point of departure, whereas C major and minor would be commenced in second position (Ex. 297). Briefly stated, Spohr begins all scales with the second finger, except, of course, those starting on G, A flat and A.

Ex. 297

The C major scale was commonly recommended in the eighteenth century as the initial scale for beginners to study, but G major gradually gained favour towards the end of the century because of its more natural distribution of the fingers on the fingerboard. Viotti gives a thorough explanation in his survey, included in facsimile in Habeneck's *Méthode* . . .:

How much there is to say about this first step! . . . . It costs one dear, it is exhausting, but with it comes success.

Everyone knows that the scale is a natural series of notes, ascending or descending. But perhaps not everyone has considered how difficult it is to perform, and what an advantage it is if, in spite of the trouble which accompanies it, one never ceases to practise it.

It is the scale which establishes good intonation, beautiful tone quality; which makes the voice or the fingers flexible; which steadies the bow on the string; which accustoms the nerves and the bodily organs to thousands of movements, to an infinite number of inflections and nuances. Finally, it is the scale which opens the arena to our stumbling footsteps, which makes us gradually steadier, helps us surmount obstacles and serves as a reliable escort through immense difficulties.

I do not need to say more to show the great *importance* I attach to it. I will add only that I, who have hardly ever practised a solo passage, have never ceased to practise scales whenever I have felt the need to convey the music as well as possible; and that if I could ever succeed in playing a perfect scale, as perfect as I can hear that it should be, then I would consider myself the best violinist in the world.

There are different ways of playing the scale or of practising scales.

First: Without inflections, which I will mark by two parallel lines = to indicate that the sound of each note should be begun, continued and terminated at the same level of loudness.

2nd: Beginning *forte* and ending *piano* ➤ .

3rd: Beginning *piano*, *crescendo* and *diminuendo* ◄ ➤ .

4th: Scales in a given key but in all the possible positions.

5th: In half-tones, or semitones, observing the same inflections as before.

6th: With a trill on each note, same inflections.

7th: Finally, practise the whole in different styles, in different positions and in various degrees of slowness or speed.

It should be observed, however, that what lays the soundest foundation and does the most good is practising extremely long sustained notes; those are what sometimes drive me mad.

All this must seem almost impossible to the absolute beginner; for the mere act of picking up the instrument, positioning the fingers and drawing the bow across the strings must recall the labours of Hercules! . . . It is therefore only to those who already have some skill that I address my reflections in this article.

The principal aim when beginning any instrument must be to play it *in tune*, or more correctly *with good intonation*. The scale which will help you most easily to achieve this aim, which will engage the pupil's attention and steady his fingers and which at the same time will cause him least trouble, is the one that should be chosen for the earliest lessons, and the scale of G, for the violin, fulfils this objective better than any other. Better than the scale of C, as many imagine. The reason is as follows: In the scale of G, the first and third fingers remain the same distance apart on all *four strings*; whereas in the scale of C, the first finger has to move back on the E string in order to play the F natural. Furthermore, in the G scale, once the fingers have been positioned on *the fourth string*, they remain the same distance apart to produce the notes on the *third*. And then, by a simple movement of the second finger, they are positioned again on the A string, remaining the same on the E string. In this way, the order or pattern is interrupted only once, instead of the two enforced interruptions in the scale of *C*, as can be seen in the following illustration:

Ex. 298

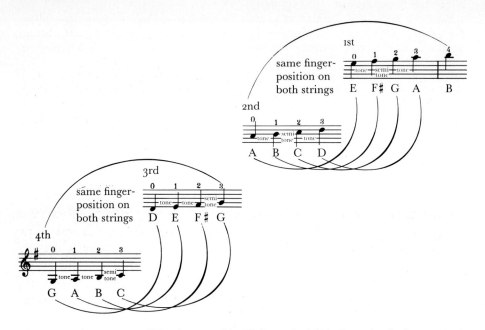

(Viotti, quoted in Habeneck, *Méthode*. . . (c.1840), pp. 33–5)

Habeneck rounds off Viotti's account by endorsing his comments, claiming that the scale is the foundation of violin technique and adding his fingering rules for ascending and descending scales.[32] He includes all the major and minor scales up to four sharps and four flats as well as some enharmonically equivalent scales similar to those cited by Baillot.[33]

Nowadays, the D major scale, which requires a finger disposition identical to that of G major, is considered the most practical for elementary study, since it requires fewer complications in the positioning of the left elbow and also the angle of the bowing arm.

Chromatic scales

Many writers who emphasise the importance of scale practice as basic technical groundwork surprisingly omit discussion of chromatic scales, L'Abbé le fils's *Principes* . . . being a notable example. Nevertheless, some methods

32. See ch. 5, p. 80.   33. Habeneck, *Méthode* . . . (c. 1840), p. 78.

devote special sections to chromatic scales and most of these adopt Leopold
Mozart's approach, involving different fingerings for those chromatic scales
written in sharps and those in flats (Ex. 287). A notable example is Habeneck's
survey, which incorporates chromatic scales in flats with fingerings identical
to those of Leopold Mozart but modifies the fingering for scales in sharps,
admitting open strings and omitting Mozart's rather awkward use of the
fourth finger (Ex. 299). Interestingly enough, Spohr stands in a position of

Ex. 299

compromise between Mozart and Habeneck, rejecting the consecutive use of
the fourth finger *in fast passages* but supporting Leopold Mozart's avoidance of
open strings, especially the harsher tonal qualities of the A and E strings, for
the scale in sharps.[34] In fairness, Leopold Mozart himself admits that the
d sharp[1], a sharp[1] and e sharp[2] of the chromatic scale in sharps may be played
with the first finger but only in *slow* pieces, preferring his indicated fingering
in quick pieces and especially if the notes e[1], b[1], or f sharp[2] respectively follow
immediately after.

The range of Habeneck's account extends beyond the first position limits of
Leopold Mozart's and includes two suggestions for chromatic scale fingerings
in the higher positions:

The first involves following the fingering of diatonic scales with regard to the position
changes and sliding forward the finger of the *sharpened* note or drawing back the finger
of the *flattened* note.

199. The second method is hardly practicable except where the chromatic scale
extends at least up to the 5th position; then the two following principles must be
applied.

I. If the scale contains an even number of notes from the open E string upwards,
the first finger should be moved to the third position on the a natural[2] and follow
the successive 1 2–1 2 fingering until the second finger has reached an interval of a
fourth below the last note of the scale, then use the fingering 2 2–3 3–4 4.

II. If the scale contains an odd number of notes from the E string upwards, the
first finger should be moved to the third position to stop the a sharp[2] or to the fourth
position to stop the b flat[2], when the scale is written in flats, and likewise follow the
successive 1 2–1 2 fingering until the second finger has reached an interval of a
fourth below the last note of the scale, then use the fingering 2 2–3 3–4 4.

34. Spohr, *Violinschule* (1832), p. 84.

Ex. 300

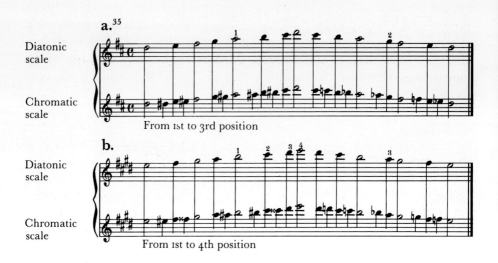

From 1st to 3rd position

From 1st to 4th position

200. The difference between the two formulae therefore lies simply in the placing of the 1st finger on the a natural^2 or on the a sharp^2 which becomes b flat^2 in scales written in flats.

Ex. 301

1 st formula: for scales comprising an even number of notes

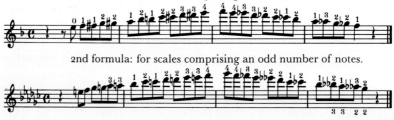

2nd formula: for scales comprising an odd number of notes.

(Habeneck, *Méthode* . . . (c. 1840), pp. 149–51)

Geminiani's recommended chromatic fingering, involving the use of one finger for each note and open strings when necessary (Ex. 302), was largely ignored by his contemporaries and immediate successors, even though it offered greater evenness, articulation and clarity – eliminating the 'smudged' *glissando* effect – than Leopold Mozart's 'slide' fingering. Signoretti, however, recommends the fingered chromatic principle in order to attain greater facility and sure intonation in quick passages but admits that the slide fingering was most commonly employed at that time.[36]

35. The minims in these scales indicate the integral notes of the common chord and they must serve to make certain of the purity of the intonation. (Habeneck's footnote)
36. Signoretti, *Méthode* . . . (1777), pt. 2, p. 25.

Ex. 302

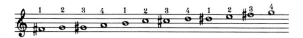

The duet

The popularity of the duet form for pedagogical purposes, especially as an intonation aid, increased considerably during the period; in addition to encouraging accurate intonation and exercising students in a number of basic technical matters, the duet helped to add informality to the relationship between master and pupil, and the accompanying second violin part guided the student in such disciplines as rhythm, harmony, style and expression. Löhlein, amongst others, incorporates numerous duets, annotated with technical instruction, into his *Anweisung* . . . , and Spohr openly acknowledges the benefits of duet practice,[37] even using the genre to illustrate the interpretation of solo passages from Rode's Seventh and his own Ninth Concertos.[38]

37. Spohr, *Violinschule* (1832), Preface and pp. 26 & 139.
38. *Ibid.*, pp. 198–245.

General remarks on expression, performance and style

In his *Allgemeine Theorie der schönen Künste* of 1771, the first work on aesthetics to devote much space to music, Johann Sulzer introduces his consideration of expression in music thus:

> The principal, if not indeed the sole function of a perfect musical composition is the accurate expression of emotions and passions in all their varying and individual nuances . . . Expression is the soul of music; without it, music is just a pleasant toy; with it, music becomes an overwhelmingly powerful language which engulfs the heart.[1]

He later summarises the varied means at the composer's disposal for the creation of such a language of the emotions, listing as his prime considerations harmony, metre, melody and rhythm, dynamic variations, the choice of accompaniment and modulation.

It is the performer's task to communicate faithfully, but nevertheless personally, the composer's intentions to his audience in a manner commensurate with the mood(s), character(s) (*Affetto, Affekt, Affect*) and style(s) of the composition in question. The eighteenth century witnessed the culmination, especially in Germany and to a certain extent England, of the 'doctrine of the affections (*Affektenlehre*) – 'Every piece of music must have a definite character and evoke emotions of a specific kind', comments Sulzer[2] – the ultimate aim of which was the musical expression of specific human emotions, depicted by specific musical devices which are to some extent standardised and identifiable. Descriptive words at the beginning of a piece, movement or section suggested in general terms its mood and, to some degree, its approximate tempo – from *Grave*, Leopold Mozart infers 'sadly and earnestly, hence very slow indeed',[3] whilst *Allegro* suggests 'a gay, but not hurried tempo' – and the violinist normally gleaned further interpretative information from matters of

---

1. *Allgemeine Theorie* . . ., ed. Sulzer (2nd edn, Leipzig, 1792–4), as quoted in le Huray and Day, *Music and aesthetics* . . ., p. 124.
2. *Ibid.*, p. 126.
3. L. Mozart, *Versuch* . . ., ch. 1, section 3, §27, pp. 48–51; see also Cartier's list of speeds in ascending order in *L'art* . . . (1798), p. 17; and Quantz's method of relating tempo descriptions to the human pulse, in *Versuch* . . ., tr. and ed. Reilly, ch 17, section 7, §47, pp.283–4.

rhythm, key, intervals, harmony and phrasing, and adapted his bowing, fingering, ornamentation, articulation, accentuation, *vibrato*, nuances, timbre and other expressive devices accordingly.[4]

Whilst the common practice of the late baroque period was to depict only one affection per movement, Quantz's numerous references to the fact that 'one passion constantly alternates with another'[5] reveals a more progressive, pre-classical approach. As Palisca puts it, 'Composers of the mid-eighteenth century found the affections too static, intellectual and lifeless; they were enticed by the possibility of continuous dynamic flux and transition of sentiment.'[6]

The imitation of nature was a complementary eighteenth-century doctrine[7] – the foundations of the composer's expressive power 'must have been laid in him by nature herself', argues Sulzer[8] – especially in France,[9] where music had invariably served a descriptive, entertaining function in connection with the theatre or the dance. However, most writers were agreed that music was best suited to express the human passions.

With the passage of time, composers tended to indicate their intentions with increasing precision, freely using more notational indications and qualifying their initial description of character, tempo or, as French writers broadly expressed it, *accent*. In his survey Baillot distinguishes four principal characters, related to four ages in life and the general progression of the human heart; he provides a table, included below (Table 3), of French and Italian words pertinent to each character; copious musical illustrations of each category follow, of which Exx. 303–6 are a selected few.[10]

Most of the technical considerations relating to aspects of expression are discussed individually elsewhere and it is within the sphere of this chapter to outline only the philosophical aspects of expression and general style in performance as typically presented in selected treatises of the period. The most complete survey of this subject is provided by Baillot, who repeats the second part of Rode *et al.*'s *Méthode . . .* verbatim as part two of *L'art . . .*, adding a brief introductory explanation for his choice of the six topics under discussion.

Expression and how to achieve it

We have now considered the violin with regard to technique and set down the practical principles required for developing in the student the physical gifts with which

4. See Quantz, *Versuch . . .*, tr. and ed. Reilly, ch. 11, §15–16, pp. 124–6 & §24–5, pp. 133–4.
5. *Ibid.*, pp. 125, 126 & 133.
6. Palisca, *Baroque music* (New Jersey, 1968), p. 4.
7. See L. Mozart, *Versuch . . .*, ch. 6, §16, pp. 119–20.
8. *Allgemeine Theorie . . .*, ed. Sulzer (2nd edn, Leipzig, 1792–4), as quoted in le Huray and Day, *Music and aesthetics . . .*, pp. 123–4.
9. Charles Batteux (1713–80) was one of the chief disseminators of this Aristotelian doctrine linking art with the imitation of both animate and inanimate nature.
10. Baillot, *L'art . . .* (1834), pp. 195–204.

Table 3

TABLEAU

des principaux accens qui déterminent le caractère

1ᵉʳ CARACTÈRE.

Simple.   Naïf.

ACCENS.		Indications correspondantes dont on s'est servi jusqu'à présent
1 -	Simple . . . . Naïf . . .	Semplice . . . . Smorfioso .
2 -	Pastoral	Pastorale .
3 -	Champêtre	Idem .
4 -	Rustique	Rustico .
5 -	Villageois	Pastorale .
6 -	Gai	Allegro - Gaio - Scherzoso .
7 -	Vif et Léger	Vivace - Leggiere .
8 -	Doux et Gracieux	Dolce - Grazioso .
9 -	Tendre et Affectueux	Tenere - Affettuoso .

(accolade: Nuances du caractère Naïf)

2ᵐᵉ CARACTÈRE.

Vague.   Indécis.

ACCENS.		
10 -	Vague . . . . Indécis . . .	Fantastico - Caprizioso .
11 -	Animé	Mosso - Vivace - Brioso - Spiritoso .
12 -	Agité . . . . Plaintif . . .	Agitato - Flebile .
13 -	Retenu	Ritenuto - Rallentando .

3ᵐᵉ CARACTÈRE.

Passionné   Dramatique

ACCENS.		
14 -	Passionné	Appassionnato - Furioso - Disperato .
15 -	de Mélancolie	Malinconico .
16 -	de Tristesse	Mesto .
17 -	Pénétrant	Espressivo - Con intimissimo sentimento .
18 -	de Douleur	Con Dolore .
19 -	Voilé. Concentré	Con Sordini - Sotto voce - Che a pena si sente .
20 -	Brillant	Brillante .
21 -	Energique	Energico .
22 -	Véhément	Stiracchiato .
23 -	Dramatique	Drammatico .
24 -	Martial	Militare - Tempo di marcia .
25 -	Résolu. Fier	Risoluto - Imperioso .
26 -	Noble. Grandiose	Nobile - Grandioso .

4ᵐᵉ CARACTÈRE.

Calme   Religieux

ACCENS.		
27 -	Calme . . . . Tranquille	Moderato - Tranquillo .
28 -	Majestueux	Maestoso - Grande
29 -	Religieux	Religioso .
30 -	Enthousiastique. Sublime	Con fuoco .

(Baillot, L'art . . ., (1834) p. 195)

Ex. 303

ACCENT

1st character: simple, naive
(Boccherini: Quintet no. 40)

a.

Naive accent

(Beethoven: Symphony no. 6, 'Pastoral')

b.

Pastoral accent

(Same Symphony)

c.

Rustic accent

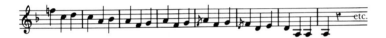

Ex. 304

2nd character: vague, undecided
(Tartini: Sonata no. 10, 'La Didone abbandonata')

a.

Plaintive and
begging accent

(Haydn: Quartet no. 80)

b.

Lively accent

(Boccherini: Quintet no. 52)

c.   Finale: Allegro ma non presto

Passionate and agitated accent

Ex. 305

3rd character: passionate, dramatic
(Viotti: Duo no. 16)

a.   Agitato assai con molto moto ($\downarrow$ = 126)

Passionate accent

(Mendelssohn: Quartet no. 2)

b.   Adagio non lento

Dramatic, noble and passionate accent

(Haydn: Symphony no. 100 ('Military'))

c.   Allegretto

Martial accent

Ex. 306

4th character: calm, religious
(Beethoven: Quartet no. 17)

a.   Lento assai e cantante tranquillo

Calm accent

Ex. 306 (cont.)

(Haydn: Quartet no. 79)

Calm and
religious accent

(Viotti: Concerto no. 3)

Majestic accent

Nature may have endowed him; when he has conquered these elementary difficulties, he should be encouraged to apply them to a good selection of music of progressive difficulty, capable of shaping both his playing and his taste, for he will never be able to rise above the common level and achieve great things unless he studies what has already been achieved. He should therefore follow up the history of the violin, so to speak, by having put before him the works of the oldest masters successively up to those of the present day.[11]

The violin thus takes on a character of its own, all that is merely technique disappears and feeling rules in its place; now feeling must win the day over artifice, show itself supreme and make us forget the means that it employs to arouse our emotions.

The student who has become competent in violin technique should therefore not believe that his studies are at an end; let him consult his [expressive] powers before he proceeds further. *Expression* now opens up possibilities for his talent, limited only by the capacity of the human heart; for him to be born sensitive is not enough, he must bear with his soul that expansive force, that warmth of feeling which spreads out from itself and imparts itself to others, penetrates, burns. This is the sacred fire that an ingenious fiction has made Prometheus steal in order to give life to mankind.

'Expression consists in giving utterance with conviction to all the ideas that the musician has to impart and all the feelings that he has to express.'[12]

Means of expression

True expression depends on sound quality, movement, style, taste, precision and genius of execution.

11. One should point out as the best compositions of this kind those of Corelli, Handel, Tartini, Geminiani, Locatelli, Ferrari, Stamitz, Leclerc, Gaviniès, Nardini, Pugnani and Viotti. (Baillot's footnote)

12. *Dictionnaire de Musique*, ed. Rousseau, article 'Expression'. (Baillot's footnote)

Sound quality

Each instrument has a peculiar quality of tone related to its structure, its size, the materials from which it is made and the means employed to cause it to vibrate; it is this tone quality which gives it a pronounced character such that the least trained ear can readily recognise. 'But', says Rousseau,[13] 'there is no instrument which affords a wider and more varied range of expression than the violin. This admirable instrument forms the basis of every orchestra and a great composer will always be able to obtain from it all those effects which inferior musicians seek in vain to achieve by blending numerous different instruments.'

In fact, in its high register, the violin can attain the brilliance of the clarinet, or the simple, pastoral tone of the oboe; in its middle range, the soft, tender sounds of the flute; and in its low register, the melancholy tones of the bassoon or the touching, noble sounds of the horn; this variety depends on the talent of the performer.

But besides this flexibility of tone which is peculiar to the instrument, there is a second quality which depends on the extent of the musician's sensibility and which so modifies the tone that the same violin played by two different musicians is hardly ever recognisable.

Before a melody has run its course or before the listener has linked an idea with what is being played, it is the *sound* that first strikes his senses and proceeds to move his soul; it is to the ear what beauty is to the eye; the first sound, like the first look, casts the spell and makes such a profound impression that it never fades. The sound that Tartini and Pugnani drew from their violins is remembered well enough to compare the differences and evoke the kind of expression which characterised their playing; although we have for too long been deprived of hearing the expressive sounds of Viotti, we have been so moved by them that nothing can ever make us forget them; their echoes will not die away, they remain forever in the memory as well as in the heart.[14]

Let those who wish to acquire a fine quality of tone begin to prepare for it by the technical means that we have indicated;[15] but let them not hope to find it beyond the bounds of their own sensibility; they must devote themselves to drawing it from the depths of their souls, for it is only there that they will find its source.

Movement

The old masters had divided music into three types in relation to its effect on the soul: *tranquil, active* and *enthusiastic* music.[16]

13. *Idem*. (Baillot's footnote)
14. Again we must draw attention here to the fact that this second part of the 1st method was written more than 30 years ago and that we have since had some happy occasions of hearing Viotti and of seeing how well-founded was our former admiration of his talents; the years have only augmented our esteem and our fondness for this fine genius whose accents were so true, natural and at the same time so lofty that they gave the most agreeable and noble character to all his inspirations. (Baillot's footnote)
15. See article 'Son', 1st part [p. 138]. (Baillot's footnote)
16. The ancient philosopher had divided music into three types, with regard to its effects on the soul: *tranquil, active* and *enthusiastic* music; the first was a solemn melody of moderate speed, which resulted in it being called *moral*. The second was a more animated melody which was suited to the passions. The third seized upon the soul and filled it with intoxication. (Notes by the Abbé Lebatteux on the poetics of Aristotle.)
   Plutarch says that there are three principles of music: *gaiety, sadness* and *enthusiasm*.
   Music may be divided into three types: music of *affliction*, of *gaiety*, of *calm* (the Greek musician Aristides-Quintilian).
   Euclid establishes three characters of melody, that which *elevates the soul*, that which *weakens* and *softens it* and that which *soothes it*.
   The distinction made by Aristides-Quintilian relates to these three words: *Adagio, Andante, Allegro*.

These principal characteristics are contained in the three grades of movement known under the terms of *Adagio, Moderato, Presto*.

The character of a piece of music depends in great part on its pace; there is nobody who has not tried to change the speed of a melody and who in so doing has not made a very gay piece out of the saddest *Adagio* or a touching air from the most lively *Presto*.

Expression demands therefore that the music that one is playing shall be given as precisely as possible a speed appropriate to its fundamental character, if one wishes to have the character appropriate to its speed.

It is necessary, moreover, to preserve this character and to do nothing which might change it; thus one will avoid inserting rapid passages in an *Adagio* or giving it a mood foreign to the character which its speed implies, but one will make the embellishments more ample, the *appoggiaturas* slower, the trills more supple and flowing, and the bowing sustained with much slower strokes than in the *Allegro*.

The *Allegro* should be played in a firmer manner and with more lively bowing. The ornaments and *appoggiaturas* should still be executed broadly but with more frequent bow strokes and the trills should be tossed off more rapidly.

All possible lightness, vivacity and spirit should be introduced into the *Presto*, and even in passages of greatest abandon, the fingers and bow will always retain some lively clarity and brilliance.

Moreover, one only has to put students on the right path in order to prevent them losing their way; there is an infinite number of other things that one could tell them, and the more intelligent will already have guessed that there are gradations of speed which have some of the characteristics of the three about which we have just spoken, such as the *Larghetto, Andante, Moderato, Allegretto* etc.; then it is up to one's musical sense to bring out more or less with these different speeds one or other of the three principal characteristics that we have been discussing.

It will soon be seen that all that has just been said concerns the material of expression and that there is another way of considering it.

Style

The manner of expression, the choice of expressions, the mood given to each piece are what characterise its *style*. Thus, in accordance with what has just been said, the *Adagio*, the *Allegro* and the *Presto* each have a particular style that one must take care not to confuse.

Each composer possesses a seal that he impresses upon all his work, a style of his own which depends on his manner of feeling and expression.

It is this which is the stumbling-block for many performers; one player perhaps has the power of doing justice to the music of one composer but cannot play that of another; his fingers, his bow, his playing, all object, because he has not within him the flexibility necessary to enter into all the styles, or he is not sufficiently well organised to seize upon the different ways of phrasing and the different moods to be given to those phrases; for this latter evil there is no remedy; but if the pupil be held up by physical obstacles only, let him endeavour to modify and vary his playing by studying

---

He considers the *Adagio* as being more sad than tender. My opinion differs from his on this point. The *Andante* depicts calmness and such gentle emotions that they do not destroy the idea of tranquility. The *Allegro* expresses gaiety as the name by itself indicates. Would Aristides-Quintilian, who makes no mention of enthusiastic music, have conceived like me that the *Allegro* becomes enthusiastic when there are added to it the properties of noise and all the devices of imitation? (Observations on Music, by Mr. de C) (Baillot's footnote)

all the genres [of music] and every composer; let him begin by imitating great models, that in turn he himself may be looked up to as a model, and let him not fear to remain an imitator. From among the best works of the best masters, he will at first adopt the style which has the closest analogy with his own way of feeling, but as feelings vary infinitely with each individual and as the smallest nuances in impression produce diversities of style, if he has the seed of true talent, he will eventually build up a style of his own in which he will express himself entirely and which will assume that characteristic of originality peculiar to those who say what they feel and who write or who play only according to the inspirations of the heart and the impulses of the imagination.

But this originality, which must never be aimed at, should be natural; one cannot affect it without betraying oneself and becoming bizarre; it is for good taste to avert this misfortune, which is more common than one might imagine.

Taste

Natural taste is nothing other than a sense of propriety, an imperceptible tact which disposes us to give to everything the tone, the character and the place most proper to it. It precedes the process of thought and, without knowing it, always chooses well.

There is another kind of taste formed as a result of comparisons, by judgement, by experience; this is *refined taste*, which adds to natural taste that intimate knowledge of the proprieties of which we have just spoken; it is at one and the same time a gift of nature and the fruit of education; it requires thought as much as instinct; it does not consist, as many believe, in introducing into a stretch of melody agreeable turns and embellishments but in abstaining from them when the subject requires it, or employing them only where appropriate, and in deriving the ornaments from the very nature of the expression of the melody, as we have already said. [17] It is the teacher's duty therefore to support his pupil, to encourage the development of his taste by convincing him that a touching and impassioned piece is not a bravura composition and that an *Adagio* has nothing in common with the sudden, hasty movements of the *Allegro*; that he must not play a quartet with the same firm and expansive manner as a concerto, that he must measure his playing to the dignity of his subject, modify his sounds and organise his resources, as passages of different expression may require, and finally that he should do nothing which does not correspond to the principal character of the piece.

But in vain shall we hope to guide the pupil if his sensibility is not ahead of what he is taught and if he requires similar observations to be repeated to him; in the end one can make an imitator of him but not a man of talent; the best lesson in taste is not the one that the teacher gives but the one that the pupil can learn for himself.

Precision

To obtain precision it is not sufficient to keep the time strictly from bar to bar; it is necessary also to observe the greatest exactness in each subdivision of the bar and to acquire such a perfect mastery of one's playing that the movement may always be regular.

Expression sometimes allows for a slight alteration in the time, but either this alteration is graduated and virtually imperceptible or the beat is simply merely disguised, that is in pretending to miss it for a moment, one finds oneself soon afterwards following it exactly as before.

17. s.v. 'Ornemens', pt. i, [p. 347]. (Baillot's footnote)

If this freedom is abused, the music loses the charm given to it by regularity of movement, and the ear, accustomed to this rhythm, to this division of time which determines the character of a piece so well, soon tires of any diversity and confusion of speeds that destroys the beauties of the whole.

Some believe that they give warmth to their performances by hurrying the time slightly in difficult passages, as if warmth of expression consisted in rapidity! Are we then to give up instilling *Adagios* with any warmth? This method is merely an artificial means of compensating for lack of genuine warmth. The latter is clearly shown in the way one performs a passage with zest, energy and with that expansiveness of the soul which must come into play as much in the *Adagio* as at other speeds.

Precision, together with accuracy, is the rarest quality in performance; by playing in front of a metronome set in tempo, one can see that nothing is more difficult than keeping regularly to the beat and the bar. It is almost as if it is the movement of the blood which has made rhythm necessary to us and that the origins of time are owed to the beating of the heart. In portraying the passions do we not in fact follow those emotions, sometimes quick, sometimes slow, those more or less animated (*accélérés*) movements that love, hatred, pleasure, grief, fear or hope excite in our breasts? It is these which act as a ruling force in the composer's choice of rhythms and time; but by their very nature they cannot be mathematically regular; furthermore, differences will be introduced which arise from the make-up of each individual, and hence comes the great difficulty of maintaining precision and following a given speed.

In order to succeed, the head must be accustomed early to moderate the liveliness of the senses and to regulate those passions which must move the performer; if he allows himself to be carried away by them, there will no longer be any sense of the beat, nuances nor pleasing effects; if he is too reserved, his performance will be cold; art consists in maintaining a balance between the feelings that carry you away and those which hold you back; as one can see, this is a different kind of precision from that which aims solely at the exact division of the beat and the bar; it is the result as much of good practice as of maturity of talent. (Baillot, *L'art . . .* (1834), pp. 264–8).

Baillot's insistence on rigorous time-keeping, allowing at the same time for some freedom of expressive effect within the 'outlines' of the pulse, reflects the general view of most theorists of the period.[18] The chief means of such freedom for expressive melodic effect was *tempo rubato*, which, often regarded as a species of ornament, seems to have been applied to four different expressive techniques during the period; the most common involved a natural flexibility of the prescribed rhythm within a constant tempo, after which the ensemble between melody and accompaniment is restored.[19] The term also extended in certain cases to the modification of dynamics and/or the displacement of natural accents (resulting, for example, in unaccented 'strong' beats of the bar);[20] the expansion of the bar(s) to incorporate more notes than the time-signature theoretically allows, and a flexible yet rhythmically controlled performance of these passages;[21] or flexibility of tempo by introducing arbitrary, unwritten

18. Quantz, *Versuch . . .*, tr. and ed. Reilly, ch. 17, section 7, §48, p. 284; L. Mozart, *Versuch . . .*, ch. 7, section 2, pp. 144–6; Tosi, *Opinioni . . .*, tr. Galliard, pp. 63–4 & p. 99.
19. See, for example, Tosi, *Opinioni . . .*, tr. Galliard, pp. 129 & 156; L. Mozart, *Versuch . . .*, ch. 12, §20n, p. 263; Spohr, *Violinschule* (1832), pp. 199 & 202; C. P. E. Bach, *Versuch . . .*, tr. Mitchell, ch. 3, §8, pp. 150–1; Türk, *Klavierschule . . .*, tr. Naumburger, p. 40.
20. See Türk, *Klavierschule . . .*, tr. Naumburger, p. 40.
21. C. P. E. Bach, *Versuch . . .*, tr. Mitchell, ch. 3, §28, pp. 160–1.

accelerandos or *ritardandos*.[22] In his brief survey, Baillot goes much further than the concept, reiterated throughout the seventeenth and eighteenth centuries, that 'good notes' (*note buone*)[23] should be held slightly longer than their written values and 'bad notes' shortened by way of compensation. Nevertheless, the flexibility offered by the 'good/bad' note principle is perhaps at the root of his textual discussion, which incorporates examples of the first two of the above *rubato* types:

There is a way of altering or breaking the pulse which derives from syncopation and is called *tempo rubato* or *disturbato, stolen* or *troubled time*. This *stolen time* is very effective but it would become by its very nature tiring and unbearable if it were used often. It tends to express trouble and agitation and few composers have notated or indicated it; the character of the passage is generally sufficient to prompt the performer to improvise according to the inspiration of the moment. He must only make use of it in spite of himself, as it were, when, carried away by the expression, it apparently forces him to lose all sense of pulse and to be delivered by this means from the trouble that besets him. We say that he only appears to lose the sense of pulse, that is he must preserve a sort of steadiness that will keep him within the limits of the harmony of the passage and make him return at the right moment to the exact pulse of the beat. This is a case where we may make the following observation: *Often a beautiful disorder is an artistic effect.*

This disorder will thus be of such a nature as to be pleasing and even to be found beautiful; it will become an *artistic effect* if it results from effort and inspiration and if the artist can use it without being forced to think of the means he is employing.

Up to a certain point this device can be notated, but like all impassioned accents it will lose much of its effect if it is performed according to the book.

We give examples of this kind of accent here simply in order to shed light on its use and to prevent any misuse that might be made of it.

Stolen time

Ex. 307

(Viotti: Concerto no. 19)

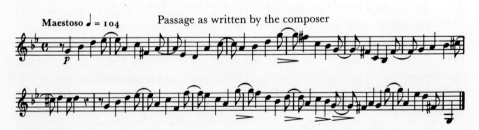

Maestoso ♩ = 104   Passage as written by the composer

22. See Koch, 'Ueber den technischen Ausdruck Tempo rubato', *Allgemeine musikalische Zeitung*, Leipzig, 1808, no. 33.
23. See ch. 12, p. 302.

General indication of the way of rendering this passage.

Ex. 308

(Viotti: Concerto no. 18)

Presto ♩ = 116

General indication of the way this passage may be rendered *the last time* it is repeated in this rondo.

Presto

(Baillot, *L'art* . . . (1834), pp. 136–7)

Finally, a type of *rubato* typical of the classical style deserves mention. Pinpointed by Rosen,[24] it is the result of composers compelling performers to extend 'the limits of harmony' and create artistic effect through harmonic disorder. The second movement of Haydn's String Quartet Op. 54 no. 2 is a prime example, the arabesque of the first violin part comprising a written-out *rubato* which delays the expected melodic notes and results in dissonance through enforced harmonic overlapping (Ex. 309).

Ex. 309

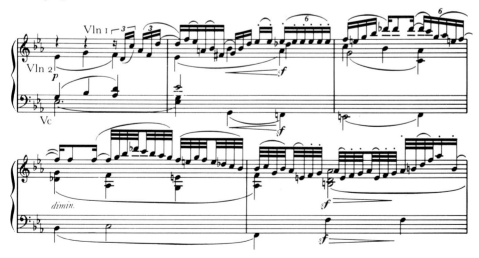

24. Rosen, *The classical style*, pp. 139–40.

Ex. 309 (cont.)

Genius of execution

It is this which grasps at a glance the varying character of music, which by a sudden inspiration identifies itself with the genius of the composer, follows it in all its intentions and reveals them with equal facility and precision, which even anticipates effects in order to make them sparkle more brilliantly, which gives to the playing of an instrument the colour which best suits the style of the composer; which knows how to unite grace with feeling, simplicity with grace, strength with gentleness and to bring out all the nuances which determine contrasts; to pass in a moment to a different expression, to adapt itself to every style and accent; to emphasise without affectation the most striking passages and throw a skilful veil over the most vulgar ones; to become imbued with the genius of a piece even so much as to lend it charms which are not indicated; even to go so far as to create effects which the composer often leaves to instinct; to interpret everything, to bring everything to life, to conjure up in the soul of the listener the very sentiment that the composer had in his own; to bring back to life the men of genius of past centuries and finally to render their sublime accents with an enthusiasm appropriate to this noble and touching language, which, like poetry, has been so rightly called the *language of the gods*.

One part of the means of expression of which we have spoken above depends upon art and shows what is required in order to do well, but genius of expression leads us to do still better; it is this which, urged on by feeling, wings its bold flight into the vast empire of expression to make new discoveries; here is no more conscious thought, no more calculation; the artist gifted with a superior talent is so accustomed to subordinate his playing to the rules of art that he follows them subconsciously and easily so that, far from chilling his imagination, they serve only to make his ideas blossom and to imbue him more fully with what he is to perform.

His sensibility prepares him for whatever he is going to play; scarcely has he caught sight of the introductory notes of the theme than his soul lifts itself to the level of the subject.

The *sonata*, a kind of concerto divested of its accompaniments, gives him the means of displaying his powers, of developing a part of his resources, of letting himself be heard alone, without pomp, without pause and without any support other than an accompanying bass; left entirely to himself, he draws his nuances and his contrasts from his own resources, and by the variety of his intentions restores the effects in which this type of music may be lacking.

In the *quartet*, he sacrifices all the riches of his instrument to the general effect; he enters into the spirit of this other type of composition, whose charming dialogue seems to be a conversation among friends, who convey to each other their feelings,

their sentiments, their mutual affections; their sometimes different opinions give rise
to an animated discussion to which each gives his own development; they soon take
pleasure in following the stimulus given by their leader, whose ascendancy carries
them along, an ascendancy which he makes felt only by the power of thought that he
displays, and which he owes less to the brilliance of his playing than to the persuasive
sweetness of his expression.

Such is not the case in the *concerto*; here the violin must develop all its power; born
to rule, it is here that it reigns as sovereign and speaks as master; made therefore to
seduce a greater number of listeners and to produce grander effects, it can now
choose a vaster theatre and demand a greater space; an orchestra of numerous players
obeys its voice and the symphony, which serves as its prelude, announces it with
dignity. In all that it does, it tends rather to elevate than to subdue the soul; it employs
in turn majesty, strength, pathos and the most powerful means of moving the crowd.
This may be either an elegant and simple subject which reappears in different forms
and yet always preserves the attraction of novelty, or a proud and noble opening
which the musician utters with candour and whose character he develops, perhaps in
brilliant passages played with great energy, or with sweetly-rendered melodic lines.

Deeply moved in the *Adagio*, he sustains the most touching sounds with slowness
and solemnity; at one moment he allows his playing and his thoughts to wander sur-
rounded by a grave and religious harmony, at another he sighs in a plaintive, tender
piece and varies his moods with all the abandonment of grief, and yet again, noble
and majestic, he rises above every vulgar sentiment and gives free rein to his own
inspiration; the violin is no longer an instrument, it is a resonant soul; travelling
through space, it proceeds to strike the ear of the least attentive listener and to find in
the depths of his heart a sensitive chord and set it vibrating.

The *Presto* offers the performer a new kind of expression; quick to vary the mood
and the character of the music, he gives free rein to all his vivacity, he communicates
to those who hear him the fire which animates him, he carries them along with him in
all his outbursts, he strikes, he astonishes by his boldness, he touches by virtue of that
sensibility which never forsakes him, he makes the most energetic passages as brilliant as lightning, and then, with the abandonment of passion, he softens his playing,
his strength seems exhausted, either by the noisy outbursts of joy or by the agitation
of grief; soon he gradually comes to life again, adds to the intensity of the sound,
increases his effects and carries emotion to its highest pitch until enthusiasm takes
possession of the audience as well as the musician, electrifies them all at once, and
causes them to experience those transports so full of charms which true expression
always brings with it.

Happy the man whom Nature has endowed with a profound sensibility! He possesses within himself an inexhaustible source of expression. The years will only serve
to increase his riches, give him new feelings, vary his situations, modify his sentiments; the more his ideas ripen the more enlightened his mind will become and the
greater simplicity he will acquire in his means and energy in his effects. For him
expression has outstripped the limits of art and becomes so to speak the story of his
life; he sings his memories, his regrets, the pleasures that he has enjoyed, the evils
that he has endured; he turns to the advantage of his art what would only spoil a commonplace talent; sorrow sharpens his sensibility and lends to his accents the delicious
charm of melancholy; even the test of adversity, by arousing his energies, excites his
imagination and inspires in him those sublime emotions, those bold ideas born of
great obstacles and seeming to spring from the heart of the tempest; finally, whatever
may be the fate that carries him along, melody will be his interpreter, his faithful
friend; it will give him the purest of all enjoyments by revealing to him the secret of

communicating to others the full range of his sensations and of interesting his fellow
men in his destiny.   (Baillot, *L'art* . . . (1834), pp. 268–9)

Spohr concentrates rather more on style, dealing first with matters of
interpretation in general before considering in turn various performing situations. In his section devoted to concerto performance he includes detailed
commentary on the interpretation of the solo passages in Rode's Seventh Concerto and an explicitly notated (with a general introductory explanation but
no commentary) edition of his own Ninth Concerto, chosen on account of its
exploitation of several techniques (for example, chromatic scales, double stopping, *staccato*) not encountered in the Rode concerto; both works are presented
with an accompanying violin part. However, there is no available space either
to include these works in the extract from Spohr's treatise, or to reproduce his
third section, devoted to methods of studying new concerto material.

On interpretation
Section one: on interpretation in general

Interpretation means the manner in which the singer or player conveys to the listener
what the composer has conceived and written down. If it is restricted to a faithful rendering of details prescribed by notes, signs and technical terms, one speaks of a correct interpretation; but if the executant has the capacity also to draw upon his own
inner resources and give spiritual life to the work he is interpreting, so that the intentions of the composer can be appreciated and shared by the listener, then this is
known as a fine interpretation, being one which combines accuracy, sensibility and
elegance.

A fine interpretation naturally presupposes a correct one. Thus it is mainly to the
latter that the instruction in the foregoing sections relates; but they include also all
the technical expedients necessary for a fine interpretation, and it thus only remains
here to show how they can be applied.

Indeed no training in fine interpretation can do more than this, since that which
transforms a correct interpretation into a fine one, namely the ability to appreciate
the character of the work to be interpreted and to share in and reveal its predominant
mood, is an inborn gift of Nature, which can indeed be awakened and fostered but
cannot be taught.

First, however, the essentials for correct interpretation must be enumerated once
more, so that the student may judge whether he has mastered them completely and
has thus acquired the capacity to aim at a fine interpretation.

For a correct interpretation the following are pertinent: (1) pure intonation, (2) the
exact division of each bar into its note durations, (3) steadiness of tempo without hurrying or holding back, (4) a strict observance both of the prescribed nuances of loud
and soft and of (5) the types of bowing, slurs, turns, trills etc.

For a fine interpretation, the following technical expedients are necessary in addition to the foregoing: (1) the finer gradations of bow management with regard not
only to the character of the sound from loud or even harsh down to a soft flute-like
tone, but also particularly to the accentuation and articulation of the musical
phrases, (2) the skilful use of positions chosen not for convenience or ease of playing
but with a view to expression and tone quality, with which can be included also gliding from one note to another [*portamento*] and changing the finger on the same note,

(3) the *vibrato* in its gradations and (4) speeding up of the tempo in fiery and impassioned passages, together with holding back [the tempo] in those which have a tender or sad, melancholy character.

But all these means of expression will result in a fine interpretation only if good taste keeps guard over their use and the player's soul guides the bow and animates the fingers. Hence if the student's development is sufficiently advanced for him to be in some measure master of the mechanics of playing, then it is time for his taste also to be developed and his sensibility aroused. This will happen most surely if he can be given frequent opportunity of hearing good music and excellent singers and virtuosi, and if his attention while doing this can be directed by his teacher both to the beauties of the composition and also to the means of expression employed by the singer and virtuoso to affect the sensibilities of the audience.

Section two: on the interpretation of a concerto

As a concerto is performed in a large hall before many listeners and accompanied by an extensive orchestra, the requisites include (1) above all a full, powerful tone. This, however, in no way precludes the more delicate nuances of performance, since it is a characteristic of the violin that even its very softest tones can be heard at a considerable distance. Even when performing a concerto, therefore, the player may deploy the whole wealth of gradations in strength of tone of which the violin is capable.

Since the most obvious aim of concerto playing is to display the player's virtuosity, it is essential here to have (2) complete mastery over every technical difficulty. The student should therefore not venture to perform a concerto or other solo piece in public until he has become so familiar with it by practising it thoroughly that his success is no longer likely to be marred by external influences, such as a high temperature in the hall, or initial self-consciousness in front of the public, or an unresponsive accompaniment.

It is not enough, however, merely to conquer the difficulties; this must be accomplished (3) elegantly and without the slightest apparent effort. Only then will the listener be able to enjoy an unspoilt artistic experience.

In concerto playing the most thorough training in technique must be allied also to (4) an interpretation full of sensibility, since without this the most brilliant playing will excite only cold admiration, never a more intimate sense of participation.

To arouse the latter one needs (5) a composition full of sensibility and sophistication. The student should therefore see to it when choosing a work for public performance not only that it gives him the opportunity to display his virtuosity but also that it is a composition of some merit in itself, which will be satisfying to the cultivated listener quite apart from the arts of the virtuoso . . .

(Spohr, Violinschule (1832), pp. 195–7)

Section four: interpreting a quartet

Recently a type of quartet has arisen in which the first violin takes a solo part and the other three instruments merely accompany. To distinguish them from genuine quartets they are known as solo quartets (*quatuors brillants*). Their purpose is to give the soloist an opportunity to display his virtuosity in smaller musical circles. From the point of view of interpretation they thus belong to the category of concerto music, and everything that was said in the preceding sections about the interpretation of a concerto is fully applicable to these and similar solo pieces with a three- or four-part accompaniment (such as variations, *potpourris* and suchlike), but with the sole proviso that here, in a small space and with a light accompaniment, the tone of the instrument must not be allowed to swell to its greatest volume, and any roughness in the playing, which would be lost in the concert hall through the remoteness of the audience, must be scrupulously avoided.

The interpretation of a genuine quartet, however, is subject to quite different requirements. The intention here is not that one single instrument should shine, but that all four should in identical manner become conversant with the composer's idea and bring it to life. The first violinist must therefore not attempt to stand out from the others either in the strength of his tone or in the style of his interpretation; he must rather contrive to work most intimately in keeping with the rest and even subordinate his own part in passages where it is not the leading voice.

Since the style of an interpretation should proceed always from the idea and spirit of the composition, the soloist must whenever he plays a quartet be able to disown his own personal style of solo playing and adapt to the particular character of the quartet before him. Unless he can do this, he will not be successful in bringing out clearly either the character of the individual movements of the quartet or the diversity of style in the works of our classical quartet composers.

The student will understand from this that for the perfect interpretation of a quartet, although perhaps less technical skill is required than in concerto playing, many other things are needed that can readily be dispensed with in a concerto, but above all an easily aroused sensibility, cultivated taste and a command of composition.[25]

Although it is only through a combination of these qualities that one becomes a perfect quartet player, there is nevertheless nothing more suitable for acquiring and fostering them than diligent quartet playing itself. The student should therefore not miss any opportunity that may be offered him of participating in good quartet music. But he should begin with the second violin part and learn first of all the difficult art of accompaniment. This consists in the skill of following the first violin most precisely in everything, for example in strength of tone, in any slight changes of tempo that may perhaps be instigated by the first violinist, and also in the interpretation of the figures that are developed thematically, whenever these appear in the second part; and furthermore in the most precise adherence to the prescribed bowings, slurs, and also to the nuances of *p* and *f*, without however standing out shrill and overloud in the latter unless the figure given to the second violin expressly requires it.

If the student has thus prepared himself for a while by accompanying; if in so doing he has become familiar with the way quartet music is played by following a good model and if he now wishes to attempt the first violin part, it is absolutely necessary for a start that he should mark his part beforehand and practise it exactly as he did with the concerto. Our most excellent quartet composers were not violinists, or at least not sufficiently so to be particularly familiar with the mechanics of violin playing; the indication of bowings and of contrived position-work etc. is thus as a rule even more inadequate than in concerto music and must therefore of necessity be supplemented by the player. In so doing, however, greater care and restraint are needed than with the concerto, since here the intention is not to show off one's virtuosity but to bring the composer's idea to life. For this reason any bowings, for instance, which form part of the distinctive expression of a musical thought and which recur in the other parts, must not be altered arbitrarily, however capable the player might be of substituting more convenient or striking ones. The quartet player must also take care with the addition of other means of expression such as are customary in solo playing,

25. If the student has not already begun to study the theory of composition, then it is now high time that he should do so. (Spohr's footnote)

since this can easily disturb the ensemble and distort the composer's idea. Only those passages where he clearly has the solo part and is simply accompanied by the others may be embellished in the manner customary in solo work. Moreover, to be able to mark a quartet impeccably, one must have it before one in score or be already thoroughly familiar with it from hearing it frequently.

A carefully considered marking of the bowings, positions etc. in this way must continue to precede the actual performance of any quartet until such time as the student has acquired sufficient skill to determine immediately upon reading the notes the most suitable division of the bow strokes and the application of any other expedients appropriate for bringing the interpretation to life. This skill, which at first will include only what is most crude and obvious, must be cultivated with increasing subtlety by the student as his taste becomes more refined and his insight into the art deepens, until it finally ranks as the most perfect interpretation.

Section five: orchestral playing and accompaniment

For the violinist, the most essential difference between concerto or quartet playing and orchestral playing is that in the latter the same part is played by several players at once. Each individual must therefore take pains to match the others as closely as possible in (1) intonation, (2) the divisions of parts of the bar, (3) the accentuation of the same, (4) the execution of the prescribed nuances of p and f and (5) the division of the bow strokes.

With regard to (1) intonation, there is only one intonation that is correct; the more each individual aims at this, therefore, the more certainly he will also be in agreement with the other players.

(2) The division of the parts of the bar according to their time values must be most strictly observed in orchestral playing, since without it perfect unanimity of the players would be impossible. Any dwelling on single or several notes (*Tempo rubato*), which is often so effective in solo playing, must therefore be avoided here.

(3) Accentuation must be limited to the normal practice of accenting the strong beats of the bar. Any other of the kind customary in solo playing to make the interpretation more striking is inadmissible here, unless it is expressly prescribed and thus to be executed by all the players.

(4) Similarly the orchestral player must confine himself to the precise observance of p and f as marked, and must not add new nuances of loud and soft on his own account as in solo playing.

The most difficult task, however, is to achieve (5) complete unanimity among the players in the division of the bow strokes. In this regard therefore much remains to be desired even in the best rehearsed orchestras. But the difficulty lies mainly in the fact that (1) the marking of the bowing is usually even more slipshod and inadequate in orchestral parts than it is in concerto and quartet music and that (2) the violinists in an orchestra are never products of one and the same school,[26] and thus all have different styles of bowing and consequently different bowing habits. And yet it is not simply very pleasing to the eye, but also of great importance for the accentuation, for uniformity in loudness and softness, in a word for the whole ensemble, that the up and down strokes of all the violinists playing the same part should always coincide. To achieve this end as completely as possible, the orchestral player must conform strictly to the old rule which prescribes: take the strong beats in the bar with the down bow, the weak beats with the up bow, and thus begin every bar with a down bow and

26. The only exception to this is found in the orchestras of the Conservatoires (in Paris, Prague, Naples), which is why such admirable results are achieved there in the ensemble of the violinists [see ch. 1, p. 31]. (Spohr's footnote)

end it with an up bow. In addition the leader has the responsibility of supplementing any deficiencies in the marked bowing (particularly when there are several rehearsals, as in operas, oratorios, symphonies) and thus ensuring the most perfect unanimity possible in the bowing.

Further recommendations for the orchestral player are: to refrain from all superfluous *appoggiaturas*, turns, trills and the like, and similarly all contrived position-work, sliding from one note to another, changing the finger on one note, in short, to avoid everything that pertains simply to the embellishment of solo playing and would disturb the smoothness of the ensemble if transferred to orchestral playing. If *appoggiaturas* and turns are present in an orchestral part, then the length of the first and the manner of executing the second must be determined by the leader, and be performed by everyone uniformly in accordance with his decision.

With regard to the time, the orchestral player must obey the indications of the director precisely, whether this be the leader or a conductor. He also has a duty to glance frequently at the latter over his copy, so that he may not only remain always in the correct time according to the given beat, but also follow quickly if by chance the beat is held back or increased.

When accompanying, it is the orchestral player's duty to subordinate himself totally to the soloist. He should therefore adjust the strength of his accompaniment to that of the solo line and take care that he never obscures or overpowers it. The *f*. or *fz*. which may occur in the accompaniment during a solo must therefore never be brought out as loudly and forcefully as in a tutti. The volume of tone should altogether be regulated always according to the kind of music and the size of the premises.

The accompanying player should beware both of forcing the soloist forward in tempo and of holding him back, yet he should follow the soloist instantly if he happens to permit himself any slight deviation from the beat. This does not apply, however, to any *tempo rubato* in the solo part, where the accompaniment has to continue its steady, regular course.

All the above applies equally to the accompaniment of singing. Since this however is normally conducted, the conductor's beat must be watched and followed with regard to the tempo and any changes in it. One type of vocal music, however, is particularly difficult to accompany, namely recitative, because here the regular beat ceases completely. In order to follow the vocal line more easily, it is customary to add the vocal part on a separate line above the accompaniment. The accompanist has to follow this line and also at the same time pay constant attention to the indications from the conductor who thus signals the entry of the accompaniment. Since these indications are not the same for all conductors, no explanation of them can be given here. An attentive orchestral player will however soon learn to understand and follow those of his own conductor, assuming the latter is consistent in them and always gives the same ones.

The tuning of the orchestra should take place as quietly as possible. The leader should take his A from the oboe, or even safer, from all the wind instruments together, and then let each individual violinist, cellist etc. tune to his A. Once each is ready, he must avoid disturbing the tuning of the others with pointless preliminary flourishes. Once all are correctly tuned, several minutes' general silence should ensue; this greatly enhances the opening effect of the music.

If the student now re-examines the prescriptions given here for orchestral playing, he will find that the chief merit of a good orchestral player consists in willingly subordinating himself to the whole and giving up his independence as a soloist.

The student should now do this for as long as he takes part in an orchestra.

(Spohr, *Violinschule* (1832), pp. 246-9)

12

Phrasing and accentuation

The art of phrasing involves dividing a piece into its constituent sections and subsections (rounded off in most cases by cadences of varying strength) and linking or separating musical ideas by means of phrasing off, minute silences (the articulation silence being taken either from the value of the last note of the phrase concluded or inserted as 'stolen time'[1] for a momentary break in the tempo before the beginning of the subsequent phrase) and suchlike, in order to give shape to a melodic line. It is sparsely documented in violin methods of the period but such evidence as exists, which tends to be vague rather than specific, indicates that it is generally considered analogous to the function of punctuation marks in language or breathing in vocal music; it clarifies the sense, structure and to a certain extent the expression of the musical 'sentence'. Baillot explains:

Notes are used in music like words in speech; they are used to construct a sentence, to give shape to an idea; consequently full stops and commas must be used, just as in a written passage, to distinguish its periods and their constituent parts and to make it easier to understand.[2]
(Baillot, L'art . . . (1834), p. 163)

Campagnoli, like Rode et al.[3] and many other writers, gives a vocal analogy:

The principles laid down for the management of the breath in singing are applicable to the employment of the bow, which performs the office of respiration and marks the points of repose, in which the art of phrasing principally consists. To play well, said Tartini, it is necessary to sing well.
(Campagnoli, Metodo . . . (1797?), tr. Bishop, pt. 2, no. 115)

However, Habeneck provides perhaps the most concise and comprehensive survey, incorporating numerous examples to illustrate the various techniques of phrase articulation employed.

---

1. See ch. 11, p. 273.
2. One may easily understand that the silences expressed in music by crotchet, quaver and semiquaver rests are the equivalent of the full stops and commas used in speech. (Baillot's footnote)
3. Rode et al., Méthode . . . (1803), pp. 135–6.

On the proper manner of phrasing

38. In a melody, as in speech, there are periods, phrases, and figures which make up the phrases.

39. A period may contain several phrases.

40. A phrase may contain several figures.

41. The phrase most usually consists of 4 bars. There are nevertheless 2- and 3- and even 5-bar phrases, but we shall not enter into more detail on this subject because such matters fall rather within the province of composition, and we wish simply to explain to our violin pupils how they may best perform the phrases they have in front of them.

42. To phrase properly, the figures, the phrases and the periods must each be brought out in such a way that the whole is easily intelligible to the audience; and for that it is necessary to make a clear distinction between the beginning and the end of each figure, phrase and period.

43. We shall call this *musical punctuation*.
We shall put forward several melodies in succession which we shall analyse in order to make the study of this matter easier for the student.

Ex. 310

(Viotti: Concerto no. 18)[4]

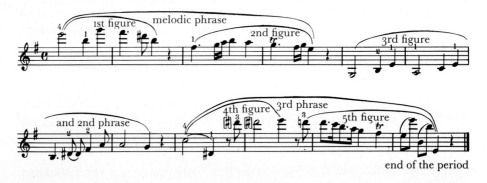

end of the period

44. In this period each figure is cut short by a rest; it is thus a very simple matter to scan it in a manner satisfying to the listener. If all melodies were as conveniently segmented, the art of phrasing would not be a difficult one.

45. But there are plenty where there are no rests until the end of a period but where the figures must be separated from each other, nevertheless, by a certain slackening of the sound.

Ex. 311

(Viotti: Concerto no. 9)

end of the period

4. In the whole of this section, the slur ⁀ is in no way to be applied to the bowing; it is used merely to separate the figures, phrases and periods. (Habeneck's footnote)

46. In this period, since the 1st figure ends on the 2nd f² in the 2nd bar, this f² must be considerably reduced in volume before attacking the a² that follows, so as to separate the two figures.

Ex. 312

(Rode: *Air varié* no. 2)

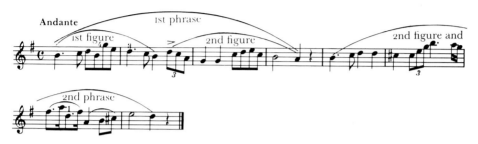

47. In this phrase, the sound must be reduced on the b¹ in the 2nd bar, and the d² that follows taken a little louder to show the start of the 2nd figure, then down again on the a¹ in the 4th bar, which forms an imperfect cadence and the end of the phrase. This leads us to put forward the following general rule:

48. The volume should be reduced at the end of every figure, phrase or period.

Ex. 313

(Baillot: Concerto no. 2)

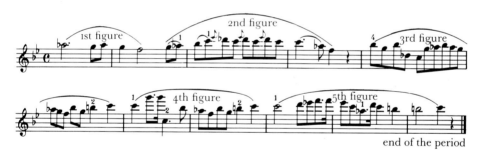

49. Here is another period where the rests come always on the 3rd beat of the bar.

Ex. 314

(Baillot: Concerto no. 5)

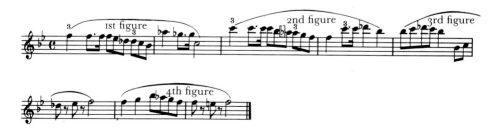

50. We will conclude this article with the analysis of the following melody, which presents certain difficulties because of the dovetailing of its periods and phrases.

Ex. 315

(Baillot: Concerto no. 3)

51. All these examples are analysed only with regard to their musical punctuation. If they are played simply according to these indications, they will be comprehensible, but they will lack that expression which gives charm to a melody. In the sections on Nuance and on Accent we shall speak of the methods that must be used to give this expression without which any performance is tedious for the audience.

(Habeneck, *Méthode* . . . (c. 1840), pp. 107–8)

Music of the classical period was characterised by well-defined articulations and a tendency towards balanced, complementary phrasing – the four-bar phrase formula was the most common – as opposed to the short motifs, ornamental *figurae* and the feeling of continuous flow given by the texturally

veiled phrase endings of much baroque music. However, matters of phrasing
were generally the performer's responsibility since few composers or theorists
were accustomed to notating phrasing marks in their works. Couperin (*Pièces
de clavecin*, books 3 and 4), who used a comma sign (') to indicate phrasing,
Schulz and Türk,[5] who employed various different signs to indicate phrase
separations or notated phrasings through note-groupings by 'breaking the
beams' at phrasing points in groups of quavers and semiquavers, were notable
eighteenth-century exceptions in instrumental music. Even in the nineteenth
century special signs were employed only rarely to clarify phrase-structure, as
Baillot confirms. He provides a lengthy explanation of methods of terminating phrases and concentrates in particular on the technique of 'phrasing off',
making wherever necessary a *diminuendo* on or just before the last note of a
phrase.

But slight separations, rests of very short duration, are not always indicated by the
composer; they must therefore be introduced by the performer, when he sees the need
for them, by letting the final note of the phrase or the entire period die away, and even
in certain cases fading this note a little before the end of its value; for example:

Half-rests or commas

Ex. 316

(Viotti: Concerto no. 27)

a. Adagio non troppo

Execution

(Kreutzer: Concerto in A)

b. Allegro moderato

Execution

Melodic final notes

At the conclusion of a melody, the final note is nearly always preceded by an *appoggiatura* or *note that one must lean on*; consequently, this final note should be no more
audible than the mute *e* is at the end of words.

5. Schulz, in *Allgemeine Theorie* . . . ed. Sulzer, s.v. 'Performance'; Türk, *Klavierschule* . . . .

Ex. 317

(Baillot: Air varié, Op. 5)

Harmonic final notes

When the conclusion is a harmonic one, that is to say, is made on one of the notes of the chord, without an *appoggiatura*, the note should be played neither harshly nor too softly, except at the end of its value, where one must let the sound fade away in order to announce the conclusion of the phrase or piece.

Ex. 318

(Baillot: Air varié, Op. 15)

Rests or full stops

The *full closes* or terminations which are indicated by a *full stop* in speech are best announced in a melody by slowing down and at the same time softening the last notes which end the phrase or the piece.

Ex. 319

(Baillot: Concerto no. 5)

But *full closes* made with the notes of a chord or harmonic final notes must be accented firmly so as to give the feeling that the sense of the phrase or piece ends on these notes as if there were a *full stop*.

In the following examples the last notes should be articulated freely and decisively, cut short and not dragged out as is often done; flabbiness should be avoided in concluding phrases of this nature, both in the principal part and in the bass, and the notes should be separated cleanly but without affectation.

Ex. 320

(Viotti: Sonata no. 1)

(Viotti: Sonata no. 5)

There are some cases where it is necessary to sustain the upper note when striking all the final notes of a chord firmly, as in the following examples where this effect is written in.

Ex. 321

(Mozart: Piano Quartet in G minor)

(Beethoven: Quartet no. 4)

In order better to indicate the end of a piece, the chords are often written with sustained notes, even in a presto; here is an example:

Ex. 322

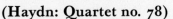

(Baillot, *L'art* . . . (1834), pp. 163–4)

In addition to the performer's artistic feeling and general musicianship, effective and meaningful phrasing thus requires first and foremost considerable artistry in bow management. This might involve the adoption of bowing appropriate to the character of the phrase, the application of nuances, accentuation, the use of the optimum part of the bow for the attack and effect desired, or bow apportionment, although the left hand naturally contributes much to the art in the form of rational fingering, *vibrato* colouring and rhythmic control.

During the first half of the eighteenth century, dynamics invariably served as a framework for the structural design of a piece or movement, with either dynamic unity or dynamic contrast between sections (although not necessarily in the extreme 'terraced' manner so often adopted in performances nowadays) as a prevailing feature. Such baroque works as Piani's sonatas (1712), Geminiani's Op. 1 (revised in 1739) and Veracini's Op. 2, which incorporate all kinds of signs for dynamic gradation, excepted, the classical style in general witnessed a more graduated and expansive approach to dynamics, prompted no doubt by the numerous suggestions regarding their application by such writers as Leopold Mozart, Tartini and Quantz. The notation of *crescendos* and *diminuendos* as well as other effects (*fz*, *m.v.*, *fp* etc.) became increasingly more prevalent with most composers around the turn of the nineteenth century, even though much was still left to the performer's discretion. Haydn's six quartets of 1793, which appeared in two sets, Opp. 71 and 74, arguably the first works of their genre to have been composed expressly for the public concert hall, are prime cases in point.

Parallels between music and speech were commonly cited by theorists in their instructions regarding the shaping and colouring of phrases by the addition of nuances. Cartier, for example, comments:

As all good music should be composed in imitation of speech, these two ornaments [the *piano* and *forte*] are intended to give the same effects as an orator produces by making his voice louder and softer.   (Cartier, *L'art* . . . (1798), pt. 1, p. 5)

Nuances were thus generally applied (whether notated or not) in order to establish the 'peaks' and general contours of phrases as well as their expressive content and were also freely employed to highlight certain dissonances, ornaments, chromatic notes, cadences (especially interrupted cadences), *roulades* and suchlike; for example, the relevant dissonance might be stressed or even swelled and the resolution relaxed by means of a *decrescendo.* C. P. E. Bach confirms:

But in general it can be said that dissonances are played loudly and consonances softly, since the former rouse our emotions and the latter quiet them.

(Bach, *Versuch . . .*, tr. and ed. Mitchell, pt. 1, ch. 3, §29, p. 163)

Habeneck considers nuance as the basic element of musical expression, providing phrases with colour and character, and he gives some general advice, with appropriate examples, on the application of nuances:

I. Every note of any duration must be 'spun out'.

Ex. 323

II. Every ascending phrase must increase in volume.[6]

Ex. 324

III. Every descending phrase must decrease in volume.

Ex. 325

IV. Any note foreign to the harmony, placed on the strong beat[7] of the bar or on the strong part of the beat, must be emphasised more strongly if it is of any length.

Ex. 326

6. Baillot adds an exception to this rule for very high notes, which must, on the contrary, be played softly to prevent them sounding harsh.
7. In a bar with 2 beats, the 1st is strong, the 2nd weak. In a bar with 3 beats, the 1st beat is always strong, the 2nd is sometimes strong and sometimes weak. The 3rd beat is always weak. In a bar with 4 beats, the 1st beat is strong, the 2nd weak, the 3rd strong and the 4th weak. In general the 1st half of the beat is always strong and the 2nd half always weak, and in a succession of equal notes arranged in twos or fours there is always an alternation of strong and weak. (Habeneck's footnote)

V. Any modified note foreign to the scale of the key one happens to be in must be emphasised more strongly than the surrounding notes.

Ex. 327

(Habeneck, *Méthode* . . . (c. 1840), p. 109)

Baillot claims that nuances are for music what *chiaroscuro* and the play of light are for painting[8] and endorses Habeneck's general rules for their introduction. He stresses particularly the performer's role of introducing appropriate and carefully graduated expression in suitable proportions (when none is indicated), according to the character of the music.

Nuances must be observed with the greatest care and, when they are not indicated at all, the artist must use his talents to make good the omission; this is quite clear, but the main object of one's attention must be *a proper sense of proportion in the use of nuances*; it is essential to observe not so much the letter as the spirit, and in particular the spirit of the piece being performed. How many steps there are indeed between the *forte* which has to sustain the voice or the principal part without ever hiding it, and the *forte* of an oratorio where the choruses are combined with the orchestra or between the strength of sound in a small space where the intensity needs to be moderated, and the strength of playing required in a vast theatre!

Each kind of music, each place where music is played requires a particular proportion in the *nuances*; one should not lose sight of this rule, since music is at an end once noise and confusion set in, and on the other hand there can be no effect if the cause has no power to make itself felt.

There is in addition an extremely simple way of increasing the effect of nuances and contrasts, that is by accustoming the ear to soft sounds by taking softness and lightness as the basis of one's playing, as the overriding principle of one's performance;[9] when the listener's senses are trained in this way, every nuance has far more hold over his soul, and the performer's power is increased for he has used only limited means to move his audience.   (Baillot, *L'art* . . . (1834), p. 145)

The theories behind the application of nuances were put into practice in the eighteenth century through the cultivation of the so-called divisions of the bow, four types of bowings categorised by Leopold Mozart (Division 1 = ⊏◁▷⊐ ; Division 2 = ▷⊐ ; Division 3 = ⊏◁ ; Division 4 = ⊏◁▷⊏◁▷⊐), which helped the player 'to apply strength and weakness in all parts of the bow'.[10] Many of Leopold Mozart's successors closely imitated his bow divisions,[11] most notably Campagnoli, who, following Mozart's text and presentation closely, includes one notable amendment: he omits reference to the 'small softness'[12] at the beginning or end of the bow

8. See also Campagnoli, *Metodo* . . . , (1797?), tr. Bishop, pt. 1, no. 41.
9. One may easily understand, however, that in fact one should take an intermediate stage and give the nuances a means of coming through at a lower and a higher level, below the intensity being used as well as above it, in a word one should take a middle course. (Baillot's footnote)
10. L. Mozart, *Versuch* . . ., ch. 5, §4–8, pp. 102–4.
11. For example, L'Abbé le fils, *Principes* . . . (1761), p. 1; Cartier, *L'art* . . . (1798), pp. 2–3; Campagnoli, *Metodo* . . . (1797?), tr. Bishop, pt. 1, no. 41.
12. L. Mozart, *Versuch* . . ., ch. 5, §3, p. 102. See Campagnoli, *Metodo* . . . (1797?), tr. Bishop. pt. 1, no. 41.

stroke, which suggests that he employed a bow similar to Tourte's model in design and musical effect (with its immediate attack):

First division – Notes gradually swelled and then diminished in tone. The stroke of the bow, whether upwards or downwards, is commenced softly; then the sound is insensibly swelled to the middle of the bow, where the greatest power is employed; and afterwards it is gradually diminished, until, at the end of the bow, it dies away entirely.

This must be practised very slow[ly], keeping back the bow as much as possible, to acquire the ability to sustain a long note, in an *Adagio* movement, in a clear and agreeable manner.

In playing soft, the bow should be removed a little farther from the bridge than usual, and the fingers be slightly pressed on the strings. In playing loud, on the contrary, the bow must approach the bridge, and the fingers be firmly pressed down.

In each division of the bow, and particularly in the first, the finger should make certain little movements alternately towards the bridge and the nut. These movements must be very slow in the *piano*, and somewhat quicker in the *forte*; this manner of sustaining a note should, however, be seldom employed.

Second division – Notes gradually diminished. This bowing is commenced loud, then insensibly diminished, and finished very soft.

The preceding divisions must be practised both with the up and with the down bow. This mode of sustaining notes is used more frequently in quick than in slow movements.

Third division – Notes gradually swelled. Here the bowing is commenced soft, then insensibly augmented, and concluded loud. This also must be practised with the up and with the down bow. It is also necessary to observe, that the bow should be drawn very slowly in the *piano*, a little quicker when the power is augmented, and very quick in the *forte*, with which the bowing terminates.

Fourth division – Notes performed with different shades or gradations of tone: This bowing is divided into five parts, that is into three weak and two strong accents. No. 1 indicates the weak, and No. 2 the strong accent. This latter has always a delicate *piano* before and after it, both in the up and in the down bow. By the constant practice of these four divisions of the bow, the pupil will acquire a facility in managing it, and by this management obtain a pure quality of tone [Ex. 328, p. 294].

(Campagnoli, *Metodo* . . . (1797?), tr. Bishop, pt. 1, no. 41)

Thus the divisions of the bow were probably not exclusive to the pre-Tourte bow but provided excellent scope for the cultivation of tonal purity and complete mastery of the bow, as well as variety of nuance and expression.

Nevertheless, the term 'bow division' in the nineteenth century was generally applied more to the actual division of the bow into parts (middle, upper third, lower half etc.) for the classification and technical description of bow strokes than to the execution of nuances; on the other hand its mastery was still of vital importance in the art of phrasing. Baillot incorporates copious examples in his detailed survey of bow division, included below.

Dividing the bow is determining which part of the bow should be used to express specifically and in the best possible way a certain effect or accent.

Too many kinds of divisions imposed as absolute rules would simply overwhelm and paralyse the performer and give the study of the instrument a tendency to over-

Ex. 328

The 4 divisions of the bow

subtlety which is to be avoided in matters of sentiment. Too much finesse diminishes the stature of objects; one should strive to treat them on a large scale in order to give a bold outline to their nature and their characteristics, which in no way rules out the delicacy and finesse that can be put into the details later when the appropriateness of the expression requires it.

Taking account of the size of the bow, its shape and the manner of holding it, here is the *division* which we think we have arrived at successfully.

Three equal parts

Point	Middle	Heel
Weakness	Balance	Strength

The *heel* has strength as its portion; it marks the beats, strikes the chords and gives an energetic indication of the accents which demand a certain strength of tone. It is also capable of exercising strength for control (see slow bow stroke),[13] and in singing, the nearest equivalent is breathing in.

The *middle* holds the balance where strength is tempered by sweetness; it is mellow when heavy, resilient when light; it is, as it were, the expressive centre where the bow can *breathe* steadily.

The *point*, furthest from the source of movement, is nevertheless not beyond its influence. Its lack of elasticity makes it suitable for muffled sounds, the 'dead' accents of the *martelé* stroke and, through the natural weakness of its tip, it is here that an expressive melody can *breathe* its last.

To find these three divisions, or if preferred, each of these parts of the division of the bow, no measuring instruments are needed, and one could tell with one's eyes shut the point where each division is most effective for what one is trying to achieve; in any case, a given passage may need to be played with the part of the *heel* that is nearest the nut, while another needs the part where the middle begins, and so on; since these divisions come one after another, it is clear that the end of one becomes the beginning of the next.

But where one finds the simple indication: *at the heel, with the middle, at the point* of the bow, then one should generally use the middle of each of these divisions.

The two extremities of each division will be more suitable where more strength or more weakness is needed in the tone.

Once the three divisions or the three parts which constitute the *general division* of the bow have been properly determined and practised in their full range, the intelligent pupil will have no difficulty in finding the *exact point* he needs to characterise passages or figures in accordance with their speed.

Division of the bow applied to the following examples.

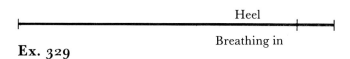

Heel

Breathing in

Ex. 329

**Strength for control
(Viotti: Concerto no. 22)**

13. See ch. 8, p. 178.

Ex. 330

Strength for emphasis
(Haydn: Quartet no. 56)

a.

(Viotti: Concerto no. 17)

b.

(Baillot: Concerto no. 2)

c.

Ex. 331

(Beethoven: Symphony no. 5)
All the chords in a down bow at the heel

Middle

Steady breathing

Ex. 332

Mellow in the melodic line
(Viotti: Concerto no. 22)

(Haydn: Quartet no. 71)

Elasticity in a running passage: slightly lengthened (détaché un peu allongé)

The notes must be separated by the elastic movement of the stick, by a slightly lengthened but imperceptible bouncing of the bow.

Ex. 333

(Viotti: Concerto no. 24)

Execution

Extremely curtailed détaché (détaché de très peu d'étendue)

The same separation produced by the elasticity of the bow. The bow stroke here should be *extremely* curtailed, by reason of the speed of this finale, and all the notes must be even, separate, rounded like pearls, which is why this bow stroke is called *perlé*.

Ex. 334

(Haydn: Quartet no. 63)

Point

Breathing out

The tone at its weakest and most remote

In these two examples one must begin at the heel of the bow and finish at the very tip of the point, allowing the bow gradually to take its own weight and letting the tone die away little by little. The second example demands the greatest control since the four bars must all be played in a single down bow.

Ex. 335

1st example

2nd example

'*Muted' accents in passage-work*: martelé

Ex. 336

(Viotti: Concerto no. 17)

f slightly lengthened *martelé*, away from the bridge

(Viotti: Trio no. 3)

Longer *martelé* than the 1st, always with mellow tone

(Rode: Caprice no. 1)

very short and briskly articulated *martelé*

remain in position

Ex. 336 (cont.)

(Baillot: Concerto no. 3, Op. 7)

d. slightly lengthened *martelé* interspersed with melodic notes

Allegro ♩ = 124

Observation regarding the division of the bow

When speaking of the *division of the bow*, we suggested that it resulted from the size of the bow, from its shape, and from the manner of holding it, and that it was allocated as follows: at the *heel*, strength for emphasis and likewise for control; at the *middle*, balance, and at the *point*, weakness.

According to these properties, a note which has to begin loud and then gradually *diminuendo* is naturally played from the heel to the point of the bow.

Nevertheless, singing often requires extreme control in the gradation of the sound as it leaves the lungs where it is held back when breathing in; in imitation of the voice, the bow, too, must exercise this breathing in and this control that it has, and must like the singer give only a weak sound at first *which will gradually increase in strength*, from which it would seem that the principle regarding the division of the bow is illusory.

But far from destroying this principle, the exceptions serve, on the contrary, simply to confirm it, by reason of the trouble one has in bringing about this reversal of strength; these exceptions prove also that there must exist in the hand of a skilful artist a power capable of drawing on strength for emphasis or for control where appropriate, and even where necessary of giving the point of the bow a strength which is not in its nature.

To obtain this power, one must devote oneself to the study of *sustained notes, swelling* and *decreasing sounds* and notes that are spun out or syncopated; and to the study of *contrary* bow strokes, *with nuances in the opposite direction*, if one wishes one's bow to obey all these varieties of expression which produce such fine effects.

Furthermore, there can be few phrases in music which do not provide evidence for the principle of the division of the bow such as we have described, since the laws of physics require it to be thus as a first resource; as for the artificial resources involved, they must be considered as inversions or reversals of the bow with which it is imperative to familiarise oneself.   (Baillot, *L'art* . . . (1834), pp. 92–7)

The earlier method by Rode *et al.* tackles bow division rather differently, concentrating on the modification of lengths of bow strokes according to the tempo indications and the character of the music.

Neatness of execution, fullness of tone and the characteristic accent given to passages, more particularly to detached notes, depend upon the manner in which the bow is divided, that is to say on that part of it which is applied to the strings and on the different length given to each stroke. As it is absolutely necessary to lengthen the stroke when one requires to infuse energy and breadth into a passage, to decrease its length when the pace and character of the piece require it, to make it even shorter and

more incisive in those cases where variety of expression demands it, the following
examples are given as general principles, whose application must be left to the
judgement of the student, otherwise he will never succeed in applying the appropriate
accent in an infinite number of modern compositions.

In the *Adagio*, where all the sounds must be sustained slowly, the bow will be used
from one end to the other and all the notes will be slurred as much as possible.

Ex. 337

If they must necessarily be detached, they should be sustained for their full value,
with the same length of bow.

Ex. 338

In the *Allegro maestoso* or *Moderato assai*, where the bow stroke must be more rapid
and decisive, the *détaché* must be given as much length as possible, from about the
middle of the stick, so that the sound is full and the string is made to vibrate fully. The
up and down bows should also be played briskly and a kind of short rest inserted
between each note. For example . . .

Ex. 339

In the *Allegro*, the bow stroke will be shorter; the note should be begun about three
quarters of the way up the stick, and the notes played without separating them with
rests.

Ex. 340

In the *Presto*, where the bow stroke has to be still more rapid and lively, less length will be given to the *détaché*, which is likewise played at the three-quarter point of the bow; but one must be careful to use enough bow for the string to vibrate equally well, so that the sound may carry as far as possible and each note may stand out and strength and warmth may be given to one's playing.

Ex. 341

The more these bow strokes are lengthened, the more effective they will be if they are placed correctly; but nothing must be exaggerated and one must strive to govern one's bow in accordance with one's talents.

One may observe, furthermore, that this division of the bow is concerned only with passage-work, and that in melodic passages the bow must be lengthened or held back in accordance with the pace and character of the piece in question.

(Rode *et al.*, *Méthode* . . . (1803), pp. 129–30)

Closely interrelated with bow division in the interests of meaningful phrasing is the problem of bow apportionment, for which Galeazzi in particular provides two significant rules especially relevant to pre-Tourte bows. However, violinists nowadays using Tourte-model bows may consider Galeazzi's first rule (Rule V) a pernicious doctrine; they are likely to claim that equal status of all parts of the bow should be encouraged when sustained playing is concerned.

150. There are two rules that we can give regarding the measurement of the bow which merit great attention. They are the following:

Rule V

When playing long notes or slurring several notes smoothly, the bow should be divided unequally according to the number of notes to be played or their length. In a down bow, two-thirds of the note value or of the number of slurred notes must be played before reaching the middle of the bow with the other third bowed in the remaining half. An up bow can be drawn a little faster at first, playing almost one half of the note value of the long note or one half the number of slurred notes in the first half of the bow with the remaining half taken in the other half of the bow. Remember, however, that it is always better to play many slurred notes with a down bow rather than an up bow.

Illustration and Explanation

The most valuable part of the bow, which it is important to manage well, is the lower third. With the greater weight there, the bow must be pulled very slowly and fully to draw a sound that equals that of the other two parts. With this knowledge and that which we have given previously, it is not difficult to understand that in playing, for example, twelve notes in a bow, the first six would be too loud and the others too weak if we were to play the first six in the first half of the bow and the last six in the last half. Therefore, having to moderate the strength of the lower third of the bow and to increase the strength of the upper third with greater speed, we must distribute the bow unequally in respect of the number of notes that we must play by bowing, for example, eight notes in the lower half of the bow and four in the upper half. Again we say that the bow must be greatly held back in the lower half until the middle and thereafter pulled faster towards the tip, thus compensating more or less weight with less or more speed. The same is true in long notes. The greatest study and attention is to be given to this golden rule, for be assured that he who knows how to control the bow will be an excellent performer. On that account, I am always anxious to reiterate to my students that *waste the first third of the bow and all is wasted*. Therefore, the most scrupulous economy must be practised.

Rule VI

151. Since the division of the bow is one of the most essential factors, especially in playing slowly and lyrically, it must be observed that, except in the cases identified and included in the preceding rule, the bow must be well apportioned to the length of the notes. Thus, if one has to play a crotchet and a minim, it would be wrong to give more bow to the first than to the second, since the latter is the longer value. If one has to bow a single note and four slurred notes all of equal value, it would be wrong to give more bow to the first single note than to the four others. If one has to play an *appoggiatura*, it would be wrong to give more bow to it than to the note to which it belongs etc.   (Galeazzi, *Elementi* . . . (1791), vol. 1, pt. 2, art. 9, pp. 152–4)

Accentuation and, in some cases, prolongation (i.e. the so-called agogic accent) of important notes within the phrase are vital for the listener's comprehension of the performer's, and hence the composer's, intentions. The first note of a phrase, a note that is longer or markedly higher or lower than its predecessors, and dissonant notes within the phrase are common instances when prolongation of the note in question invariably provides a flexible musicianly solution,[14] while the *note buone*, notes of rhythmic stress (for example, the first note of each bar or various accented beats of the bar) were accommo-

14. See also ch. 11, pp. 272–4.

dated, especially in France and Germany, by the traditional rule of down bow; this long-standing principle, formulated by the Italians early in the 17th century or even before, required such notes to be played with the stronger down bow and the unaccented beats with the weaker up stroke. Strongly influenced by Leopold Mozart's detailed survey of the down-bow rule,[15] Petri writes:

As the down stroke has more strength and emphasis than the up stroke, this is, of course, the reason why the down bow is required for the good notes and good parts of the bar, and the up stroke for the bad.   (*Petri*, Anleitung . . . (1767), pt. 3, p. 393)

The greater strength of the down bow was due to a combination of factors, notably the downward force of gravity, the weight exerted on the bow stick by holding it from above with the hand in a palm-down position and the natural weight of the arm.[16] Curiously enough, Galeazzi excepted, few Italian violinists adhered rigidly to the down bow rule, attitudes ranging from Geminiani's outright rejection of that 'wretched rule of down bow'[17] to Tartini's more flexible compromise:

As regards bowing, there are no definite rules for determining whether one should begin with a down bow or up bow. On the contrary, all passages should be practised in both ways, in order to gain complete mastery of the bow in both up and down strokes.   (Tartini, *Traité* . . ., ed. Jacobi, p. 56)

Nevertheless, the rule of down bow has remained a guiding force in bowing to this day even though, as the eighteenth century progressed, it was the subject of constant modification notably for purposes of articulation and tone production, by theorists of various nationalities, most of whom aimed 'to give the up and down stroke equal importance'.[18] Quantz, as early as 1752, claims:

The equal strength and dexterity of the up stroke and down stroke . . . is most necessary to the current musical style . . . Although certain notes must necessarily be taken with a down stroke, an experienced violinist with the bow completely under control can also express them well with an up bow.

(Quantz, *Versuch* . . ., tr. and ed. Reilly,
ch. 17, section 10, p. 222 and section 11, p. 223)

Furthermore, the fifteenth edition of Corelli's sonatas, Op. 5, by Cartier includes the following statement:

It is a mistake to believe that one should always use an up bow on the up beat and a down bow on the strong beat of the bar. The school of Corelli does not acknowledge this slavish rule and the Corelli of France, Gavinier [sic], has never prescribed it either. The bow should be free and the beauty of sound depends on the manner in which one is able to employ it.

(Here quoted in translation from Laurencie,
L'École française de violon . . ., vol. 2, p. 314 n. 4)

The Tourte bow's greater strength of attack at the point brought nearer to reality the quest for equality of strength in the up and down bow; even so, a

15. L. Mozart, *Versuch* . . ., ch. 4, pp. 70–100.   17. Geminiani, *The art* . . ., Ex. VIII, p. 4.
16. *The new Grove* . . ., s.v. 'Bowing'.   18. Reichardt, *Ueber die Pflichten* . . . (1776), p. 28.

down bow was still generally employed at the beginning of most phrases, especially those commencing on the strong beats of the bar, as confirmed by Baillot's short summary:

General rules for employing the down or up bow.

It is generally necessary to use a *down bow* when the phrase begins on a strong beat.

Ex. 342

(Viotti: Concerto no. 18)

Use an *up bow* when the phrase begins on an up beat:

Ex. 343

(Viotti: Concerto no. 27)

Exclude from this rule passages composed of several notes and several bow strokes.

Ex. 344

(Viotti: Concerto no. 22)

Use an *up bow* on the final cadence, since its resolution takes place on the strong beat of the following bar.

Ex. 345

(*idem*)

Use a *down bow* on long notes which constitute a pause, above all on final notes, since as the bow falls of its own accord from its strong to its weak part, that is to say from the heel to the point, the sound constantly decreases by the natural movement of the arm, which comes gradually to rest.   (Baillot, *L'art* . . . (1834), p. 16)

13

Specific ornamentation (*agréments du chant*)

Adequate discussion of such a treacherous area as ornamentation is wellnigh impossible in the limited space available, for practically every composer was to some extent a law unto himself. However, the schematic outline of this volume justifies an attempt at a broad survey of the art if only to present the reader with some of the plain facts, provide the performer with some general interpretative guidelines and set into a historical context the various treatise extracts quoted. It is hoped also that the glossary of specific ornaments, collated from the treatises which have contributed most significantly to this volume, will highlight the range of ornaments generally documented in contemporary instruction books and further confirm the impossibility of presenting a definitive interpretation of most ornament signs. Performers should be warned of the danger of applying rigidly theoretical instructions on ornamentation, as musical contexts invariably require such principles to be modified.

Of the three different approaches to ornamentation distinguishable during the period, that involving the use of free improvisation by the performer, practised for the most part by the Italian school, is discussed separately in chapter 14. For the moment, it is symbolic notation that concerns us, either specific stereotyped figures indicated by some sort of written sign (Quantz's *wesentliche Manieren*, essential graces or *agréments*) or ornaments written out in some sort of approximate notation. The essential ornaments or *agréments* comprised primarily the *appoggiatura*, mordent, trill and turn, and were of more or less fixed form and small melodic range, serving not merely as additional embellishment to a preconceived melody but essentially forming an organic part of the melody. C. P. E. Bach holds no doubts as to their value or function:

No one disputes the need for embellishments. This is evident from the great numbers of them everywhere to be found. They are, in fact, indispensable. Consider their many uses: they connect and enliven tones and impart stress and accent; they make music pleasing and awaken our close attention. Expression is heightened by them; let a piece be sad, joyful, or otherwise, and they will lend a fitting assistance. Embellishments provide opportunities for fine performance as well as much of its subject matter. They improve mediocre compositions. Without them the best melody is empty and ineffective, the clearest content clouded.

305

2. In view of their many commendable services, it is unfortunate that there are also poor embellishments and that good ones are sometimes used too frequently and ineptly.

3. Because of this, it has always been better for composers to specify the proper embellishments unmistakably, instead of leaving their selection to the whims of tasteless performers.

4. In justice to the French it must be said that they notate their ornaments with painstaking accuracy. And so do the masters of the keyboard in Germany, but without embellishing to excess. Who knows but that our moderation with respect to both the number and kinds of ornaments is the influence which has led the French to abandon their earlier practice of decorating almost every note, to the detriment of clarity and noble simplicity?

(Bach, *Versuch . . .*, tr. Mitchell, pt. 1, ch. 2, sections 1–4, p. 79)

During the eighteenth century the use of symbols to indicate conventional ornaments therefore increased, especially in France and North Germany, largely for reasons of convenience in writing in such a shorthand. However, signs for ornamentation were never mandatory and it was not customary to indicate every ornament required; obligatory ornaments such as the cadential trill, demanded by convention and context, were not always notated, especially in most non-keyboard music,[1] and in many cases a general sign was employed (for example, + or ×), even in the more exacting French school, to indicate the possible incidence of some embellishment, the exact detail of which was undefined and left to the performer, according to mood, tempo and genre. Although this practice undoubtedly resulted in less precision in performance, it also offered numerous advantages, notably in the flexibility of interpretation and nuance according to the character of the music and the taste of the performer, the prevention of further ornamentation and the clarification of the overall musical structure. Signs with more specific intentions were also employed (for example, J. S. Bach's list of thirteen ornament signs in his 'Explicatio' in the *Klavierbüchlein vor Wilhelm Friedemann Bach*, 1720), many with certain implied interpretative formulae relating to such matters as expression, nuance, emphasis, and rhythmic subtleties. Unreliable calligraphy, ambiguous indications, casual performance,[2] inconsistent terminology employed by theorists and a variety of different regional and personal styles combine to make up a very confusing picture from which a definitive interpretation of the countless small details of ornaments, often so subtle and flexible in rhythm and pitch that they defy expression in ordinary musical notation, is in most cases impracticable.

During the second half of the eighteenth century the three main channels of ornamental theory and practice[3] – the French, German and Italian (English

1. C. P. E. Bach, *Versuch . . .*, tr. Mitchell, pt. 1, ch. 2, §14, p. 82.

2. Mondonville, for example, in his *Pièces de clavecin en sonates avec accompagnement de violon* Op. 3 (1734), employs different signs for similar ornaments in the harpsichord and violin parts. But his Op. 5 shows a different, more uniform approach, the ornaments in the violin and harpsichord parts being notated identically.

3. Naturally such divisions were not as rigid as this implies. For example, German ornamental practice

and other national practices largely comprised a hybrid mixture of Italian, German and French customs) – gradually merged into some measure of general agreement. The French school's complicated system of symbols was adopted with increasing thoroughness and consistency in some German schools. This was mainly the work of Quantz, Marpurg, Agricola and especially C. P. E. Bach, who, amidst the emerging homophonic *style galant*, modified and extended French practices into a more international language of ornaments governed by the *Affektenlehre*, a language that was more harmonic than melodic (hence the quest for *das vermischte Geschmack*, a combination of the best qualities of Italian, French and German types of ornamentation).[4] Without cataloguing signs and contexts for every ornamental figure available to the performer – in some circumstances, such as the cadential trill, ornamentation was an accepted, unmarked convention – C. P. E. Bach's *Versuch* . . . became a model for numerous subsequent treatises on the subject, even though his *theoretical* inflexibility of ornamentation practice contradicts the nature and function of ornament itself. Most of his contemporary compatriots were a little more flexible in approach and some national schools, particularly the Italian, still left ornamentation largely to the spontaneous invention of the performer.

Many French writers began to rebel against the practice of various excesses in ornamentation for brilliant effect[5] and advocated the incorporation of *agréments* into ordinary musical notation. Furthermore, prompted by the influence in France of Italian violinists such as Viotti and the first publication entirely devoted to ornamentation to appear in France, Tartini's *Traité des agrémens*, translated by P. Denis (1771), a more international language began to emerge. This was confirmed in Cartier's compromise of international styles and technique in *L'art* . . . . Italian practices also yielded to international influence, as illustrated in the first section of Tartini's *Traité*. . ., devoted to essential ornaments, and in Galeazzi's survey of ornaments,[6] in which, even though the *agréments* are regarded as fundamentally improvisatory, internationally used signs are employed for their indication.

Moreover, by the end of the eighteenth century many theorists were coming out in favour of indicating their ornamental intentions as precisely as possible, using a minimum of signs and writing out all complex ornaments in such a way that their interpretation, apart from a certain rhythmic freedom in some instances, could not be doubted.[7] Some fifty years earlier, J. S. Bach had been scathingly criticised for this practice by Scheibe.[8] Apart from trills, mor-

itself comprised a hybrid mixture of national customs, parts of the country (for example, Celle) being primarily French-influenced, parts (for example, Salzburg) Italian-influenced and so on.

4. C. P. E. Bach, *Versuch* . . ., tr. Mitchell, pt. 1, ch. 2. §25, p. 85; Quantz, *Versuch* . . ., tr. and ed. Reilly, ch. 18, §87–9, pp. 341–2.

5. For example, Bollioud de Mermet, *De la corruption du goût* . . ., p. 28; Le Pileur d'Apligny, *Traité sur la musique* . . ., p. 160.

6. Galeazzi, *Elementi* . . . (1791), vol. 1, pt. 2, art. 15, pp. 190–7.

7. For example, Milchmeyer, *Die wahre Art das Pianoforte zu spielen*, ch. 3, p. 37.

8. See Scheibe, *Der critische Musicus*, vol. 1, p. 6.

dents and turns, it gradually became more customary to write out ornaments in full, either in normal-sized notes as an integral part of the rhythmic scheme, in small notes extra-rhythmically or in a compromise between the two.

Since the French school was foremost in the representation of essential ornaments, Baillot's survey, an expanded account of the study by Rode *et al.*, is presented sectionally below. In order to avoid a one-sided view of contemporary ornamentation practice,[9] additional comments that bear upon national and individual variations of approach have been drawn from several other sources and are included where appropriate between the main divisions of Baillot's survey.

Agrémens du chant

Agrémens du chant are named as follows;
1. *Petites notes* or *appoggiaturas*.
2. *Ports de voix.*
3. *Trills, brisés* and *double trills.*
4. *Petits groupes.*
5. *Mordants.*

Petite note or appoggiatura

That is, a note that one must lean on. When the *petite note* is written above, it can be a tone or a semitone:

Melodic *appoggiatura*

Ex. 346

a.

Written below, it must always form an interval of a semitone:

b.

Nevertheless, it can also be a whole tone when this is a repeated note:

c.

The *petite note* is normally half the value of the note that follows it, and this value is subtracted from that of this same following note.

It is called a *prepared appoggiatura* when it is preceded by a main note at the same pitch; it is always given half the value of this main note:

9. For comprehensive surveys of eighteenth-century *agréments* the reader is referred to Neumann, *Ornamentation in baroque and post-baroque music* . . . and Aldrich, 'The principal agréments of the seventeenth and eighteenth centuries . . .' (unpublished Ph. D. degree thesis, Harvard University, 1942).

Ex. 347

Although the *appoggiatura* must be leaned on, as its name implies, one must not lean too much or too little, for fear of exaggerating or weakening its gentle and tender character.

As a consequence of the accent given to the *appoggiatura*, one should sound the following note only lightly.

Thus when two notes are slurred at the end of a phrase, the first must be leaned on and the second allowed to die away like a mute *e*:

Ex. 348

(Beethoven: Quartet no. 9)

(Viotti: Concerto no. 14)

One can play a double *appoggiatura*:

Ex. 349

One can also play the *appoggiatura* a third lower; it is then quick and light and the note that follows is leaned on like a *principal appoggiatura*.

Ex. 350

Wherever there are two *appoggiaturas* in succession, the longer one should stand out.

Finally one can play the *appoggiatura* a semitone below the main *appoggiatura*; if the same finger is used to play it, it gains in grace and expression.

Ex. 351

Appoggiatura played with the same finger as the previous note.

Ex. 352

These last ornaments are rarely marked. Another way of playing the *appoggiatura* a semitone below.

Ex. 353

(Viotti: Concerto no. 22)

Here is a double *appoggiatura* which is played by articulating the two grace notes evenly and lightly and leaning on the main note.

Ex. 354

All the *appoggiaturas* we have just spoken of can be called *melodic* because their purpose is to give grace and shape to the melodic line.

There is another kind of *appoggiatura* that must be called *rhythmic* because its aim is to mark, emphasise and bring out the rhythm, that is the beat, the measure of a piece. There are numerous examples to be found among the better composers.

It must be played quickly and almost on the main note. In lively movements it will naturally be played more quickly than in slow movements; nevertheless in the latter it will still retain a certain quickness which will distinguish it from the *melodic* grace note.

Rhythmic *appoggiatura*

(Baillot, *L'art* . . . (1834), pp. 74-5)

Before c. 1750, the *appoggiatura*, sometimes written out in full but otherwise
variously indicated and flexibly interpreted, although in accordance with certain contextual standards (for example, conduct of melody, tempo, phrasing
etc.), fulfilled primarily a melodic function with little, if any, harmonic or
rhythmic implication. But increased exploitation of its essentially dissonant
nature led to the establishment for it of interpretative criteria, systematised
largely by C. P. E. Bach and his German contemporaries and based upon a
more 'vertical' appreciation of the music. The ornament was then divided into
two main types: the long, or variable, *appoggiatura* (*veränchlicher Vorschlag*) and
the short *appoggiatura* (*kurzer Vorschlag*). Despite isolated attempts to distinguish graphically between these two types for correctness of interpretation
(for example, indicating *appoggiaturas* in values as close as possible to their
intended durations, or pointing the hooks of the cue-sized *appoggiatura* note in
the direction of the note from which the time is to be taken, as in Ex. 356),[10] no
consistent notational distinction was employed. A cue-sized note of varying,
usually meaningless, value was the norm and, although indeterminate as
regards *appoggiatura* lengths, it served the necessary functions of defining the
ornament type and preventing the addition of further ornamentation which
might spoil the harmony.[11] Such ambiguity of notation gave the performer
some latitude in interpretation for his own taste and musicianship to manifest
itself, except in the cases when rigid rules of some theorists, among them
C. P. E. Bach, dictated a more definitive manner of performance or, as in the
case of Tartini, some expressive variation (Ex. 357).

10. See, for example, Marpurg, *Die Kunst das Klavier zu spielen* (Berlin, 1751–61); C. P. E. Bach, *Versuch* . . .,
    tr. Mitchell, §5 and Fig. 69, pp. 87–8. N.B: Geminiani gives ♪ as the symbol for the long *appoggiatura*
    but appears to use ♪ or ♪ for the short variety.
11. L. Mozart, *Versuch* . . ., ch. 9, §21, p. 210.

Ex. 356

Execution

Ex. 357

The difference of expression in the second example is not in the value of the grace note, which is the same as that of the main one, but in the kind of bowing stroke or vocal attack. If this grace note were a main note, as it seems to be in this example, it should have been rendered with more force than the second, and would need a short trill. But as it is only a grace note, the bow or voice must begin it softly, increase it gradually until halfway through its length, and decrease it again till it falls on to the main note to which it is joined. This latter needs a short trill to give it more force.

(Tartini, *Traité* . . ., ed. Jacobi, pt. 1, section 1, p. 66)

Baillot summarises most varieties of *appoggiatura* employed during the period, although not in the systematic detail of C. P. E. Bach, Quantz, Leopold Mozart and some other mid-eighteenth-century writers. He stresses the additional harmonic function of his *appoggiature mélodique*,[12] the long, colouristic, descending (or superior) *appoggiatura* (variously called backfall, *appoggiatura di sopra*, *Accent fallend*, *coulé*, *chute*, *port de voix*[13] etc. *en descendant*) characteristic of the rococo 'sigh', and the ascending (or inferior) *appoggiatura* (variously called forefall, *appoggiatura di sotto*, *Accent steigend*, *coulé*, *chute* etc. *en ascendant*), both types generally being played on the beat (hence Quantz's term *anschlagende*)[14] and given more stress and volume (although Quantz advocates, like Tartini, a soft start, swelling if time permits into the main note, which is to be played more softly),[15] due to their discordant 'leaning' function, than the

12. See C. P. E. Bach, *Versuch* . . ., tr. Mitchell, pt. 1, ch. 2, section 2, §1, p. 87; Quantz, *Versuch* . . ., tr. and ed. Reilly, ch. 8, §1, p. 91.
13. Not to be confused with its modern meaning of *portamento*.
14. Quantz, *Versuch* . . ., tr. and ed. Reilly, ch. 8, §5, p. 93; but see, for example, Rousseau's pre-beat *coulé*, *Dictionnaire de musique*, s.v. 'Coulé',
15. See also Geminiani, *The art* . . ., p. 7 and Cartier, *L'art* . . . (1798), art. 19, p. 4.

ensuing main note to which they are slurred (termed *Abzug*, literally 'dying off', or *Accent*).[16] He fails to comment on those considerations of timbre which demand abstinence from open strings in the execution of *appoggiaturas*[17] and gives only a very general rule for deciding the lengths of such ornaments. He also omits either to mention necessary variations occasioned by harmony,[18] dotted main-note values (the *appoggiatura* normally took two-thirds the length of a dotted main note), different metres (in $\frac{6}{8}$ or $\frac{6}{4}$ metre, an *appoggiatura* to a dotted note tied to another note normally took the whole value of the dotted note) and the intervention of rests (the *appoggiatura* normally took all of a note before a rest, the main note being played in the time of the rest and the rest ceasing to exist)[19] or to provide illustrative examples. However, his indecisiveness is perhaps excusable on two counts, namely because expression, taste and musicianship were always the overriding deciding factors as to *appoggiatura* length (in many cases, long, expressive *appoggiaturas* took as much as three-quarters of the main note) and, by the nineteenth century, *appoggiaturas* were becoming incorporated increasingly in normal, bold notation into the written melody. Baillot's short *appoggiature rhythmique*, indicated ♪ by many nineteenth-century writers[20] but not distinguishable in notation from the longer variety in most eighteenth-century sources (L'Abbé le fils's pre-beat intentions for his *coulés brefs suivis d'un son soûtenu* provide a notable exception),[21] is essentially an equivalent of C. P. E. Bach's 'invariable' short *appoggiatura*.[22] This is most common before long notes when a note is repeated; in syncopated passages or sometimes when filling in descending thirds; when the main note is itself either an *appoggiatura* or a short note followed by more notes of the same value. It is generally played so fast that the ensuing note loses little of its notated length and stress.[23] However, Baillot finds no equivalent for the descending *appoggiatura* by leap, employed notably by Tartini, C. P. E. Bach and their disciples (Ex. 358), or the so-called 'passing' *appoggiatura* (*coulé, Nachschlag, durchgehender Vorschlag*),[24] graphically indistinguishable from other varieties and inappropriately named because it is not a genuine *appoggiatura*,[25] being taken as an unaccented, normally descending passing note between two main beats a third apart in order to 'sharpen and brighten the expres-

16. C. P. E. Bach, *Versuch* . . ., tr. Mitchell, pt. 1, ch. 2, section 2, §7, p. 88.

17. See, for example, L. Mozart, *Versuch* . . ., ch. 9, §8, p. 199.

18. See Quantz, *Versuch* . . ., tr. and ed. Reilly, ch. 8, §10, p. 96; C. P. E. Bach, *Versuch* . . ., tr. Mitchell, pt. 1, ch. 2, §14, p. 92 & §17, p. 95.

19. See Quantz, *Versuch* . . ., tr. and ed. Reilly, ch. 8, §7–11, pp. 95–6; but see also Dolmetsch, *The interpretation* . . ., pp. 115–16.

20. For example, Spohr, *Violinschule* (1832), p. 171.

21. L'Abbé le fils, *Principes* . . . (1761), p. 16.

22. C. P. E. Bach, *Versuch* . . ., tr. Mitchell, pt. 1, ch. 2, §13 & 14, pp. 91–2. See also Quantz, *Versuch* . . ., tr. and ed. Reilly, ch. 8 and Habeneck's *acciaccatura, Méthode* . . . (c. 1840), p. 110.

23. L. Mozart, *Versuch* . . ., ch. 9, §9, pp. 199–200.

24. Quantz, *Versuch* . . ., tr. and ed. Reilly, ch. 8, §5 & 6, pp. 93–4; L. Mozart, *Versuch* . . ., ch. 9, §17, p. 206; Tartini, *Traité* . . ., ed. Jacobi, p. 69.

25. See Marpurg, *Anleitung* . . ., 2nd edn, pt. 1, art. 9, p. 4; C. P. E. Bach, *Versuch* . . ., tr. Mitchell, pt. 1, ch. 2, §25, p. 98.

Ex. 358

sion'.[26] He also omits mention of the possible desirability of adding *appoggia-*
turas, for particular expressive effect, when not specifically indicated.[27] Baillot
includes some varieties of double *appoggiatura* (*port de voix double, Anschlag,*
Doppelvorschlag), including a remarkable duet of highly expressive species,
incorporating *portamento* effects, but provides little interpretative instruction,
especially with regard to Ex. 354, the so-called slide (*coulé, flatté, Schleifer* etc.),
two conjunct *appoggiaturas*, played on the beat with speed varying according to
context, approaching the main note from a third above or below. Only one of
the basic slide types is illustrated and no mention is made of the numerous
dotted (*punctierte Schleifer*) and other rhythms, although it must be admitted
that these were more common in the keyboard music of the late eighteenth
century.

As Baillot's survey confirms, the *appoggiatura* tradition of the late eighteenth
century persisted virtually unchanged well into the nineteenth century,
although, if anything, the long *appoggiatura* was liable to be extended (see
glossary); in many cases it was written out in normal notation as part of the
rhythmic scheme. However, although there is little supporting verbal evidence, apart from that of the 'passing' *appoggiatura* described by many
eighteenth-century authorities,[28] it appears that the less detailed nineteenth-
century accounts of the ornament and the consequent, arguably more flexible
and confusing interpretations of its symbols led many performers to play
short *appoggiaturas* unaccented and before the beat, taking the time of the
previous instead of the ensuing note. Indeed, some early-nineteenth-century
composers actually indicated these anticipatory *appoggiaturas* by placing them
when convenient before the bar-line (for example, Schumann and Chopin).
Musical evidence suggests that this practice of taking short *appoggiaturas* before
the beat was widely imitated (for example, in Liszt's Ballade no. 1 (1848), bar
115); however, for the purposes of the period under discussion, the rules of the
rococo period, adopted flexibly and, above all, musically, should be our
guiding principles.

Ports de voix

There are two ways of 'carrying on' the line or notes.

26. Tartini, *Traité* . . ., ed. Jacobi, p. 70.
27. C. P. E. Bach, *Versuch* . . . tr. Mitchell, pt. 1, ch. 2, §8 & 9, p. 88; Quantz, *Versuch* . . ., tr. and ed. Reilly,
ch. 8, §12, pp. 96–7.
28. For example, Quantz, *Versuch* . . ., tr. and ed. Reilly, ch. 8, §6, pp. 93–4; L. Mozart, *Versuch* . . ., ch. 9,
§17, p. 206; Tartini, *Regole* . . ., facsimile edn, p. 7.

The first is when several notes of equal value, proceeding by steps or leaps, are slurred, as in this example.

Ex. 359

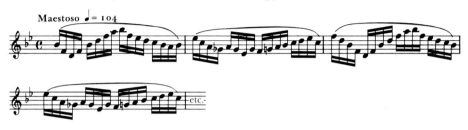

**1st manner of 'carrying on' the sound
(Viotti: Concerto no. 19)**

These notes should be articulated evenly and distinctly, without being separated by any marked movements of the fingers or bow. It is necessary to play them *broadly*, which means not with a large amount of bow but by sustaining each note steadily for its entire length yet without slowing down the beat.

The second way is used between two notes that form an interval of some size and that proceed by disjunct degrees only; it consists of a very light slurring that moves on at the very end of the first note to pass to the next, anticipating it.

Ports de voix

Ex. 360

(Mozart: Quintet in C [K. 515])

The *port de voix* can also be played in this way:

Ex. 361

Included among the *ports de voix* are passages where there is a *slight sliding* from one note to the next, with the same finger:

Ex. 362

(Fiorillo: Étude no. 13)

For this *port de voix*, slide the 1st finger a little, touching the B sharp only very lightly, and carry the sound over directly to the G which must be played with a crescendo.[29]

Ex. 363

(Viotti: Concerto no. 18)

When one passes from a note to a distant interval, it should generally be done freely and without letting anything be heard as one moves the finger directly to the separate note, either up or down, *without port de voix*:

Ex. 364

(Baillot: Concerto no. 1)

(Haydn: Quartet no. 76)

---

29. Baillot's instructions are somewhat ambiguous here but as no B sharp is actually printed in his example he presumably intends the opening bars to be executed as shown in Ex. 363b.

Since the *port de voix* provides an expression of tenderness, it would become insipid if it were used too often.

One must take the greatest pains to avoid draggings or slidings which allow intermediate notes to be heard, as in the following; the effect is particularly unpleasant:

Ex. 365

(Viotti: Concerto no. 18)

The descending *port de voix* is played by sliding the finger a little, not the one on the note that is being played but the one on the note that is about to be played, when the finger will just barely touch the semitone above the last note:

Ex. 366   **(Haydn: Quartet no. 38)**

General rule

From low to high, shade from *soft* to *loud*.

Ex. 367

From high to low, shade from *loud* to *soft*.

There are a few exceptions to this rule for *ports de voix*. These are more for passages where very high notes require to be softened.

Ex. 368

(Baillot, *L'art* . . . (1834), pp. 76–8)

Baillot here gives two more meanings of the term *port de voix*, including the modern *portamento* equivalent, to add to the common seventeenth- and eighteenth-century French *agrément*, an inferior or ascending suspension or on-beat *appoggiatura*, often accompanied by a *pincé* (mordent). (L'Abbé le fils describes two kinds, the *port de voix feint*, emphasising the grace note and tapering into the main note, and the *port de voix suivi d'un son plein et martelé*, a compound ornament adopting the reverse dynamic formula and incorporating a mordent on the principal note.)[30] Baillot's inclusion of these two types of *port de voix*, apparently related only by their slurred execution, as essential ornaments, is somewhat surprising since they are indicated only by fingering implication (if, indeed, fingering is included) and only rarely, if at all, by any specific sign.[31]

Trill

The trill consists of a pulsating oscillation between two notes which must always be a tone or a semitone apart.

The trill on a whole tone is *major*; that on a semitone is *minor*.

It is also known as a *cadence* because it is normally played over a movement in the bass which is introducing a state of harmonic repose into which the melody is about to fall (*cadere*).

There are three things to consider in a trill: 1. the *preparation*. 2. *oscillation*. 3. the *termination*.

Four preparations are normally used.

Ex. 369

Indication

The 1st is formed by the actual note on which the trill is marked.
The 2nd is formed by the note above.

Execution
1st preparation   2nd preparation

---

30. L'Abbé le fils, *Principes* . . . (1761), pp. 15–16.
31. For further discussion of this expressive ornament and its relationship to the mechanics of shifting, see ch. 5, p. 98.

Ex. 369 (cont.)

The 3rd by the note below.
The 4th by the note a third below.

Since the last three examples begin with *appoggiaturas*, one must lean on these first notes, which will then give the finger a certain thrust and more grace and suppleness for making the trill.

Likewise four terminations can be used.

The 1st is played by adding *one* note to the oscillations, before the final note.

The 2nd by adding *two* notes.

Ex. 370

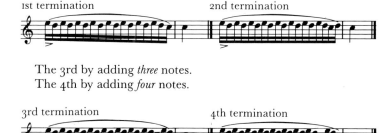

The 3rd by adding *three* notes.
The 4th by adding *four* notes.

Any one of the four *preparations* can be used with each of the *terminations*, according to the characteristics of the phrase in which the trill occurs; the choice is left to taste; taste is exposed in this choice, in particular, which is the touchstone of sentiment, for a bad termination to a cadence is enough to demonstrate that the passage or sometimes the whole piece has not been understood.

The 2nd *preparation* is the one most frequently used.

The 1st *termination* is generally more suitable for simple melodies.

Ex. 371

(Du Caurroy (attrib.): Air, 'Charmante Gabrielle')

As for *ornamented terminations*, numerous examples will be found following the article on *cadenzas*.

See no. 2, letter A, for *cadenzas* or *turns* to introduce a final cadence. And nos. 1 and 2, letter B, for *terminations* to cadences in all keys [pp. 363 & 364].

The *trill* is more easily made, above all in fast passages, by pressing only very lightly with the stopped finger during the oscillations of the other finger; these oscillations are then freer as a result. When making the trill, one must avoid stiffness or any kind of force, which would result in a bleating sound; it must, on the contrary, be given flexibility and be played with a sort of reticence so that it is even and brilliant, that is to say, so that the finger falls at the same speed, with elasticity, and with a slight click on the string in an *Allegro*; for in an *Adagio* the cadence should be gentle and unctuous conforming to the character of the movement.

In a succession of trills it is often better to use two different fingers than to make the cadence with the same one:

Ex. 372

(Viotti: Concerto no. 2)

The cadence should be terminated at the same speed as the trill:

Ex. 373

Exceptions to this rule are found in the final cadences of an *Adagio* or occasionally in cadenzas, for example:

Ex. 374

Sometimes cadences can also be played, in both these cases, beginning slowly, gradually increasing the speed, and then likewise decreasing it to end slowly; for example:

Ex. 375

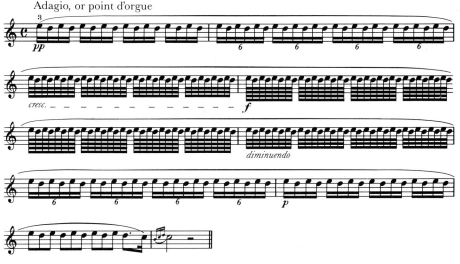

(Baillot, *L'art . . .* (1834), pp. 78–80)

The trill (*cadence, tremblement, trille, pincé renversé, Triller, shake, trillo*), invariably indicated by such signs as *tr, t,* ⌣, ⌣, +, and × and applied particularly at cadences, was modified considerably in individual cases by the addition of preparations or terminations to the fundamental ornament and by varying the number, rhythm, speed and nuances of the notes comprising the ornament. Violin treatises of the period paint only a very narrow and often belated picture of actual performance practice. Apart from a few accepted conventions outlined below, these variations were left entirely to the performer's discretion, according to the tempo and character of the phrase concerned. Tartini, for example, draws an interesting distinction between the trill 'on a full close' and one on imperfect or interrupted cadences:

Trills on imperfect and interrupted cadences should consist of three notes [i.e. trill plus termination] [Ex. 376]. When there is time, to the three notes of this trill is added a passing grace note.   (Tartini, *Traité . . .*, ed. Jacobi, pt. I, pp. 79–80)

Ex. 376

a.

b.

He warns against over-using the ornament, equating its application with the use of salt in cookery – 'Too much or too little salt spoils the result and it should not be put in everything one eats.'[32] – and he provides one of the few known exceptions to Baillot's instruction regarding the normal tone or semi-tone trill, a trill over an augmented second (Ex. 377); this trill type, on his own admission, is better replaced by a natural or artificial ornamental figure on account of its difficulty, lack of taste (Quantz rejects its use for voice and all instruments except bagpipes!) and its consequent ineffectiveness.[33]

Ex. 377

By the addition of one example (iv) to the survey of Rode *et al.* Baillot gives four of the myriad elaborate trill preparations, which were varied according to the tempo and character of the phrase, the length of the trill note and the taste of the performer. His claim that the preparation on the note above is the most commonly employed backs up the theories and practices of most eighteenth-century writers/performers, who tend to emphasise the harmonic as opposed to the melodic function of this ornament, especially at a cadence. Trills were generally well accented and commenced on the beat on the note a semitone or tone above the written note, depending on the position of that written note in the scale, but his survey serves to remind us that other designs coexisted with the upper auxiliary preparation and therefore should not be discounted as valid interpretations.[34] Indeed, Quantz, apart from certain specific instances, is non-committal as to whether his trills should be preceded by a long on-beat (*anschlagende*) or a short pre-beat (*durchgehende*) *Vorschlag*, while Tarade, contrary to Baillot, suggests that the upper auxiliary preparation was losing its popularity by the late eighteenth century and implies by his examples that the main-note 'preparation' (often variously termed *cadence jetée, précipitée* or *coupée* in France, according to author, or *trillo imperfetto* in some Italian sources, for example, Galeazzi's *Elementi . . .*) was the most popular alternative:

The French always prepare their trills; although these old preparations are still used in operas and old songs, they are not any more in modern music and still less by foreigners.   (Tarade, *Traité. . .* (1774), p. 47)

32. Tartini, *Traité . . .*, ed. Jacobi, pt. 1, p. 74; although Galeazzi suggests that the trill and *mordente* were abused and overused by the Tartini school (*Elementi . . .* (1791), vol. 1, pt. 2, art. 15n, p. 195).
33. Tartini, *Traité . . .*, ed. Jacobi, pt. 2, p. 75 and L. Mozart, *Versuch . . .*, ch. 10, §4, p. 218. See Quantz, *Versuch . . .*, tr. and ed. Reilly, ch. 9, §4, p. 102.
34. See Neumann, *Ornamentation in baroque and post-baroque music . . .*, pp. 272–86.

Certainly, many late-eighteenth-century theorists appear to have endeavoured to highlight the predominant melodic line by such means as holding the main note prior to the trill-beating[35] or, as implied by L'Abbé le fils's *cadence subite ou jetée*,[36] in which the heavily printed main note seems to invite the stress of the metrical accent, making the auxiliary an anticipatory note. Whilst the upper-note start appears to have been most common well into the nineteenth century, many writers admit the use of a main-note trill either in specific contexts (such as in some continuous chains of trills, with certain prolonged trills employed for melodic, as opposed to harmonic, intensification, in figures involving short, quick trills and in cases where ungrammatical harmony – for example, consecutive fifths – would otherwise result)[37] or apparently on a regular basis.[38] However, taste, contextual requirements and musical instinct were inevitably the deciding factors as to the treatment of this flexible and versatile ornament.

From about the second quarter of the nineteenth century onwards most German sources (for example, Hummel's *Anweisung*. . . and Spohr's *Violinschule*, which quotes Hummel's work as its authority but incorrectly states that the main-note start was first advanced by Hummel) argue on melodic grounds or for brilliance of effect in favour of a main-note 'preparation' as the norm but such an interpretation is not without exception. On the other hand, in most cases when an alternative, more harmonically based interpretation was required, composers tended to indicate the first note of the trill by means of a small grace note, as in Ex. 378.

Ex. 378

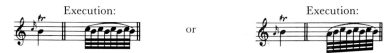

Baillot includes here the two standard terminations (*Nachschläge*), those ending with a turn (no. 2) and, the most common eighteenth-century type for simple melodies, with a note of anticipation (no. 1). He adds two more elaborate, interrelated possibilities, incorporating what Spohr describes as an 'inferior and superior turn' (no. 3)[39] as well as, in the case of the fourth example, an anticipatory note, referring the reader elsewhere for more complex compound ornaments. Baillot is adamant that the speed of repercussion should remain constant to the end.[40] Yet on the evidence of many other theorists of

35. Cartier, *L'art* . . . (1798), §21, p. 5.
36. See glossary.
37. For example, Quantz, *Versuch* . . ., tr. and ed. Reilly, ch. 17, section 2, §24, pp. 229–30; Habeneck's 'Trille appelé improprement cadence' (see glossary), *Méthode* . . . (c. 1840), p. 111.
38. Kürzinger, *Getreuer Unterricht* . . . (1763), p. 36.
39. Spohr, *Violinschule* (1832), p. 154.
40. Like C. P. E. Bach, *Versuch* . . ., tr. Mitchell, pt. 1, ch. 2, section 3, §15, p. 104; Quantz, *Versuch* . . ., tr. and ed. Reilly, ch. 9, §7, p. 103.

the period this was not always the case, especially, of course, with the more expressive accelerating trill (in which case the terminating turn adopts the speed reached at the end of the acceleration) and when articulation was required between the trill and its ensuing note (especially anticipatory terminations, unless slurring is indicated). Furthermore, many writers preferred the main trill note to be impressed rather more on the ear and thus prescribed that it should be dwelt upon immediately prior to the termination;[41] this was especially the case with the anticipatory termination. There is also some conflicting evidence from Rellstab that the fashion towards the turn of the century was to make the trill termination slower than the trill and to add further embellishment, but it seems that this could by no means be called standard practice.[42]

The choice of termination was normally determined by taste and context. However, if an anticipatory termination was required, the anticipatory note was invariably notated in the music; this was especially necessary in the early nineteenth century when, despite Baillot's comment, the terminating turn, whether indicated or not, became the vogue in contemporary compositions (although the note values used to indicate it varied considerably, the turn was executed as a continuation of the trill itself). Furthermore, Spohr, among others, describes trills which on account of their shortness or context remain without termination, a type which was rare in the eighteenth century.[43]

Apart from his variations for final cadences in *Adagios* or cadenzas, Baillot does not venture into the detail of many eighteenth-century sources regarding the speed of the trill (Quantz, for example, considers the ordinary speed of a typical long, final trill to be eight demisemiquavers in the time of мм $\downarrow$ = 80 but necessarily admits that speeds should vary according to context),[44] merely suggesting that this should always be regular[45] and should conform with the tempo and character of the music.[46] Cartier, quoting Leopold Mozart for the most part, takes other points into consideration:

The trill should not be executed very fast in general in order not to acquire the habit of bleating. It is better to make the trill slower and even than too fast and uneven. Furthermore, the trill can be made faster on the thinner strings than on the thicker ones; because the vibration of the latter is slow, whereas that of the former is much faster. However, it is also necessary to consider the place where one is performing one's solo. The fast trill is very effective in a small room where the audience is quite close. Conversely, the slow trill is better in a resonant room and when the audience is further away.   (Cartier, *L'art*. . . (1798), pt. 2, art. 7, p. 32)

Tartini mentions three cadential trill speeds (slow, 'for serious, pathetic and

---

41. Rode *et al.*, *Méthode* . . . (1803), p. 127; Tartini, *Traité* . . ., ed. Jacobi, p. 77; L. Mozart, *Versuch* . . ., ch. 10, §6, p. 220.
42. Rellstab, *C. P. E. Bachs Anfangsgründe mit einer Anleitung* (Berlin, 1790), p. ix.
43. Spohr, *Violinschule* (1832), p. 155; after Hummel, *Anweisung* . . ., pt. 3, p. 387.
44. Quantz, *Versuch* . . ., tr. and ed. Reilly, ch. 9, §6, p. 102 and ch. 17, section 7, §55, p. 288.
45. See also L. Mozart, *Versuch* . . ., ch. 10, §8, p. 221; Spohr, *Violinschule* (1832), p. 156.
46. See also Froehlich, *Vollständige theoretisch-praktische Musikschule* (1810), vol. 4, §6, pp. 43–4; L. Mozart, *Versuch* . . ., ch. 10, §8, p. 221.

sad pieces', moderate, 'for moderately gay ones', fast, 'in pieces which are gay, lively and swift')[47] and specifies that changes from one speed to another faster speed should be anticipated by an appropriate acceleration (Ex. 379). In keep-

Ex. 379

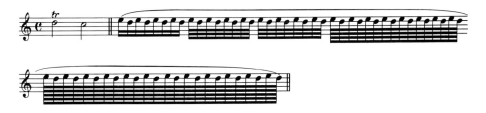

ing with this, Leopold Mozart gives four trill-speeds – slow, medium, rapid and accelerating[48] – the latter being employed for cadential or final cadenza trills, but does not include Baillot's eventual speed reduction. Likewise, Spohr, while advocating the accelerating trill, is adamant that a trill should never begin fast and end slowly; furthermore, he continues:

> The beats of the semitone trill should be taken somewhat slower than those of the whole-tone trill, because the ear cannot distinguish the quick interchange of the close interval as easily as the larger interval.   (Spohr, *Violinschule* (1832), p. 156)

Early-nineteenth-century theorists appear to have been less concerned than their eighteenth-century counterparts about the addition of nuances to accompany trills. Baillot certainly makes no reference to the addition of any dynamic expression but such additions may well have been accepted nineteenth-century practice which required no further textual explanation. It appears, however, that a *crescendo* or *diminuendo* was often applied to trills, according to context, notably to the long[49] and in particular to the accelerating trill, in which the increase in speed was invariably matched by an increase in volume.[50]

Although omitted by Baillot, open-string trills were generally avoided where possible (by means of a shift, normally to modern third position) in the interests of preserving uniformity of tone colour. Cartier for one is adamant that only double trills should involve a first-finger trill on an open string, since the player has no other option.[51] Nevertheless, some writers like Herrando fail to take timbre into account and Tartini recommends regular practice of the open-string trill as a means to an end:

47. Tartini, *Traité* . . ., ed. Jacobi, pt. 1, p. 76.
48. L. Mozart, *Versuch* . . ., ch. 10, §7, pp. 220–1.
49. Froehlich, *Vollständige theoretisch-praktische Musikschule* (1810), vol. 4, §6, p. 43.
50. For example, L. Mozart, *Versuch* . . ., ch. 10, §7, pp. 220–1; Spohr, *Violinschule* (1832), p. 156; Cartier, *L'art* . . . (1798), pt. 2, art. 6, p. 32.
51. Cartier, *L'art* . . . (1798), pt. 2, art. 8, p. 32. See also L. Mozart, *Versuch* . . ., ch. 10, §10, p. 222; Habeneck, *Méthode* . . . (c. 1840), p. 111, etc.

You must attentively and assiduously persevere in the practice of this embellishment, and begin at first with an open string, upon which, if you are once able to make a good shake with the first finger, you will with the greater facility acquire one with the second, the third and the fourth or little finger.

(Tartini, *Traité* . . ., ed. Jacobi, appendix, p. 139)

Writers continually stress the importance of trill practice in every key and with each finger, even the weakest little finger, and many provide exercises accordingly. Such facility was especially significant in the execution of consecutive trills, generally of considerable technical difficulty, chains of which became longer and more common as the period progressed. Even so, contrary to Baillot's instructions, most writers recommend the use of the same fingers continuously in a succession of trills, ascending or descending, and invariably with a main-note start.[52] Leopold Mozart provides three alternative fingerings, while Rode *et al.* give three detailed alternatives to the use of one finger regarding the execution of a succession of trills, one commencing with the upper note and two on the main note, the final example complete with termination.[53] Habeneck likewise recommends the addition of terminations in slow movements but suggests an interesting compromise for successions of trills in quick tempos, employing the same two fingers throughout (and in rather unorthodox fashion) but alternating on each trill between a main-note and an upper-note start.[54] With Spohr, only the last of a succession of trills generally terminates with a turn, especially when the trills are on short notes, but he does admit a terminating turn on each of a chain of long trills.[55]

Like Baillot, most writers of the period emphasise certain basic left-hand requisites for optimum trill execution, namely keeping the trilling finger absolutely supple, even, and in one place for intonation purposes, and raising it high above the string so that its tip falls on the string with some impact, in order to obtain clarity of articulation in keeping with the intended brilliant effect.[56] However, many of these requisites contrast markedly with the views of modern writers, who generally stipulate that the fingers should neither be lifted high nor allowed to strike the string with great force, on the grounds that both faults cause tension and impede the speed and fluency of the trill.[57] Apart from the attentions of a few German writers[58] concerned mainly with the adjustment of bow speed to suit the length of the trill, in order to avoid a bow change in the middle of a long trill, bow management with the trill suffers surprising neglect in late-eighteenth-century and early-nineteenth-century methods.

52. See Mazas, *Méthode* . . . (1830), p. 116; Tartini, *Traité* . . ., ed. Jacobi, pt. 1, p. 78.
53. See glossary, Rode *et al.*, 'Suite de trilles'.
54. See glossary.
55. Spohr, *Violinschule* (1832), p. 158.
56. See Reichardt, *Ueber die Pflichten* . . . (1776), pp. 43–4; Campagnoli, *Metodo* . . . (1797?), tr. Bishop, pt. 2, no. 125; Rode *et al.*, *Méthode* . . . (1803), p. 126; Mazas, *Méthode* . . . (1830), p. 116; Spohr, *Violinschule* (1832), p. 155.
57. See Galamian, *Principles of violin playing and teaching*, p. 30.
58. L. Mozart, *Versuch* . . ., ch. 10, §9, p. 221; Reichardt, *Ueber die Pflichten* . . . (1776), pp. 44–5: Froehlich, *Vollständige theoretisch-praktische Musikschule* (1810), vol. 4, §6, pp. 43–4.

Finally, two unusual types of trill warrant special mention, the two trills in harmonics (Ex. 241) incorporated in L'Abbé le fils's famous *Menuet* and imitated later by numerous virtuosi, and Tartini's peculiar compromise between trill and *vibrato*:

The two notes that make it up join in such a way that the two fingers never quite leave the string. It is not done, like the others, by raising the finger but by using the wrist to carry the whole hand, and thus also the finger, in a rippling motion, so that this kind of trill is 'rippled' and not 'struck'. It sounds well in playing *con affetto* and when the two notes are only a semitone apart.   (Tartini, *Traité. . .*, ed. Jacobi, pt. 1, pp. 78–9)

Brisés

The *brisé* is a trill that is begun only on the written note or on the note above and is not finished off. Example:

Ex. 380

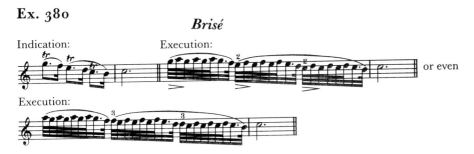

Brisé

It is indicated by the ordinary trill sign *tr*, or sometimes by this: ⌇⌇⌇

Ex. 381   **(Viotti: Trio no. 3 and Concerto no. 5)**

(Baillot, *L'art . . .* (1834), p. 80)

Baillot's *brisé* (called *mordant* by Rode *et al.*),[59] a form of shortened trill, is similar to the true German *Pralltriller*[60] repopularised by C. P. E. Bach and his contemporaries in the 1750s; it may not be but usually is prepared, taken on

59. Rode *et al.*, *Méthode . . .* (1803), p. 127.
60. See C. P. E. Bach, *Versuch . . .*, tr. Mitchell, pt. 1, ch. 2, section 3, §30, p. 110. The terms *Pralltriller* and *Schneller* were confused and often used interchangeably by many theorists, probably because their normal speed of execution made them difficult to distinguish.

the beat and executed rapidly but it is rarely terminated and occurs most commonly in passages descending by step. Baillot's textual comment is sparse compared with that of Habeneck, who warns against incorporating more notes into the *brisé* than time will comfortably allow, since this can cause stiffness of the wrist and fingers. He claims that finger speed should not exceed reasonable limits and should be related to the duration of the *brisé* with the fingers kept upright for articulation purposes in order to achieve a brilliant effect without distorting the rhythm.[61]

Mordant

The *mordant* is also a *brisé* or a trill which is not finished off. It is similarly indicated by the sign *tr* or by this other sign ∿ .

Ex. 382

(Viotti: Divertissement no. 1)

(Baillot, *L'art.* . . (1834), p. 80)

Baillot's *mordant* is the equivalent of the German *Schneller*,[62] an unprepared main-note trill of one repercussion, which is taken on the beat and occurs most typically in the eighteenth century in passages descending by step; it was employed largely in order to avoid consecutives (resulting from a prepared long trill) or when there was insufficient time to play even a normal short trill. It was applied and performed more freely in the nineteenth century under various names (it was described by Hummel (1828) as *mordente* and also confusingly called *Pralltriller* by some nineteenth-century writers); towards the end of our period it was commonly performed as a pre-beat ornament according to the expressive context.

Baillot omits mention in his survey of the mordent (otherwise variously called *pincé, martellement, mordente* etc.), most probably because the ornament was often absorbed by the ordinary notation towards the end of the eighteenth century.[63] It is a very rapid alternation of the main note, normally taken on

61. Habeneck, *Méthode* . . . (c. 1840), p. 113.
62. C. P. E. Bach, *Versuch* . . ., tr. Mitchell, pt. 1, ch. 2, §1, p. 142.
63. Donington (*The interpretation of early music*, p. 202) suggests that from the second quarter of the nineteenth century onwards, the normal assumption appears to be that an 'inverted mordent' (alternation of the main note with an upper auxiliary a tone or semitone above), as opposed to the standard mordent, is intended.

the beat (although it may be prepared by an accented lower auxiliary note, treated in *appoggiatura* fashion) with a lower auxiliary a tone or semitone below; even so, a case may be made according to some writers' implications for a pre-beat interpretation.[64] On longer notes, more than one repercussion may be appropriate (Ex. 383), thus prolonging the ornament and producing a

Ex. 383

Written:

Played:

less brilliant, slower effect but ending without exception on the main note without termination (C. P. E. Bach indicates a short mordent by ♦ and a mordent of over three notes by ♦♦). Tartini claims that the mordent may comprise two, four or six notes according to finger speed and duration of note and that it is appropriate in bright, lively pieces. Leopold Mozart extends the mordent category by adding two similar 'biting' ornaments, which, on his own admission (1787 edition), resemble respectively a disjunct double *appoggiatura* and a slide (ascending or descending).[65] Cartier relates various interpretations of the ornament to certain expressive ideals and claims that it can express anger, resolution, horror, sadness, affection, pleasure, and so on.[66]

The double trill

The same principles hold for the *double trill* as for the single trill.

Nevertheless, one is obliged sometimes to make changes in the final notes of a cadence. Here are some examples:

Ex. 384

Indication: Execution:
a.

b.

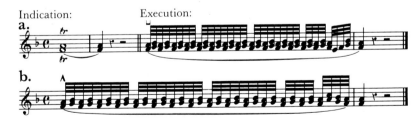

64. See L. Mozart, *Versuch* . . ., ch. 11, §8, p. 242 & §13, p. 244.
65. Tartini, *Traité* . . ., ed. Jacobi, p. 91; L. Mozart, *Versuch* . . ., ch. 11, §8–14, pp. 242–3.
66. Cartier, *L'art* . . . (1798), art. 27, p. 6. See glossary.

Ex. 384 (cont.)

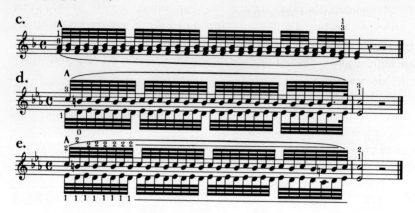

Here is a kind of trill which, though not a double trill, is played in double stopping:

Ex. 385

(Baillot: *Thème varié*, Op. 17)

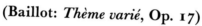

The name *closed trill* is given to a trill which like the previous one is not actually double, but which again is played in double stopping and between two notes which oblige two fingers to be left in place.

Ex. 386

(Tartini: *L'art de l'archet*, Var. 36)

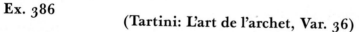
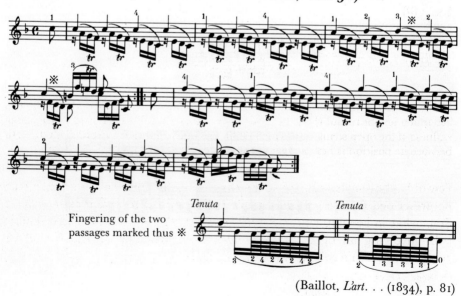

(Baillot, *L'art*. . . (1834), p. 81)

Baillot's consideration of the double trill, immediately followed by two pages of trills involving major and minor scales, omitted from our survey, is rather limited in scope, neglecting many of the added technical complications caused by double stopping, notably bow management and even finger action. Although he claims that the same principles apply to the double as to the single trill, his examples of preparations and terminations, like those of most writers, lack thoroughness, including only double trills in thirds and sixths beginning on the main note. Spohr, however, whilst starting all his trills on the main note (unless expressly indicated), adds that in cases when the closing turn requires a position-change (Ex. 387) the shift should be made as quickly as possible, so that there is no break between the trill and the turn.

Ex. 387

Double trills in thirds were most common and caused fewest technical problems, although their execution in the higher registers was by no means easy. Examples and exercises for the perfection of double trills in thirds were incorporated into many methods and the fingerings prescribed were generally orthodox and straightforward. One notable exception is L'Abbé le fils's curious fingering for such trills involving the use of an open string. This fingering (Ex. 388) involves an unnecessary contraction of the left hand and it is a moot point whether it could ever be employed successfully unless approached by simple position-work. L'Abbé le fils explains:

Ex. 388

I have noticed in our best masters that the double trills with the first and third fingers are much less beautiful than those with the second and fourth fingers, because the stiffness of the open string repels the first finger, which, furthermore, has less strength because its position is not as erect as the others.

(L'Abbé le fils, *Principes* . . . (1761), p. 65)

Few of L'Abbé le fils's successors appear to have adopted this fingering, which he prescribed for use with all double trills in thirds involving open strings. Somewhat in keeping with L'Abbé's example, Rode *et al.* claim that double trills involving an open string should not be terminated and should be employed only in a succession of double trills.[67]

67. Rode *et al.*, *Méthode* . . ., (1803), p. 128.

The execution of double trills in sixths is technically more complex, commonly requiring the consecutive use of one and the same finger on different strings. Leopold Mozart provides a notable example of this problem (Ex. 389) and explains:

Ex. 389

. . . the first finger must never be lifted, but must be brought across to the D string by means of a movement of the whole hand, with the foremost part only and with a slight sideways movement.   (Mozart, *Versuch* . . ., ch. 10, §31, p. 235)

This trill in sixths was only rarely employed as a special effect, usually to bring some finality to a cadenza. Bornet provides a similar example (without instructive text), called the *cadence du diable* and both Lorenziti and Campagnoli include exercises for the perfection of double trills in sixths, the latter, like Tonelli, employing similar principles to Baillot's fourth alternative double trill and recommending some very unusual fingerings (although few fingerings match Baillot's 'slithery' fifth suggestion for bizarrerie).[68]

Double trills in octaves and unisons were even less commonly employed than the sixth trill. These involved considerable finger extension and could not be accomplished by players with small hand-spans. Notable examples are incorporated in Romberg's Sonata Op. 32 no. 2 (Ex. 390) and in particular in many of Paganini's works (Ex. 391).

Ex. 390

Ex. 391

---

68. Bornet, *Nouvelle méthode* . . . (1786), p. 80; Campagnoli, *Metodo* . . . (1797?), tr. Bishop, pt. 2, no. 138; Lorenziti, *Principes* . . . (1798), p. 28.

Examples of the closed trill, a trill involving double stopping in which only one note actually trills, are commonly included in contemporary methods but, as here, are generally not accompanied by any individual textual instruction. Spohr, however, provides the following instruction for his accompanied trill:

The 9th bar sees the beginning of the most difficult of all trills, namely the trill accompanied by another voice. A double difficulty has to be overcome here, since the onset of the accompanying voice must not impede or disturb either the oscillations of the trilling finger or the sweep of the bow stroke. In order that the second finger may play the c² in the accompanying voice without having to be lifted from the trilled note, the g², it must be placed on the g² right from the start in such a way that it almost touches the A string and can cover this string also with only a slight movement towards it. During the pauses in the accompaniment the bow must be lifted only very slightly above the A string, so as to be able to touch it again at once without any great movement as soon as the accompaniment begins afresh. The changes of bow must always take place during the pauses in the second voice; this trill is therefore to be divided into four bows, of which the first (a down bow) takes up four crotchets, the second, three, the third, again three, and the last, two crotchets. A method for making the change of bow imperceptible to the ear has been taught earlier. This accompanied trill, when properly played, must sound as if it is being performed by two people.

Ex. 392

(Spohr, *Violinschule* (1832), p. 165)

Among other notable examples of this trill type should be included Woldemar's *gammes de cadence dite du diable*, incorporating the problems of fingered octaves with the first and extended third finger and a fourth-finger trill on the top note (Ex. 393), and Schweigl's even greater finger extension, requiring trills on the lower note of consecutive stopped tenths (Ex. 394).

Ex. 393

Ex. 394

Petit groupe

Ex. 395

Petit groupe of three notes

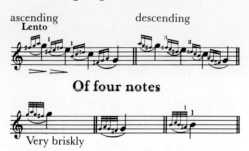

Of four notes

This is an ornament consisting of three and sometimes four notes. These notes must constitute among themselves a minor third or a diminished third, otherwise the *petit groupe* would have a harsh effect.

The 1st note must be emphasised a little more strongly than the others and held on longer in a melody; but in a passage in a lively movement, the *petit groupe* must be played in a brisk and abrupt manner suited to the pointing of the rhythm. For example:

Ex. 396

The *petit groupe* can be embellished in this and many other ways, principally in a melodic line.

Ex. 397

Here is an ornament which has something of the mordent and of the *petit groupe*.

The next one is called by the Italians *il mordente impertinente*. As it consists here of four notes, we are including it among the *petits groupes*.

Ex. 398

Ex. 399

(Tartini: L'art de L'archet, Var. 3)

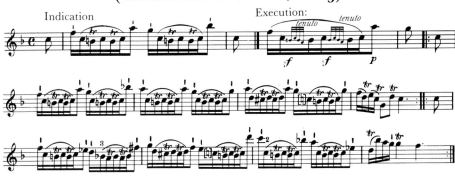

Note: The small notes must be played quickly and lightly, with a small *sforzando* and 'dragging' the b[1] that comes after.   (Baillot, *L'art* . . . (1834), p. 84)

Baillot restricts these brilliant ornamental notes (otherwise termed *gruppo*, *gruppetto*, although some theorists – for example, Leopold Mozart – restricted the use of the term to certain specific instances), employed essentially to connect main notes, to groups of three or four and to a prescribed melodic range. Quite logically, he includes the turn in this classification of embellishment, an ornament comprising the alternation of a main note with two auxiliaries a tone or a semitone away. He illustrates the two main rhythmic varieties of turn, the so-called *accented* type (called double turn or *mordente* by Spohr, Galeazzi and Tartini), played on the beat, accented, before the main note and indicated by a sign directly above the note, and the *unaccented* type, played after the main note and indicated by a sign above but slightly to the right of the main note, but he omits the less common turn form, the inverted (inferior) turn, from his discussion. Spohr discusses both formal varieties and claims that the sign should indicate whether the superior or inferior variety is intended – a sign with the first hook or notch bent upwards indicated an inferior turn;[69] however, few composers were reliable or consistent on this score, many employing small grace-notes which were invariably ambiguous as to the type of turn intended. Consequently, further into the nineteenth century, it became the custom to write out turns in full in ordinary notation, thus leaving no doubt as to the intended interpretation.

69. Spohr, *Violinschule* (1832), p. 168. See glossary.

The rhythm of the turn was generally even (as in Baillot's elaborate unaccented type) but both accented and unaccented types also occurred in a variety of unequal rhythms. C. P. E. Bach, for example, prefers an uneven rhythm for accented turns in slow tempos (Ex. 400) because of that ornament's predominantly brilliant character and customary rapid execution.

Ex. 400

The constituent notes on the more melodic, unaccented variety, however, were invariably allotted rhythms which would best suit the musical context. Ex. 401a might be interpreted as Ex. 401b or 401c or 401d or 401e, or in other rhythms and speeds determined by the performer's musical instinct; the general tendency in such dotted rhythms was to delay and shorten the note after the dotted note.

Ex. 401

A few other figures were described or illustrated as specific ornaments in some methods (for example, Galeazzi's *conducimento* and *volata*, or Leopold Mozart's *groppo*, *tirata* and *circle*)[70] but these are arguably more accurately classified as *ornements*, embellishments more closely associated with free (improvised) ornamentation, than as *agréments*.

Finally, compound ornaments, combinations of two or more specific ornaments, appeared in abundance during the period, extending considerably the available vocabulary of embellishments. Thus, a mordent may be 'prepared' by an *appoggiatura*, an *appoggiatura* may be prefixed to a turn, a turn may be combined with an *appoggiatura* and short trill and so on, creating for the performer a more varied ornamental language, founded essentially on the basic principles governing each individual ornament, from which to draw.

70. See glossary and L. Mozart, *Versuch* . . ., ch. 11, §18–22, pp. 247–51.

14

Improvisation

The eighteenth and early nineteenth centuries saw the culmination of the art of improvisation (especially at the keyboard), whether in the form of melodic ornamentation, cadenzas, preludes, continuo realisations or the type of independent extemporisation for which Bach, Handel, Mozart and Beethoven, among others, were renowned. A tradition of free embellishment was omnipresent during the period but it was practised in varying degrees and in different forms, according largely to date, venue, individual practices and national styles.[1] Furthermore, since the very nature of improvisation is arbitrary, spontaneous, wide-ranging in style and inconsistent with any rigid rules and structural definition and since for obvious reasons melody instruments were rather more limited in scope for improvisation than keyboard instruments, theorists normally include only very general observations on the art. Instead they prefer to instruct by musical example rather than textual discussion[2] and encourage students to listen to performances by the great masters.

In respect of the violin and its treatises, the incidence of improvisation can be subdivided into four main areas – the variation of melody, the decoration of fermatas and the extemporisation of both cadenzas and preludes – although cases have been made for the inclusion of dynamic nuances, *vibrato*, *tempo rubato* and articulation under the category of improvised embellishment as elements of variation contributing towards an expressive goal.[3]

VARIATION OF A MELODY

Improvised variation of a melody, otherwise termed 'divisions' or *diminuzioni*, involved the performer in the free and usually spontaneous addition of

1. See Quantz, *Versuch* . . ., tr. and ed. Reilly, ch. 10, §13, p. 113.
2. For example, Zuccari's *The true method of playing an Adagio* . . ., comprising twelve *Adagios* with *basso continuo*, each presented in its simple form and in an embellished version but with no explanatory text; Franz Benda's Op. 1 violin sonatas (Paris, 1763), most movements of which are written out in both simple and varied versions. See also Schmitz, *Die Kunst der Verzierung im 18. Jahrhundert*, pp. 135–9.
3. See, for example, Quantz, *Versuch* . . ., tr. and ed. Reilly, ch. 14, §15–20, pp. 167–8; Galeazzi, *Elementi* . . . (1791), vol. 1, pt. 2, p. 197 & p. 202.

melodic figures[4] that were too variable to be indicated satisfactorily by signs, as well as the conventional stereotyped ornaments classified and discussed in the previous chapter, that is to say Quantz's 'arbitrary' (*willkührlich*) as well as his 'essential' (*wesentlich*) ornaments and the early-nineteenth-century French school's *ornements* as well as their *agréments du chant*. Such melodic variation, confined in theory (although apparently not always in practice) to solo contexts or passages of ensemble music in which a solo texture prevails,[5] required the performer to understand elementary harmony and appreciate the harmonic progressions as the basic foundations of the melody, whose shape could be refashioned with various melodic elaborations, figurations and other formulae.[6]

Approaches towards melodic ornamentation, and improvised embellishment in particular, varied enormously from composer to composer, performer to performer, country to country and even region to region. The knowledge of how and when to introduce embellishments was a largely unwritten performing tradition passed down through the generations from teacher to pupil. Three national styles of performance predominated in the mid eighteenth century – a French approach in which essential ornaments were generally specifically indicated and arbitrary ones played little part (although the occasional *roulade* or *tirade* was left to the performer's discretion until about 1780, as well as the variation of *agréments*, in repeated sections),[7] an Italian approach which admitted both categories of ornament but only seldom with any indication as to their application, and a German compromise in which Italian influence was paramount but nevertheless restrained by a more expressive and selective use of ornaments (both essential and arbitrary) in keeping with the *Affektenlehre* or doctrine of the affections,[8] especially in the North German school. C. P. E. Bach deliberately refrains from detailed discussion of improvised ornamentation, arguing that its implementation is too variable to classify and that it was becoming customary in his circles to write it out in full.[9] Quantz, however, makes the following distinction:

The *Italian manner of playing* is arbitrary, extravagant, artificial, obscure, frequently bold and bizarre, and difficult in execution; it permits many additions of graces, and requires a seemly knowledge of harmony; but among the ignorant it excites more admiration than pleasure. The *French manner of playing* is slavish, yet modest, distinct, neat and true in execution, easy to imitate, neither profound nor obscure, but com-

4. But see Quantz, *Versuch* . . ., tr. and ed. Reilly, ch. 18, §11, p. 301.
5. See L. Mozart, *Versuch* . . ., ch. 11, §22, p. 251.
6. Galeazzi, *Elementi* . . . (1791), vol. 1, pt. 2, p. 199.
7. See Quantz, *Versuch* . . ., tr. and ed. Reilly, ch. 14, §4, p. 163; Algarotti, *An essay on the opera* (London, 1767) p. 59; *Dictionnaire de musique*, ed. Rousseau, p. 366. See also Aldrich, 'The principal agréments of the seventeenth and eighteenth centuries . . .' (unpublished Ph. D. degree thesis, Harvard University, 1942) pp. 145-7.
8. See Wessel, 'The Affektenlehre in the eighteenth century' (unpublished Ph. D degree thesis, University of Indiana, 1955); see also, for example, Quantz, *Versuch* . . ., tr. and ed. Reilly, ch. 8, §16, p. 98, ch. 11, §15, pp. 124-5 & ch. 14, §8, p. 165; L. Mozart, *Versuch* . . ., ch. 12, §2, p. 252.
9. C. P. E. Bach, *Versuch* . . ., tr. Mitchell, ch. 2, pp. 79-80.

prehensible to everyone, and convenient for amateurs; it does not require much
knowledge of harmony, since the embellishments are generally prescribed by the
composer; but it gives the connoisseurs little to reflect upon.

In a word, Italian music is arbitrary, and French is circumscribed. If it is to have a
good effect, the French depends more upon the composition than the performance,
while the Italian depends upon the performance almost as much as upon the composition, and in some cases almost more.

. . . .

If one has the necessary discernment to choose the best from the styles of different
countries, a *mixed style* results that, without overstepping the bounds of modesty, could
well be called *the German style*, not only because the Germans came upon it first, but
because it has already been established at different places in Germany for many
years, flourishes still, and displeases in neither Italy nor France, nor in other lands.[10]

(Quantz, *Versuch* . . ., tr. and ed. Reilly, ch. 18, §76, p. 335 and §87, p. 341)

Increasing foreign influence both before and after the revolution prompted
significant changes in the French style. Rousseau and his followers championed the Italian style; there was a French translation of Tartini's treatise on
ornamentation (1771); Cartier's *L'art du violon* included a notable collection of
music of the Italian school; and, latterly, Viotti settled in Paris. All these combined to spread the Italian performing style, especially with regard to ornamentation. Framery[11] confirms that French musicians tended to invent ornaments rather more than previously, even though French composers, unlike
the Italians, still consistently specified their required 'essential' ornaments,
thus setting certain limits to the play of free ornamentation. The German
compromise persisted to some extent in the late eighteenth century; however,
because of their selective and expressive approach towards ornamentation
German musicians had begun well before 1750 to notate precisely the interpretative details of their compositions and thus write pretty fully ornamented
melodies. The first movement of J. S. Bach's sonata in G minor for unaccompanied violin (BWV 1001), a kind of free fantasia with written-out embellishment, is a prime example, as are many of Bach's instrumental obbligatos,
which severely limit the performer's freedom to embellish, essentially
restricting such opportunities to the varied reprise.[12] Dr Burney, on visiting
the court of Frederick the Great, remarked:

. . . if any of his Italian troops dare to deviate from strict discipline, by adding, altering or diminishing a single passage in the parts they have to perform, an order is sent,
de par le Roi, for them to adhere strictly to the notes written by the composer, at their
peril. This, when compositions are good, and a singer is licentious, may be an excellent method; but certainly shuts out all taste and refinement.

(Scholes, ed., *Dr Burney's Musical Tours in Europe* (London, 1959) vol. 2, p. 207)

The design and content of the melodic elaborations are impossible to cata-

10. See also Quantz, *Versuch* . . ., tr. and ed. Reilly, ch. 14, §1-4, pp. 162-3 & ch. 10, §13, p. 113.
11. Framery, Ganguené & de Momigny, eds., *Encyclopédie méthodique* (Paris, 1791), vol. 1, p. 182, s.v.
'Broderies'.
12. See Scheibe's criticism of Bach's approach and Birnbaum's defence of it in David & Mendel, *The Bach
reader*, pp. 238-48.

logue in detail because of the wide range of styles employed, the degree and type of variation differing greatly in character from one musician to another and one movement genre to another. However, we may be guided by a number of eighteenth-century works which have survived, for some reason or other, with embellishments added – for example, the various available embellished versions of Corelli's Op. 5 violin sonatas with embellishments respectively by Corelli himself, Geminiani, Dubourg, Tartini and three unidentified composers/violinists, one of whom is thought to have been Castrucci (Ex. 402);[13] the *Zwölf methodische Sonaten für Violine oder Flöte und Basso Continuo*

Ex. 402

by Telemann (Hamburg, 1728 and 1732); the *Sechs Sonaten für Clavier mit veränderten Reprisen* by C. P. E. Bach (Berlin, 1760); and Franz Benda's 32 three-movement sonatas for violin and bass (composed before 1763). These works represent arguably a surer guide to improvisatory ornamental practice than contemporary treatises, the Benda sonatas, for example, incorporating at least one embellished version (presented below the original solo line) in all but two movements.

Additions were most prolific in slow movements (especially those written in the common 'skeletal outline' manner of the Italian style) and helped to sus-

13. See Marx, 'Some unknown embellishments of Corelli's violin sonatas', *Musical Quarterly*, vol. 61 (1975), pp. 65–76.

tain musical interest in repeated sections (for example, in binary form movements in which each section is repeated; in ternary or da capo aria form in
which the first A section is repeated; in rondo refrains; in recapitulations of
sonata form movements and in the concerto soloist's repetitions of tutti
material).[14] They range from the inclusion of merely a few trills and *appoggiaturas* to a complete reworking of the entire structure. Generally speaking,
however, most of the embellished versions comprise a balanced variety of note
values and rhythms. They adhere closely to the overall melodic contour of the
original, its salient structural points (cadences, principal notes, phrases etc.)
being emphasised through the addition of both stereotyped ornaments (such
as *appoggiaturas*, trills, turns and mordents) and ornamental figures such as
Leopold Mozart's *battement, ribattuta, groppo, tirata, mezzo circulo*, Galeazzi's
gruppo, conducimento, volata, diminutions,[15] passage-work of varying kinds or
even simple arpeggios, especially at the approach to a cadence or modulation.
Rhythmic patterns like those of Ex. 403 (a compilation by the author from

Ex. 403

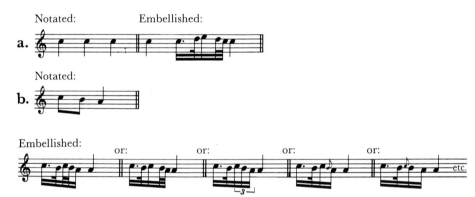

various sources chiefly of ornamentation attributed to Tartini) were also commonly employed, as well as upper and lower auxiliary notes, simple passing
notes, single-note repetitions, two- or three-note *Schleifer* and scale passages
normally of no more than an octave span, the latter figures generally filling in
the intervals between the notes of the given melody. In more isolated cases, and
then generally at cadences, the melodic outline was temporarily distorted and
dissolved into smaller note values faithful only to the harmonic constitution of
the original (i.e. Tartini's *modi artifiziali* as opposed to the *modi naturali*).[16] The

14. See Burney, *History of music*, 1935 edn, vol. 2, p. 545. However, not all reprises were embellished; see
    Quantz, *Versuch . . .*, tr. and ed. Reilly, ch. 12, §27, pp. 134-5.
15. L. Mozart, *Versuch . . .*, ch. 11, §15-21, pp. 245-51; Galeazzi, *Elementi . . .* (1791), vol. 1, pt. 2, pp. 190-1.
    See also Elmer, 'Tartini's improvised ornamentation as illustrated by manuscripts from the Berkeley
    collection of eighteenth-century Italian instrumental music' (unpublished M. A. degree thesis,
    University of California at Berkeley, 1962) for a description of a manuscript collection of ornamenta-
    tion, by Tartini, which most probably served as a supplement to his *Regole . . . .*
16. Tartini, *Regole . . .*, facsimile edn, pp. 20-43.

reverse process was also exploited, involving the lengthening of note values and condensing of melodic figuration (Ex. 404) in addition to a type of *tempo rubato*, featuring either rhythmic displacement (Ex. 405) or the accommodation of an irregular grouping of notes within the bar (Ex. 406).[17] Multiple

Ex. 404

(F. Benda: Sonata XXVII)

Ex. 405

(F. Benda: Sonata XVIII)

Ex. 406

(F. Benda: Sonata VIII)

stopping was invariably substituted for arpeggiated passages, or vice versa, and short cadenzas were sometimes included, Benda's sonatas providing a number of instances, especially in the slow movements. Finally, the importance of changes of articulation, phrasing and bowing should not be underestimated in the process of melodic variation.

17. See also ch. 11, p. 273.

Performers generally aimed to achieve a progressive and cumulative ornamental effect, a melody normally being performed as written or very simply on its first occurrence and its variations, attendant sequences or repeated passages becoming increasingly more elaborate at each recurrence without deforming the melody and disrupting the unity of the piece.[18]

Although one of the principal objects of extempore embellishment was to demonstrate the skill of the performer, such invention was supposed to serve an expressive role and, certainly towards the end of the eighteenth century, to be kept within the bounds of moderation and discretion. However, despite theorists' recommendations, some performers, especially Italians, indulged in the addition of excessive and over-florid embellishment, which was in bad taste and in the final reckoning injurious to the overall musical effect. Löhlein expresses his disapproval of extravagant ornamentation thus:

> It has already been said that ornaments, like clothing or other finery worn on the body, must be consistent with the music or the content of the piece. One must also not to be too extravagant about it, otherwise one would be like those who, in order to beautify their figures, wrap themselves in so many layers of colourful clothing and ornaments that one is scarcely aware that there is a human figure underneath it all. Ornaments in music are like spices in food. They must be introduced sparingly and in the right place; otherwise they will spoil rather than improve. One finds with young scholars that those who have the least wit are anxiously concerned to appear witty at every opportunity and mostly out of place. The same situation is found with musicians. Those who have the least amount of good taste take great pains to show their listeners how tastefully they can play by means of all-too-frequent, ill-advised ornaments and in this very way they betray their weakness rather than their fine taste to people of sense.   (Löhlein, *Anweisung*. . . (1774), ch. 10, §72, pp. 51-2)

Furthermore, Burney remarked of Geminiani that 'he transformed Corelli's solos and six of his sonatas into concertos, by multiplying notes, and loading, and deforming, I think, those melodies, that were more graceful and pleasing in their light original dress'.[19] The *Adagio varié*, published by Cartier as a supplement to his *L'art* . . .,[20] provides notable examples of complex and over-florid embellishment, which otherwise comply fully with the general principles of melodic elaboration described above. The Nardini sonatas published in elaborate versions in the same treatise and Woldemar's *Grande méthode* . . . provide an interesting, if less wide-ranging choice of ornamental possibility (Ex. 407).[21]

Such 'malpractices', along with stylistic and social changes and the desire to reproduce the proper *affect* or character of a piece, were responsible for a marked increase in written-out embellishment (see, for example, C. P. E. Bach's *Sonaten*. . . *mit veränderten Reprisen* (1760, 1766 and 1768); the decorated reprises are written out in full because according to C. P. E. Bach such a prac-

18. See Galeazzi, *Elementi* . . . (1791), vol. 1, pt. 2, p. 199.
19. Burney, *History of music*, 1935 edn, p. 993.
20. Reproduced in Donington, *The interpretation of early music*, pp. 534-7.
21. Woldemar, *Grande méthode* . . . (c. 1800), pp. 63-9.

Ex. 407

Light
embellishment

Extensive
embellishment

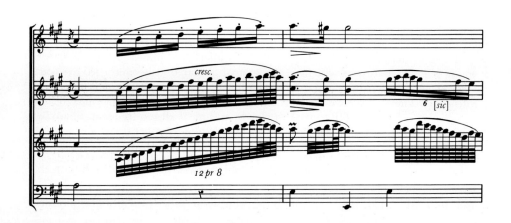

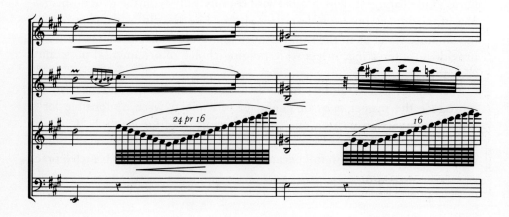

Ex. 407 (cont.)

tice best illustrates how variations can be tastefully achieved, and the composer is better placed than the performer to vary a melody according to his original intentions).[22] Consequently, with the advent of the high classical style, the performer's freedom of extensive improvised ornamentation was curtailed, even though we learn that Mozart[23] and Beethoven varied their ornamental figuration in performance, especially in their slow movements.[24] Certainly by the beginning of the nineteenth century a more or less international approach towards ornamentation had emerged and composers generally endeavoured to indicate their intentions as precisely as possible, using a minimum of signs and defining clearly any complex or unfamiliar embellishments in the few cases required by the 'complete' melodies of the time. Milchmeyer explains:

> Formerly, the embellishment of a melody as indicated by small notes was considered unimportant in the early stages of instruction and was omitted in playing because it was believed that beginners did not possess sufficient perfection of musical feeling to perform them well. Just as our taste has, however, improved in the past twenty years in very many compositions, so now the greatest composers write out all the embellishments of their pieces mostly in large, normal notes, according to the true value that each should have. I, myself, find this very good, the beginner will not be confused and the pieces will be less disfigured by the player, since so much depends on good performance of ornaments. An ornament introduced at the wrong time or badly performed spoils the finest phrases and shows the player's bad taste.
>
> (Milchmeyer, *Die wahre Art das Pianoforte zu spielen*, ch. 3, p. 37)

Interestingly enough, Galeazzi subscribes to Milchmeyer's view, thus indicating a slight change in Italian attitude from one in which the performer was pre-eminent in the selection of embellishment to one in which the composer was considered to be better placed than the performer to determine the type and extent of melodic ornamentation best suited to his music.[25] He considers the tasteful improvisation of 'diminutions', the introduction of appropriate bowing and the effective implementation of graded dynamics as the principal elements of expression.[26]

Thus, an equivocal attitude reigned, which on the one hand recognised the necessity and value of tasteful ornamentation in order to emphasise and articulate structure, and on the other attempted to control the practice, inhibiting the interpretative freedom and spontaneity of the performer and allowing the composer to emerge as the dominant partner. Burney confirms:

> It was formerly more easy to compose than to play an *adagio*, which generally consisted of a few notes that were left to the taste and abilities of the performer; but as the

22. See C. P. E. Bach, *Versuch* . . ., tr. Mitchell, pt. 1, ch. 3, §31, pp. 165–6, and the preface to the *Sonaten mit veränderten Reprisen* (1760), also quoted in Haas, *Aufführungspraxis der Musik*, p. 242.
23. Reported by Reinecke; as quoted in Haas, *Aufführungspraxis der Musik*, p. 259.
24. For example, in answer to his sister's complaint about the sketchy form of the slow movement of his Piano Concerto in D major, K. 451, Mozart sent her an ornamented variant, possibly implying that he expected the performer to provide free ornamentation.
25. Galeazzi, *Elementi* . . . (1791), vol. 1, pt. 2, pp. 190–1 & p. 199.
26. *Ibid.*, p. 197.

composer seldom found his ideas fulfilled by the player, *adagios* are now more *chantant* and interesting in themselves, and the performer is less put to the torture for embellishments.   (Burney, *History of Music* (London, 1776), 1935 ed., vol. 2, p. 10)

Nevertheless, Paganini evidently could scarcely ever resist the opportunity of giving free rein to his flight of fancy, especially when playing the works of others; and Ferdinand David, when leading his string quartet in the 1830s, was renowned for his addition of enterprising free ornamentation to the recapitulation sections of Haydn's quartets, a practice to which even the purist Spohr evidently would not have objected. Spohr praises the manner in which the younger Eck embellished 'the poorest spots' of a quartet by Krommer with 'the most tasteful of flourishes'[27] and further remarks in his advice on string quartet playing:

In passages, *decidedly solo*, the usual embellishments may be allowed.
                                                        (Spohr, *Violinschule* (1832), p. 246)

The recapitulations in many movements of the period, however, are recast in a different, more dramatic light and such improvised ornamentation proved largely superfluous on structural grounds in the classical style. Rosen claims that 'the music of Haydn after 1775 cannot be ornamented' and continues:

The idea of the recapitulation as a dramatic reinterpretation of the exposition attacks the practice of decoration at its root: the structure itself now does the work of the improvised ornaments. The ornamentation of the repeat of the exposition becomes an actual embarrassment: it implies either that the material heard in a dramatically different form in the recapitulation will be less ornamented and inevitably less elaborate than the repeat of the exposition, or that the recapitulation must also be ornamented, which can only obscure and minimize the structural changes with their radically different expressive significance.   (Rosen, *The classical style*, pp. 100–1)

To complete this section, Baillot's general historical survey of improvised melodic ornamentation is reproduced below. It provides a nineteenth-century view of the gradual convergence of national approaches described above, with the predominant eighteenth-century tradition of violin improvisation, the Italian school, most closely under the microscope, and the eventual pre-eminence of the composer over the performer in the determination of melodic embellishment as well as other interpretative details.

[*Improvised*] *ornamentation*

The chief merit of simplicity is that it discloses unity, that attribute of the truly beautiful. These two things combine to capture the interest or the admiration by concentrating all the faculties of the soul together on the character of the subject. But simplicity does not always exclude *ornemens*; an interpretation can be enhanced by such graces provided that it is never eclipsed by them.

The imagination invents *ornemens*, while good taste concerns itself with their variety, their different character and their appropriate use. Taste allows them, selects

27. Spohr, *Autobiography*, Eng. tr., vol. I, p. 31.

them and must often exclude them, for it is not sufficient that the *ornemens* should be graceful and florid, they must above all be used only at suitable moments.

Composers have notated their music in two different ways: *Corelli* and *Tartini*, the earliest for violin music, although they wrote out their fugues and faster-moving pieces as they should be performed (with regard to their nuances and accents), have, however, written out only the outline of their *Adagios*: the evidence can be seen in some old editions of their sonatas where the decorated melody is placed under the simple melody.

But towards the end of the last century, *Haydn*, *Mozart* and, later, *Beethoven* defined their intentions by notating the melodies exactly as they wanted them to be performed, at least as regards the notes, generally leaving scarcely anything to the discretion of the performer in this connection; this usage has spread and indeed for some years now composers have endeavoured to omit nothing which might enable their thoughts to be conveyed more precisely and they have not only notated the *ornemens*, but furthermore indicated *nuances*, *fingerings*, *bowings*, the *character* and all the principal elements of the *accent*.

It is up to the performer to recognise in which kind of way the music he is going to play is notated, in order to comply with its requirements. This is not as easy to determine as one might think if one considers that the positive manner of notating [ornaments] has come to be accepted only little by little and that one comes across many pieces of music where in some of the principal passages the *ornemens* and graces in the melody are simply stated or located [i.e. not fully notated] as if to advise the performer that here he can give free rein to his imagination.

The result is, therefore, as we have already said, that there are several ways of notating [music]; here are some examples:

Ex. 408

Plain note leaving the *ornemens* to be made by the performer
(Corelli: Sonata no. 1, Op. 5)

Ex. 409

Ornemens notated by Corelli

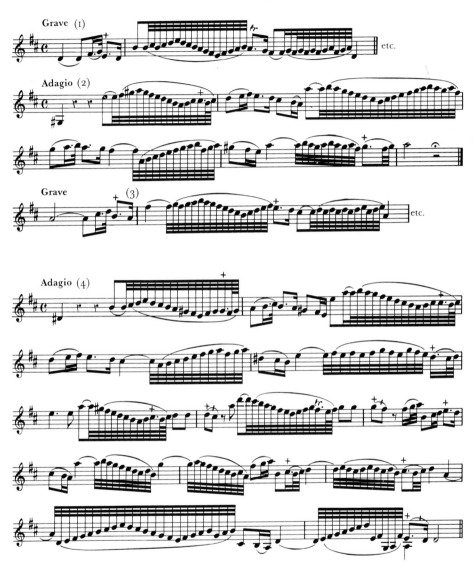

Plain note

(Tartini: Sonata)

Ex. 409 (cont.)

Ornemens notated by Tartini in 17 different ways and cited in J. B. Cartier's *L'art du Violon*

Ex. 410

Plain note without any indications of *ornemens* (Viotti: Adagio from the first concerto he composed, no. 3 in numerical order)

One can see that nothing has been indicated in the way of *ornamentation* in this *Adagio* except for some *appoggiaturas* and some trills, and even they are only specified without any of the details that could give them grace and expression. The constituent parts of phrases in bars 9, 10, 11, 12, 13 and 14 should evidently be ornamented, for if it is natural and necessary, in general, to add some embellishments to a passage which is repeated, there is all the more reason for giving variety to one whose values are the same six times in succession.

Ex. 410 (cont.)

Manner in which this Adagio may be embellished

In the following two *Adagios*, some figuration is indicated yet at the same time the final notes are notated in such a manner as to require a more florid ending.

Ex. 411

(Viotti: Concerto no. 10)

Ornemens that could be added to this ending:

Ex. 412

Simple melody which should be performed as written by the composer
(Mozart: Quartet no. 6)

Here, far from wanting to embellish this melody, it is essential to play the *plain* note only [i.e. the written notes only], with all the charm that it possesses; by preserving the beauty of his design, the composer's ornaments will stand out later with all their elegance and expressiveness. Woe betide anyone who would wish to add anything! – This is not the moment to create, it is a time to allow oneself to be possessed by the profound feeling that this sublime piece inspires.

Ex. 413

Same melody, embellished by Mozart

Finally, such broad melodies as those in the following examples must be rendered with simplicity: the fewer notes there are, the more richness of *accent* there can be.

Ex. 414

(Viotti: Concerto no. 24)

(Baillot: Concerto no. 1, Op. 3)

In the examples taken from the works of Corelli and Tartini, it has been possible to see that the manner of notating employed by these composers was not only simple, but could even be called bare in the *Adagios*, whereas they overloaded them with *ornemens* whenever they performed them. It should be remarked on this subject that the more instrumental music has spread, the more widely this manner of notating the melody has extended, while performance, for the very same reason, has become less arbitrary.

This change in the notation came about as a result of the progress of dramatic music, which has caused a more positive type of melody, adapted to the lyric scene and to the more passionate *accents*, to be substituted in instrumental music for melodies that were for the most part full of charm but vague in their expressiveness.

The violin, more than any other instrument, was to participate in this progress by reason of its similarity with the voice, a similarity which prompts it to imitate the voice even to the very accents of speech. (Baillot, *L'art*. . . (1834), pp. 156–62)

Baillot proceeds with a brief discussion of the remarkable development in dramatic melodic expression in all musical genres towards the end of the eighteenth century and concludes that it culminated for the violin with Viotti's concertos, on account of their sustained character and their noble, expressive melodies, which seem to have been based on words. He continues:

This tendency towards the dramatic style[28] was to give rise to the need to increase the number of signs and to notate evey inflection in order to correspond as closely as possible to the wishes of the composer. This is what modern composers have done and this is what makes music written before this era much more difficult to perform and to interpret well: we stress this point in order that students may not be discouraged at all at the prospect of the large number of works where the absence of signs makes an appeal to their intelligence which is bound to turn to their advantage if they will only take the trouble to deepen their studies.

The abundance of signs is favourable to music in that it can prevent any number of misinterpretations and serve as a guide to those who cannot manage without them, but it may end by stifling the genius of performance which takes pleasure above all in guessing, in creating in its own way. This disadvantage will be avoided by studying old music and never losing sight of it: it will always leave a vast field open to the imagination.

Summary relating to ornemens

1. Make the *ornemens* suitably, that is to say, when they are necessary.
2. Make them appropriate to the subject.
3. Do not play too many or too few.
4. Abstain from them entirely when the subject demands.

(Baillot, *L'art* . . . (1834), p. 162)

PRELUDES

The prelude, originally a short improvisation played immediately before a formal performance, served a variety of purposes, benefiting both performer and listener. It enabled the performer to check his tuning and call for silence, to loosen his fingers and accustom himself to the acoustic and general atmosphere of the concert venue, to verify or display his current proficiency in certain technical areas and to establish for the listener the tonality and mood of the more formal music to come.

Textual documentation regarding the art of preluding is sparse in violin methods of the period but many incorporate examples of written-out preludes in various keys for students to study.[29] Baillot, however, was one of the few writers to examine the by then dying art specifically in terms of the violin, discussing both the written-out and improvised prelude, in harmonic and melodic forms, together with examples and general rules for their application and employment.

28. Demonstrated, as Baillot points out in a footnote, by the increasing practice of qualifying tempo markings with expressive indications representing the 'passions'.
29. For example, L'Abbé le fils, *Principes* . . . (1761), pp. 68–71.

'The *prelude* is a melodic passage whose purpose is to announce the key by running through its principal chords, to command silence, to verify that the instrument is in tune and to prepare the ear for what it is going to have played to it.'[30]

There are two kinds of prelude: the *written-out prelude* and the *improvised prelude*.

The *written-out prelude* has been used in several forms. The earliest composers, *Corelli*, *Geminiani* and others, made it a kind of introduction in several parts; *Sebastian Bach* made frequent use of this type of prelude in his harpsichord pieces; but in the sonatas he composed for solo violin, the form of the prelude is almost that of the other pieces. Modern composers have finally given the written prelude the form of a melodic passage.

This melodic passage or line may be performed according to its nature; it may be presented also in another guise, that is to say, invested with chords.

In the first case the prelude is *melodic*, in the second it is *harmonic*.

Ex. 415

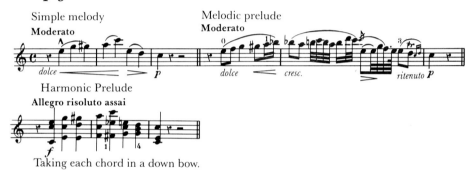

Taking each chord in a down bow.

The *improvised prelude* allows the virtuoso to give entirely free rein to his inspiration. This type of prelude was employed for the piano or organ by *Handel*, *Bach*, *Mozart*, *Clementi* and *Beethoven*; modern organists and pianists have by no means neglected it but amongst violinists Rodolphe Kreutzer is the only one we can mention, to the best of our knowledge, who has indulged in it with any success; yet even he never improvised in public, although he was well equipped to do so. Improvisation demands a habit acquired through constant practice; some great talents have lacked only persistent study in this respect. Study cannot impart genius but it can provide the means of bringing ideas into play and drawing the best from them.

Our object here is not to discuss improvisation; we must restrict ourselves to working a simple improvised melodic line or harmonic passage into a prelude of some bars' length destined to prepare the ear or to command silence. It is with this aim in view that we have placed below some preludes and some harmonic progressions, 1. in order to regulate the use of the prelude, whose application has become confused; 2. to draw attention to the danger of preluding inappropriately.

We have said, in the introduction, that the violin lent itself to harmony to such an extent that it could play broken chords like the harp and simultaneous chords like the piano, the first by means of *arpeggios*, the second by means of *struck chords*. The study of chords having been too much neglected, we have placed, after the *melodic preludes*, exercises in *harmonic preludes*, in order to make more familiar one of the most beautiful of violin effects, chords, and to make students rather better equipped to perform all the fugues and sonatas of Corelli, Tartini, Geminiani and the sonatas of Sebastian

---

30. *Dict[ionnaire] de musique moderne*, ed. Castil-Blaze. (Baillot's footnote)

Bach, whose fugue in C, illustrated below, would alone require one to devote oneself to this kind of study in order to succeed in conveying all its beauties:

Ex. 416

Chords have been used with success in several modern compositions; but as this aspect of playing seems to us still capable of much greater expansion, we have considered it our duty to assign some special studies to it.

General rules

As the *improvised prelude* is not generally destined to serve at all as preparation or introduction, it can be called a fantasy prelude or improvisation; it is free in its movement, in its forms, in its length; all praise to the man who, following the impulse of his genius, can exploit at the same time all the resources of the art in this kind of fancy which allows him to reach the sublime!

But the improvised prelude which serves as preparation or introduction cannot enjoy the same freedom. Let us add that it becomes harmful when it is unnecessary and that only a feeling for the proprieties can determine the need for it.

Once this need has been established, 4 bars of melody will suffice, played gracefully or tossed off with a flourish, to prepare for or introduce a piece. Such will be the *melodic prelude*.

A few chords struck resolutely will likewise suffice to determine the key and command silence: such should be the *harmonic prelude*.

But silence is, most often, the only preparation that it is suitable to use; it should in all instances come after the prelude.

The famous *Crescentini* always used to make a space between the last chord of the ritornello and the beginning of the melody. Our admirable *Garat* likewise used to use this holding back with exquisite feeling; it had an extraordinary effect.

In the preparatory prelude, certain parts want to be animated, others slowed down, above all from the last beat of the penultimate bar to the end. It is well to remark here that the same generally applies to the ending or a suspension in any melodic piece; there is a better lead up to the ending, and the pause is made more understandable if there is a slight slowing down to initiate and introduce it.

On what occasions and in what manner the prelude may be used.

One must never prelude when the violin does not play the leading role.

The prelude can be placed before a first piece; but if several pieces follow one another in the same work, one intended to contrast with another, complete silence becomes indispensable to the enjoyment of this contrast. Woe betide the player who is careless about tuning his instrument quietly, or who puts in a prelude where there should be nothing but silence, and in this way betrays the state of his soul! He makes it only too clear that having been casual in what he has just said, he is likely to be equally so in what he is going to say next.

Let a few introductory chords suffice if one needs to command silence; but, after this warning, one should remember that nothing succeeds better in disposing the audience to silence than silence observed by the performer himself.

One should thus beware particularly of those trifling preludes which antagonise the listener instead of disarming him, those preludes of ill omen which presage only too clearly the fate from which he cannot escape.

The prelude and the cadenza, both children of the imagination, should be concerned above all with responding only to its call, for once the artist has undertaken them, they become for him one more hidden danger or cause for triumph, and if he has the misfortune not to succeed, one is all the less indulgent when one knows that he could have avoided taking the risk in the first place.

Ex. 417 [selected examples only]

24 PRELUDES in all the keys

HARMONIC PRELUDES
50 exercises in chords in all the keys.
No. 2

Harmonic progressions

(Baillot, *L'art* . . . (1834), pp. 183–90)

FERMATAS AND CADENZAS

A fermata or pause ($\curvearrowright$) was open to various interpretations throughout the period according to context, ranging from a straightforward prolongation, at the performer's will, of the note, chord or rest thus indicated to improvised embellishment of that note or chord or even an extended cadenza. In the latter case, a passage or section of variable length and indefinite form was normally extemporised by the performer but sometimes written out (the older type of written-out quasi-cadenza normally above the *tasto solo* bass, as exemplified in Corelli's sonatas, still persisted in the eighteenth century), perhaps even playing a fully integrated part in the structure of the movement (as in the harpsichord cadenza in the first movement of Bach's Fifth Brandenburg Concerto). Derived from the vocal aria as a natural result of ornamenting cadences (*cadenza* means 'cadence' in Italian), it was generally introduced near the end of a composition (normally a concerto) or movement on a pause either on the dominant of the key or, in the case of the classical concerto, on the tonic six-four chord. Ending with a trill on the dominant chord, it served as a vehicle for technical display, although, certainly in the mid eighteenth century, musicianship and tasteful expression were the prime considerations of most theorists.

Although preceded by Tosi's rather limited survey, Quantz's account appears to be the first comprehensive and fully illustrated eighteenth-century discussion of cadenzas and it served as a model for many later studies, especially that of Türk.[31] Quantz was the first writer to expand the largely ornamental early-eighteenth-century concept of the cadenza, normally comprising mere elaborations of the final cadence, into a more meaningful part of the musical design, recommending that cadenzas should be constructed of the main motifs of the composition. However, it appears that such a recommendation was commonly ignored, soloists too often succumbing to the temptation of displaying virtuosity at the expense of musicality.[32] Indeed, even the conservative Leopold Mozart admitted the use of special effects such as the trill in sixths and the accelerating trill with *crescendo* in cadenzas; nevertheless, musicianship predominates and these effects represent his rare concessions to technical display.[33] The actual length of the cadenza – one only was deemed sufficient in the mid eighteenth century – depended to some extent on the solo instrument, Quantz advising singers and wind players to make their cadenzas last no longer than a single breath but claiming that 'a string player can make them as long as he likes, if he is rich enough in inventiveness. Reasonable brevity, however, is more advantageous than vexing length.'[34] Quantz also

31. Tosi, *Opinioni* . . ., tr. Galliard, ch. 8, pp. 128-9; Quantz, *Versuch* . . ., tr. and ed. Reilly, ch. 15, pp. 179-95; Türk, *Klavierschule* . . ., ch. 5, section 2.
32. Quantz, *Versuch* . . ., tr. and ed. Reilly, ch. 15, §18, pp. 185-6.
33. L. Mozart, *Versuch* . . ., ch. 10, §7, pp. 220-1 & ch. 10, §31, p. 235.
34. Quantz, *Versuch* . . ., tr. and ed. Reilly, ch. 15, §17, p. 185.

mentions cadenzas for two soloists but emphasises that, for obvious reasons, such examples should be pre-planned by the soloists concerned.

The classical and early romantic eras witnessed an expansion in the scope of the cadenza. It was normally of considerable length and meaningful musical substance and fulfilled an architectural function, with its climactic passage for the soloist balancing the orchestral exposition in the concerto structure, as well as the dramatic one of allowing the soloist free rein for unfettered solo display. Some cadenzas were written out by the composer either for use in performance or as models for students to imitate. Most of the authentic cadenzas (after c. 1777) by Mozart for his piano concertos (for example, K. 271 and K. 488) and to a certain extent the written-out cadenza in his *Sinfonia Concertante* in E flat major for violin and viola, K. 364 serve as excellent models of the classical cadenza. Although they display great variety and a wide range of imagination in their content, the majority of extant piano concerto cadenzas adopt a tripartite design (with the exception of some second and third movement examples) bound together, as it were, in one harmonic progression, the first (and largest) subdivision commencing either with one of the chief themes of the movement (for example, K. 453, first movement) or with an energetic flourish (which may also have thematic affinities; for example, K. 271, first movement) emanating naturally from the six-four chord. This is followed by a more reflective section, invariably sequential in nature, passing through but rarely establishing a variety of close keys and incorporating thematic and/or motivic material from the main part of the movement. A descent to a sustained chord or long note in the lower register eventually serves as a point of departure for further technical display, incorporating scalic runs, arpeggios and suchlike, prior to the brief, normally non-thematic (the first movement of K. 453 is one notable exception) closing transition to the final cadential trill on the dominant seventh.

The early nineteenth century witnessed further changes. Beethoven, whilst preserving the tradition of cadenza improvisation in his first four piano concertos and his violin concerto (later rewritten for piano with a written-out cadenza for piano and solo timpani), composed cadenzas as an integral part of his Fifth Piano Concerto, Op. 73 ('The Emperor'). This precedent was imitated by many of his successors (for example, Schumann and Brahms), together with the increased practice of writing out independent cadenzas in full (as, for example, in Mendelssohn's Violin Concerto in E minor, Op. 64) in order to counteract the abuse of virtuoso technique and lack of invention displayed by contemporary performers at a time when the art of improvisation was essentially on the decline.

Baillot's survey of cadenzas, which is unequalled in a violin manual during our period, concentrates mainly on eighteenth-century practice and considers fermatas and cadenzas together, probably because of the common difficulty of differentiating between certain ornamental passages and true cadenzas. He defines ten types of cadenza (*point d'orgue*) and includes appropriate examples.

Pauses

There are several types of pauses; they are all indicated only by this sign . . .⌢ ‿

However, they should not all be played in the same manner; it is necessary to define them, each in detail in order to avoid all uncertainty and confusion.

No. 1 Pause. To which nothing is added.

Ex. 418

(Viotti: Concerto no. 9)

No. 2 Pause. After which a small passage may be added between the *cadenza*-sign or *pause* and the following note.

Ex. 419

(Haydn: Quartet no. 20)

No. 3 Total pause or silence. After which the note must cease.

Ex. 420

(Beethoven: Quartet no. 14)

(Beethoven: Quintet no. 3)

(Haydn: Quartet no. 38)

One cannot recommend too strongly that with these concluding pauses or silences one should hold the rest long enough for the effect to be noticeable. For the silence to contrast with the movement that has gone before, it needs to be of a certain duration to be effective. Reason demands that it should be so, but feeling does more, for it can make silence most eloquent at the right moment: 'The musician's creative genius holds sway over the entire universe with his art, he paints every picture in sound, he makes silence itself speak.' (J. J. Rousseau)

No. 4 Cadenza (*Point d'orgue*).

It is a *pause* so called because originally the organ sustained the tonic or dominant throughout its duration.

When this *pause* is on the *tonic*, it is only a *suspension* which demands only a simple *turn* (*tournure*) of very little extent.[35]

Ex. 421

Suspensions and turns on the *tonic*

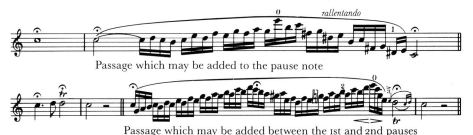

Passage which may be added to the pause note

Passage which may be added between the 1st and 2nd pauses

Turn on the *dominant*, to lead to the final cadence

Passage which may be added between the 2nd pause and the trill.

See, below, the examples of *suspensions* and *turns* in all the keys, at letter A and letter B.

'The cadenza strictly defined is that which is made on the *dominant* and to which a certain development is given. It is called *cadenza*, because it is used on the 1st note of a final cadence, and it is also called *arbitrio*, on account of the freedom that is allowed to the performer to give rein to his ideas and follow his own taste.'[36]

But there are several types of *cadenza* which it is important not to confuse, since nothing can succeed in being good, above all in matters of embellishment, unless it is done properly.

Therefore one can play a *cadenza* with or without barlines, written out or not, or equally one may make it more or less extensive according to whether it is introduced on a larger or smaller scale by the movement of the bass or the *Tutti* which precedes it.

35. The term 'suspension' should not be understood here in the harmonic sense of a note of one chord sustained during the sounding of another chord (of which the suspended note forms no part). Instead, it has affiliations with the eighteenth-century *agrément*, indicated by a fermata-like symbol, in which the written note is delayed by a short rest (for example, $\widehat{P}$ = ᜎ); however, here the delay is caused by a 'turn' (in this case not the specific ornament discussed in the previous chapter but simply an embellishment of variable and undefined length around the note in question).

36. *Dictionnaire de musique moderne*, ed. Castil-Blaze. (Baillot's footnote)

Examples of all kinds of cadenzas

We will divide the *cadenzas* in this way.
1. Suspensions or turns on the *tonic* .... letter A. 1
2. Slightly extended *cadenzas*, or turns on the *dominant* to lead up to the final cadence .... letter A. 2, B. 1 and B. 2.
3. *Cadenzas* with a pedal or bass note sustained to the end .... letter C.
4. Without pedal and without modulation .... letter D.
5. With accompaniment and modulation .... letter E.
6. Without accompaniment, with modulation .... letter F.
7. Drawn from the subject .... letter G.
8. Subject mixed with passages played at whim .... letter H.
9. Entirely according to one's fancy .... letter I.
10. Returning to the theme without interruption and being linked to it by what is called a re-entry .... letter J.

The *cadenzas* which have just been designated are presented below as *examples* and cannot be given as *models*, as this type of embellishment is left to the taste of the performer; but no matter what type of *cadenza* is used, it is particularly necessary to note that as the *cadenza* is by its nature a *pause*, one should begin by establishing this pause by playing a long held note to separate it from what has gone before, then by means of slight intermediate pauses evoke its origin, its independent and capricious pace and its inspired dreaming and then lastly make a final pause with a trill of more than two bars' length, in order to define the conclusion clearly.

Ex. 422

CADENZAS

called turns or suspensions, on the tonic

CADENZAS

of little length, or turns on the dominant, to lead to the final cadence

TERMINATIONS OF CADENCES

Other terminations in C major

Ex. 422 (cont.)

SAME TERMINATIONS OF CADENCES
In all the keys.

Letter B. 2

CADENZA
with pedal or bass note sustained until the end

Letter C.

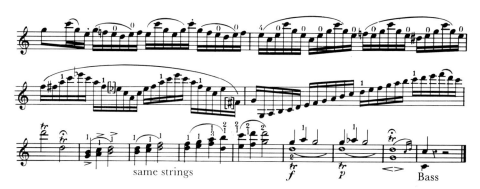

Without pedal and without modulation

With accompaniment and modulation
(Viotti: Concerto no. 22)

Ex. 422 (cont.)

Subject mixed with passages played at whim

Letter H

(Baillot, *L'art* . . . (1834), pp. 165–82, selected examples only)

Appendix

Instruction books for the violin c. 1760 – c. 1840, arranged in chronological order by country of publication

France & Belgium

c. 1760   Tessarini, C., *Nouvelle méthode pour apprendre par théorie dans un mois de tems à jouer du violon divisée en trois classes avec des leçons à deux violons, par gradation* (Liège [1760], 2nd edn, Paris & Amsterdam [1760], 3rd edn, Paris & Amsterdam [1760])

         Lolli, A., *L'école du violon en quatuor, œuvre 8* (Paris, c. 1760)

         Anon., *Nouvelle méthode pour apprendre à jouer du violon et à lire la musique. Divisée en deux parties* (Tours, c. 1760)

1761   L'Abbé le fils (J.-B. Saint-Sevin), *Principes du violon pour apprendre le doigté de cet instrument, et les différens agrémens dont il est susceptible* (Paris [1761]/R1961, 2nd edn, 1772)

1763   Brijon, E. R., *Réflexions sur la musique et la vraie manière de l'exécuter sur le violon* (Paris, 1763/R1972)

1766   Anon., *Tablature idéale du violon jugée par feu M. Le Clair l'aîné être la véritable* (Paris, 1766)

1768   Leone, P., *Méthode raisonnée pour passer du violon à la mandoline et de l'archet à la plume ou le moyen seur [sic] de jouer sans maître en peu de temps par des signes de convention assortis à des exemples de musique facile* (Paris, 1768, 2nd edn, c. 1770, 3rd edn, [1773])

1771   Anon., *Manière de graduer un violon* (Paris, 1771)

1772   Labadens, J. B., *Nouvelle méthode pour apprendre à jouer du violon et à lire la musique, divisée en quatre parties* (Paris [1772], 2nd edn, 1797)

c. 1774   Tarade, T.-J., *Traité du violon ou règles de cet instrument à l'usage de ceux qui veulent en jouer avec la parfaite connoissance du ton dans lequel on est* (Paris, c. 1774/R1972)

c. 1775   Dupont, J.-B., *Principes de violon* (Paris, c. 1775)

1779   Bailleux, A., *Méthode raisonnée pour apprendre à jouer du violon* (Paris, 1779, 2nd edn [1798])

1782   Corrette, M., *L'art de se perfectionner dans le violon* (Paris [1782]/R1973)

         Anon., *La parfaite connoissance du manche du violon* (Paris, 1782)

1786   Bornet (*l'aîné*), *Nouvelle méthode de violon et de musique* (Paris [1786], 2nd edn, c. 1795, 3rd edn, c. 1799)

c. 1790   Cambini, G. G., *Méthode de violon* (Paris, c. 1790)

         Thiémé, F., *Principes abrégés de musique à l'usage de ceux qui veulent apprendre à jouer du violon* (Paris, c. 1790)

         Anon., *Principes pour apprendre facilement à jouer du violon* (Paris, c. 1790)

368

1791   Alban (*l'aîné*), *Méthode de violon* (Paris, 1791?)

c. 1795   Alday (*l'aîné*), *Nouvelle méthode de violon* (Lyons, c. 1795)

Cambini, G. G., *Petite méthode de violon* (Paris, c. 1795)

1796   Durieu, *Méthode de violon* (Paris, 1796)

1798   Cartier, J.-B., *L'art du violon ou collection choisie dans les sonates des écoles italienne, françoise et allemande précédée d'un abrégé des principes pour cet instrument* (Paris [1798], 2nd edn, [1799]/R1977, 3rd enlarged edn, c. 1801)

Lorenziti, B., *Principes ou nouvelle méthode de musique pour apprendre facilement à jouer du violon suivis de douze duos progressifs* (Paris [1798], 2nd ? edn, 1800)

c. 1800   Anicot (*l'aîné*), *Principes de violon rendus assez clairs et assez détaillés pour apprendre en peu de tems* (Paris, c. 1800)

Bedard, J.-B., *Nouvelle méthode de violon courte et intelligible précédée d'un abbrégé des connaissances essentielles de la musique en général* (Paris [1800])

Henry, B., *Méthode de violon* (Paris, c. 1800)

Lachnith, L. W., *Exercices sur les quatre cordes du violon; ou méthode simple et facile pour apprendre les premiers principes de cet instrument* (Paris, c. 1800)

Lolli, A., *L'art du violon* (Paris, c. 1800)

Marcou, F. (Pierre?), *Principes de musique, pour faciliter les personnes qui veulent apprendre rapidement et sans confusion cet art. Suivis de principes de violon* (Paris, 1800)

Woldemar, M., *Grande méthode ou étude élémentaire pour le violon* (Paris, c. 1800, 2nd edn, c. 1800)

Abrégé de la grande méthode de violon (Paris, c. 1800)

1801   Woldemar, M., *Méthode de violon par L. Mozart rédigée par Woldemar, élève de Lolli. Nouvelle édition* (Paris, 1801)

1803   Baillot, P. M. F. de S., Rode, P., & Kreutzer, R., *Méthode de violon* (Paris, 1803/R1974)

Cambini, G. G., *Nouvelle méthode théorique et pratique pour le violon divisée en trois parties* (Paris [1803]/R1972)

1804   Marcou, F. (Pierre?), *Méthode simple et facile, par demandes et par réponses, pour apprendre rapidement et sans confusion la musique, suivie des principes du violon et de l'explication des termes italiens* (Paris [1804])

1804   Bruni, A. B., *Nouvelle méthode de violon très claire et très facile* (Paris, 1806, 2nd? edn, c. 1810)

1808   Demar, J., *Nouvelle méthode abrégée pour le violon* (Orléans & Paris, 1808)

Lottin, D., *Principes élémentaires de musique et de violon à l'usage des commençans* (Paris, 1808)

c. 1810   Demar, J. S., *Méthode de violon, avec 40 duos faisant suite de la méthode* (Paris, c. 1810)

Martinn, J. J. B., *Méthode élémentaire pour le violon* (Paris, c. 1810, 2nd? edn, c. 1815)

1812   Hering, K. G., *Les commandemens du violon* (Paris, 1812)

c. 1815   Dupierge, F. T. A., *Méthode de violon* (Paris, c. 1815)

Perrin, *Méthode de violon* (Paris, c. 1815)

1817   Billiard, J.-P., *Méthode de violon* (Paris, 1817)

Vaillant, P. M. G., *Méthode de violon* (Paris, c. 1817)

1818   Baillard, *Méthode de violon* (Paris, 1818)

c. 1820   Cadot, C., *Méthode élémentaire pour le violon* (Paris, c. 1820)

Chevesailles, *Petite méthode de violon* (Paris, c. 1820)

Fauré, F., *Nouveaux principes de violon à l'usage des commençants pour servir d'introduction à la Méthode du Conservatoire* (Paris, c. 1820, 2nd rev. edn, c. 1825)

Frey, G., *Méthode élémentaire de violon* (Paris, c. 1820)

c. 1822   Garaudé, A. de, *Méthode de violon* (Paris, c. 1822)

c. 1825   Alday (*fils*), *Première grande méthode pour le violon* (Lyons, c. 1825)

Turbry, F. L. H., *Méthode de violon sympathique* (Paris, c. 1825)

c. 1826   Martinn, J. J. B., *Grande méthode de violon* (Paris, c. 1826)
    Petite méthode de violon (Paris, c. 1826)
    Anon., *Gamme de violon avec les principes de la musique* (Paris, c. 1826, 2nd? enlarged edn, c. 1827)
    Méthode petite de violin (Paris, c. 1826)
c. 1827   Müller, *Méthode de violon* (Paris, c. 1827)
    Roy, C. E., *Petite méthode de violon* (Paris, c. 1827, rev. J. Javelot, Paris, 1884)
    Roy, P., *Méthode de violon* (Paris, c. 1827)
c. 1828   Le Carpentier, A. C., *Méthode de violon* (Paris, c. 1828)
1830   Mazas, J. F., *Méthode de violon, suivie d'un traité des sons harmoniques en simple et double corde Oe. 34* (Paris, 1830, rev. V. Bretonnière, Paris, c. 1850)
    Pastou, F. J. B., *Méthode élémentaire pour le violon avec une théorie nouvelle sur la manière d'employer l'archet* (Paris, c. 1830)
c. 1831   Corret (*l'aîné*) *Méthode de violon, Oe. II* (Paris, c. 1831)
c. 1832   Mazas, J. F., *Petite méthode de violon extraite de la grande* (Paris & Bonn, c. 1832)
1834   Baillot, P. M. F. de Sales, *L'art du violon: nouvelle méthode* (Paris, 1834)
c. 1836   Wanski, J. N., *Grande méthode de violon* (Paris?, c. 1836)
1837   Bergerre, A. B., *Méthode de violon adoptée par le Conservatoire de Paris, Oe. 46* (Paris, 1837)
c. 1839   Fontaine, A., *Méthode élémentaire et progressive de violon* (Paris, c. 1839)
    Gasse, F., *Méthode de violon d'après les principes du Conservatoire et servant d'introduction à la Méthode publiée par cet établissement* (Paris, c. 1839)
c. 1840   Guichard, *Ecole du violon* (Paris, c. 1840)
    Habeneck, F. A., *Méthode théorique et pratique de violon, précédée des principes de musique et quelques notes en facsimile de l'écriture de Viotti* (Paris, c. 1840)
    Roger, A., *Grande méthode de violon Oe. 19* (Paris, c. 1840)
    Wanski, J. N. *Grande méthode de violon* (Paris?, c. 1840)
    Petite méthode de violon pour les commençants (Paris?, c. 1840)

Germany & Austria

1763   Kürzinger, I. F. X., *Getreuer Unterricht zum Singen mit Manieren, und die Violin zu spielen* (Augsburg, 1763, 2nd edn, 1780, 3rd edn, 1793)
1767   Petri, J. S. *Anleitung zur praktischen Musik für neuangehende Sänger und Instrumentalspieler* (Leipzig, 1767, 2nd rev. edn, 1782/R1969)
1774   Löhlein, G. S., *Anweisung zum Violinspielen, mit praktischen Beyspielen und zur Übung mit vier und zwanzig kleinen Duetten erläutert* (Leipzig & Züllichau, 1774, 2nd rev. edn, 1781); ed. J. F. Reichardt (Leipzig & Züllichau, 1797)
1776   Reichardt, J. F., *Ueber die Pflichten des Ripien-Violinisten* (Berlin & Leipzig, 1776)
1786   Schweigl, I., *Verbesserte Grundlehre der Violin, zur Erleichterung der Lehrer und zum Vortheil der Schüler* (Vienna, 1786, 2nd rev. edn, 1794)
1787   Kauer, F., *Kurzgefasste Violinschule für Anfänger* (Vienna, 1787)
    Kobrich, J. J. A. B., *Johann Anton Kobrichs praktisches Geig-Fundament, das sich mehr in Zeichen und Noten, als in vielen ausgesinnten Erklärungen für schwächere Lehrlinge leicht ausgezeichnet* (Augsburg, 1787)
c. 1790   Campagnoli, B., *L'art d'inventer à l'improviste des fantaisies et cadences pour le violon* (Leipzig, c. 1790)
1792   Hiller, J. A., *Anweisung zum Violinspielen, für Schulen und zum Selbstunterrichte* (Leipzig [1792], 2nd edn, 1795)
1795   Schweigl, I., *Grundlehre der Violin* (Vienna, 1795)
c. 1800   Lefils (or Fils), *Méthode très-facile pour jouer au violon les sons harmoniques dans tous les tons majeurs et mineurs* (Vienna, 1800)

Kauer, F., *Neuverfasste Violinschule nebst Tönstücken zur Uebung* (Vienna, c. 1800)

1803 Fenkner, J. A., *Anweisung zum Violinspielen* (Halle, 1803)

1804 Wranitzky (or Wraniczky), A., *Violin Fondament nebst einer vorhergehenden Anzeige über die Haltung sowohl der Violine, als auch des Bogens* (Vienna, 1804)

1807 André, J. A., *Anleitung zum Violinspielen in stufenweise geordneten Uebungsstücken, Op. 30* (Offenbach, 1807)

1810 Hering, K. G., *Praktische Violinschule nach einer neuen, leichten und zweckmässigen Stufenfolge* (Leipzig, 1810)

Froehlich, F. J., *Vollständige theoretisch-praktische Musikschule für alle beym Orchester gebräuchliche wichtigere Instrumente* (Cologne & Bonn, 1810–11)

1812 Blumenthal, J. von, *Kurzgefasste theoretisch-praktische Violinschule* (Vienna, 1812)

1815 Maass, J. G. E., 'Ueber die Flaschinettöne, besonders der Saiten', *Allgemeine musikalische Zeitung* (July 1815), cols. 477–87

Froehlich, F. J., *Violinschule nach den besten Meistern bearbeitet* (Mainz, c. 1815)

Schiedermayer, J. B., *Neue theoretische und praktische Violinschule: ein zweckmässiger Auszug aus L. Mozarts grosse Violinschule* (Mainz, c. 1815)

Waldenfeld, H. von, *Kleine Violinschule bei ersten Unterrichte* (Brunswick, c. 1815)

1819 Küster, J. H., 'Einiges über die Ausübung der Flageolettöne auf der Violine', *Allgemeine musikalische Zeitung* (October 1819), cols. 701–7

c. 1823 Anon., *Gamme et positions sur le violon* (Berlin, c. 1823)

c. 1825 Kieninger, J. M., *Theoretische und praktische Anleitung für angehende Violinspieler, nach den besten Methoden eingerichtet* (Graz, c. 1825)

Anon., *Violinschule praktische, oder Sammlung leichter Arien . . . aus neuen Werken berühmter Componisten* (Leipzig, c. 1825)

c. 1826 Schall, C., *Scalen für 2 Violinen zum Gebrauch für Lehrer und Schüler, mit einer kurzgefassten Violinschule* (Leipzig, c. 1826)

Anon., *Gamme pour violon, alto et violoncelle* (Offenbach & Augsburg, c. 1826)

1829 Guhr, C., *Ueber Paganinis Kunst die Violine zu spielen; ein Anhang zu jeder bis jetzt erschienen Violinschule nebst einer Abhandlung über das Flageoletspiel in einfachen und Doppeltönen* (Mainz [1829]; Fr. tr., Paris [1830]; It. tr., Milan, 1834; Eng. tr., London [1915])

Blumenthal, J. von. *Abhandlung über die Eigenthümlichkeit des Flageolet als Anleitung zur praktischen Ausübung desselben auf der Violine, Op. 43* (Vienna, c. 1829)

c. 1830 Dominik, F., *Neue theoretisch-praktische Violinschule in zwei Abtheilungen* (Augsburg, c. 1830)

1832 Spohr, L., *Violinschule . . . mit erlaeuternden Kupfertafeln* (Vienna [1832]; Fr. tr., Heller, Paris, c. 1870; It. tr., Chiasso, c. 1840; Eng. tr., C. Rudolphus, London [1833], J. Bishop, London [1843], F. Marshall, rev. H. Holmes, London [1878])

Mazas, J. F., *Traité des sons harmoniques Oe. 35* [extracted from the *Méthode de violon*] (Bonn, c. 1832)

André, J. A., *Lehrbuch der Tonkunst* (Offenbach, 1832–43)

1834 Barnbeck, F., *Theoretisch praktische Anleitung zum Violinspiel für Dilettanten, namentlich auch Schullehrer, Seminaristen und alle Solche, denen es an Gelegenheit oder Mitteln zu einem gründlichen Unterrichte in der Violinspielkunst fehlt, daher mit besonderer Rücksicht auf den Selbstunterricht* (Stuttgart, 1834)

c. 1835 Kastner, J. G., *Elementarschule für die Violine mit einem Anhang von Übungstücken* (Leipzig, c. 1835)

c. 1840 Birgfeldt, *Neue praktische Violinschule* (Hamburg, c. 1840)

Eckhardt, *Praktischer Unterricht zur Erlernung der Violine* (Bonn & Elberfeld, c. 1840)

Gébauer, M. J. le jeune, *Principes élémentaires de la musique: positions et gammes de violon Oe. 10* (Mainz, c. 1840)

Kindscher, L. *Elementarunterricht für Violinspieler, oder Anleitung auf die Violine bald sicher und rein greifen lernen* (Chemnitz, c. 1840)

Meilhan, P. C., *Die Schule der Geläufigkeit, in sechzehn Studien Op. 7* (Leipzig, c. 1840)

Michaelis, F. A., *Praktische Violinschule* (Breslau, c. 1840)

Straub, C. G., *Kurze Anleitung zum Violinspielen nebst 40 stufenmässig geordneten Duetten für die ersten Anfänger* (Stuttgart, c. 1840)

Volckmar, A. V. W., *Violinschule zum Gebrauch für Schullehrerseminarien und Seminar-präparandenschulen Op. 2* (Kassel, c. 1840)

Wohlfahrt, H., *Der Violinfreund; ein progressiver Violinunterricht für Kinder, in zwei Heften* (Meissen, c. 1840)

Schule der Anfänger im Violinspiel (Meissen, c. 1840)

Violinschule für Kinder, oder musikalischer Elementarunterricht in einer Naturgemäss (Meissen, c. 1840)

Zimmermann, C. F. A., *Praktische Violinschule vollendet von Franz Schubert* (Dresden, c. 1840)

Italy

1770   Tartini, G., *Lettera del defonto Signor Giuseppe Tartini alla Signora Maddalena Lombardini inserviente ad una importante lezione per i suonatori di violino* (Venice, 1770; Eng. tr., C. Burney, London, 1771/R1967, 2nd edn, 1779; Ger. tr., H. L. Rohrmann, Hanover, 1786)

1781   Anon., *Riflessioni d'un professore di violino sopra un discorso morale e politico intorno il teatro recitato nella Congregazione dei Signori di Codogno nel giorno 22 di Ottobre dello scorso anno 1780, ed indi stampato in Piacenza* (Piacenza, 1781, 2nd edn, Lugano, 1782)

1791   Galeazzi, F., *Elementi teorico-pratici di musica, con un saggio sopra l'arte di suonare il violino analizzata, ed a dimostrabili principi ridotta* (2 vols., Rome, 1791-6, 2nd edn, 1 vol., 1817)

c. 1797   Campagnoli, B., *Metodo della mecanica progressive per violino diviso in 5 parti distribuite in 132 lezioni progressive per 2 Violini e 118 studi per violino solo Op. 21* (Milan, 1797?/R1945, 2nd edn, 1803, 3rd? edn, c. 1828; Fr. & Ger. tr., Leipzig, 1824; Eng. tr., J. A. Hamilton, London, c. 1830, 2nd edn, 1834, tr. J. Bishop, London, 1856)

1811   Scaramelli, G., *Saggie sopra di doveri di un primo violino direttore d'orchestra* (Trieste, 1811)

1823   Tonelli, L., *Metodo completo per il violino, diviso in due parti* (Milan [1823])

c. 1827   Giovanni, N. de, 'Metodo teorico pratico per ben fare sul violino gli armonici semplici, trillati e doppi' (MS, privately owned, dating from c. 1827-8)

Great Britain

c. 1760   Bremner, R., (attrib.), *The compleat tutor for the violin* (London, c. 1760, 2nd edn, c. 1765, 3rd edn, c. 1770)

Anon., [*The Muses delight*] *The complete tutor or familiar instructions for the voice, violin, harpsichord, German-flute, hautboy, French-horn, common-flute, bassoon and bass-violin* ([Liverpool], c. 1760)

1762   Zuccari, C., *The true method of playing an Adagio made easy by twelve examples, first in a plain manner with a bass, then with all their graces. Adaptet [sic] for those who study the violin* (London, 1762)

c. 1765   Tessarini, C., *An accurate method to attain the art of playing ye violin, with graces, in all the different keys, how to make proper cadences, and ye nature of all ye shifts, with severall duets and lessons for that instrument* (London, c. 1765)

1766   Philpot, S., *An introduction to the art of playing on the violin, on an entire new plan, calculated for laying a regular foundation for young beginners, explained by such easy rules and principles as will enable a scholar to acquire a proper method for performing on that instrument* (London, 1766, 2nd edn, 1767)

c. 1775   Geminiani, F. (supposititious work?), *New and compleat instructions for the violin* (London, c. 1775, 2nd edn, c. 1790, 3rd edn, c. 1799, 4th edn, c. 1806)

c. 1780   Gehot, J., *Complete instructions for every musical instrument. Containing a treatise on practical music in general, to which is added the scale or gamut for thirty five different instruments* (London, c. 1780)

1790   Gehot, J., *A complete instructor for every instrument* (London, 1790)

   The art of bowing on the violin, calculated for the practice and improvement of juvenile performers (London, c. 1790)

   Barthélemon, F. H., *A new tutor for the violin, in which is introduced principal rules . . . of music* (London, c. 1790)

c. 1792   Geminiani, F. (supposititious work?), *The entire new and compleat tutor for the violin* (London, c. 1792, 2nd edn, c. 1800, 3rd edn, c. 1800, 4th edn, c. 1800)

c. 1795   Anon., *Compleat instructions for the violin, containing the easiest and best methods for learners to obtain a proficiency, with some useful directions, lessons, graces . . . by Geminiani* (London, c. 1795)

c. 1796   Tashanberg, J., *The compleat school or the art of playing the violin with seventy-one variations, cadences, preludes and capricios* (London, 1796?)

c. 1800   Perry, J., *New and improved tutor for the violin, comprising the rudiments of music and method of tuning etc.* (London, c. 1800)

c. 1805   Jousse, J., *The modern violin preceptor* (London, 1805?)

1810   Goodban, T., *A new and complete guide to the art of playing on the violin* (London, 1810)

1811   Jousse, J., *The theory and practice of the violin* (London, 1811)

1813   Keith, R. W., *A violin preceptor on an entirely new principle calculated to lay a regular and stable foundation for young practitioners and to facilitate their early progress on that instrument* (London, 1813)

c. 1815   Paine, J., *Treatise on the violin: showing how to ascertain the true degree of time, by a peculiar method of bowing; exemplified by a tune attached to each degree* (London, c. 1815, 3rd edn, 1820?)

1820   Cobham, C., *Harmonic system for the violin. A treatise on single and double harmonics* (London [1820])

1824   Loder, J. D., *A general and comprehensive instruction book for the violin* (London, 1824, 2nd edn, 1828, 3rd edn, 1837, 5th edn, 1841)

1825   Challoner, N. B., *Instructions for the violin. In which, in addition to the rudiments progressively arranged, care has been taken to introduce lessons expressly adapted to the instrument with the view of facilitating the progress of the pupil and preventing unnecessary trouble to the master* (London, 1825)

   Howell, T., *Original instructions for the violin, illustrated by precepts and examples* (Bristol, 1825)

1829   Howell, T., *Practical elementary examples for the violin, consisting of a systematic progression of original lessons with copious rules for obtaining an effective and elegant method of bowing. Designed as an auxiliary work to the author's Original Instructions for the Violin* (London, 1829)

c. 1830   James, W. *A new and compleat tutor for the violin, wherein the science is clearly explained especially in the art of bowing, with a selection of favourite airs* (London, c. 1830)

   Präger, H. A., *Elementary and practical school for the violin, in three parts* (London, c. 1830)

   Campagnoli, B., *A complete treatise on harmonics for the violin Op. posth.* (London, 183–?)

1831   Anon., *Practical rules for producing harmonic notes on the violin* (Bury St Edmunds & London, 1831)

c. 1835 Hack, R., *New and original instructions for the violin* (London, c. 1835)

1840   Thomson, A., *New and improved violin instructor, with a catechism for the violin, to which is added a collection of popular tunes* (London [1840])

Glover, C. W., *An elementary treatise on the violin* (London, c. 1840)

Hamilton, J. A., *Catechism of the violin* (London, c. 1840, 5th edn, 1848)

A complete and popular course of instructions for the violin (London, c. 1840)

West, W., *The art of playing the violin on a new principle by which the progress of the learner is greatly facilitated* (London [1840])

Anon., *Paganini's method of producing the harmonic double stops* (London, 1840)

Other countries

1771   Ferandiere, D. F., *Prontuario músico, para el instrumentista de violin, y cantor* (Malaga, 1771)

1777   Signoretti, P. (Giuseppe?), *Méthode contenant les principes de la musique et du violon* (The Hague, 1777)

1784   'I. A.' (attrib. I. Astachofi), *Ecole de violon ou l'enseignement du jeu du violon* (St Petersburg, 1784)

1800   Holyoke (or Holycke), S., *The instrumental assistant* (Exeter, New Hampshire, 1800)

1805   Delarue, J., *New method of music taken from Italian solphège to learn readily this art and those of playing on the instrument violin, in a very short time: to wich [sic] is added a select collection of songs, airs, marches and different pieces of Paris opera* (New York, 1805)

c. 1815 Anon., *Tabelle pour le violon* (Amsterdam, c. 1815)

c. 1828 Anon., *Violin instructor, containing a plain and easy introduction to the rules and principles of the violin, together with a choice and valuable selection of popular music* (Hallowell, Maine, 1828?, 5th edn, c. 1835)

1833   Wlczek (or Vlcek), K., *Erörtete und erläuterte Geheimnisse der Violine* (Prague, 1833)

c. 1840 Schmidt, J., *Principes de violon* (Amsterdam, c. 1840)

Glossary of specific ornaments as documented in late-eighteenth- and early-nineteenth-century treatises

This glossary has been collated from the major violin treatises published during the period c. 1760–c. 1840, outlined in the Introduction, which have contributed most significantly to this volume (Baillot's survey is omitted here as it is presented in the main body of chapter 13). Arranged in chronological order by country, it is intended to summarise the range of specific ornaments generally documented in the late eighteenth and early nineteenth centuries, to catalogue some of the myriad interpretations of the (often conflicting) symbols employed to indicate specific ornaments and to complement what are arguably the most significant and detailed eighteenth-century surveys of such embellishments, namely those incorporated in Geminiani's *The art* . . . (1751), Quantz's *Versuch* . . . (1752), C. P. E. Bach's *Versuch* . . . (1753), Leopold Mozart's *Versuch* . . . (1756) and Tartini's *Traité* . . . (1771). These five surveys are excluded from this glossary for a number of reasons, not least the dates of publication of the Quantz, Bach, Geminiani and Mozart works (which place them essentially out of the period under scrutiny), the very different biases of the Quantz, Bach and Tartini volumes compared with the others discussed (for they are not primarily violin methods) and the fact that they are all easily available in splendid modern editions/translations.

Surviving evidence, though more plentiful and standardised during the late eighteenth and early nineteenth centuries than in the baroque period, is nevertheless inconsistent and rife with ambiguity. Some of the major treatises of the period fail to include any special section devoted to specific ornaments (for example, Woldemar's *Grande méthode* . . . and Guhr's *Ueber Paganinis Kunst* . . .) and have therefore been omitted from this glossary. Others admit a surfeit of examples, of which only a selection can justifiably be included in such a compilation as this, whereas a few omit explicit musical examples regarding the interpretation of ornament signs, leaving considerable interpretative onus on the student. In this latter case, where dual consideration of text and example allows a definitive interpretation to be determined, a method of execution has been suggested and marked thus (✳) to indicate that it represents my own interpretation of the available evidence. In the cases where this has not been possible – and information regarding the execution of certain ornaments is both sparse and unclear in some treatises – the example has been left untouched. Any text which may accompany these examples is included in the glossary (in abridged form) only when it is vital to clarify the correct performance of the ornament(s) concerned.

Finally, a word of warning. A glossary of this nature is liable to be somewhat arbitrary. Most ornaments, even trills and mordents, allow scope for individuality of execution, not only in the actual notes from which they may be constituted but also in the speeds, rhythm and timing adopted, the subtle application of stresses, nuances and general expression and many other variables.

FRANCE

L'Abbé le fils: Principes . . . (1761)

Des cadences

La cadence appuyée

Written:

Played:

La cadence subite (ou jettée)

Written:

Played:

La cadence feinte

Cadences Feintes préparées. Cadences feintes jettées.
Written:

Played:

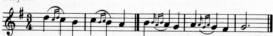

La cadence tournée

Le martellement

Written:

Played:

Le port de voix

Written:

Ports de voix suivis d'un son feint

Played:

Written:

Ports de voix suivis d'un son plein et martelé.

Played:

L'accent

Written:

Played:

Le coulé

Coulés soûtenus, suivis d'un son feint.

Coulés brefs, suivis d'un son soûtenu.

Corrette: L'art de se perfectionner . . . (1782)

[The length of the small note of the *port de voix* is according to the taste of the player and the character of the music.]

Cartier: L'art du violon (1798)

Du tremblement uni, simple

[for fast tempos]

Du tremblement tourné

[fast; expresses gaiety or tenderness, according to manner of execution]

Du port de voix

Du port de voix d'en-haut (ou supérieur)

[expresses love, affection, pleasure when long; *appoggiatura* takes half or more of value of succeeding note]

Du port de voix d'en-bas (ou inférieur)

[similar qualities as preceding: make a *pincé* on the succeeding note]

De la tenue

Du détaché

De l'anticipation

[often made with a *pincé* and *tremblement* and swelling the sound]

De la séparation

[used to span intervals of a 2nd or 3rd ascending or a 2nd descending. If the *pincé* and a *crescendo* are added on the first note then a *port de voix* should be added on the second note for the expression of tenderness.]

Du pincé [adaptable to express many 'passions']

Du tremblement

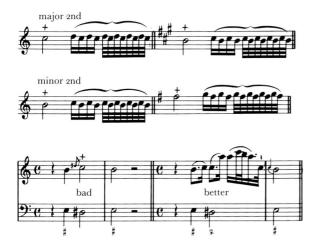

Préparations

[without preparation]

[prepared with a slow *coulé*]

[prepared with a *port de voix* and *coulé*]

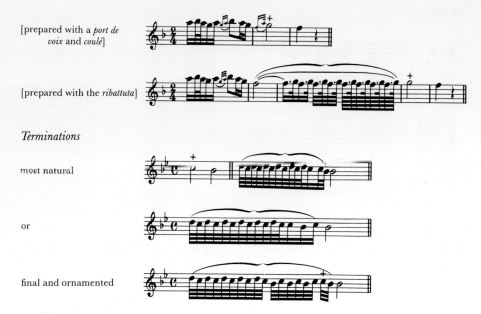

[prepared with the *ribattuta*]

Terminations

most natural

or

final and ornamented

Tremblements tournés

[All short *tremblements* (or *tremblements tournés*) are made with a fast *coulé* and two notes, of which the first descends and the other ascends diatonically.]

Accelerating trill

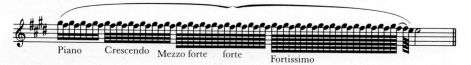

Piano   Crescendo   Mezzo forte   forte   Fortissimo

[appropriate for concluding a piece with suitable dynamics]

[Trill sequence avoiding use of open strings]

Des doubles cadences

[in 3rds involving open string]   (L'Abbé le fils)

[in 6ths]

(L. Mozart)

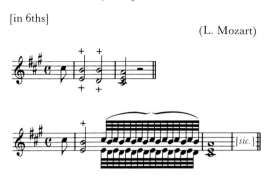

Trillo accompagnato

(L. Mozart)

(L. Mozart)

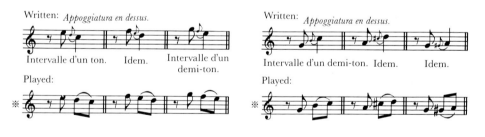

Rode, Baillot & Kreutzer: Méthode de violon (1803)

Petite note or appoggiatura

Written: *Appoggiatura en dessus.*

Intervalle d'un ton.   Idem.   Intervalle d'un demi-ton.

Played:

Written: *Appoggiatura en dessus.*

Intervalle d'un demi-ton.   Idem.   Idem.

Played:

Appoggiatura préparée

Written: préparation   préparation

Played:

Double appoggiatura

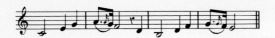

Portamento or port de voix

Trille

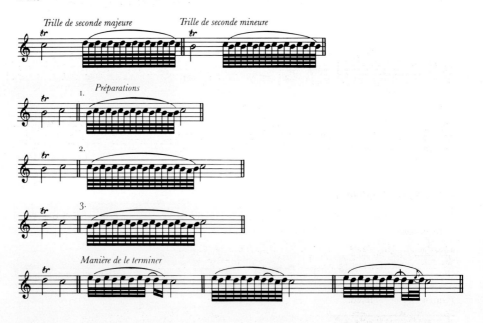

Mordant

Written: Played (i):

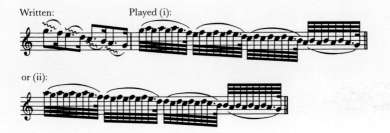

or (ii):

Suite de trilles

Petit grouppe or grupetto [*sic*]

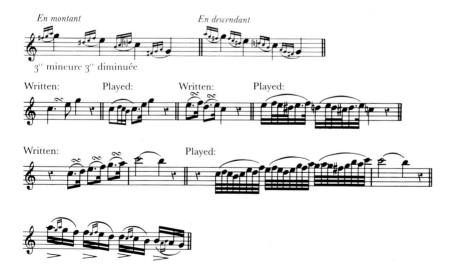

Habeneck: Méthode théorique et pratique . . . (c. 1840)

La petíte note (or appoggiatura)

Written:

Played: etc.

Acciaccatura

Written:

Played:

Le gruppetto (or mordant)

(a)
3 notes

good   good   bad   good   good
                    major 3rd

Written:

(b)
                    (*sic*)
Played:

4 notes

Written:

(c)

Played:

5 notes

Le trille appelé improprement cadence

Written:

Played:

Le brisé or petit trille

or in slower tempo

GERMANY

Spohr: Violinschule (1832)

Trill (Triller)

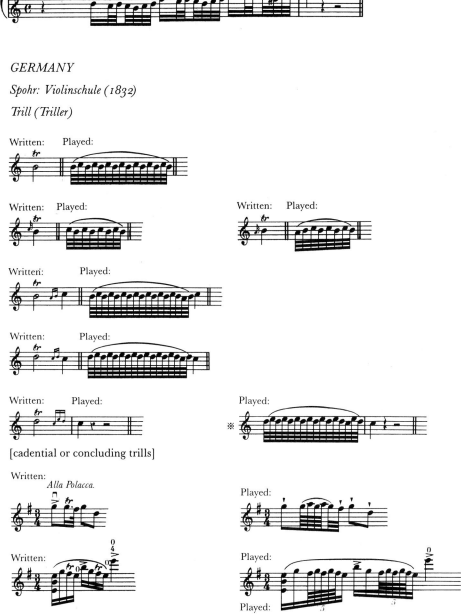

[cadential or concluding trills]

Schneller or Pralltriller

Written:

Played:

Turn (Doppelschlag)

Direct turn
Written:

Played:

Inverted turn
Written:

Played:

Written:

Played:

Written:

Played:

Written:

Played:

Written:

Played:

Written:

Played:

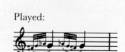

Written:

Played:

Written:

Played:

Appoggiatura (Vorschlag)

i) long

Written:

Played:

Written:

Played:

Written:

Played:

Written:

Played:

Written:

Played:

Written: Played:

ii) short

Written: Played:

Grace notes (Verzierungen)

ITALY

Galeazzi: Elementi . . . (1791–6)

Appoggiatura

(a), (b), (d) = appoggiatura di sopra
(c), (e), (f) = appoggiatura di sotto

Gruppo

Mordente [indicated by ∽ or ⌇]

mordente (or mordente discendente)   *mordente roverso (or mordente ascendente)*

Trillo

Mezzo trillo   *Trillo*   *Trillo imperfetto*

Conducimento

ascending   descending

Volata

(a)

(b)

Campagnoli: Metodo . . . (1797?)

Appoggiatura

Written:

Adagio non troppo   **Andantino grazioso**

(a)   (b)   etc.   *Dol.* [*dolce*]   (b)   *cresc.*   *f*

Played:

Written:

Allegretto

scherzando   (c)   (c)

Played:

(a) = long appoggiatura
(b) = longer appoggiatura
(c) = short appoggiatura

Written:

Larghetto

etc.

Played:

Select bibliography

With the exception of the instruction books for violin (c. 1760 – c. 1840), listed in the Appendix in chronological order by country of publication, the principal sources consulted in the preparation of this volume include the following:

Abbado, M., 'La scordatura negli strumenti ad arco e Nicolo Paganini', *La Rassegna Musicale*, vol. 13 (1940), pp. 213-26

Abbot, D. & Segerman, E., 'Gut strings', *Early Music*, vol. 4 (1976), pp. 430-7

Aldrich, P. C., 'The principal agréments of the seventeenth and eighteenth centuries: a study in musical ornamentation' (unpublished Ph.D. degree thesis, Harvard University, 1942)

    'The "authentic" performance of baroque music', in *Essays on music in honor of Archibald Thompson Davison by his associates* (Cambridge, Mass., 1957), pp. 161-71

    'Bach's technique of transcription and improvised ornamentation', *Musical Quarterly*, vol. 35 (1949), pp. 28-35

Allgemeine Theorie der schönen Künste, ed. J. G. Sulzer (2nd edn, Leipzig, 1792-4)

[Ancelet], *Observations sur la musique, les musiciens et les instruments* (Amsterdam, 1757)

André, J. A., *Lehrbuch der Tonkunst* (6 vols., Offenbach 1832-43)

Auer, L., *Violin playing as I teach it* (New York, 1921)

Avison, C., *An essay on musical expression* (London, 1752)

Axelrod, H. R., see Sheppard, L.

Babitz, S., *The violin: views and reviews* (Urbana, Illinois, 2nd edn, 1959)

    'Violin staccato in the eighteenth century' (Letters), *Musical Times,* vol. 96 (1955), p. 376

    'Learning to use the eighteenth-century violin and bow', *The Strad,* vol. 64 (1954), pp. 274-6

    'Differences between eighteenth-century and modern violin bowing', *The Score,* vol. 19 (1957), pp. 34-55

    'The problem of rhythm in baroque music', *Musical Quarterly*, vol. 38 (1952), pp. 533-65

    'Modern errors in Mozart performance', *Mozart-Jahrbuch*, vol. 15 (1967), pp. 62-89

    'Recent findings in eighteenth-century performance style', *American String Teacher*, vol. 15 (1965), pp. 10-15

    'Concerning the length of time that every note must be held', *Music Review*, vol. 28 (1967), pp. 21-37

    'Identifying the renaissance, baroque and transition violins', *The Strad*, vol. 76 (1965), pp. 9-13

Bach, C. P. E., *Versuch über die wahre Art das Clavier zu spielen* (vol. 1, Berlin, 1753/R1957, 2nd edn, 1759, 3rd rev. edn, 1787; vol. 2, Berlin, 1762/R1957, 2nd rev. edn, 1797); both vols. tr. W. J. Mitchell as *Essay on the true art of playing keyboard instruments* (New York, 1949)

Bachmann, A., *An encyclopedia of the violin* (New York, 1925/R New York, 1966)

    Le violon (lutherie, œuvres, biographies) (Paris, 1906)

Badura-Skoda, E. & P., *Mozart-Interpretation* (Vienna, 1957); tr. L. Black as *Interpreting Mozart on the keyboard* (London, 1962/R London, 1970)

Barbour, J. M., *Tuning and temperament* (Michigan, 1951)

'Violin intonation in the eighteenth century', *Journal of the American Musicological Society*, vol. 5 (1952), pp. 224-34

Barnett, D., 'Non-uniform slurring in 18th-century music: accident or design?', *Haydn Year Book*, vol. 10 (1979), pp. 179-99

Bennati, F., *Notice physiologique sur Paganini* (Brussels, 1831)

Berlioz, L. H., *Traité de l'instrumentation et d'orchestration moderne* (Paris, 1843); tr. M. C. Clarke as *A treatise on modern instrumentation* (London, 1858)

Béthizy, J. L. de, *Exposition de la théorie et de la pratique de la musique suivant les nouvelles découvertes* (2nd enlarged edn, Paris, 1764/R 1972)

Bibliographie musicale de France et de l'étranger ou répertoire général systématique de tous les traités et œuvres de musique vocale et instrumentale (anon., Paris, 1822)

Biographie universelle des musiciens et bibliographie générale de la musique, ed. F. J. Fétis (8 vols., Paris, 1835-44)

Biographisch-bibliographisches Quellenlexikon der Musiker und Musikgelehrten der christlichen Zeitrechnung bis zur Mitte des neunzehnten Jahrhunderts, ed. R. Eitner (10 vols., Leipzig, 1900-4)

Bollioud-Mermet, L., *De la corruption du goût dans la musique française* (Lyons, 1746)

Bonaventura, A., *Niccolo Paganini* (Modena, 1911)

Boomkamp, C. van L., & Meer, J. H. van der, *The Carel van Leeuwen Boomkamp collection of musical instruments* (Amsterdam, 1971)

Borrel, E., *L'interprétation de la musique française (de Lully à la révolution)* (Paris, 1934)

'Un cours d'interprétation de la musique de violon au XVIIIᵉ siècle par Cambini', *Revue de musicologie* (1929), pp. 120-4.

Boyden, D. D., *The history of violin playing from its origins to 1761* (London, 1965)

Catalogue of the Hill collection of musical instruments in the Ashmolean Museum, Oxford (London, 1969)

'The violin', in A. Baines, ed., *Musical instruments through the ages* (Harmondsworth, 1961)

'Violin' (1-11), *The new Grove dictionary of music and musicians* (London, 1980)

'Bow' (1: 2-4, 11), *The new Grove dictionary of music and musicians* (London, 1980)

'Der Geigenbogen von Corelli bis Tourte', in V. Schwarz, ed., *Violinspiel und Violinmusik in Geschichte und Gegenwart* (Vienna, 1975), pp. 295-310

'The violin bow in the eighteenth century', *Early Music*, vol. 8 (1980), pp. 199-212

'The violin and its technique: new horizons in research', *Bericht über den siebenten internationalen musikwissenschaftlichen Kongress Köln 1958*, ed. G. Abraham, S. Clercx-Lejeune, H. Federhofer & W. Pfannkuch (Kassel, 1959)

'The violin and its technique in the eighteenth century', *Musical Quarterly*, vol. 36 (1950), pp. 9-38

'Geminiani and the first violin tutor', *Acta Musicologica*, vol. 31 (1959), pp. 161-70

'A postscript to "Geminiani and the first violin tutor" ', *Acta Musicologica*, vol. 32 (1960), pp. 40-7

'The missing Italian manuscript of Tartini's *Traité des Agrémens*', *Musical Quarterly*, vol. 46 (1960), pp. 315-28

'Prelleur, Geminiani and just intonation', *Journal of the American Musicological Society*, vol. 4 (1951), pp. 202-19

'Dynamics in seventeenth- and eighteenth-century music', in *Essays on music in honor of Archibald Thompson Davison by his associates* (Cambridge, Mass., 1957), pp. 185-93

Bremner, R., *Some thoughts on the performance of concert music* (London, 1777/R London, 1972)

Brossard, S. de, 'Fragments d'une méthode de violon' (MS, c. 1712, Bibliothèque Nationale, Paris)

Burney, C., *The present state of music in France and Italy* (London, 1773/R New York, 1969)
  The present state of music in Germany, the Netherlands and United Provinces (London, 1775/R New York, 1969)
  A general history of music (4 vols., London, 1776–89)
Busby, T., *A general history of music* (2 vols., London, 1819)
Chesnut, J. H., 'Mozart's teaching of intonation', *Journal of the American Musicological Society*, vol. 30 (1977), pp. 254–71
Cohen, A., 'A cache of 18th-century strings', *Galpin Society Journal*, vol. 36 (1983), pp. 37–48
Corrette, M., *L'école d'Orphée, méthode pour apprendre facilement à jouer du violon dans le goût françois et italien* (Paris, 1738/R Geneva, 1973)
Courcy, G. I. C. de, *Paganini the Genoese* (2 vols., Norman, Oklahoma, 1957)
Crome, R., *The fiddle new model'd* (London, c. 1750; 3rd edn, London, c. 1775)
Curry, P. B., 'The François Tourte violin bow: its development and its effect on selected solo violin literature of the late-eighteenth and early-nineteenth centuries' (unpublished Ph.D. degree thesis, Brigham Young University, 1968)
Dannreuther, E., *Musical ornamentation* (2 vols., London, 1893–5)
Dart, R. T., *The interpretation of music* (London, 1954)
David, H., & Mendel, A., *The Bach reader: a life of Johann Sebastian Bach in letters and documents* (New York, 1945)
Day, J., see le Huray, P. G.
Day, L. A., *Niccolo Paganini of Genoa* (New York, 1929/R London, 1966)
Dictionnaire de musique, ed. S. de Brossard (Paris, 1703/R 1964)
Dictionnaire de musique, ed. J.-J. Rousseau (Paris, 1768/R 1969); tr. W. Waring as *A complete dictionary of music* (2nd edn., London, 1779)
Dictionnaire de musique moderne, ed. F. H. J. Castil-Blaze (Paris, 1821)
Dolmetsch, A., *The interpretation of the music of the seventeenth and eighteenth centuries* (London, 1915)
Donington, R., *The interpretation of early music* (London, 1963; 3rd revised edn., London, 1974)
  The performer's guide to baroque music (London, 1973)
  String playing in baroque music (London, 1977)
  'Ornaments', *The new Grove dictionary of music and musicians* (London, 1980)
  'James Talbot's Manuscript', *Galpin Society Journal*, vol. 3 (1950), pp. 27–45.
Dorian, F., *History of music in performance* (New York, 1942)
Dubourg, G., *The violin; some account of that leading instrument and its most eminent professors, from the earliest date to the present time* (4th edn, London, 1852)
Du Rivage, *Réflexions d'un artiste sur le talent de Paganini* (Paris, 1831)
Eberhardt, S., *Paganinis Geigenhaltung* (Berlin, 1921)
Ellis, A. J., 'The history of musical pitch', *Journal of the Society of Arts*, vol. 28 (1880), pp. 293–336; reprinted in A. Mendel ed., *Studies in the history of musical pitch* (Amsterdam, 1968), pp. 11–54
Elmer, M., 'Tartini's improvised ornamentation as illustrated by manuscripts from the Berkeley collection of eighteenth-century Italian instrumental music' (unpublished M.A. degree thesis, University of California at Berkeley, 1962)
Encyclopédie de la Musique, ed. A. Lavignac & L. de la Laurencie (11 vols., Paris, 1920–31)
Encyclopédie, ou dictionnaire raisonné des sciences, des arts et des métiers, ed. J. le R. d'Alembert & D. Diderot (11 vols., Paris, 1751–72)
Eymar, A.-M. d', *Anecdotes sur Viotti, précédés de quelques réflexions sur l'expression en musique* (Geneva, 1800)
Farga, F., *Geigen und Geiger* (Zurich, 1940): tr. E. Larsen as *Violins and violinists* (London, 1950, 2nd rev. edn, London, 1969)
Fayolle, F. J. M., *Notices sur Corelli, Tartini, Gaviniès, Pugnani et Viotti* (Paris, 1810)
  Paganini et Bériot; ou avis aux jeunes artistes qui se destinent à l'enseignement du violon (Paris, 1831)
Fellinger, I., *Verzeichnis der Musikzeitschriften des 19. Jahrhunderts* (Regensburg, 1968).

Ferand, E. T., *Die Improvisation in der Musik* (Zurich, 1938)
   Die Improvisation in Beispielen aus neun Jahrhunderten abendländischer Musik (2nd rev. edn, Cologne, 1961)
Ferguson, H., *Keyboard interpretation from the fourteenth to the nineteenth century: an introduction* (London, 1975)
Fétis, F. J., *Antoine Stradivari, luthier célèbre* (Paris, 1856; tr. J. Bishop, London, 1864/R 1964)
   Notice biographique sur Nicolo Paganini (Paris, 1851); tr. W. E. Guernsey as *Biographical notice of N. Paganini, followed by an analysis of his compositions and preceded by a sketch of the history of the violin* (London, 1876)
Fischer, K. von, 'Eine Neubearbeitung von L. Mozarts Violinschule aus dem Jahre 1804', *Die Musikforschung*, vol. 2 (1949), p. 187
Flesch, C., *Die Kunst des Violinspiels* (2 vols., Berlin, 1923–8); tr. F. H. Martens as *The art of violin playing* (New York, 1924–30)
   Alta scuola di diteggiatura violinistica (Milan, 1960); tr. B. Schwarz as *Violin fingering, its theory and practice* (London, 1966)
Forster, S. A., see Sandys, W.
Galamian, I., *Principles of violin playing and teaching* (London, 1964)
Gehot, J., *Complete instructions for every musical instrument* (London, c. 1780)
Gelrud, P. G., 'A critical study of the French violin school (1782–1882)' (unpublished Ph.D. degree thesis, Cornell University, 1941)
Geminiani, F., *The art of playing on the violin* (London, 1751; facsimile ed. D. Boyden, London, 1952); Fr. tr. as *L'art de jouer le violon* (Paris, 1752); Ger. tr. as *Gründliche Anleitung oder Violin Schule* (Vienna [1782])
   Rules for playing in true taste on the violin, German flute, violoncello and harpsichord, particularly the thorough-bass Op. 8 (London, c. 1746)
   A treatise of good taste in the art of musick (London, 1749/R London, 1969)
Gerhartz, K., 'Zur älteren Violintechnik', *Zeitschrift für Musikwissenschaft*, vol. 7 (1924–5), pp. 6–12
   'Die Violinschule von Leopold Mozart', *Mozart-Jahrbuch*, vol. 3 (1929), pp. 245–302
   'Die Violinschule in ihrer musikgeschichtlichen Entwicklung bis Leopold Mozart', *Zeitschrift für Musikwissenschaft*, vol. 7 (1924–5), p. 553
Giazotto, R., *Giovan Battista Viotti* (Milan, 1956)
Giehne, H., *Zur Erinnerung an Ludwig Spohr: ein kunstgeschichtlicher Vortrag über dessen Leben und Wirken* (Karlsruhe, 1860)
Glasenapp, F. von, *Georg Simon Löhlein: sein Leben und seine Werke, insbesondere seine volkstümlichen Musiklehrbücher* (Halle, 1937)
Göthel, F., *Das Violinspiel Ludwig Spohrs: unter Berücksichtigung geigentechnischer Probleme seiner Zeit* (Grosschönau, 1935)
Gruenberg, E., *The violinist's manual: a progressive classification of technical material, études, solo pieces and the most important chamber works* (New York, 1896)
Gruenberg, M. P. E., *Führer durch die Literatur der Streichinstrumente* (Leipzig, 1913)
Haas, R. M., *Aufführungspraxis der Musik* (Potsdam, 1931)
Handbuch der musikalischen Litteratur, ed. C. F. Whistling (Leipzig, 1817/R 1975; 2nd edn, Leipzig, 1827–8; 3rd edn, Leipzig, 1845)
Hart, G., *The violin: its famous makers and their imitators* (London, 1875)
   The violin (London, 1880)
   The violin and its music (London, 1881)
Hawkins, Sir J., *A general history of the science and practice of music* (5 vols., London, 1776)
Heim, E., *Neuer Führer durch die Violin-Literatur* (Hanover, 1889)
Henley, W., *Universal dictionary of violin and bow makers*, vols. 1–5 (Brighton, 1959–60); vol. 6 ed. C. Woodcock as *Dictionary of contemporary violin and bow makers* (Brighton, 1965)

Heron-Allen, E., *De fidiculis bibliographia* (2 vols., London, 1890–4)
  Violin making as it was and is (London, 1884)
  'Nicolo Paganini and his Guarnerius', *Musical Times*, vol. 27 (1886), pp. 266–70
Hickman, R., 'The censored publications of *The art of playing on the violin* or Geminiani un-
  shaken', *Early Music*, vol. 11 (1983), pp. 73–6
Hill, W. H., A. F. & A. E., *Life and work of Antonio Stradivari* (London, 1902/R New York, 1963)
Historisch-biographisches Lexicon der Tonkünstler, ed. E. L. Gerber (2 vols., Leipzig, 1790–2/R
  1964–7)
Hofmann, R., *Führer durch die Violin-Literatur* (Leipzig, 1904)
Huet, F., *Etude sur les différentes écoles de violon depuis Corelli jusqu'à Baillot: précédée d'un examen sur
  l'art de jouer des instruments à archet au XVIIe siècle* (Chalons-sur-Marne, 1880)
Hummel, J. N., *Ausführliche theoretisch-practische Anweisung zum Piano-fortespiel* (Vienna, 1828;
  Eng. tr., London, 1829)
Istel, E., *Nicolo Paganini* (Leipzig, 1919)
  'The secret of Paganini's technique', *Musical Quarterly*, vol. 16 (1930), pp. 101–16
Jacobi, E. R., 'G. F. Nicolai's manuscript of Tartini's *Regole per ben suonar il violino*', *Musical
  Quarterly*, vol. 47 (1961), pp. 207–23
Kapp, J., *Paganini* (Berlin & Leipzig, 1913)
Keller, H., *Phrasierung und Artikulation* (Kassel, 1955); tr. L. Gerdine (London, 1966)
  Die Bedeutung der Zeichen Keil, Strich und Punkt bei Mozart (Kassel, 1957)
Kendall, R., 'Notes on Arnold Schlick', *Acta Musicologica*, vol. 11 (1939), pp. 136–43
Kirkendale, W., 'Segreto comunicato da Paganini', *Journal of the American Musicological Society*,
  vol. 18 (1965), pp. 394–407
Kolneder, W., *Das Buch der Violine* (Zurich, 1972)
  'Die Gründung des Pariser Konservatoriums', *Die Musikforschung*, vol. 20 (1967), pp. 56–7
Laborde, J.-B. de, *Essai sur la musique ancienne et moderne* (4 vols., Paris, 1780)
Laphalèque, G. I. de, *Notice sur le célèbre violoniste Nicolo Paganini* (Paris, 1830; tr. L. F. L'Heritier,
  London, 1830)
Lassabathie, T., *Histoire du Conservatoire impérial de musique et de déclamation* (Paris, 1860)
Laurencie, L. de la, *L'école française de violon de Lully à Viotti* (3 vols., Paris, 1922–4/R Geneva,
  1971)
  'Gaviniès et son temps', *La Revue musicale* (1922), pp. 135–48
Lee, D. A., 'Some embellished versions of sonatas by Franz Benda', *Musical Quarterly*, vol. 62
  (1976), pp. 58–71
Lefort, A., see Pincherle, M.
le Huray, P. G., & Day, J., *Music and aesthetics in the eighteenth and early-nineteenth centuries* (Cam-
  bridge, 1981)
Le Pileur d'Apligny, *Traité sur la musique et sur les moyens d'en perfectionner l'expression* (Paris, 1779)
Mackerras, J., 'Problems of violin bowing in the performance of eighteenth-century music',
  Canon, vol. 17 (1965), pp. 25–30
Malibran, A., *Louis Spohr, sein Leben und Wirken* (Frankfurt, 1860)
Marguerre, K., 'Forte und piano bei Mozart', *Neue Zeitschrift für Musik*, vol. 128 (1967),
  pp. 153–60
Marpurg, F. W., *Die Kunst das Clavier zu spielen* (Berlin, 1750; 4th rev. and enlarged edn, Berlin,
  1762/R 1969)
  Anleitung zum Clavierspielen (Berlin, 1755; 2nd edn, Berlin, 1765/R 1969)
Marx, H. J., 'Some unknown embellishments of Corelli's violin sonatas', *Musical Quarterly*,
  vol. 61 (1975), pp. 65–76
Mayer, D. M., *The forgotten master: the life and times of L. Spohr* (London, 1959)
Meer, J. H. van der, see Boomkamp, C. van L.

Melkus, E., 'Zur Ausführung der Stricharten in Mozarts Werken', *Mozart-Jahrbuch*, vol. 15 (1967), pp. 244–66

Memoir of Signor Paganini with critical remarks on his performances (anon., Liverpool, 1832)

Mendel, A., 'On the pitches in use in Bach's time', *Musical Quarterly*, vol. 41 (1955), pp. 332–54 & 466–80

    'Pitch in the sixteenth and early-seventeenth centuries', *Musical Quarterly*, vol. 34 (1948), pp. 28–45, 199–221, 336–57 & 575–93

    'Pitch in Western music since 1500: a re-examination', *Acta Musicologica*, vol. 50 (1978), pp. 1–93

    See also David, H.

Meyer, F., *Führer durch die Violinliteratur, Geschichte der Violine und des Bogens u.s.w.* (Leipzig, 1910)

Milchmeyer, J. P. *Die wahre Art das Pianoforte zu spielen* (Dresden, 1797)

Monosoff, S., 'Fingering' (II: 1–3), *The new Grove dictionary of music and musicians* (London, 1980)

Moser, A., *Geschichte des Violinspiels* (Berlin, 1923, rev. 1966–7)

    'Die Violin-Skordatur', *Archiv für Musikwissenschaft*, (1919), pp. 573–89

Mozart, L., *Versuch einer gründlichen Violinschule* (Augsburg, 1756; 2nd edn, Augsburg, 1769 & 1770; 3rd edn, Augsburg, 1787; 4th edn, Frankfurt & Leipzig, 1791 and Augsburg, 1800; Dutch tr., Haarlem, 1766; Fr. tr., ed. V. Roeser, Paris [1770]; Eng. tr., E. Knocker, London, 1948; 2nd edn, 1951); ed. J. Pirlinger as *Neue vollständige theoretische und praktische Violinschule für Lehrer und Lernende* (Vienna, 1799–1800)

A musical dictionary, ed. J. Grassineau (London, 1740/R1967)

Nelson, S. M., *The violin and viola* (London, 1972)

Neumann, F., *Ornamentation in baroque and post-baroque music, with special emphasis on J. S. Bach* (Princeton, 1978)

Nunamaker, N. K., 'The virtuoso violin concerto before Paganini: the concertos of Lulli, Giornovichi and Woldemar (1750–1815)' (unpublished Ph.D. degree thesis, Indiana University, 1968)

Otto, J. A., *Treatise on the construction, preservation, repair and improvement of the violin and all bow instruments*, tr. T. Fardely (London, 1833)

Paneraj, V., *Principi di musica* (Florence, c. 1780)

Piccoli, G., *Trois siècles de l'histoire du violon, 1617–1917* (Nice, 1954)

Pierre, C. V. D., *Histoire du concert spirituel 1725–90* (Paris, 1875)

    B. Sarrette, et les origines du Conservatoire (Paris, 1895)

Pincherle, M., *Les violonistes, compositeurs et virtuoses* (Paris, 1922)

    The world of the virtuoso (London, 1963)

    Feuillets d'histoire du violon (Paris, 1927)

    'On the rights of the interpreter in the performance of seventeenth- and eighteenth-century music', *Musical Quarterly*, vol. 44 (1958), pp. 145–66

    'L'exécution aux XVIIe et XVIIIe siècles: instruments à archet', *Report of the eighth I. M. S. Congress*, ed. J. La Rue (New York, 1961), pp. 220–31

Pincherle, M., & Lefort, A., 'Le violon', *Encyclopédie de la Musique*, (Paris, 1927)

Pougin, A., *Viotti et l'école moderne de violon* (Paris, 1888)

    Le violon, les violonistes et la musique de violon du XVIe au XVIIIe siècle (Paris, 1924)

    Kreutzer (Paris, 1868)

Pulver, J., *Paganini, the romantic virtuoso* (London, 1936)

    'Violin methods old and new', *Proceedings of the Royal Musical Association*, vol. 50 (1923–4), pp. 101–27

Quantz, J. J., *Versuch einer Anweisung die Flöte traversiere zu spielen* (Berlin, 1752; 3rd edn, 1789/R1953); tr. E. R. Reilly as *On playing the flute* (London & New York, 1966)

Rangoni, G. B., *Essai sur le goût de la musique avec le caractère des trois célèbres joueurs de violon, Messieurs Nardini, Lolli et Pugnani* (Livorno, 1790)

Reilly, E. R., 'Quantz on national styles in music', *Musical Quarterly*, vol. 49 (1963), pp. 163–87
  Quantz and his Versuch: three studies (New York, 1971)
Retford, W. C., *Bows and bowmakers* (London, 1964)
Reuchsel, M., *L'école classique du violon* (2nd edn, Paris, 1906)
Reuter, F. von, *Führer durch die Solo Violinmusik* (Berlin, 1926)
Rhodes, J. J. K., & Thomas, W. R., 'Schlick, Praetorius and the history of organ pitch', *The Organ Yearbook*, vol. 2 (1971), p. 58 & vol. 4 (1973), p. 112
  'Pitch' (2–5), *The new Grove dictionary of music and musicians* (London, 1980)
Roda, J., *Bows for musical instruments of the violin family* (Illinois, 1959)
Rosen, C., *The classical style* (London, 1971)
Rothschild, F., *The lost tradition in music* (2 vols., London & New York, 1961)
Rudimenta panduristae, oder Geig-fundamenta (attrib. G. C. Wagenseil, Augsburg, 1751; 4th edn, Augsburg, 1770)
Russell, T., 'The violin scordatura', *Musical Quarterly*, vol. 24 (1938), pp. 84–96
Saint-George, H., *The bow, its history, manufacture and use* (London, 1896)
Sandys, W., & Forster, S. A., *History of the violin* (London, 1864)
Saussine, R. de, *Paganini le magicien* (Paris, 1938; tr. M. Laurie, London, 1953)
Savart, F., *Mémoire sur la construction des instruments à cordes et à archet, lu à l'Académie des sciences, le 31 mai 1819* (Paris, 1819)
Scheibe, J. A., *Der critische Musikus* (Hamburg, 1738–40; 2nd enlarged edn, 1745/R1970)
Schering, A., 'Zur instrumentalen Verzierungskunst im 18. Jahrhundert', *Sammelbände der internationalen Musikgesellschaft*, vol. 7 (1905–6), pp. 365–85
Schletterer, H. M., *Ludwig Spohrs Werke* (Leipzig, 1881)
Schmitz, H.-P., *Die Kunst der Verzierung im 18. Jahrhundert* (Kassel & Basel, 1955)
Schottky, J. M., *Paganinis Leben und Treiben als Künstler und als Mensch* (Prague, 1830)
Schroeder, C., *Guide through violin literature* (London, 1903)
Schubert, F. L., *Die Violine, ihr Wesen, ihre Bedeutung und Behandlung als Solo- und Orchesterinstrument* (Leipzig, 1865)
Schütz, F. C. J., *Leben, Charakter und Kunst des Ritters, Nicolo Paganini* (Leipzig, 1830)
Schwarz, B., 'Beethoven and the French violin school', *Musical Quarterly*, vol. 44 (1958), pp. 431–47
Segerman, E., see Abbot, D.
Sheppard, L., 'The English Tourte', *The Strad*, vol. 81 (1971), pp. 579–80
Sheppard, L., & Axelrod, H. R., *Paganini* (New Jersey, 1979)
Sibire, L'Abbé, *La chelonomie, ou le parfait luthier* (Paris, 1806)
Simpson, A., 'A short-title list of printed English instrumental tutors to 1800', *Royal Musical Association Research Chronicle*, vol. 6. (1968), pp. 24–50
Skeaping, K., 'Some speculations on a crisis in the history of the violin', *Galpin Society Journal*, vol. 8 (1955), pp. 3–12
  'A baroque violin from Northumberland', *Galpin Society Journal*, vol. 14 (1961), pp. 45–8
Smi'es, J. E., 'Improvised ornamentation in late-eighteenth-century music; an examination of contemporary evidence' (unpublished Ph.D. degree thesis, Stanford University, 1976)
  'Directions for improvised ornamentation in Italian method books of the late-eighteenth century', *Journal of the American Musicological Society*, vol. 31 (1978), pp. 495–509
Spohr, L., *Autobiography* (Eng. tr., London, 1865)
Stoeving, P., *The story of the violin* (London, 1907)
Stolba, K. M., 'A history of the violin étude to about 1800' (unpublished Ph.D. degree thesis, University of Iowa, 1965)
Stowell, R., 'The development of violin technique from L'Abbé le fils to Paganini (unpublished Ph.D. degree thesis, University of Cambridge, 1978)
Stradner, G., 'Eine Ausstellung: zur Entwicklung der Geige', *Violinspiel und Violinmusik in Geschichte und Gegenwart*, ed. V. Schwarz (Vienna, 1975), pp. 314–23

Straeten, E. S. J. van der, *The history of the violin* (2 vols., London, 1933/R New York, 1968)
   The romance of the fiddle (London, 1911)
Stratton, S. S., *Nicolo Paganini: his life and work* (London, 1907)
Swalin, B. J., *The violin concerto: a study in German romanticism* (Chapel Hill & London, 1941)
Tansur, W., *A new musical grammar and dictionary* (3rd edn, London, 1756)
   The elements of musick display'd (London, 1767)
Tartini, G., *Traité des agrémens de la musique* (Fr. tr., P. Denis, Paris, 1771; Eng. tr., ed. E. R. Jacobi, Celle & New York, 1961)
   Regole per arrivare a saper ben suonare il violino (MS, Bologna); facsimile edn as supplement to *Traité des agrémens . . .* ed. E. R. Jacobi (Celle & New York, 1961)
Tessarini, C., *Grammatica per i principianti di violino* (Rome, c. 1745)
   A musical grammar which teaches an easy and short method of learning to play to perfection the violin in parts (Edinburgh, c. 1765)
Themelis, D., 'Entstehung der Violinetüde; allgemeine, spieltechnische und musikalische Voraussetzungen bis zur Gründung des Pariser Conservatoire' (unpublished Ph.D. degree thesis, University of Munich, 1964)
Thomas, W. R., see Rhodes, J. J. K.
Tibaldi-Chiesa, M., *Paganini* (Milan, 1944)
Tosi, P., *Opinioni de' cantori antichi e moderni* (Bologna, 1723); tr. J. E. Galliard as *Observations on the florid song* (London, 1742)
Tottmann, A., *Führer durch den Violin Unterricht: ein kritisches, progressiv geordnetes Repertorium der instructiven, sowie der Solo- und Ensemble Werke für Violine* (Leipzig, 1874)
Türk, D. G., *Clavierschule, oder Anweisung zum Clavierspielen für Lehrer und Lernende* (Leipzig & Halle, 1789); abridged tr. C. G. Naumburger as *Treatise on the art of teaching and practising the pianoforte* (London, 1802)
Vannes, R., *Dictionnaire universel des luthiers* (2nd edn, 2 vols., Brussels, 1951–9/R1972)
Vatelot, E., *Les archets français* (Nancy, 1976)
Vidal, L.-A., *Les instruments à archet* (3 vols., Paris, 1876–8/R1961)
   La lutherie et des luthiers (Paris, 1889)
Vinquist, N., & Zaslaw, N., *Performance practice: a bibliography* (New York, 1971)
Wasielewski, W. J., *Die Violine und ihre Meister* (4th edn, Leipzig, 1904)
Wassmann, C., *Entdeckungen zur Erleichterung und Erweiterung der Violintechnik durch selbstständige Ausbildung des Tastgefühls der Finger* (Berlin, 1885)
Weidmann, G., 'Die Violintechnik Paganinis' (unpublished Ph.D. degree thesis, University of Berlin, 1950)
Wessel, F. T., 'The Affektenlehre in the eighteenth century' (unpublished Ph.D. degree thesis,' University of Indiana, 1955)
White, E. C., 'Giovanni Baptista Viotti and his violin concertos' (unpublished Ph.D. degree thesis, Princeton University, 1957)
   'The violin concertos of Giornovichi', *Musical Quarterly*, vol. 58 (1972), pp. 24–45
Williams, M. D., 'The violin concertos of Rodolphe Kreutzer' (unpublished Ph.D. degree thesis, Indiana University, 1973)
Wilson, J., ed., *Roger North on music: being a selection from his essays written during the years c. 1695–1728* (London, 1959)
Wirsta, A., 'Ecole de violon au XVIIIème siècle d'après les ouvrages didactiques' (unpublished degree thesis, University of Paris, 1955)
   'L'enseignement du violon au XIXème siècle' (unpublished degree thesis, University of Paris, 1971)
Wunderlich, F., *Der Geigenbogen: seine Geschichte, Herstellung und Behandlung* (2nd edn, Leipzig, 1952)
Yampolsky, I. M., *The principles of violin fingering*, tr. A. Lumsden (London, 1967)
Young, P. M., *The concert tradition* (London, 1965)

Zaslaw, N., 'The compleat orchestral musician', *Early Music*, vol. 7 (1979), pp. 46–57 & vol. 8
    (1980), pp. 71–2
    'Toward the revival of the classical orchestra', *Proceedings of the Royal Musical Association*,
    vol. 103 (1977), pp. 179–187
    'The size and composition of European orchestras, 1775–95', in J. P. Larsen, H. Serwer &
    J. Webster, eds., *Haydn Studies: Proceedings of the International Haydn Conference, Washington,
    DC (1975)* (New York, 1981) pp. 186–8
    See also Vinquist, N.

Index